SHOCKS
and
RIVALRIES
in the
MIDDLE EAST
and
NORTH AFRICA

SHOCKS

and

RIVALRIES

in the

MIDDLE EAST

and

NORTH AFRICA

IMAD MANSOUR
WILLIAM R. THOMPSON

Editors

Georgetown University Press / Washington, DC

The publisher is not responsible for third-party websites or their content. URL links were active at time of publication.

Library of Congress Cataloging-in-Publication Data

Names: Mansour, Imad, editor. | Thompson, William R., editor.
Title: Shocks and Rivalries in the Middle East and North Africa / Imad
    Mansour, William R. Thompson, editors.
Description: Washington, DC : Georgetown University Press, 2020. |
    Includes bibliographical references and index.
Identifiers: LCCN 2019025952 (print) | LCCN 2019025953 (ebook) | ISBN
    9781626167674 (hardcover) | ISBN 9781626167681 (paperback) | ISBN
    9781626167698 (ebook)
Subjects: LCSH: Middle East—Foreign relations. | Africa, North—Foreign
    relations. | Middle East—Politics and government. | Africa,
    North—Politics and government.
Classification: LCC DS63.18 .S54 2020 (print) | LCC DS63.18 (ebook) | DDC
    327.56—dc23
LC record available at https://lccn.loc.gov/2019025952
LC ebook record available at https://lccn.loc.gov/2019025953

♾ This book is printed on acid-free paper meeting the requirements of the American National Standard for Permanence in Paper for Printed Library Materials.

21 20   9 8 7 6 5 4 3 2   First printing

Printed in the United States of America.
Cover design by Jeremy John Parker.

For Giulia, Tiberio, and Leandro.
—IM

In memory of John Mikhail,
a promising political scientist who
did not survive Middle Eastern rivalries.
—WRT

Contents

Illustrations

FIGURES

TABLES

Acknowledgments

The papers that evolved into chapters for this book were first presented at a workshop at Qatar University in Doha on December 14–15, 2016. We thank Qatar University for fully funding the workshop, in addition to the immense support we received from the College of Arts and Sciences, especially its then-dean Rashid Al-Kuwari, and the Department of International Affairs, especially its then-chair Ahmed H. Ibrahim. Special thanks go to Sherin Naguib at the College of Arts and Sciences for her mighty support in making the workshop possible. Finally, we thank our discussants, who provided valuable feedback to the papers presented there: Mazhar Al-Zo'by, Hassan Barari, Mark Farha, Steven Wright, and Mahjoob Zweiri.

At Georgetown University Press, we would like to thank our commissioning editor, Don Jacobs, for his collegiality and the great support he had for this project from the beginning. We also thank the anonymous reviewers, whose feedback considerably helped us improve our work.

1

Introduction

A Theory of Shock and Rivalry

Imad Mansour and William R. Thompson

This edited volume introduces explicit analysis of state-to-state rivalries in the international relations of the Middle East and North Africa (MENA). In the past two decades, international relations (IR) scholars have made significant advances in analyzing rivalries. This statement may sound strange. Surely we are all aware of the existence of rivalries. After all, they have been around as long as there have been Sumerian city-states, thousands of years ago. But that is the point. We are well aware of the existence of interstate rivalries, but we have been quite slow in addressing them as rivalries per se. Part of this process of making their study more explicit involves specifying which relationships qualify and which ones do not. We define an interstate rivalry as encompassing dyads of states that regard each other as competitive, threatening enemies.[1] We can identify which relationships count because decision-makers acknowledge in various ways who they select as prominent adversaries. They refer to them frequently in foreign policy speeches, and they orient their military preparations to cope with their threats.

As soon as we begin focusing on rivalry behavior, one fact jumps out clearly. Most of the conflict in international politics is recidivist in nature. If one counts all the possible dyadic ways to connect an ensemble of states, only a small number of the dyads are responsible for most of the conflict. Rivalries, then, are the best place to understand why conflict occurs and persists. This is all the more the case in the MENA, which has more contemporary experience with rivalries than any other region. Thus, it is a good regional theater for testing propositions as well as describing significant patterns of regional change.

For MENA-dedicated studies, it is common to find loosely defined concepts of rivalry used in studying regional conflict and various forms of security relations (Halliday 2012, chap. 6). Rivalry is often described as pertinent to understanding regional politics (Lawson 2016). In explaining rivalries and their effects, some place emphasis on "the international dimension," that is, external politics (Phillips 2016, 3); others place emphasis on material and ideational factors (Mabon 2013). However, very few works on the MENA provide theoretically driven analyses and engage rivalry as a distinct field of study. In this volume we explicitly engage rivalry as an empirical phenomenon from a theoretical perspective. Moreover, we seek to contribute to theory building in the field of rivalry analysis from the complexity and descriptive "thickness" of regional politics.

It is not enough to simply identify which states are rivals and describe their interactions. We must also understand the dynamics of rivalry origins, maintenance, escalation, and termination. Some of these dynamics are found in many cases. For instance, rivalries tend to emerge from disputes over borders and relative position. Some of it is, of course, idiosyncratic. In the Middle East a good example is the way in which the extended Hashemite family looms large in the earlier history of the region's rivalries; familial relations, hence, are often analyzed in how they affected the politics of Iraq, Jordan, Saudi Arabia, Syria, and other states born in the twentieth century. Thus, MENA has provided plenty of such idiosyncratic causes of rivalry. This volume is different in that it allocates more attention to the general factors of MENA rivalries while simultaneously probing the course of specific rivalries.

Furthermore, an important complementary goal for this volume involves stressing the role of shocks (as abrupt and jarring changes to an equilibrium or status quo) in understanding how rivalries and rivalry fields (as networks of interdependent rivalries) undergo transformation. We think that the impact of political shocks on rivalries remains seriously understudied. The MENA is not only an arena with a large number of dyadic and multiple-actor rivalries; it also has experienced quite a few shocks, especially at the regional level, with varied effects. These effects will be explored in our propositions. Thus, in our volume one effect that is highlighted is the contributory role of shocks in beginning and ending rivalries. Moreover, an important contribution of our volume is explicating how shocks affect fluctuations in interstate rivalry and rivalry field dynamics in between the onset and termination of these adversarial relationships.

RIVALRIES AND SHOCKS

The more formal study of rivalries emerged from the realization that militarized interstate disputes were not randomly distributed across time and space. Some pairs of states (dyads) engaged in them serially and disproportionately compared to other dyads.[2] Thus, the initial identification of enduring rivalries tended to be carried out by isolating the spatial and temporal density of conflict. Enduring rivalries were pairs of states that participated in X militarized interstate disputes within a specified period.[3] Such an approach singles out the pairs of states that were involved in the most conflict. But that implies that rivalries must fight when it is not clear that all do clash conspicuously or frequently. An alternative approach emerged that focuses on inventorying decision-maker perspectives about who their interstate enemies were. Some of these strategic rivalries were characterized by frequent militarized interstate disputes, and some were distinctive in rarely coming to physical blows despite ample, if fluctuating, displays of hostility.

Both approaches to identifying rivalry exist today, with most empirical analysts using one approach or the other.[4] Neither approach can claim to be liability free. Enduring rivalries begin and end when sufficient conflict breaks out and stops. Relationships with off-and-on hostilities tend to be slighted. A focus on enduring rivalries also tends to emphasize dyads in which very powerful states fight very weak states, however briefly. Whether these highly asymmetrical relationships should count as rivalries similar to the more protracted contests between more symmetrical powers continues to be debated.

Identifying strategic rivalries is a more subjective game and requires knowing more about foreign policy attitudes and interactions than is sometimes knowable by analysts. For instance, Egypt and Israel were once very clearly enduring rivals fighting wars in four consecutive decades, and then they stopped fighting each other. From an enduring rivalry perspective, the rivalry ended some four decades ago. From a strategic rivalry perspective, however, neither side seems to rule out the possibility of a return to conflict. The rivalry thus de-escalated after the Camp David Accords without terminating.

While there is certainly considerable overlap in the rivalries identified by either perspective, the consequent identifications are not the same. One needs to choose which approach seems more appropriate.[5] Nonetheless, both approaches attempt to isolate conflict recidivists. That is, a disproportionate amount of interstate conflict is generated by a very small group of states that feud with each other repeatedly. It follows, then, that we need to look more closely at the recidivists to best understand why conflict persists in the ways that it does. That means more than merely identifying rivalries. We also need to better understand their origins, dynamics, and endgames.[6]

Yet it is one thing to say that we should focus more on conflict recidivists to best understand why conflict occurs. It is quite another thing to say *how* we should focus on conflict recidivists. We can certainly describe their behavior, and unsurprisingly, many of the descriptions of conflict in international relations are implicitly about rival interactions. There is nothing wrong with these descriptions. They add to, or more precisely, can add to our knowledge and understanding. Yet their explanatory payoffs are limited in the sense that they can tell us something about what specific actors did at specific times— or what an author thinks they might have done. Would it not be advantageous if we also had general explanations of what states are likely to do in certain situations?

This is where theories of foreign policy enter the picture. To develop theories of foreign policy, we need to move away from saying the Saudis did X to the Iranians and the Iranians responded with Y. One parsimonious view of foreign policy considers international interactions something like a tennis match. One state does or says something to another state, and in turn that state responds at the same level or chooses to escalate (tit for tat in the absence of escalation). Yet we know that this approach is not sufficient to capture all or most of the variance in foreign policy interactions.

Another explanatory factor is path dependency. States tend to keep on doing the same things to other states until or unless something makes them stop. If we know what two states did to each other last year, there is some probability that they will do much the same next year. Yet we also know that a combination of tit for tat and path dependency does not suffice to explain interstate interactions either. States radically change course at times. At other times they escalate or de-escalate out of proportion to the stimuli to which they are responding.

One of the constructs for capturing abrupt departures from tit for tat and path dependency is the notion of shocks; they alter the landscapes in which decision-makers operate. Shocks are unexpected reconfigurations of the political-military and economic landscapes within which decision-makers try to find solutions to the problems they choose to address (we define shocks in more detail later). Economists rely on them extensively to make sense of radical changes in prices, supply, and demand because they view them as overt disruptors of processes that otherwise demonstrate considerable stability. We need to make more use of them in international relations for the same reason.

In the study of rivalries, shocks have already been prominently associated with the origins of rivalries and their termination. Most prominently, Diehl and Goertz (2000) were the first to apply "independence shocks" to explain the onset of enduring rivalries (see also Colaresi 2001; Goertz and Diehl 1995a). For this line of inquiry, scholars found that the moment of political independence—Westphalian statehood—constituted a shock when emerging entities came into existence with dispute boundaries with neighbors; these disputes transformed into rivalries. On one side of the equation, that is, ending the rivalry, Rasler, Thompson, and Ganguly (2013) applied the notion of shock to rivalry terminations. For them, to de-escalate a rivalry, one or both sides needed to appreciate a much different approach to dealing with an established enemy, and shocks were the conduits to changes in strategic assessments of the other. Through historical and empirical analysis, they found that defeat in war, a major loss of capability, or radical regime change with different preferences—all of which constitute varying types of shocks—might encourage de-escalations. Therefore, as the findings of the two seminal works on shocks and rivalry analysis confirm, without some kind of significant environmental shift, foreign policy inertia should be expected to prevail, which means that rivalries should be maintained infinitely. The termination of rivalries, however, highlights the need to study sources of change in these conflictive relationships; specifically, what happens to change the ways decision-makers in rival states see each other?

Accordingly, we are proposing to focus on shocks in this volume as a way to understand not only beginnings and endings but also how rivalries are maintained and whether they escalate or de-escalate over time. In other words, we believe shocks are critical to making sense of the ups and downs of rivalry fluctuations. To do that in a nondescriptive way, a theory is needed. We develop one in the next section of this introduction.

THE SHOCK THEORY

To theorize about shocks and rivalries, we begin with two central assumptions:

Assumption 1: Foreign policy is characterized by substantial inertia that has to be overcome in some way for changes in policies to occur.

Assumption 2: Rivalries are characterized by variable levels of intensity or activity—that is, they are associated with a normal range of behavior that is susceptible to change during the course of a rivalry. Rivalries with higher intensity levels are more likely to experience militarized conflict than are rivalries with lower basic rivalry levels.

We define a shock as a rapid departure from a state of equilibrium—that is, an abrupt and significant change in the properties of a physical, social, political, or economic system. Shocks may be internal, such as an economic crisis (with implications for regime change or the ability to cope with external threats), regime change, or civil conflict. Shocks may also be external, such as a shift in power configurations at the system level (e.g., the end of the Cold War), interstate war, or the emergence of a revolution that overthrows the status quo in another state (through active calculated designed interventions or as a result of ensuing anarchy and violence spillovers). As disruptive events, shocks are perceived to significantly alter threat environments in some way and, therefore, encourage responses to the changes. Such events alter policymakers' calculations about their external and domestic environments. Events that interrupt the status quo, therefore, alter what decision-makers perceive they should and can do about others. Decision-makers perceive these shocks not only as threats but also as opportunities to expand their interests and roles in the region, to alter balances of power, and to consolidate themselves domestically. It is here that we can introduce a third assumption on how shocks have the *potential* to impact political processes externally and domestically through policymaking:

> Assumption 3: Shocks contribute to opening windows to change by overcoming inertia, at least for some states or actors. Shocks need not be prime drivers for change; they only have to create some potential for change. Whether actors jump through the windows is another matter.

In sum, shocks increase the probability of change in foreign policy generally, with the magnitude and direction of change varying with the type and magnitude of the shock. Thus, shocks can contribute to rivalry onset or termination and to shifting basic rivalry levels upward (escalation/inflammation) or downward (de-escalation/dampening) of hostilities.

Finally, shocks can sometimes "cluster" and thus have even more sizable effects. This means that there are, at least occasionally, circumstances in which a series of shocks in rapid succession significantly affect rivalry intensity or dynamics. For example, multiple shocks affected the Iran–Saudi Arabia rivalry in 1988–91, including the end of the Iran-Iraq War, leadership changes occurring in both Iran and Saudi Arabia, the end of the Cold War, and the launching of the Gulf War to liberate Kuwait. In this case the cluster of shocks moved the Iran–Saudi Arabia rivalry toward temporary détente.

Following from the preceding discussion, we offer several propositions about how shocks affect rivalry dynamics, including onset, termination, and importantly, persistence and fluctuation.

> Proposition 1: Shocks, in conjunction with other factors, increase the probability of rivalries beginning, escalating, de-escalating, and terminating if they introduce new sources of threat (beginnings) or devalue old sources of threat (terminations).
>
> Proposition 2: A cluster of shocks in a relatively short period, other things being equal, is more likely to increase the probability of change in foreign policy.

Proposition 3: A series of major shocks with considerable scope is likely to destabilize foreign policies regionally, especially if the region is closely interconnected (as opposed to loosely interconnected).

Proposition 4: Regions characterized by multiple shocks and rivalries are apt to experience more conflict than regions less characterized by shocks and rivalries.

These propositions will be empirically studied in this volume's individual chapters, each of which will demonstrate how shocks work with reference to a specific case. Studying multiple rivalries as well as varied observations within a single rivalry would give us a theoretical edge: it would help map out varieties of shocks and explain how they act on rivalry dynamics. Moreover, mapping out varieties of shocks would help unearth deeper societal and historical factors to explain rivalries. We need to be cautious in bestowing too much causal credit on shocks alone, however. It stands to reason that shocks will have greater impact in places that are more susceptible to them. For example, studying the importance of shocks while attending to societal and historical contexts would allow for a more accurate interrogation of how the Iran–Saudi Arabia rivalry was built on conflicts that had emerged before the 1979 revolution. Or how and why the Morocco-Algeria rivalry can be traced back to the mid-nineteenth century, that is, long before the two states' independence in the 1950s and 1960s, respectively.

Individual chapters vary in how closely they adhere to testing these propositions, but all address the role of shocks in their selected settings. One reason why they vary is that authors privilege differently general versus specific analyses about how their rivalries work. Some focus on one rivalry exclusively or even one side of one rivalry, others compare two rivalries, and still others focus on the region or subregions as wholes. We think this makes for a good mix in our attempt to make sense of the generalities and the specifics of MENA rivalries. Rivalry conceptualization and theory testing in the MENA remain in their infancy. We think that we make considerable headway in this volume vis-à-vis attaining our multiple goals. Yet much more work remains to be done before we can tell the full extent to which this approach offers significant, value-added, explanatory power.

NOVELTIES

The strength of this project encompasses two novelties. First, MENA contemporary international relations are analyzed in terms of rivalries, rivalry processes, and rivalry fields. Second, the new emphasis on shocks expands the analysis of rivalries and is particularly relevant to exploring and explaining MENA political and economic history.

As reflected in our propositions, our study brings forth a novel analytical approach to the MENA that moves beyond considering it as simply a macro-geographic entity. To highlight this strength, we need to underscore that an important dimension of our project is interpreting and comprehending MENA international relations from a rivalry perspective as conceptual structures and processes. This is a novel approach for studying MENA international relations that allows us to go beyond discussing the region in terms of what country X did to country Y in year Z. In our analysis we approach the MENA as a collection of "systems" (and also subregional systems) where units (mostly states and also substate actors) interact along certain issue areas. Such an approach allows us to understand the dynamics of rivalries being affected by shocks to issue areas of interest for involved states (e.g., revolution in a contiguous state, the birth of alliances, ideational and identity-based conflicts, societal contestation and revolts).

In such an approach we appreciate the diffusion effects of rivalries. By diffusion we mean that rivalries feed into existing conflict structures across the region even if rivals are not directly involved in a particular conflict. Diffusion exacerbates these conflicts and feeds back into fueling rivalries. Our initial findings tell us that conflict gets diffused more quickly in regions such as the MENA, where there is neither a dominant regional power nor a resident major power to help organize the regional order.

Moreover, the MENA is quite susceptible to extra-regional penetration, and those intrusions are particularly powerful in creating additional conflict, even independently of rivalries (although the intrusions can also be motivated by extra-regional rivalries). The actions of Great Powers and other powerful external actors (e.g., Britain before 1971; the United States and, to a lesser extent, Russia, ever since; and France in the Maghreb) repeatedly and forcefully affect regional rivalries. External interventions, if nothing else, make multiple shocks, sometimes originating from afar, more probable.

Building on the earlier argument on the analytical benefit of thinking of regions as open systems, the volume contributes to the development of the concept of a rivalry field. Rivalries can be viewed in terms of multi-actor dynamics—as "complexes" or "constellations"—rather than simply as dyads or pairs of states (the way the literature mostly looks at them now). These rivalries also interact and intersect with each other, whereby significant changes in the trajectory of one could reverberate to or strongly affect others. Moreover, focusing on rivalry fields allows us to better understand how shocks operate. For example, shocks to the Iran-Iraq rivalry as the result of the 1991 and 2003 interventions (mostly by the United States) affected the Iran–Saudi Arabia rivalry—the former fostered détente, while the latter inflamed the rivalry. Combining rivalry fields with the notion of shocks improves the explanatory and predictive power of our overall framework.

In comparison to other regions, the contemporary MENA hosts an unusually high number or frequency of rivalries, coupled with an unusually high number of violent interstate confrontations and protracted conflicts. The MENA ranks highest for both the number of rivalries and the levels of militarized interstate disputes (MIDs) occurring across the past four decades. We suspect these findings to be sustained when comparing regions according to rivalry fields as well.

It is here that we can add another motivation driving this volume: unpacking contemporary MENA politics. The rivalry field in the MENA has undergone radical empirical change, in part owing to the shocks that we are stressing as critical to interpreting the course of regional events. Arab-Israel hostilities, which have persisted for decades, have given way to a Sunni-Shi'a / Iranian–Saudi Arabian cleavage. In essence, the rivalry field of the MENA has radically altered—which is not a common finding in the rivalry literature. This finding will be of interest to scholars of conflict, war, and IR more broadly.

As a consequence, and building on the finding that the rivalry field has radically altered, knowing how regional politics once worked may not be all that useful in the future. This simple statement should be important in advocating for precision and analytical modesty when using analogies, predicting, and generalizing; it also reflects our championing of embedding rivalry analysis in deep historical and societal contexts. A better understanding of their roots and implications should improve our understanding of international relations in general as well as advance our ability to comprehend what is going on in the region.

CHAPTER SEQUENCE AND SUMMARY OF FINDINGS

After this introductory chapter, which lays out propositions primarily about the influence of shocks on rivalry dynamics as well as about the explanatory significance of rivalry fields, chapter 2 places MENA rivalries in a comparative global perspective and tests the effects of several variables. Thomas J. Volgy, Kelly Marie Gordell, and Paul Bezerra are interested in how "comparative regional analysts may identify a range of variables driving political relationships within all regions." In their chapter they find three salient issues about Middle East rivalries: (1) ideology has given way to sectarianism as a source of contention; (2) there has been a reduction, especially in the past decade, of the intensity of the rivalry field in the Middle East (making the region look more "normal" compared to others globally); and (3) shocks left important impacts. Among their conclusions is a recommendation to dedicate more attention to how nonstate actors are important in Middle East rivalries.

In chapter 3 William R. Thompson maps out the shift in the MENA rivalry field, with attention to the changing density and intensity of conflicts in the region. He finds that the stability of the MENA rivalry field has been undermined by a series of shocks that have rendered traditional enmities in the region less meaningful. It is hardly the case that MENA has suddenly been transformed into a highly cooperative setting. Adversarial relationships definitely remain, but they are now less likely to be structured in the form of conventional interstate conflicts. The chapter finds that the contemporary MENA rivalry field no longer resembles what it was a decade and a half earlier: the shift occurred, primarily, in a manner that places Iran at the center of MENA rivalry activity.

The following chapters attend to the dynamics of intra-MENA rivalry activities, locating Iran as a common actor. It should be noted here that the finding that the rivalry field shifted regionally toward a "Gulf-centric" one was not intended; we did not go looking for authors who would confirm this claim. While we had our suspicions about how MENA rivalries had changed over the past years, we were somewhat surprised (and pleased) that empirical descriptions from the chapters confirm that proposition.

In chapter 4 John Calabrese studies factors responsible for the onset and persistence of the Iran–Saudi Arabia rivalry. The Iranian Revolution catalyzed the rivalry, after which the trajectory of the rivalry was affected by a cluster of shocks in the 1990s, including an Iranian exhaustion owing to the war with Iraq (leading to Iran "swallowing the bitter pill"), a change in leadership in Riyadh, and the ebbing of the Cold War and collapse of the Soviet Union. The 2003 American invasion of Iraq shocked the Iran–Saudi Arabia rivalry into escalation and widened its geographic scope. Adding to this escalation and the geographic spread of rivalry, Calabrese finds, were the 2011 Arab Spring uprisings, from which emerged new actors and fields of competition.

In chapter 5 Thomas Keith Wilson provides an illustration of how Iranian behavior is embedded in domestic politics. To that end, the chapter examines intense points in the Iran–Saudi Arabia rivalry between 1979 and 2015, with specific attention to Iranian behavior. The chapter presents an explanatory model that accounts for decision makers' perceptions vis-à-vis the rival in their political institutional framework, as well as the role of the United States. Employing event data, content analysis, and process tracing to validate initial event data, the chapter argues that "rivalry outcomes are the product of environmental triggers, but only following internal bargaining processes between actors within distinct governing structures."

Chapters 4 and 5 highlight the centrality of Iran in a Gulf-centric rivalry field. Moreover, the following three chapters empirically find that Iran has been involved in "inter-subregional" active rivalries; this pattern of rivalry has mostly concerned activity that connects the Gulf to the Levant.

In chapter 6 Marwan J. Kabalan draws conclusions on how triadic rivalries operate by studying the rivalry among Iran, Iraq, and Syria since the mid-twentieth century and explaining the impact of shocks on its fluctuating patterns. The chapter studies the effects of four shocks: revolution in Iraq (1958), American invasion of Iraq (2003), revolution in Iran (1979), and revolt and civil war in Syria (2011). The chapter demonstrates how a shock in one of these countries affects this complex relationship, moving it closer to or distant from a rivalry.

In chapter 7 Meliha Benli Altunışık explains how the Iran-Turkey relationship contains elements of cooperation and intense competition, presenting characteristics of rivalry, especially mutual distrust and threat perceptions. The chapter studies effects of seven shocks or clusters of shocks, some of which were systemic (e.g., the emergence of the modern state system and the rise and end of the Cold War), domestic (e.g., the Iranian Revolution and the Arab uprisings), or regional-global (especially the 2003 American invasion of Iraq and efforts at rebuilding Syria after the collapse of the Islamic State of Iraq and the Levant [ISIL]). Altunışık concludes with the observation that the Iran-Turkey relationship is about status and influence and has been influenced by ideological/identity competition and domestic/regime security. This competition has manifested itself in the Middle East, Central Asia, and the South Caucasus.

In chapter 8 Imad Mansour studies the rivalry between the Islamic Republic of Iran and the state of Israel to demonstrate the explanatory power of narratives (as ideational structures) in rivalry analysis, especially as these are noncontiguous states. The chapter also empirically traces how shocks affect a dyadic rivalry dynamic and explores shocks that initiate the rivalry and others that have since influenced its intensity. Studying the Iran-Israel rivalry allows for an added elaboration as to what goal incompatibility means and where it could be rooted.

Chapters 9 and 10 provide explanations to MENA rivalry patterns, with attention to historic legacies, state-building pressures, and revolutionary zeal. They also highlight two observations. First, and before the shift of the rivalry field southward, the Egypt–Saudi Arabia rivalry left effects that reverberated broadly across the MENA, influencing the regional order at a critical time in its formation; these effects were transmitted in North Africa–Gulf connections via foreign policy activism, alliances, and relations with major powers, among others. Second, the two chapters confirm our claim about the noted shift in the rivalry field.

In chapter 9 Karen Rasler tests the influence of revolutions and revolutionary ideologies on rivalry onset, studying the Egypt–Saudi Arabia rivalry after the 1952 Egyptian Revolution and the Iran–Saudi Arabia rivalry after the Iranian Revolution of 1979. The chapter finds that revolutionary leaders pursued radical foreign policies (driven by their zeal and sense of mission), and some of these policies singled out certain regional states as competitors. These foreign policies, in turn, threatened neighbors that mobilized resources to counter these threats, which led to the creation of rivalries.

In chapter 10 Yahia H. Zoubir studies the Morocco-Algeria rivalry and explains how negative images and perceptions of the other, which emerged in the pre-independence period and persist to this day, were constructed and have since been reshaped by decision-makers. Shocks, this chapter explains, have had the effect of entrenching negative images of the other. In addition to novel empirical evidence, the chapter references interviews with high-level decision-makers conducted by the author.

In the concluding chapter there is an assessment of the shocks and rivalry theory we propose in this volume, which is based on the case studies. We offer three observations on (1) the importance of examining rivalries as rivalries, that is, as explicit adversarial relationships; (2) what shocks are, from where they can emerge, and at what level they act; and (3) why analyzing regional dynamics by applying the prism of rivalry fields has powerful explanatory value.

NOTES

1. "Competitive" means that these relationships tend to be restricted within leagues of roughly equivalent power. That is, Great Powers tend to focus on other Great Powers, and weaker states are more likely to single out proximate states of similar weaker states. It does not imply that very strong and very weak states never develop rivalry relationships but only that it is relatively rare. It also does not imply that rivalry relationships must reflect symmetrical power dyads. Two minor powers may have asymmetrical capabilities—India and Pakistan are a good example—but various other factors, such as geography, allies, or nuclear capability, may work to sustain unequal confrontations. The "threatening enemies" component is essential in differentiating actors that may be quite competitive but who are not perceived as representing existential threats from those that do.

2. Some of the early, pre-rivalry work included Leng (1983) and Gochman and Maoz (1984). Vasquez (1993) preceded most of the empirical work on rivalry.

3. Initially, there were a number of different operational schemes put forward by Diehl and Goertz (1992, 2000); Bennett (1996, 1997b, 1998); Wayman (2000); and Maoz and Mor (2002).

4. While the Diehl and Goertz approach fared best within the enduring rivalry, their approach has undergone some conceptual and empirical changes (see Klein, Goertz, and Diehl 2006, 2008;

Goertz, Diehl, and Balas 2016). The strategic rivalry approach has been fairly consistent, but its historical span has expanded with time (Thompson 1995, 2001; Colaresi, Rasler, and Thompson 2007; Thompson and Dreyer 2011).

5. Or one can evade choosing by focusing on selected rivalries. See, for instance, Thompson (1999), Leng (2000), or Paul (2005, 2018).

6. For an overview and selective integration of a large number of rivalry termination models, see Thompson (2018).

2

Crucial Fault Lines in the Middle East

Interstate Rivalries in Comparative Perspective

Thomas J. Volgy, Kelly Marie Gordell, and Paul Bezerra

Area specialists are advantaged in their studies by developing deep and thorough knowledge of the unique features of their region of interest. By the virtue of their training, orientation, and the extent to which they create a deep familiarization with both the historical and current features of their region, area specialists carry extensive knowledge of how such political arenas operate. At the same time, through their intense focus (and since it is virtually impossible to develop in-depth expertise on all regions), area specialists tend to emphasize *the uniqueness* of their focus of expertise. Too often Latin America, Africa, East Asia, Europe, or Middle East area specialists argue for the distinctive nature of their geographical area.

By contrast, international relations scholars, and particularly those who focus on comparative regional analysis (a sample of such scholarship is given in Volgy et al. 2017, 2018), often lack the expertise developed by area specialists. Instead, international relations scholars bring to their analysis a search for patterns that are applicable across regions in the context of their knowledge of international politics. Comparative regional analysts approach a geopolitical area such as the Middle East by assessing variation in the commonalities regions share (rather than their unique characteristics), commonalities that should help explain patterns of cooperation or conflict within any region.[1]

It may well be that both perspectives eventually identify a region as being unique, although they may do so for different reasons. Area specialists may focus on sets of regional characteristics not exhibited in other regions (common religious preferences, colonial heritage, topography, an unusual set of political systems, or a distinct political culture, etc.). Comparative regional analysts may identify a range of variables driving political relationships within all regions; on some of those salient characteristics a region may register uniquely from others, and its placement on that variable may be strongly linked to the dependent variable in question. For example, our focus here is on regional rivalries, their densities, and the way such considerations affect levels of intra-regional conflict. Regional rivalries are salient for all regions; what may be unique for the Middle East is that it has a substantially thicker clustering of such rivalries than any other geopolitical area in international politics. This makes the Middle East unique even from the standpoint of comparative regional analysis. What is more, such uniqueness may help account for why in post–World War II international politics the Middle East has been consistently the most conflict prone of all regions.

Both approaches have helped advance knowledge concerning how regions operate, and both approaches provide theoretically interesting answers to the question of why some regions are more conflictual than others. The approach we bring to this project is from the second school and reflects our own bias toward comparative regional analysis. In the following we first offer a theoretical framework suggesting the variety of conditions under which regions may experience different levels of intra-regional conflict or cooperation. Applying the framework, we find that while it works relatively well in accounting for which regions are more conflictual or pacific, it also indicates that on at least one crucial dimension—the extent to which interstate rivalries dominate relations between states—the Middle East region stands out as truly unique. Once we have demonstrated that uniqueness, we explore fluctuations in the Middle East rivalry field over time, link those fluctuations to regional shocks, and suggest consequences both for the region and for other regions in world politics.

A CONCEPTUAL AND THEORETICAL FRAMEWORK

Our primary interest is why some regions are conflict prone, others are pacific, and others still have moved from one category to another. Figure 2.1 illustrates the sets of considerations helping to explain variation in intra-regional conflict in world politics.

We have discussed this framework elsewhere (Volgy et al. 2018); here we briefly summarize its dimensions. We contend that three large sets of forces account for how much

Figure 2.1. Theoretical framework regarding intra-regional conflict and cooperation

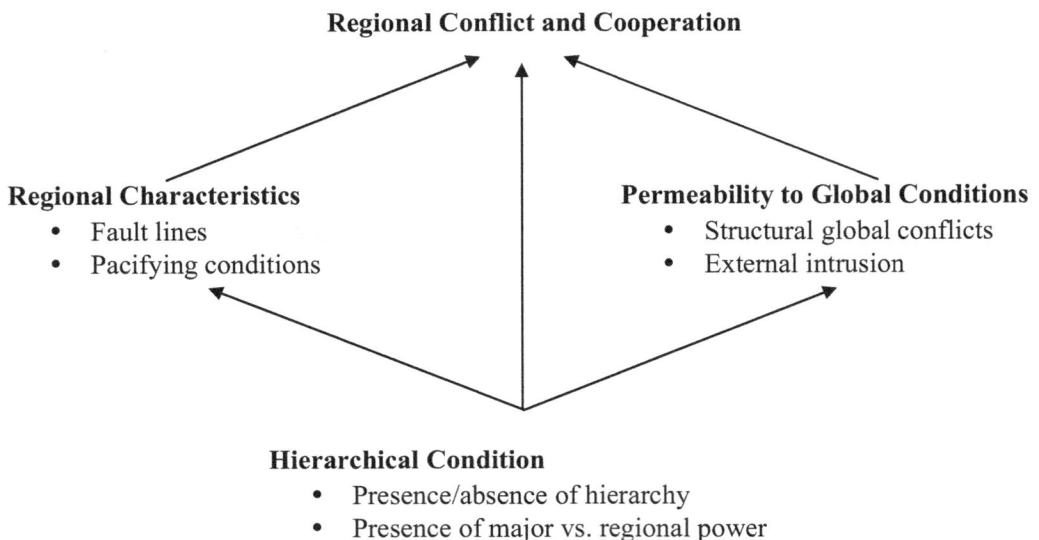

Regional Conflict and Cooperation

Regional Characteristics
- Fault lines
- Pacifying conditions

Permeability to Global Conditions
- Structural global conflicts
- External intrusion

Hierarchical Condition
- Presence/absence of hierarchy
- Presence of major vs. regional power

interstate conflict exists in a region. The first is the argument that regions vary with respect to certain characteristics internal to the region, conditions that either exacerbate conflicts or encourage cooperation between states. *Fault lines* refer to conditions— demonstrated empirically by extant research focusing on dyadic conflicts—that exacerbate conflict. Prime candidates include interstate rivalries, territorial claims, and civil wars, which may spread across the region.[2] The more these conditions exist in a region, the more likely the region will experience substantial conflict.

Additionally, regions vary with respect to a variety of *pacifying conditions*, conditions likely to encourage cooperation between states in the region. Again, based on previous research, we suggest three such conditions: intra-regional trade dependence, the extent to which regional states are democracies, and the extent to which regional states share membership in intergovernmental organizations (IGOs). None of these three factors should be surprising; the literature on the Kantian peace is not uncontroversial, but much of the evidence indicates that these forces encourage cooperation between states.[3]

There is not much originality in our specifications of either fault lines or pacifying conditions for regions; they merely reflect extant scholarship on states and dyads. However, conceptualizing these conditions as regional characteristics is more novel and raises two important points. First, regions are not created equal. Some regions are endowed with substantial fault lines (e.g., the Middle East), other regions with ample pacifying conditions (e.g., North America). Managing relations in a region riddled with fault lines is fundamentally more difficult for foreign policy makers than for those who live in regions endowed with substantial pacifying conditions.

Second, our framework places the concept and importance of interstate rivalries in a larger perspective. It is not surprising that interstate rivalries often lead to conflicts and that the presence of numerous interstate rivalries in a region would also lead to substantial intra-regional conflict. The larger issue, however, may be determining the relative salience of rivalries compared to other fault lines. Are rivalries more important in accounting for conflict between members of a region than the possible diffusion of civil wars or unresolved, festering territorial claims? Are rivalries trumped by competing pacifying conditions, such as a predominance of democracies in the region, or by the presence in the region of a dominant power seeking order, or by external interference into a region by outside powers? Our framework is designed to probe for answers to these questions.

The second dimension of our framework draws attention to the notion that regions do not exist in a vacuum. Regions are also part of the global international system and likely vary in terms of their permeability to global forces and global powers. The "bipolar" global conflicts of the Cold War touched, to one extent or another, virtually every region; the key to comparative regional analysis is understanding the extent to which some regions were able to resist Cold War intrusion more so than others. Similarly, in the post–Cold War environment, major powers, such as the US, China, and Russia, have actively intervened in regional affairs in some regions albeit not uniformly in all;[4] an appropriate question is to ask about the conditions that may facilitate the extent of regional resistance to such intervention and the effects of such interventions on intra-regional relations.

The third aspect of our framework focuses on whether (and the extent to which) intra-regional relationships play out in the context of power hierarchies. Some regions contain one or more major powers with the capability (and often the willingness) to dominate relationships within the region or to seek favorable regional security and economic orders. Other regions may contain a dominant regional power seeking the same. Finally, there are numerous regions in world politics containing neither regional nor major powers; the intra-regional relationships in several of those regions (including the Middle East) resemble conditions consistent with the anarchy assumption argued by neorealists.

We consider the presence or absence of hierarchy and the type of hierarchy that may exist within a region to be particularly salient to intra-regional relationships.[5] This is so for two reasons. The first is that a dominant power in the region would likely find it in its interest to impose order in the region. Consistent with its own foreign policy objectives, a dominant power would formulate security and economic rules, norms, and institutions favoring it, with a view toward minimizing regional conflicts that may be disruptive to its interests. How much of such order a dominant power can create in its region (and to what extent it will seek conformance by other states in the region) likely depends on its capabilities, willingness, and competence to do so.

The second reason why the distinction is important is the relationships among hierarchy, regional characteristics, and regional permeability to global dynamics. Strong dominant powers in a region may seek to minimize fault lines or their diffusion across the region, encourage the development of regionally pacifying trends (e.g., trade interdependencies or the creation of IGOs), or prevent the intrusion of outside powers that might take a counteractive role in the region. Presumably, these outcomes would require dominant states that have substantial capabilities and the willingness to act—capability and willingness greater than some regional powers may possess.

Applying our framework to the Middle East allows us to assess conditions that are unique to the Middle East as well as conditions that fit regions similar to the Middle East. In comparative perspective the region scores high on fault lines and low on pacifying conditions. While we demonstrate later that the Middle East is unique with respect to the nature of its rivalries, it also shares some important characteristics with other regions that help shape its conflict orientation. For instance, the region experiences more civil wars (~2.5 versus ~1.5) and is characterized by more territorial disputes (~0.7 versus ~0.4) than more pacific regions. It is also characterized by an absence of conditions that might otherwise restrain states from violent contestations. In terms of pacifying conditions, Middle Eastern states are not particularly interdependent on one another for trade, and the region is nearly absent of democracies. The Kantian peace likely collapses in the absence of a single leg, let alone two or even, possibly, all three. Additionally, the Middle East lacks any semblance of hierarchy, as is recognized by major and regional power scholars, and it is heavily penetrated by outside forces, such as the United States and Russia, with said forces often taking opposite sides of the same disputes.[6] These examples foreshadow our emphases in the remaining chapter: (1) the Middle East is uniquely conflict-prone, but rivalries are only a part of the explanation—not the whole of it—and (2) rivalries in the Middle East may be changing over time with important implications for peace.

A FEW KEY CONCEPTS

Before addressing the salience of rivalries, we note a few critical concepts.[7] First, we define a region as a geopolitical space of three or more states in close proximity, where states have the capacity to reach each other and demonstrate some unique willingness to do so at a frequency typically greater than with states outside the region.[8] We measure the existence of regions and state membership in those regions by aggregating our indicators at ten-year intervals. Thus, we map regions and regional membership by decades, and as a result, the primary unit of our subsequent analysis is the region year.[9]

Our methodology requires regional membership to be mutually exclusive: a state cannot belong to two regions at the same time. However, since both membership in a region and the very existence of a region are empirically determined, states, within geographical limits, can move from one region to another (e.g., Turkey). Further, not only can new regions emerge but existing regions can disappear.[10] Most but not all states are classified as belonging to a region at any point in time, although some states do not fit into any region.[11] Between 1951 and 2010 the number of regions varies by decade, ranging from eight in the 1950s to eleven in the 2000s.

In this context, our approach to the Middle East is somewhat different from the approach in chapter 3 of this book, which indicates three fixed regions in the Middle East subsystem. Our empirical indicators exclude the Maghreb as part of the Middle East and treat it as a separate region when the indicators so warrant; the states in the Levant and the Gulf are classified as belonging in the Middle East.

We opt for delineating rivalries as strategic rivalries consistent with the conceptualization and measurement offered by Thompson (2001) and Thompson and Dreyer (2011). We also identify rivalry fields (see chapter 3 in this volume) as the overarching, prevailing pattern of rivalries within a single region. Rivalry fields are distinct from individual rivalries in that the field is thought to condition each region member's behaviors even if a member is not a party to any rivalries within its region. As an example, during the 1960s Lebanon had no rivalries in the Middle East but was nonetheless conditioned by the dense rivalry field of the Middle East (see fig. 2.10). The density of the rivalry field refers to the extent of rivalries within said region.

As a second key concept, political shocks are defined as major abrupt and unanticipated political disturbances to domestic, regional, or global environments (Goertz 2000). Although shocks have tremendous potential to alter interstate relations by cutting through path dependencies and policymakers' inertia, they have not been systematically studied, nor is there a semblance of agreement over their definition and method of identification.[12] We chose the Diehl and Goertz definition as it appears to be most consistent with common scholarly usage.

As our third key concept, whether a region contains a hierarchy is identified by the presence or absence of either a major power or a regional power in the region.[13] Major and regional powers are identified consistent with Volgy et al. (2011) and Cline et al. (2011), respectively. These approaches to major or regional power designation require a set of thresholds that need to be met in order for a state to be identified as a major or regional power. For the former, a state must possess unusual amounts of military and economic capacity compared to other states (both in terms of sheer size and the ability to use this capacity across large distances), be willing to act globally, and be recognized as having the status of a major power. Regional powers need to meet similar criteria but with respect to the states within their own region. Our empirical analysis indicates that for the Middle East, and while there have been numerous contenders, no single state has emerged since 1945 that meets all the threshold requirements for regional power status.[14]

PLACING RIVALRIES IN CONTEXT

Why is the Middle East the most conflict prone of all regions (Volgy et al. 2018)? Is it due to the nature of regional interstate rivalries? Or does the presence of other fault lines or the absence of pacifying conditions better explain the prevalence of conflict? Consistent with our perspective and the framework outlined previously, we begin by asking about the relationship between rivalries and conflict (one of three fault lines identified in our framework), regardless of the region in which those rivalries are situated.

At first glance it is clear that a close relationship exists between the numbers of rivalries and the extent of conflict within a region. The simple correlation between the number of regional rivalries and the frequency of severe regional conflict (measured as severe militarized interstate disputes, or MIDs [Palmer et al. 2015]) is 0.43; the relationship between frequency of regional rivalries and the diffusion of regional conflict (the numbers of states in the region involved with severe MIDs) is even stronger at 0.52. Nonetheless, the relationship between numbers of rivalries and the extent of conflict within a region could plausibly be mitigated by other factors in our framework, and especially the presence or absence of regional hierarchy.

Can the presence of hierarchy have a mitigating impact on the number of rivalries? Our data suggest that it may. Table 2.1 compares the frequency of rivalries across regions, controlling for hierarchy.[15] There is clearly a substantial difference in the frequency of rivalries across types of regions: nonhierarchical regions experience a substantially greater frequency of rivalries than do regions containing dominant powers.[16] Of course, such limited analysis does not allow us to tell anything about the direction of impact. It is just as likely that large numbers of rivalries in a region inhibit the rise of major or

Table 2.1. Numbers of rivalries in regions, by type of region, 1951–2010

	Nonhierarchical regions	Hierarchical regions	
		Major power	Regional power
Mean number of rivalries	5.17	2.91	1.42

regional powers because dominant states successfully suppress or even preempt strategic rivalries from emerging in their regions. What we can tell, however, is that both the frequency of rivalries and the presence of hierarchy matter in assessing whether some regions are more conflict prone than others.

Table 2.2 assesses these relationships further by integrating a broader range of considerations into the equation, consistent with our theoretical perspective. The table now contains three variables associated with what we consider to be regional fault lines (rivalries, civil wars, and territorial claims), three indicators corresponding to regionally pacifying conditions (trade interdependencies, democratic regimes, and IGO membership), and two global conditions (Cold War and external alliances with major powers), along with regional differentiation based on the presence or absence of regional hierarchies.[17]

We draw several conclusions from table 2.2. First, even in this broader context, both intra-regional rivalries and the absence of hierarchy appear to have pernicious effects on the amount of interstate conflict regions experience. Second, as important as the number of strategic rivalries is in accounting for levels of regional conflict, it is by no means the only major consideration, and at least three other factors—territorial claims, the presence of hierarchy, and alliances with major powers outside the region—provide even stronger predictions to how much regional conflict occurs. Third, the suggestion raised

Table 2.2. OLS regression models for major and regional powers and regional conflict, with number of severe MIDs / number of states in region

	Base model		Major power presence		Regional power presence	
Hierarchy	–	–	-0.167***	(0.030)	-0.112***	(0.028)
Number of intra-regional rivalries$_{t-1}$	0.021***	(0.003)	0.016***	(0.004)	0.016***	(0.004)
Number of civil wars$_{t-1}$	0.020**	(0.007)	0.007	(0.006)	0.044***	(0.010)
Territorial claims$_{t-1}$	0.169**	(0.052)	0.264***	(0.070)	0.201***	(0.050)
Percentage of regional trade$_{t-1}$	-0.036**	(0.013)	–	–	0.005	(0.019)
Percentage of regional democracies$_{t-1}$	-0.118**	(0.043)	-0.047	(0.054)	-0.141***	(0.040)
IGO membership$_{t-1}$	-0.169***	(0.045)	-0.200***	(0.057)	-0.186***	(0.050)
External alliances$_{t-1}$	0.080**	(0.026)	0.050	(0.029)	0.124***	(0.026)
Cold War	-0.054**	(0.023)	-0.044	(0.024)	-0.081**	(0.027)
Time counter	-0.003	(0.004)	-0.004	(0.004)	-0.006	(0.004)
Constant	0.227***	(0.042)	0.202***	(0.049)	0.160***	(0.047)
Observations	366		261		267	
Adjusted R^2	0.322		0.408		0.445	
AIC	-157.1		-175.5		-117.7	
BIC	-118.0		-139.9		-78.26	

Note: Robust standard errors reported in parentheses.
* p < .05; ** p < .01; *** p < .001

Figure 2.2. Marginal effect of major power hierarchy and rivalries on severe MID frequencies

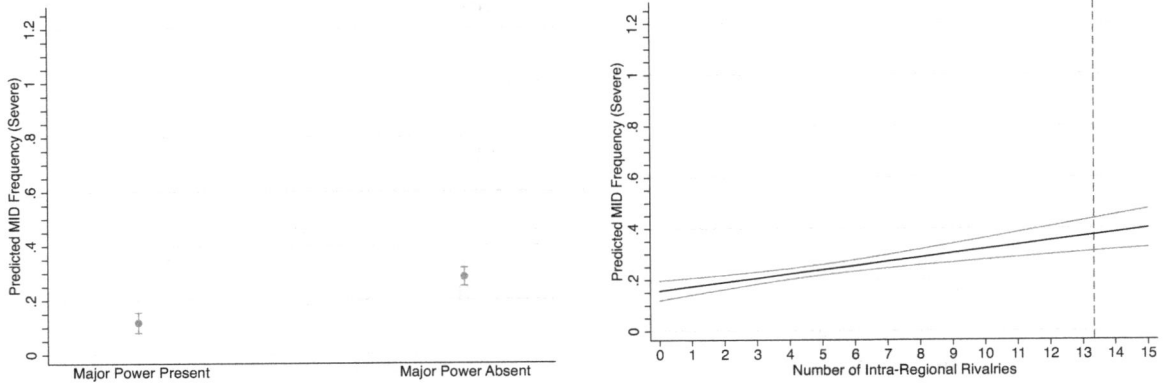

by table 2.1 continues in table 2.2: regions with dominant powers appear to be affected less by rivalry than regions without.

To better evaluate the unique impact of hierarchy versus rivalries on regional conflict patterns, figures 2.2 and 2.3 plot the marginal effects of these conditions for major power and regional power hierarchies, respectively (the latter two models in table 2.2). The left panel in figure 2.2 plots the pacifying effect of a major power within a region, and the right panel plots the conflict-exacerbating effect of an increasing number of rivalries in any given region (each level is observed in our models); the dashed line in the right panel marks 13.333 rivalries, which corresponds to the average number of rivalries in the Middle East in each of our models—a point we will revisit later in this chapter. As shown in the left panel, regions without a major power are predicted to experience nearly 141 percent more conflict than regions with a major power in terms of severe

Figure 2.3. Marginal effect of regional power hierarchy and rivalries on severe MID frequencies

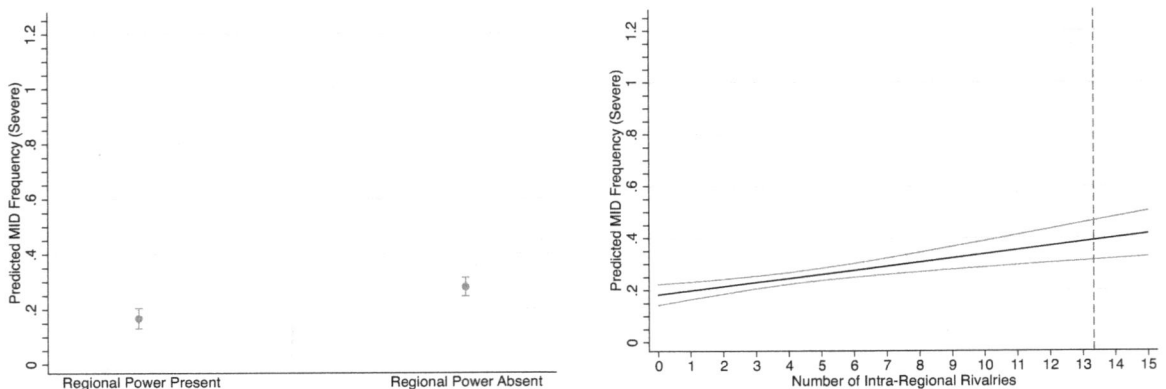

Figure 2.4. Marginal effect of rivalries on severe MID frequencies by hierarchy types

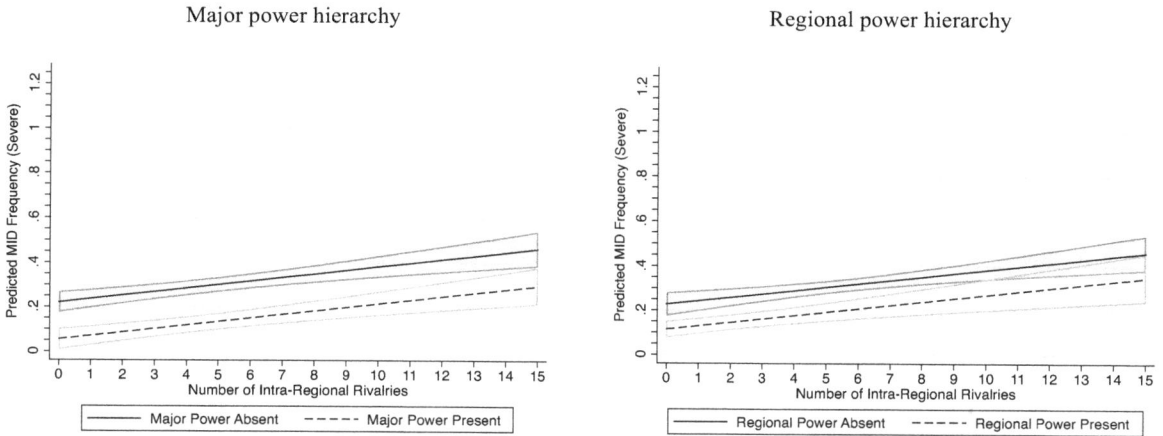

MID frequency (0.284 versus 0.118). These effects are roughly comparable, shown in the right panel, to the predicted level of severe MID frequency in regions possessing zero intra-regional rivalries (0.158) and eight intra-regional rivalries (0.287). Thus, individually, both major power hierarchy and intra-regional rivalries condition the frequency of severe MIDs—but the conflict-exacerbating effect of rivalries surpasses the pacifying effect of major power hierarchy in the upper half of our observed rivalry counts.[18]

To better capture the effect of intra-regional rivalries on severe MID frequency patterns by hierarchy type, figure 2.4 plots the predicted levels of conflict by increasing numbers of rivalries in regions with hierarchy versus regions without. In the case of major powers (left panel), regions characterized by the presence of a major power (dashed line) are always predicted to experience lower severe MID frequency than regions without such hierarchy (solid line)—no matter the number of intra-regional rivalries present. The same cannot be said of regional power hierarchies whose pacifying effect becomes indistinguishable from nonhierarchical regions as the number of intra-regional rivalries approaches the upper third of our observed intra-regional rivalry counts.

As an additional test of these relationships, we change the dependent variable from the frequency of severe conflicts annually in a region (again, controlling for region size) to the number of states engaged in severe conflicts annually in the region (also controlling for region size). This was done to approximate a measure of the extent of conflict diffusion in regions and to ascertain the extent to which rivalries create stronger diffusion effects or the extent to which hierarchies minimize diffusion effects. The results are displayed in table 2.3.[19] We do not learn a great deal more about the effects of rivalries on conflict diffusion than we did about conflict levels. While the rivalry coefficients are stronger, so are the coefficients for territorial claims. However, as shown in figures 2.5

Table 2.3. OLS regression models for major and regional powers and regional conflict, with number of states in region involved in severe MIDs / number of states in region

	Base model		Major power presence		Regional power presence	
Hierarchy	–	–	-0.285***	(0.051)	-0.141**	(0.047)
Number of intra-regional rivalries$_{t-1}$	0.052***	(0.006)	0.045***	(0.006)	0.047***	(0.008)
Number of civil wars$_{t-1}$	0.027*	(0.012)	0.009	(0.010)	0.060***	(0.017)
Territorial claims$_{t-1}$	0.247**	(0.084)	0.308**	(0.113)	0.266**	(0.084)
Percentage of regional trade$_{t-1}$	-0.071**	(0.021)	–	–	0.001	(0.032)
Percentage of regional democracies$_{t-1}$	-0.129	(0.074)	-0.033	(0.093)	-0.163*	(0.076)
IGO membership$_{t-1}$	-0.336***	(0.073)	-0.360***	(0.094)	-0.392***	(0.083)
External alliances$_{t-1}$	0.144**	(0.046)	0.097	(0.052)	0.215***	(0.047)
Cold War	-0.093*	(0.038)	-0.060	(0.042)	-0.126***	(0.046)
Time counter	-0.009	(0.006)	-0.010	(0.007)	-0.015	(0.008)
Constant	0.406***	(0.072)	0.327***	(0.080)	0.288***	(0.078)
Observations	366		261		267	
Adjusted R^2	0.378		0.455		0.465	
AIC	221.6		119.1		174.2	
BIC	260.6		154.7		213.7	

Note: Robust standard errors reported in parentheses.
* p < .05; ** p < .01; *** p < .001

and 2.6, it appears hierarchy does have a somewhat stronger impact in minimizing the diffusion of conflict than it did in minimizing levels of regional conflict.

Following the same structure outlined previously, figure 2.5 plots the unique effects of major power hierarchy (left panel) and intra-regional rivalries (right panel) and corresponds to the "Major Power Presence" model of table 2.3; figure 2.6 plots the same for regional power hierarchies and corresponds to the "Regional Power Presence" model of table 2.2. Figure 2.5 suggests regions without a major power experience approximately 144 percent more severe MID involvement (0.484 versus 0.198), and these effects are comparable to the predicted levels of involvement for a region when it is characterized by zero intra-regional rivalries (0.197) and between six (0.470) and seven (0.515) intra-regional rivalries. Unlike our previous results, regional powers demonstrate less ability to inhibit conflict diffusion than major powers. Whereas our separate models predict similar levels of conflict diffusion in the absence of major or regional power hierarchy (0.484 and 0.456, respectively), the presence of a regional power reduces this prediction to only 0.315, whereas major powers reduce the prediction to 0.198. Compared to the individual effect of intra-regional rivalries on conflict diffusion, the presence of a regional

Figure 2.5. Marginal effect of major power hierarchy and rivalries on severe MID involvement

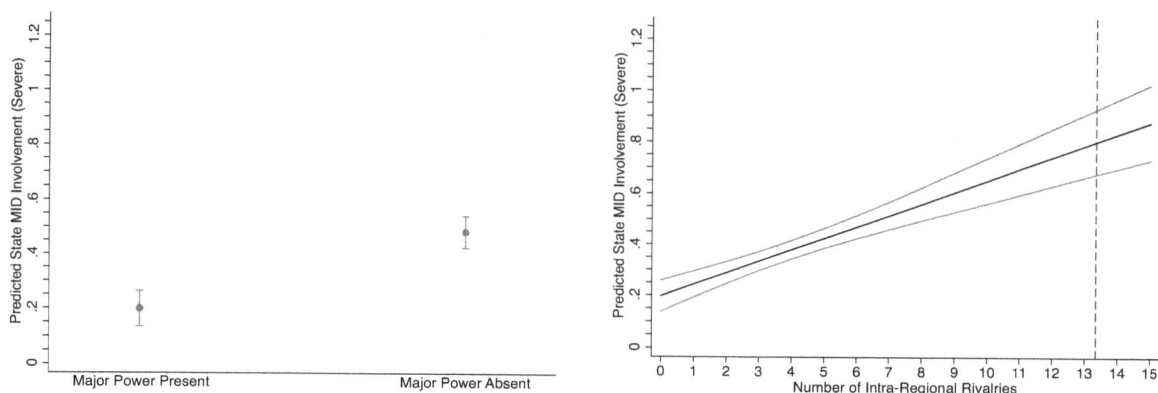

Figure 2.6. Marginal effect of regional power hierarchy and rivalries on severe MID involvement

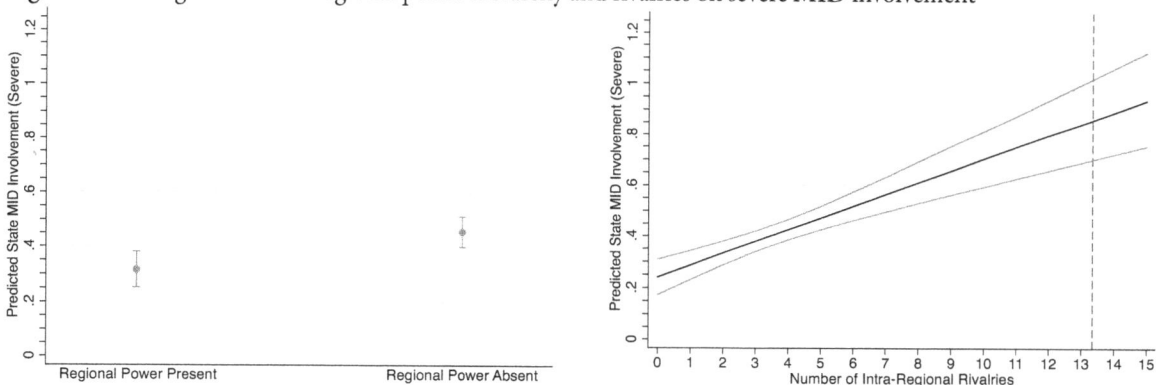

power hierarchy in a region is equivalent to roughly the presence of two rivalries (0.333), and the absence of a regional power hierarchy is equivalent to roughly between four (0.426) and five (0.472) rivalries. Thus, hierarchy and rivalries both individually influence a region's conflict-diffusion patterns, but regional powers appear to be less capable of containing diffusion than major powers.

Figure 2.7 further elaborates on the differences between major and regional powers' abilities to contain diffusion by plotting the effect of intra-regional rivalries on conflict diffusion by hierarchy type. As seen in previous results, major power hierarchies (left panel) are almost always distinguishable from regions without hierarchy in terms of their ability to mitigate conflict diffusion. The same cannot be said for regional power hierarchies (right panel). Regional power hierarchies are distinguishable from nonhierarchical regions only in a narrow range of intra-regional rivalries in the lower half of our observed intra-regional rivalry counts.

Figure 2.7. Marginal effect of rivalries on severe MID involvement by hierarchy types

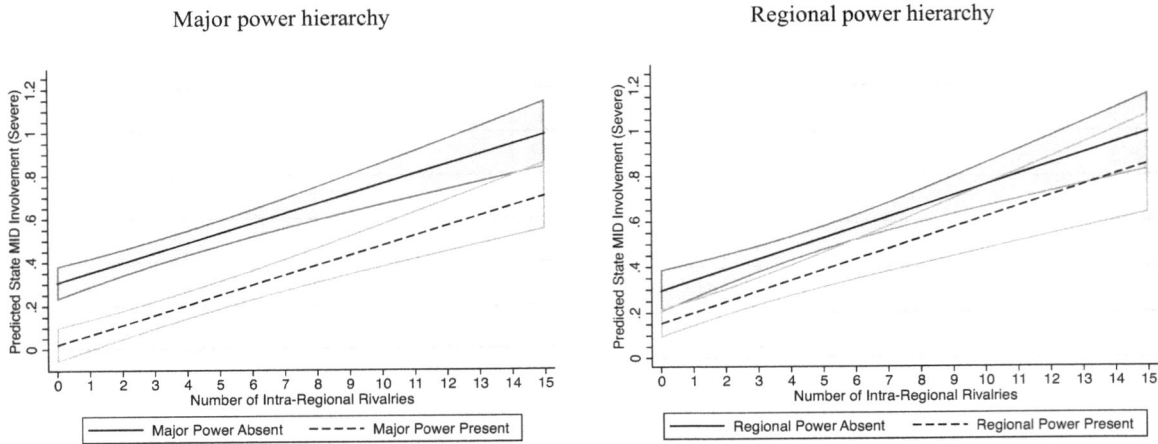

WHAT IS SO UNIQUE ABOUT THE MIDDLE EAST?

Recall that we are interested in assessing why some regions (and especially the Middle East) are unusually conflict prone. This interest requires first answering another, earlier question: What would constitute a unique region from the perspective of comparative regional analysis? From the standpoint of our framework, the Middle East ticks all the boxes associated with a high-conflict region. In terms of the region's fault lines, the Middle East ranks high on numbers of interstate rivalries (~13 on average versus ~2 in all other regions), Middle Eastern states often experience civil wars (~2.5 versus ~1.5 in all others), and disputed territorial claims exist among states in the Middle East (~0.7 versus ~0.4). In terms of pacifying conditions, the Middle East offers few: its members do not rank high on IGO membership compared to other regions, its states are not highly interdependent in terms of their trade relationships (2.87 versus 2.17 for other regions), and there are virtually no democracies in the region (~7 percent of the Middle East versus ~34 percent in all other regions). With respect to its permeability to global forces, the Middle East was an active theater during the Cold War and remains externally penetrated by major powers today—particularly by the US and Russia—as well as by allied participants of the US-led war on terrorism.[20] With respect to the possibility that the presence of a hierarchy might dampen conflict, the Middle East contains aspirants, including Egypt, Israel, Iran, and Saudi Arabia, but no dominant major or regional power (Cline et al. 2011).

Consistent with our theoretical framework, we would expect this combination of circumstances to predict a region of ongoing, substantial intra-regional conflict. Indeed, apart from the Central African region during the 2000s, the Middle East is the most conflictual of all regions in world politics. In this sense, the Middle East is an outlier among regions, and thus it is unique by both its performance on our dependent variable and on our key independent variables.[21]

Being an outlier does not necessarily create uniqueness, however; there may be several outliers and for similar reasons. Another way of looking at the notion of uniqueness is to ask whether the region exhibits some pattern associated with conflict that makes it distinctly different from other regions. The clear candidate in this volume is interstate rivalries. While we caution that it is not the only, and perhaps not even necessarily the dominant, driver of conflict relations (as suggested by tables 2.2 and 2.3, and the accompanying figures), an unusually high density of interstate regional rivalries can threaten to overwhelm a region, especially in the absence of a dominant power in the region seeking order and stability. This is precisely what we find in the Middle East.

Figure 2.8 illustrates the average density scores for Middle East states in rivalries, compared to the average of all other regions and the next-highest region exhibiting interstate rivalries. Although these data exhibit the mean scores over a large period (1951–2010) and control for region size (number of states), the Middle East density scores are incomparably large compared to all other regions. Clearly, the region is unique with respect to the density of its interstate rivalries.[22]

Figure 2.9 further underscores the uniqueness of the region. Not only is the rivalry field density incomparably high compared to other regions but most states are also actively involved in these rivalries, ranging from a low of 55 percent of all the region's states to over 90 percent of all states during the late 1960s, and nearly 80 percent of all states in the region during the late 1980s through the 1990s. This was foreshadowed by the dashed line at 12.333 in figures 2.2, 2.3, 2.5, and 2.6, which marks the Middle East's average number of intra-regional rivalries in our models; the collective average of all other regions in our models hovers near two intra-regional rivalries.[23]

Figure 2.8. Average rivalry density scores for the Middle East versus other regions, 1951–2010

Figure 2.9. Percent of Middle East states involved in regional rivalries, 1951–2015

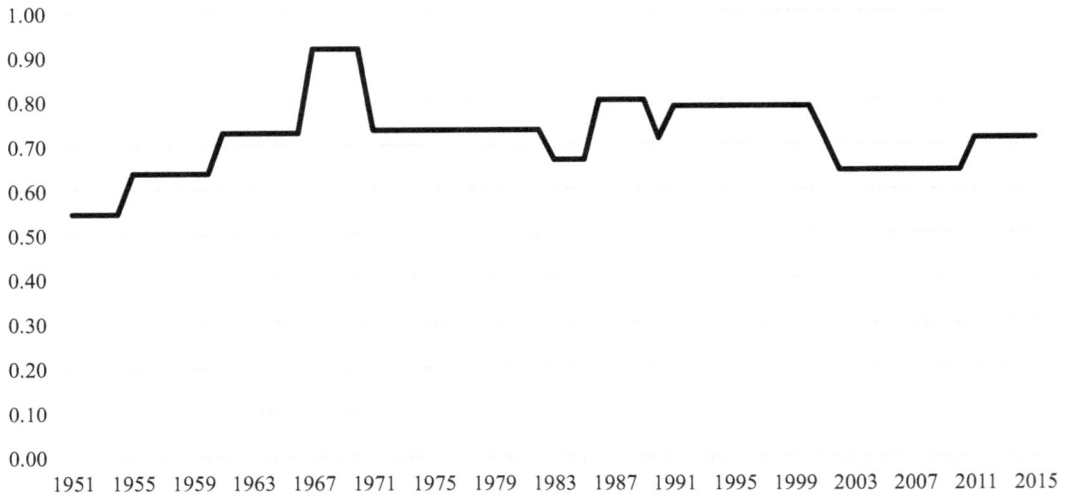

Until this point we have used a comparative delineation of regions as indicated previously. However, to focus on changes to rivalries in the Middle East only, we now keep regional membership constant for the entire period.[24] Note, however, the changing nature of the Middle East rivalry field along with some key changes regarding the state actors involved with each period: the thickness of the density field yields substantial changes over time. We illustrate with figures 2.10–12.[25]

Figure 2.10 shows the region's rivalry field in 1960; with the exception of four states (Kuwait, Lebanon, Oman, and the Yemen Arab Republic), all other region members are

Figure 2.10. Middle East rivalry field, 1960

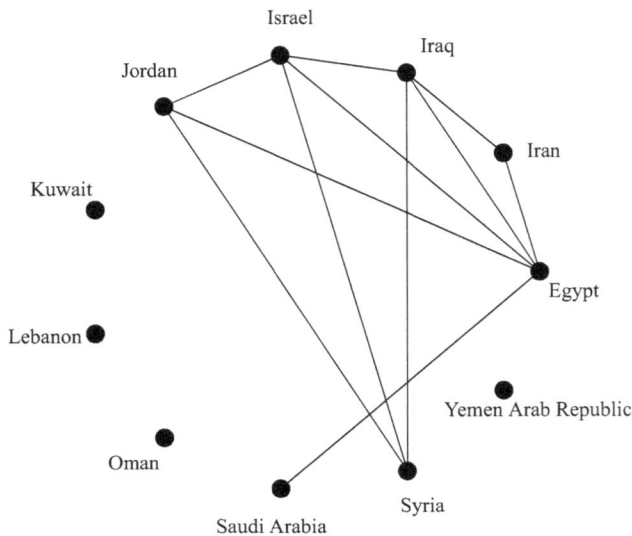

Figure 2.11. Middle East rivalry field, 1990

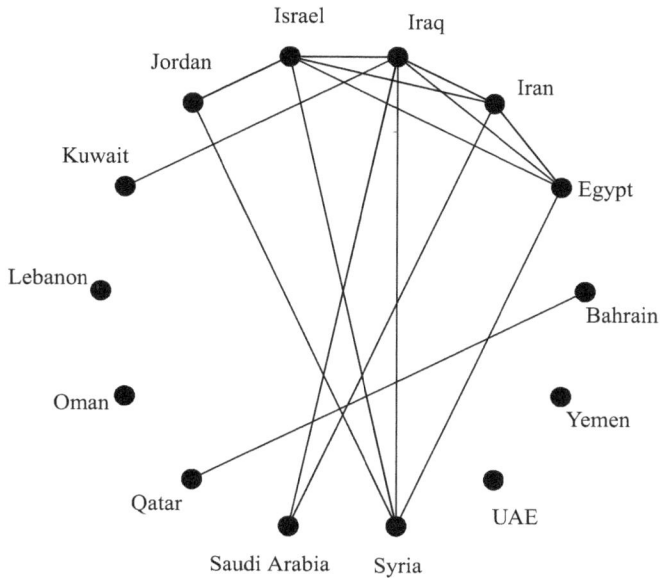

caught in rivalries. Figure 2.11 maps the rivalry field for 1990; a single set of rivalries is now bifurcated into a dominant one, and a smaller one (Qatar-Bahrain), with four, slightly changed, states remaining outside rivalries (Lebanon, Oman, Yemen, and UAE).

Figure 2.12 maps the region's rivalry field for 2015. In this latest period two obvious differences emerge. First, the number of states involved in rivalries is smaller than in

Figure 2.12. Middle East rivalry field, 2015

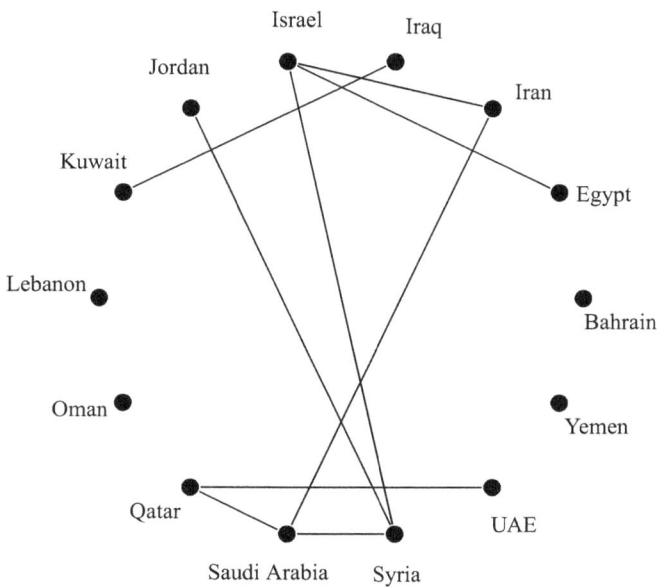

1960, and second, the number of non-connected states evolved slightly again such that four states remain outside rivalries (Bahrain, Lebanon, Oman, and Yemen).

Some obvious changes contribute to the fluctuations in the field. Egypt, which was involved in roughly 60 percent of rivalries during the 1960s, was by 2015 involved with less than 10 percent of the field. Iraq's involvement had been more prominent than even Egypt's, with a consistent involvement in nearly half of all rivalries—until 2003, after which it nearly disappears from the field. Israel's involvement in the rivalry field is also extensive, albeit not nearly as much as either Egypt's or Iraq's involvement, and Israel's lowest rate of involvement (around 23 percent) occurs from 2004 to the present. As a result of these states' reduced involvement in the Middle East rivalry field, we observe a pattern that is by 2015 more "normal" compared to other regions, but only when assessed in the context of the Middle East's much denser field before the twenty-first century. However, a word of caution is due: more "normal" in the Middle East does not equate to "typical" for a region of its type (nonhierarchical). Even in its more simplified form, the density of the field in the region remains incomparable to other major regions.

Do these changes create dramatically less conflict in the Middle East? That should not be expected. After all, even when the field is substantially reduced, it is still substantially denser than in virtually any other region. Additionally, as we noted earlier, it is not only the rivalry field that drives intra-regional conflict, as other fault lines (e.g., territorial contestation and civil wars) and external interventions continue to exacerbate conflicts. Needless to say, the absence of hierarchy does not help promote peace either, facilitating instead struggles by regional power aspirants that today include Saudi Arabia and Iran, a list that previously included Egypt and Iraq as well.[26]

Instead, what may be changing is the amount of conflict in the region that can be solely attributed to the rivalry field. Consider figures 2.13 and 2.14. Figure 2.13 shows the annual fluctuations in the Middle East rivalry field's density. Density goes beyond simply the number of states involved in rivalries by considering also the commonality of

Figure 2.13. Middle East rivalry density field, 1951–2015

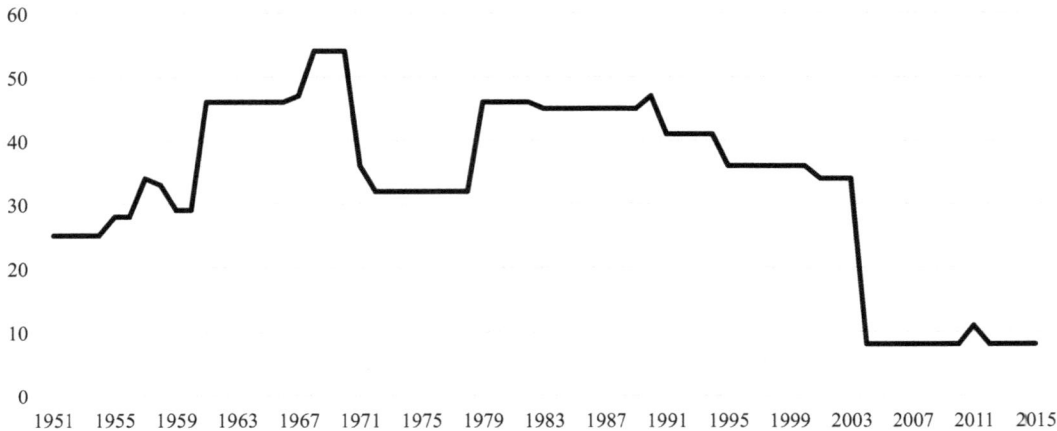

Figure 2.14. Average annual frequency of regional severe MIDs, by rivalry field type, 1951–2010

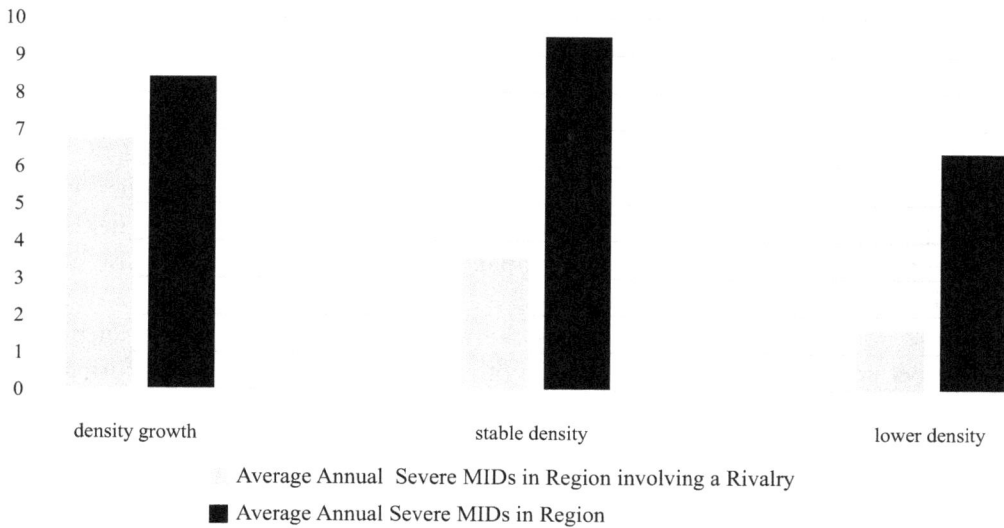

Average Annual Severe MIDs in Region involving a Rivalry

■ Average Annual Severe MIDs in Region

the actors within active rivalries each year. There appear to be roughly three periods: the first, 1951–70, is a period of growth in the field; the second, 1979–2002, is a period of stability in the field; the third represents a sharp decline in the field, following the invasion of Iraq and the dismantling of the Saddam Hussein regime.

Figure 2.14 provides some limited evidence of the declining, direct contribution of rivalry density to intra-regional conflict. We know rivalries are pernicious in terms of their impacts on conflict. We expect rivalry fields would have similar consequences. We expect, though, that different levels of rivalry field density would be associated with different levels of conflict. This is essentially what we find in terms of the changing density field in the Middle East. During the period of rivalry density growth, some 80 percent of severe MIDs occurring in the region involve rivals. During periods of stable rivalry densities, that percentage is reduced to about 54 percent, while during the period of lower densities, only some 22 percent of severe MIDs are directly associated with the rivalry field. As the figure demonstrates, clearly the most conflict associated with rivalry fields is during the growth in the field. While stable and lower density eras are associated with a lower percentage of conflicts in which rivals are directly engaged, the era of lower density demonstrates the fewest direct conflicts being generated by rivalry members with each other.

POLITICAL SHOCKS AND RIVALRY FIELDS

Note, however, that even a dramatic decline in the rivalry field fails to augur the end of substantial conflicts in the region. Although the density of the rivalry field is dramatically reduced in the period we designate as "lower density," this most recent period still exhibits nearly 70 percent of the conflicts occurring in the previous period. Furthermore, during the era of stable density, the actual number of severe MIDs is at its highest and is not directly attributable to the density field.

Nevertheless, changes to the rivalry field appear to matter for patterns of conflict in the Middle East, and this relationship raises the larger question of under what conditions the field might change. One strong argument made in this collection concerns the potential effects of political shocks on rivalry fields and thus on intra-regional conflict. Thompson's chapter 3 provides evidence that virtually all changes in the rivalry field, either terminating or initiating rivalries, are accompanied or immediately preceded by substantial political shocks in the region.

We have no valid, meaningful database with which to assess the range of political shocks experienced in the Middle East or in other regions. Collecting this information is a project worthy of further pursuit but necessarily beyond our own efforts here. We suspect, however, that the Middle East is also a likely candidate for having experienced more political shocks than any other region. Until an appropriate database is developed, that remains a suspicion, but many events in the region can be enumerated as appropriate political shocks with both short-term and long-term implications.

Consider a second look at the density of the Middle East rivalry field and four key political shocks in the region: two domestically driven political shocks (the Nasser and the Khomeini revolutions emanating out of Egypt and Iran, respectively), one external military intrusion into the region by the United States eliminating the Saddam Hussein regime in 2003, and the Cold War's end. These are matched to the rivalry field's density in figure 2.15; the starts of these shocks are represented by the dotted vertical lines.

Three of the four shocks appear to correspond to changes in the rivalry field. The Nasser revolution parallels the commencement of a substantial increase in the rivalry field's density, reflecting both clashes between radical and conservative regimes and the

Figure 2.15. Density of the Middle East rivalry field and selected regional shocks, 1951–2015

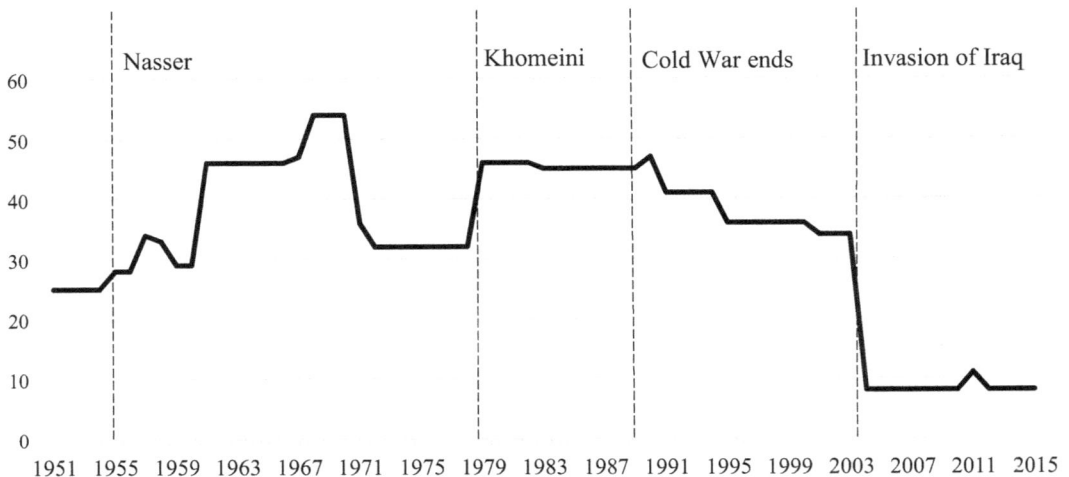

fuller entanglement of these states in the Arab-Israeli conflict; the Khomeini revolution corresponds with the beginning of a stable density field; the 2003 American invasion of Iraq immediately precedes the dramatic decline in the rivalry field's density. The 2003 invasion constitutes a very different shock since it pulled Iraq from the density field and tilted the balance in power relations in the region. This case serves as a reminder that the effects of these shocks are typically to interrupt path dependencies: they can substantially increase or reduce the rivalry field's density. If the Cold War had a substantial impact on the field, it appears that its end had an impact that is more gradual but may have minimized the Khomeini revolution's own impact over the longer term.[27]

It is also plausible that political shocks may not result in substantially greater or fewer rivalries but instead function to realign and stabilize rivalry fields. This may be the case with the Khomeini revolution in Iran. It is followed by a significant period of stability in the density field, meaning neither more nor fewer states in the region engage in rivalries after the revolution. However, the contents of many of those rivalries are altered, paralleling growing sectarian divisions in the region.[28]

Until we can systematically assess a fuller sample of both domestic and externally induced shocks in the Middle East (and elsewhere), much of this discussion can only be speculative. For instance, figure 2.15 identifies only four political shocks, yet there are many other possible candidates, as noted in chapter 3. For example, the Camp David agreements, coming shortly before the Khomeini revolution, may have, in combination with that revolution, produced the stability in the rivalry field as both effectively set in place for a period of otherwise dynamic relationships (e.g., Israel with some of its challengers and post-revolution Iran with other anti-Western regimes). Alternatively, the end of the Cold War, a system-wide political shock, was followed by another: the Iraqi invasion of Kuwait and the first US-led Persian Gulf War. Was it the end of the Cold War or the Gulf War that led to a gradual reduction in the density of the rivalry field that can be observed during the 1990s in figure 2.15? On the one hand, the end of the Cold War allowed for a global reordering of relations, including in the Middle East (e.g., reunification of Yemen), but on the other hand, the first Gulf War significantly reduced the military capabilities of a belligerent Iraq and demonstrated the West's commitment to existing patterns of sovereignty in the Middle East.

We do not have a sufficient number of observations to arrive at a systematic assessment, but it is likely that these shocks can range from being mutually reinforcing to possibly annulling one another. And whether these patterns are unique to the Middle East requires additional comparative regional analysis.

CONCLUSION

It is clear, even from a comparative regional perspective, that the Middle East is unique among the various regions in international politics. The Middle East ranks high on fault lines, ranks low on pacifying conditions, lacks a hierarchical order, and has demonstrated substantial permeability to both global forces and intrusion from external powers. Its uniqueness is especially underscored by both the unusual number of inter-state rivalries in the region and a truly unique pattern of an extremely dense rivalry field that has at times involved nearly all state members. No wonder then that it is also, at least since the end of the Second World War, the most conflictual of all regions.

Not much is static in international relations, and neither are regional dynamics. While it is clear that rivalries have dominated international politics in the Middle East, three trends have emerged to suggest the relationship between rivalry and conflict may be waning. First, the density of the Middle East rivalry field, especially over the last decade, has substantially diminished. Second, the share of regional conflicts that appear to be directly attributable to regional states in rivalry has also diminished. Third, the overall level of state-to-state regional conflict as measured by severe MIDs has declined.

These trends suggest to us three salient issues about the conflicts in the regions. First, the political dimensions over which many of the rivalries are playing out have changed, from an earlier period that was driven by radical versus traditional regimes and the Arab-Israeli conflict, to the latter period in which these dimensions appear to be becoming secondary to conflicts between Shi'a- and Sunni-based regimes.[29] In turn, such sectarian differences may simply underscore a longer-term phenomenon of (changing) regional aspirants struggling for regional leadership in the absence of a dominant power. The Saudi-Iran proxy conflict in Yemen may reflect the latest round of such struggles.

Second, the reduced density in the rivalry field suggests that the Middle East is possibly becoming "more normal" compared to other regions—especially if "normalcy" means that the Middle East becomes comparable to regions lacking a hierarchy and with substantial fault lines.[30] Of course, such a return to "normalcy" would not indicate that the region is becoming substantially more peaceful but only that considerations other than rivalries are becoming more salient in determining the level of regional conflict. As we noted earlier, the percentage of conflict directly attributed to states in rivalries during the last decade is at its lowest of the time frame we sampled, even as the region remains highly conflict prone.[31]

Third, and to the extent the region's highly dense rivalry field has created so much conflict, it is well worth probing the conditions under which the field can further diminish. Our exploration of political shocks and their impact on the region has been brief, but it does indicate such shocks can have a strong impact on the rivalry field, either substantially increasing its density or reducing it under certain circumstances. What we have failed to do, given chapter limitations and the limitations of data, is to systematically assess the conditions under which such political shocks may work in opposing directions.[32]

What remains clear is that political shocks should be integrated into any meaningful analysis of changes in regional politics. It would be useful to know, for instance, if the Middle East is also unique in facing an onslaught of political shocks (or "shock waves") fundamentally greater in volume and scope than other regions. Regional governance exposed to such shock waves becomes highly difficult and problematic. We would want to know as well if different types of shocks have different consequences for regional dynamics. Under what conditions (e.g., see chapter 9 in this volume) do domestic shocks affect the entire region? Do systemic, global shocks have the same impact in the Middle East as they do elsewhere? If so, why? Under what conditions can certain shocks offset each other or drive the region in different directions, as in the cases of the shocks generated by both the Camp David Accords and the Khomeini revolution? Under what conditions do shocks cease to be shocks? At what point are they perceived by foreign policy makers as a "normal" attribute of the region? Under what conditions does an event rise to the status of a shock in the first place?[33] Can we differentiate between shocks that have an immediate impact versus those that take substantial time to weave through the region's politics? We have answers to none of these questions, but they appear to be critical avenues worthy of further pursuit, not only for a greater understanding of the Middle East but also for more thorough explanations of regions that undergo substantial changes.

In this sense, it would be highly useful to try to link the concept of shocks to the growing literature on diffusion and contagion processes (e.g., Solingen 2012; Braithwaite 2006). We know, for instance, that the Arab Spring diffused to parts of the Middle East (e.g., Egypt) while being aggressively contained elsewhere (e.g., Qatar, Saudi Arabia). Minimizing diffusion of such shocks is more manageable in regions with a hierarchy in which the dominant power can, to some extent, anticipate such shocks or respond to them quickly to minimize their spread across the region when it is not in the interest of the dominant power to have such diffusion occur. It is far more difficult to minimize such diffusion in regions without a hierarchy. Developing a clearer understanding of conditions under which states are willing (and able) to minimize shocks by creating diffusion firewalls may be one key to a better understanding of when political shocks become more or less salient in a region.

The salience of non-state actors in the Arab Spring and regarding domestic shocks also highlights another limitation of this analysis. Both the nature of intra-regional conflict and our key independent variables are focused on state actors and state interactions. We have not considered conflicts in the region between non-state actors nor between non-state actors and states. Yet as the aftermath of the 2003 invasion of Iraq and the Syrian Civil War should remind us, numerous non-state actors operate across the region (from Hezbollah and the Islamic State to the Kurdistan Workers' Party). These actors often interact across state borders, and they often clash with state and other non-state actors. The complex interplay between shocks and rivalry fields must take them into account as well, and their activities should also be part of the assessment of how much conflict exists in the Middle East and whether it is unique in this regard.[34]

Finally, any consideration of the Middle East becoming a more peaceful region may depend in significant part on whether it can accommodate the eventual rise of a regional power. As we noted earlier from our comparative analysis, regions that contain a major power or a regional power also demonstrate substantially less intra-regional conflict, including minimizing some of the effects of intra-regional rivalries.[35] Regional powers may also be able to erect diffusion firewalls in the region to minimize the impact of political shocks. While major power hierarchies have stronger pacifying effects than regional power hierarchies, the latter type nevertheless has a significant impact on ordering relationships in the region.

If this is likely to be the case for the Middle East as well, then the question that needs exploring is what it would take to have such a regional power emerge in the Middle East. That is clearly beyond the scope of this project, but it may be a vital question to answer if there is some hope that the region may become substantially more peaceful in the future. However, we would not make that prediction for the near future. It is plausible that given the still-remaining substantial rivalry density field, the sheer weight of rivalries in the region may mean that too many of the key regional actors will strongly oppose the emergence of any one of them as a regional power. Additionally, efforts by outside powers to balance regional power contenders against one another (e.g., Iraq versus Iran or Iran versus Saudi Arabia) have also lessened the prospects of a regional power emerging.[36] Given all of that, we see little on the horizon inspiring hope for a substantially more peaceful Middle East.

APPENDIX

Table 2A. Variables, sources, and manipulations

Variable	Source	Manipulation
State MID involvement	Palmer et al. (2015)	Number of states involved in level four or five MIDs/total number of states in region
MID frequency	Palmer et al. (2015)	Number of level four or five MIDs/total number of states in region
Major power presence	Volgy et al. (2011)	Dichotomous; 1 = presence, 0 = no hierarchy
Regional power presence	Cline et al. (2011)	Dichotomous; 1 = presence, 0 = no hierarchy
Number of intra-regional rivalries	Thompson and Dreyer (2011)	Number of states involved in rivalry with states of the same region; lagged one year
Rivalry density	Thompson and Dreyer (2011)	Number of rival dyads within a region, multiplied by total number of connections/ total number of states within the region minus one
Number of civil wars	Pettersson and Wallensteen (2015)	Number of states involved in internal conflict with cumulative intensity of one thousand battle deaths or more; lagged one year
Percentage of regional trade	Barbieri & Keshk (2012); Barbieri et al. (2009)	Amount of trade among states in a region/total trade of the region; logged and lagged one year
Percentage of regional democracies	Marshall, Gurr, and Jaggers (2016)	Percent of states with Polity IV score of 7+ states/ total number of states with Polity IV scores in region; lagged one year
External alliances	Gibler (2009)	Dichotomous; 1 = presence, 0 = no defense pact between a regional state and an external major power; lagged one year
Territorial claims	Gibler and Miller (2014)	Number of territorial claims in a region/total number of states in region; lagged one year
Regional IGO membership		Number of regional IGO memberships held by states in region/all possible regional IGO memberships; lagged one year
Cold War		Dichotomous; 1 = Cold War; 0 = post-Cold War
Time Counter		Time counter for each decade

NOTES

1. For an example of a comparative perspective explicitly rejecting Middle East "exceptionalism," see Sorli, Gleditsch, and Strand (2005).

2. Either directly by diffusion or emulation or through substantial refugee flows into the neighborhood (e.g., Salehyan and Gleditsch 2006).

3. We recognize that the Kantian peace (e.g., Oneal and Russett 1999), especially its democratic peace component, is challenged by the "capitalist" peace (e.g., Gartzke 2007) and the "territorial peace" (e.g., Gibler 2012) and that all three forms may be linked to prior dynamics created by dominant global powers (e.g., Rasler and Thompson 2005). However, note that all four conditions are included to some extent in our framework.

4. It is difficult to dismiss, for example, the counterfactual of how different relations would look in today's Middle East had the United States not engaged in the second war against Iraq, starting in 2003, or if Russia had not come to the aid of the Assad regime as it fought its civil war in Syria. Nor have researchers plotted out the cumulative impact of Chinese involvement in sub-Saharan Africa from a regional, rather than a Great Power, perspective (e.g., Gao 2017).

5. Literature on the salience of hierarchy for international politics and interstate relations is highlighted in Lake (2011), Milner (1991), and Bially Mattern and Zarakol (2016). The extent to which a region can fluctuate between anarchy and hierarchy is demonstrated by Butt (2013); in that sense, we accept the notion that hierarchy, rather than being a constant, is a variable, not only across regions but plausibly within regions as well. However, some regions lack a dominant power; those regions will not exhibit hierarchy until a dominant power emerges. In other regions where a dominant power exists, hierarchy may be a variable, depending on the willingness of the dominant power to play a hierarchical role or the extent to which its dominance is contested by contenders from the region.

6. Using a very different definition of regional power than used by us, one could make an argument that there have been one or more regional powers. Possession of nuclear weapons and the ability to deliver them anywhere in the region could qualify Israel. Another definition based on the existence of surface ballistic missiles capable of reaching all region members would qualify Iran, Iraq, and Israel. In contrast, our definition is based not only on military capabilities but dominance as well in the economic sphere, a willingness to focus foreign affairs on the region, and recognition of dominant power status by both the region and the larger global community. In these terms, there are contenders for regional dominance but no dominant power in the Middle East.

7. The concepts, their operationalization, and sources used are detailed in table 2A.

8. Clearly this is not the only definition of what constitutes a region. In fact, there is no consensus nor a gold standard defining and empirically identifying the contours of regions (Volgy et al. 2017), nor has there been one (Thompson 1973).

9. For a full list of the regions, the states they contain, and the way they have changed across decades, see Volgy et al. (2018).

10. For instance, we note the formation of a Central Asian region in the 1990s; that "region" seems to have disappeared in the first decade of the 2000s.

11. These states are typically microstates or relatively inactive states in international politics.

12. This judgment is based on a survey of contemporary international relations literature using political shocks either as an independent or dependent variable of interest (Gordell 2017). The survey included publications in fourteen leading journals between 2005 and 2016.

13. We recognize that the concept of hierarchy can fluctuate across time in regions with a dominant power (see Butt 2013). However, a critical precondition for such fluctuation is the existence of a dominant power in the region.

14. Since 1951, when data became available, the Middle East has been characterized by an absence of both major and regional powers but not by an absence of challengers. Although Cline et al. (2011, 135) do not recognize the existence of any regional powers in the Middle East, Egypt, Iran, Iraq, Israel, and Saudi Arabia have all aspired to regional power status but fallen short for

various reasons. Reasons for falling short of regional power status include lack of military or economic opportunity in the region and lack of either extensive cooperative or conflict-prone involvement in the region (Cline et al. 2011, 140–49).

15. Here, and in the following tables, rivalries are measured as the number of rivalries in the region annually. Alternatively, one can control for the size of the region by dividing the annual rivalry count by the number of states in the region (opportunity to engage in rivalries). We opted for the former in order to assess the impact of the absolute levels of rivalries on a region. However, we reran these tables controlling for region size for all relevant independent variables. We find that the rivalry variable actually increases in impact on the dependent variable (MIDs) when controlling for opportunity. Other changes are noted for civil wars and territorial disputes, which reduce somewhat in impact when controlling for opportunity. Results are available from authors on request.

16. The difference between the two is statistically significant.

17. The unit of analysis is region year. We control for region size in our dependent variable, and the independent variables are lagged by one year. The variable for trade interdependence is omitted from the major power presence model owing to collinearity issues. For a greater consideration of this problem, see Volgy et al. (2018).

18. Similar, but slightly weaker, patterns are observed for the presence of a regional power in a region, so we omit its discussion for the sake of brevity.

19. Here, as in all the tables and figures, severe MIDs refers to MIDs coded as 4 or 5, involving actual hostilities between parties. Regional conflict refers to MIDs between states that are members of the region. For measurement decisions and sources for these and other variables in the analysis, see table 2A.

20. As of 2018, the United States based soldiers in Bahrain, Iraq, Jordan, Kuwait, Oman, Qatar, and the UAE (Press TV 2018). Outside its involvement in the Syrian Civil War, Russia has maintained a military facility in Tartus since 1971. Admittedly, the Tartus facility has been variously staffed over the years, but it remains Russia's only immediate port facility in the Mediterranean Sea.

21. In a previous review of empirical literature over the last decade (Volgy et al. 2017), we found that virtually all large-N empirical analyses that controlled for region in dyadic analyses found the Middle East variable, regardless of how the Middle East was delineated, to exhibit patterns that were statistically significantly different from the "base" region, regardless of which region was used as the base.

22. Rivalry density scores are created using the total number of rival dyads within a region, multiplied by the total number of connections, or linkages, between rival dyads. This number is then divided by the total number of states within the region minus one. Linkages are established between rival dyads that involve a common state actor.

23. The average of all other regions varies between approximately 1.92 and 2.41.

24. To assess the salience of a single variable over time for a region requires the regional delineation to remain stable. Therefore, we use our delineation of the Middle East region and its state membership from the 2000s as a permanent marker for the entire time frame, making adjustments to regional membership only when a state comes into existence or has no legal status (e.g., Kazakhstan before the dissolution of the Soviet Union), or when two or more states integrate or dissolve (e.g., Egypt and Syria). Thus, the membership may vary, but the region is a constant in this part of the analysis.

25. Note the network figures differ from those contained in chapter 3, and for two reasons. First, we conceptualize the Middle East differently than Thompson, as the contours of our region do not include states from North Africa. Second, we include only those rivalries that include the region's members (e.g., we exclude the US-Iran rivalry).

26. Turkey could be added as another regional aspirant if its primary focus of attention consistently becomes the Middle East.

27. Why that would have been the case is beyond the scope of this chapter. We suggest, however, that the end of the Cold War had resulted in a redistribution of global capabilities (from

bipolar conflicts to some form of unipolarity) and thus, for a while, limited the East-West competition in the region.

28. This phenomenon is also illustrated in figures 2.10 to 2.12.

29. We are not implying that these conflicts are based solely or perhaps even primarily on religious differences. Underlying them are also major conflicts over the direction of the region and states competing for regional leadership.

30. Lacking systematic data on political shocks, we cannot make a strong case that the Middle East is uniquely targeted by political shocks; however, it is plausible that the frequency of shocks may vary with the fragility of states in a region. However, there are other regions with even more fragile states that lack the extensive rivalry network exhibited within the Middle East.

31. Thompson (2018) makes a similar point in arguing that domestic conflicts and especially civil wars have become more prevalent in the region as the rivalry field simplifies. We agree, but our framework suggests such a shift to intrastate conflict can ultimately result in increased intrastate conflict in others as well and also enhanced interstate conflict through refugee flows, greater external involvement by outside powers, and the rise of non-state actors violently participating in ongoing rivalries. Certainly, the civil conflicts in Iraq, Syria, and Yemen suggest such possibilities.

32. For one promising direction in assessing external shocks, see Maoz and Joyce (2016).

33. For example, we had some difficulty classifying regional wars. Did all such wars constitute shocks to the region? Are some wars more expected than others? Do some wars, long in duration, such as the Iran-Iraq War, begin to seem normal?

34. Note that our measure of conflict is frequency of severe MIDs between states in a region, which excludes non-state actors that are not acting in behalf of a particular state. Inclusion of semi-autonomous non-state actors in the region's rivalry field could substantially change our estimates of how much smaller that field is today, compared to previous decades.

35. The one exception to this generalization is the case of South Asia, where the regional power (India) is itself engaged in a long, ongoing rivalry.

36. In an earlier time US efforts that resulted in the Camp David accords also virtually guaranteed that Egypt would not be able to emerge as a regional power either.

3

Humpty Dumpty Had a Great Fall?

Making Sense of Longer-Term Ups and Downs in Middle Eastern and North African Rivalries

William R. Thompson

The Arab [Spring] uprisings have so far brought little change to the pattern of relations among countries of the MENA region. There has been no dramatic realignment of countries. Rather, the turmoil has largely confirmed old patterns, although making cleavages deeper and some relations even closer. —Marina Ottaway

There are two predictable and nearly always mistaken responses to any great international upheaval; one is to say that everything has changed; the other is to say that nothing has changed. —Fred Halliday

Nostalgia for decades gone by reigns supreme in a number of highly developed, affluent regions. If we could only turn back the clock, somehow a former greatness would rematerialize. This is one thing on which many citizens in the United States, Britain, and Russia seem to agree. Citizens in other parts of the world, putting aside advocates for the restoration of the Caliphate or the Persian or Ottoman Empires, are less likely to agree. Change to something new is much preferred to the less-than-desirable past.

A case in point are rivalries in the Middle East and North Africa (MENA). In earlier decades the MENA was the "Rivalry-R-Us" region with almost every state in the neighborhood harboring multiple rivalries with nearby states. That is no longer the case, at least in exactly the same way. Multiple rivalries still exist, but the rivalry field in the MENA has undergone significant change. Rivalries have hardly disappeared there as they did in North America, in Europe, or almost in South America, but they have surely fluctuated in number, declining in some decades while increasing in others. We should ask ourselves what this pattern means. Rivalries and rivalry fields tell us something about how regions function. If they do have meaning and they evolve, we should be able to interpret what the emergence of new structures might imply.

Moreover, and despite the abundance of material, the analysis of rivalries as something other than billiard balls of clashing states (Riyadh did X to Damascus, Tehran did Y to Tel Aviv, and so forth) is woefully underdeveloped in the MENA. While the number of ongoing rivalries in the MENA has declined in some years, rivalry processes are hardly disappearing.[1] It is well past time that MENA rivalries be viewed from the perspective of objective, dispassionate, and comparative interstate processes.

In this chapter rivalry is first defined as a concept. The contemporary history of MENA rivalries is then summarized. Next, the evolution of the MENA rivalry fields is surveyed from the 1940s to 2018. Selected shocks are portrayed as the presumed agents of transforming rivalry fields. The fragmenting complexity of successive fields is highlighted as an indicator of structural change in MENA politics that imperfectly captures how the neighborhood context is in flux. While the Arab Spring shocks were not the only source of stimulus, the MENA rivalry field—a structural manifestation of basic interstate antagonisms in the region—has undergone a fundamental and radical revision. Expressed most simply, the former Arab-Israeli configuration has given way to a structure predicated on Iranian-Saudi hostility and polarization that makes for new and sometimes strange bedfellows.

RIVALRIES AND RIVALRY FIELDS

Strategic rivalries are interstate relationships in which the parties see their adversaries as competitive but also threatening enemies (Thompson 2001). States compete with one another on a variety of fronts. Some state pairs are rivals in commerce, athletic contests, or ideational leadership. But none of these relationships necessarily convey some sense of the possibility of serious coercive damage. In other words, they do not always lead to the type of physical threat perceptions that characterize strategic rivalries. Yet the two states also have to be in the same power leagues. Ordinarily, major and minor powers may well threaten each other, but they are not competitive with each other in terms of capabilities. Thus, minor power states are most likely to form strategic rivalries with other, often adjacent states like them in their home regions. Major powers are most likely to develop strategic rivalries with other major powers.[2] However, probability does not rule out exceptions to this tendency.

Moreover, perceptions of competition, threat, and enemy are not carved in stone once they emerge. They tend to fluctuate. They may even seem to disappear only to surge back unexpectedly. They are also rarely symmetrical in hostility, for a variety of reasons. One state may possess multiple rivalries and, as a consequence, cannot afford to obsess on a single enemy. Or a state with multiple rivalries may choose to obsess on one rival and give less attention to lesser threats. In other circumstances one state in a rivalry pair may fear the possibility of a military invasion, while the other state perceives the nature of threat in an entirely different way, as in financial, cultural, or ideological intrusions. Needless to say, these attributes can interfere with identifying who is a rival with whom and when. Any attempt to categorize these relations must be viewed with the proverbial grain of salt. In other words, some categorical errors are likely. The question is whether attempts at categorization have utility that outweighs the errors committed. Fortunately or unfortunately, it is difficult to interpret rivalries in general without knowing something about their particulars.

References to interstate rivalry are legion and long-standing, going back at least to Athens and Sparta, if not Sumer and Elam. But the references have tended to be predominantly descriptive and cloaked in proper place names. That habit may be fine for some purposes, but it misses the possibilities associated with applying more general understandings of how rivalries work. For instance, a central motivation in studying rivalry processes more systematically concerns the links between rivalry and militarized disputes, interstate crises, and war. While the propensity for rivals to go to war is high in the world at large, it is even higher in the MENA. Table 3.1 lists the ten MENA wars that satisfy the Correlates of War project on formalizing war information. In nine of ten cases MENA wars were fought by rivals on opposing sides, and in most cases opposing rivals were the primary combatants. These observations do not tell us that we can assume rivals will go to war. Sometimes they do, and sometimes they do not. It does tell us that rivals are recidivists when it comes to intense conflict, and that is the primary justification for focusing on their behavior. Most states do not fight each other, but nonrivals rarely do so. Rivals, on the other hand, do clash and sometimes wage war with their adversaries. If we are interested in deciphering conflict processes, rivalry is a good place to begin.

We also think some parts of the world have fairly dense collections of rivals (the Middle East and Northeast Africa, for instance), while others are now pretty much rival-free (the Americas, Western Europe). It follows that rivalry densities may have some linkage to how conflictual various regions are. Presumably, the more regions are rivalry free, the less conflictual they are likely to be. Yet despite their importance in identifying zones of conflict, we know less than we should about rivalry processes—that is, how they emerge, how they are maintained, and how they terminate. We know

Table 3.1. War and rivalry in the Middle East

Year	War	Rivalries involved	Other states
1948–49	Arab-Israeli	Egypt-Israel, Israel-Syria, Jordan-Israel, Iraq-Israel	Lebanon
1956	Sinai	Egypt-Israel	France, UK
1957	Ifni	Morocco-Spain	
1967	Six-Day	Egypt-Israel, Israel-Jordan, Israel-Syria	
1969–70	Attrition	Egypt-Israel	
1973	Yom Kippur	Egypt-Israel, Iraq-Israel, Israel-Jordan	Saudi Arabia
1980–88	Iran-Iraq	Iran-Iraq	
1982	Over Lebanon	Israel-Syria	
1990–91	Gulf	Egypt-Iraq, Iraq-Kuwait, Iraq-Saudi Arabia, Iraq-Syria	US, Canada, UK, Italy, Morocco, Oman, France, United Arab Emirates, Qatar
2003	Iraq Invasion		

Note: The war names in column 2 are those used by the Correlates of War project. See Sarkees and Wayman (2010).

less than we should because it was not until fairly recently that we began to take the idea of rivalry seriously. Instead of allowing "rivalry" to be a throwaway noun that can be applied equally easily to states and football teams, taking rivalry seriously means defining what constitutes rivalry, developing an information base on when and where rivalries have been prominent, and creating theories about how rivalries begin, sustain themselves, and end. Most of all, it means comparing rivalries as rivalries—as opposed to falling back on the proper place names of hostile states in making sense of what appears to be going on.

Yet only rarely are rivalries taken seriously as something worth studying in the MENA. Despite all of the ink spilled on why Iran and Saudi Arabia do not like each other much, why Algeria and Morocco cannot quite get along, or what drove Egypt and Israel to fight three or four wars (depending on how you categorize the thousand days of intermittent combat after the 1967 war), it is difficult to find a book or article that assesses MENA rivalries as comparable conflict processes.[3] If more than a handful exist, they are well hidden. It is fair to say that the study of MENA international relations has been resistant to innovation in general and conceptualization of rivalries in particular.

The stability of the MENA rivalry field was once matched only by the density and intensity of its conflicts. It was not quite a Hobbesian war of all against all, but there certainly were an unusually large number of adversarial relationships pitting non-Arabs against Arabs as well as Arabs against Arabs. The stability of the MENA rivalry field has been undermined by a series of shocks that have rendered traditional enmities in the region less meaningful. Yet it is hardly the case that the MENA has suddenly been transformed into a highly cooperative setting. Adversarial relationships definitely remain, but they are now further complicated by non-state conflicts, even while interstate conflicts persist. Earlier shocks helped construct the conventional MENA rivalry field on a rickety and very shallow, nation-state-based, regional subsystem.[4] World War I forced out the Ottomans, helped salvage the Husseini clan, and led to Sykes-Picot-inspired borders and League of Nations mandates, especially in the Fertile Crescent. Countries that had never existed before were created and coexisted with countries that had been around in one form or another for millennia. Defeats in Arab-Israeli conflicts, nationalization of the Suez Canal, and increased local control of petroleum dominated the late 1940s through the early 1970s. These initial shocks reinforced the stability of the rivalry field. It was very difficult to imagine any rivalries disappearing. But then the shocks started working in a different direction. The Camp David Accords and Palestine Liberation Organization (PLO) conflict in Lebanon and Jordan dampened the centrality of the Palestinian issue and marginalized Egyptian centrality in the region. The Iranian Revolution, among other things, greatly expanded the interests of Iranian decision-makers in playing a more salient role in the MENA. After a long but inconclusive struggle with Iran, Iraqi expansion into Kuwait led to massive external military intervention into the region. In Lebanon, Hezbollah gained prominence as an independent actor with Iranian assistance. In Palestinian territory the PLO and Hamas fought and continue to fight for control. The Second Gulf War and its aftermath hammered Iraq into a shell of what it once was and, ultimately, led to various types of Sunni-Shiʻite group warfare, including, eventually, the Islamic State of Iraq and the Levant (ISIL) and possibly the breakup of Iraq. Civil wars in Syria and Libya have led to, or facilitated, the ascendance of several non-state groups and possibly the permanent breakup of both states too. All in all, as many as four states (Iraq, Syria, Libya, and Sudan)—all prominent in the rivalry annals—have fragmented in one way or another. Yemen seems to have become a fifth.

Such changes cannot but help destabilize conventional interstate relationships, just as they encourage other nearby states such as Turkey to take renewed interest in what is going on in adjacent neighborhoods. Periodic regional, tectonic plate–style shake-ups will be manifested in interstate patterns of interaction, conflict, and cooperation. Thus, we should expect rivalry fields to reflect serious disruptions of the structure of the prevailing status quo. It worked that way after World War I, after World War II, and now again, after the latest perturbations that are linked most saliently to the renewed prominence of Sunni-Shiʻite differences: the US occupation of Iraq, the increased activity of non-state groups, and the Arab Spring. As a consequence, the contemporary MENA rivalry field no longer resembles what it was only a decade or two ago.

To explore these issues further, some foundation needs to be established by answering some basic questions. Who have been interstate rivals in the MENA? Have MENA international relations been rife with rivalry? Has that characterization changed over time, and if so, why? What difference(s) does it make to the MENA rivalry field?

As noted, the idea of rival states is no stranger to our conceptualizations of interstate politics. We have some sense of who is a rival with whom and why. Table 3.2 identifies the durations of strategic rivalries in the MENA. The first column identifies the rivals according to the three main sub-neighborhoods in the region (Mashriq, Gulf, and Maghreb).[5] When a rivalry ends and then resumes at a later point, the adversarial relationships are treated separately (as signaled by a roman numeral). The second column specifies the duration of the rivalry relationship. Some of the states in the Maghreb also play roles in other regional subsystems to the south of North Africa, but these rivalries are not identified in table 3.2 as a matter of simplification.[6]

The third column notes changes to durations as of 2018, due either to the initiation or termination of a rivalry, or a reclassification, due to changes in operating assumptions. In this case the main change in rivalry identification involves states that have either disintegrated (along Somali lines) or been occupied by foreign powers (Iraq). The old rule had been to freeze rivalries until the disintegrated state either re-emerged or the foreign power military occupation ended. But that is too conservative a coding rule if the disintegration or occupation persists for years. Moreover, there is some probability that the newly re-emerged state will be unable to engage in rivalry immediately and perhaps for some indefinite future period. Thus, it now seems better to terminate most extant rivalries unless there is some evidence that one or more persists despite disintegration or occupation.[7]

A third type of change represents what some might call coder error. There is a bias in identifying strategic rivalries as generally symmetrical in terms of ranks (e.g., minor

Table 3.2. Middle East (Mashriq and Gulf), North African (Maghreb), and Southwest Eurasian rivalries to 2015

Rivalry	Duration as of 2010	Changes as of 2018
	Mashriq	
Egypt-Iran I	1955-71	
Egypt-Iran II	1979-ongoing	
Egypt-Iraq	1945-ongoing	1945-2003
Egypt-Israel	1948-ongoing	
Egypt-Jordan	1946-70	
Egypt-Ottoman Empire	1828-41	
Egypt-Qatar		2013-ongoing
Egypt–Saudi Arabia	1957-70	
Egypt-Syria	1961-90	
Iran-Israel	1979-ongoing	
Iraq-Israel	1948-ongoing	
Iraq-Syria	1946-ongoing	1945-2011
Israel-Jordan	1948-94	
Israel-Syria	1948-ongoing	
Jordan-Saudi Arabia	1946-58	
Jordan-Syria	1948-ongoing	
Saudi Arabia–Syria I	1961-70	
Saudi Arabia–Syria II		2011-ongoing
Syria-Turkey I	1946-2004	
Syria-Turkey II		2011-ongoing
	Gulf	
Iran-Ottoman/Turkey	p1816-1932	
Iran-Russia	p1816-28	
Bahrain-Qatar I	1986-2001	
Bahrain-Qatar II		2014-ongoing
Iran-Iraq I	1932-39	
Iran-Iraq II	1958-ongoing	1958-2003
Iran-Saudi Arabia	1979-ongoing	
Iran-United States		1982-ongoing
Iraq-Kuwait	1961-ongoing	
Iraq-Saudi Arabia I	1932-57	
Iraq-Saudi Arabia II	1968-ongoing	
Oman-South Yemen	1967-82	
Qatar–Saudi Arabia		1995-ongoing
Qatar-UAE		2011-ongoing

Saudi Arabia-Yemen I	1932-34
Saudi Arabia-Yemen II	1990-2000
Yemen–South Yemen	1967-90
Maghreb	
Algeria-Morocco	1962-ongoing
Egypt-Libya	1973-92
Egypt-Sudan	1991-ongoing
Libya-Sudan	1974-85
Morocco-Mauritania	1960-69
Morocco-Spain	1956-91

Source: Thompson and Dreyer (2011), with modifications and updating.
Note: The letter *p* indicates that the rivalry began before 1816.

versus minor, major versus major). Major-minor power rivalries have always existed, but one must be very careful in identifying them as equally embraced by both sides of the conflict.[8] Iranian decision-makers had fairly consistently identified the United States as the Great Satan or enemy number one, albeit with some variation depending on who was in power in Tehran. What was less clear was where Iran ranked as a US enemy. Crist (2012) and Solomon (2016) make strong cases for US decision-makers viewing Iran as a rival for hegemony in the Gulf subsystem. Crist (2012, chapter 5) provides an account of US-Iranian relations that suggests an initiation of the rivalry in 1982, when US decision-makers feared that Iran was about to defeat and invade Iraq in the battle over control of Basra. Before that time the United States had certainly had its problems with Iranian foreign policy and student occupiers of its embassy, but in 1982 the United States adopted the role of chief containment agent of the Iranian Revolution. If Iraq fell, the rest of the Sunni world and especially the Gulf petro-states were endangered. That was a potential calamity that could not be accepted.[9]

Nonetheless, what the third column really represents or highlights are the disequilibrating changes wrought by shocks. Shocks are important in international politics because decision-makers and habitual behaviors are characterized by a great deal of inertia. There is a strong tendency to do something at time *t* along similar lines to what was done at time *t*–1 just because it was done at time *t*–1. That is how habits develop. Shocks come along and force decision-makers to rethink. The shocks do not usually force decision-makers to deviate from *t*–1 habits, but they provide an opportunity or open window for doing so. Whether decision-makers jump through the open window is another story.

Shocks are given some preeminence in rivalry research programs. Diehl and Goertz (2000, 221) argue that shocks help create new rivalries and terminate old ones. Their argument is that if "enduring rivalries are the result òf well-entrenched causes, then the end of a particular rivalry or the beginning of a new rivalry should be associated with some dramatic change in the environment or the actors. These shocks may be exogenous to the rivalry, such as the occurrence of a world war, or endogenous, such as the change in the administration or regime of one of the rivals following a civil war."

Rasler, Thompson, and Ganguly (2013) also portray shocks as one of the four most important ingredients in rivalry termination and de-escalation processes. Shocks set up situations in which some decision-makers with altered expectations can explore alternative rivalry strategies that, in turn, can lead to de-escalation if met with reciprocity and subsequent reinforcement.

Table 3.3 underlines the influential effect of shocks on rivalries. The message in the table is not that shocks dictated all the rivalry effects suggested in the second column. The rivalry changes (onsets and terminations) in column 2 can be linked to the shocks in column 1 in the sense that the probability of the effects would have been much less in the absence of the shocks.[10] The emergence of new states often brings with it the baggage of disputed territory, either in the new state or older, adjacent states, or resurrects old feuds, as in the Saud-Hashemite case going back to an older Hejaz rivalry. Wars can be fought over these opposing claims to territorial control, and the new state effect can become fused with the war effect as in the first Arab-Israeli War. But wars and revolutions can

Table 3.3. Effects of shocks on rivalries

Shock event	Rivalries affected
Independence	Iraq-Saudi Arabia I, Egypt-Jordan, Jordan-Saudi Arabia, Jordan-Syria, Syria-Turkey I, Morocco-Spain, Morocco-Mauritania, Algeria-Morocco, South Yemen-Yemen, Oman-South Yemen
1948-49 war[a]	Egypt-Israel, Iraq-Israel, Israel-Jordan, Israel-Syria
Egyptian Revolution	
1956 war	Egypt-Saudi Arabia
1967 war	
1973 war	Egypt-Libya
Camp David Accords	Egypt-Israel, de-escalated but not terminated; *Israel-Jordan*, indirectly
Iranian Revolution	Iran-Saudi Arabia, Iran-Israel, Egypt-Iran II
Iran-Iraq War	Iran-United States
First Gulf War	
Second Gulf War	*Egypt-Iraq II, Iran-Iraq II, [Afghanistan-Iran]*
Arab Spring	Egypt-Qatar, Bahrain-Qatar, Iraq-Syria, Qatar-UAE, Saudi Arabia-Syria, Syria-Turkey II
Trump administration	To be determined

Note: New rivalries in bold; terminating rivalries in italics.

[a]It is conceivable that these effects can be related to the creation of a new Israeli state and therefore should be listed in the preceding Independence row. This interesting question underscores some of the ambiguities associated with attributing causal impact to various shocks. Was the disequilibrating shock in 1948 the creation of a new state, the consequent scramble for territorial control by several states, or both?

also stimulate or highlight new grievances in the battles over leadership in the Arab world or the MENA writ large. Wars can also destroy a state's ability to operate in regional politics as an influential actor. If that state had maintained a number of rivalries before the war onset and, abruptly, it no longer can pursue them because it has lost its competitive standing, the region's rivalry field is likely to be altered significantly. The long military occupation of Iraq had just this effect.

Table 3.3 reminds us, however, that every possible shock need not produce discernible rivalry effects. The Egyptian Revolution had little direct effect on the rivalry field, while the Iranian Revolution increased the probability of three new and salient rivalries. Of the seven wars listed in column 1, four wars helped generate varying effects; three did not have direct impacts, although some of the effect-less wars nonetheless did have influences on other rivalries. An example is that the Iraqi invasion of Kuwait seems less likely if it were not for the earlier Iraqi war with Iran. But Saddam Hussein's war-induced money problems did not invent the Iraq-Kuwait adversarial relationship—it only escalated it. Similarly, one could argue that the Second Gulf War would not have happened without the outcome of the First Gulf War.[11] Thus, it is not so much that shocks sometimes have rivalry effects and sometimes do not. Shocks are likely to have both direct and indirect, as well as variable, influences. But only some shocks have helped bring about rivalry initiations and terminations.

Nor are shocks restricted to wars and revolutions. The Camp David Accords sought to ensure one very central rivalry would be de-escalated by providing considerable aid to both sides of the confrontation as long as they no longer fought. It did not end the Egyptian-Israeli rivalry. Nonetheless, the likelihood of Egyptian-Israeli conflict diminished significantly. Without Egypt, another Arab-Israeli war was out of the question. The Trump election could turn out to be another type of shock, or at least the prelude to new US-induced shocks. The anti-ISIL position was intensified. So too was the stridency of US positions on supporting Israel (as manifested in the embassy move to Jerusalem) and opposing Iran (withdrawing from the nuclear deal). The feud between Saudi Arabia / UAE and Qatar was initially encouraged despite the large US base in Qatar, but that encouragement does not seem to have been sustained. Trump policies might also eventually negate (or accelerate) the alleged US pivot to dealing with China that has been constrained by recurrent MENA problems and focus even more US resources on stabilizing or destabilizing the larger southwestern Asian region.[12]

RIVALRY FIELDS

Rivalry fields encompass the array of rivalries in one region or throughout the world.[13] Since nodes tend to be linked by one or more states possessing multiple rivalries, behavior in the region is likely to be interdependent and diffused through the rivalry network. That is, a significant change in one part of the rivalry network is likely to manifest itself in other parts of the extended network. Rivalry fields, therefore, are not merely useful for outlining structure but are also a conduit for change throughout the field. There is some question, after all, whether the world is truly and exclusively composed of multiple dyadic relationships. States are clustered by a variety of mechanisms and processes, including rivalry. We should anticipate, therefore, that "neighborhood" effects may be as influential as direct dyadic interactions in determining how states handle their conflict relationships.

Rivalry fields can be depicted by a diagram showing which states are linked through rivalry. Thus, they serve as a partial indicator of regional conflict structures.[14] The main problem with such diagrams, though, is that they are highly static. If the rivalry field is evolving, there is a need for multiple diagrams to capture the changing structure.

Figures 3.1–3.3 sketch the MENA rivalry field at six selected time points: 1949, 1956, 1975, 2000, 2005, and 2018. The idea is that these six time points offer the best vantage point for observing structural change in this regional rivalry field. An annual depiction of the field would no doubt be more comprehensive but unnecessary since the field does not change on an annual basis. Some of the observed points were selected for their timing in terms of post-shock changes, while others emphasize continuity in structure.

Figure 3.1 portrays the rivalry fields at their earliest constructions. The 1949 field captures the structure immediately after the First Arab-Israeli War. The structure emphasizes the eastern segment of the MENA, the Mashriq, with four states centered on rivalries with Israel. Yet, at the same time, all the Arab actors had adversarial relationships with

Figure 3.1. 1949 and 1956 Middle East rivalry fields

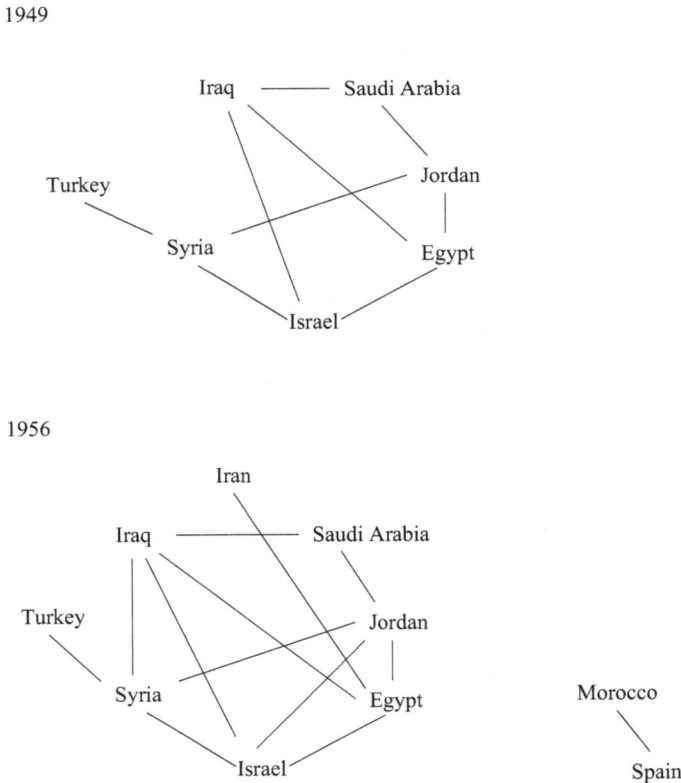

other Arab actors. Jordan had four Arab rivalries, Egypt had three, and Syria had two, but also one with non-Arab Turkey. Seven years later, the 1956 rivalry field did not look too much different. Israel still had the same four rivalries with Arab states. Jordan had reduced its rivalry exposure. Egypt now had four rivalries with the addition of another two monarchical opponents in Saudi Arabia and Iran. One could say that the eastern MENA had become more extended with greater Iranian participation, but the Maghreb or western portion was also becoming more alive with the addition of two more independent states (Tunisia and Morocco), one of which added a rivalry with Spain over Spanish colonial territory in Northwest Africa to the mix.

Figure 3.2 compares the 1975 and 2000 rivalry fields. The antagonism toward Israel—perhaps the defining feature of the earlier rivalry fields—persisted through 1975 but was lessening by 2000. The 1975 structure has a stronger Maghreb segment with three rivalries. The Gulf subsystem is also coming through more strongly with an Iraqi-centered focus (rivalries with Iran, Saudi Arabia, and Kuwait) that might be linked to the new rivalries on the southern Saudi peninsula (Oman–South Yemen and South Yemen–Yemen). Otherwise, the Mashriq component looks fairly similar, albeit with less emphasis on the waning contest between monarchs and Nasserite socialism.

Figure 3.2. 1975 and 2000 Middle East rivalry fields

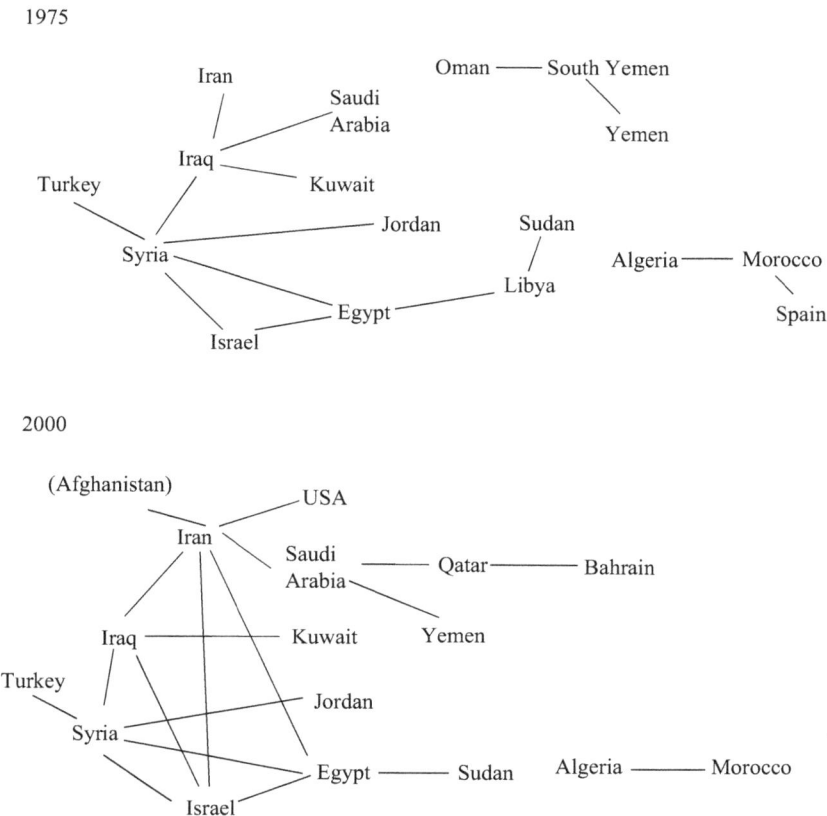

By 2000, though, the southern Saudi peninsula rivalries had been resolved, at least for the time being. New Gulf rivalries emerged (Bahrain-Qatar, and the about-to-end Saudi-Yemen rivalry might be included in this segment as well). The Maghreb rivalries have been reduced to the persistent Algerian-Moroccan anchor and a new Egyptian-Sudan antagonism. The Mashriq maintained its focus on Israel, but with the de-escalation of the Egyptian-Israeli relationship, the focus had become less defining.

Figure 3.3 outlines more recent variations on the MENA rivalry field. In 2005 the field looks much less complex than it had before. A few rivalries survive, but a number have disappeared. The 2000 rivalry field showed seventeen connections, while the 2005 field shows only thirteen. This 24 percent reduction in rivalry linkages in a very short period primarily reflects the ending of rivalries in the Gulf and the Arabian Peninsula. Note that the US retaliation against its perceived 9/11 enemies had the effect of ousting the Taliban in Afghanistan and Saddam Hussein in Iraq, thereby inadvertently removing two of Iran's most proximate rivals in one fell swoop.

By 2018 the simplification of Mashriq rivalries was altered by the Syrian Civil War and what might be termed Saudi-Iranian polarization. The Turkish rapprochement with Syria had ended. The Syrian rivalries with Israel and Jordan had been put on a back burner while the intense civil war was being waged within Syria. The Iraq-Kuwait and

Figure 3.3. 2005 and 2018 Middle East rivalry fields

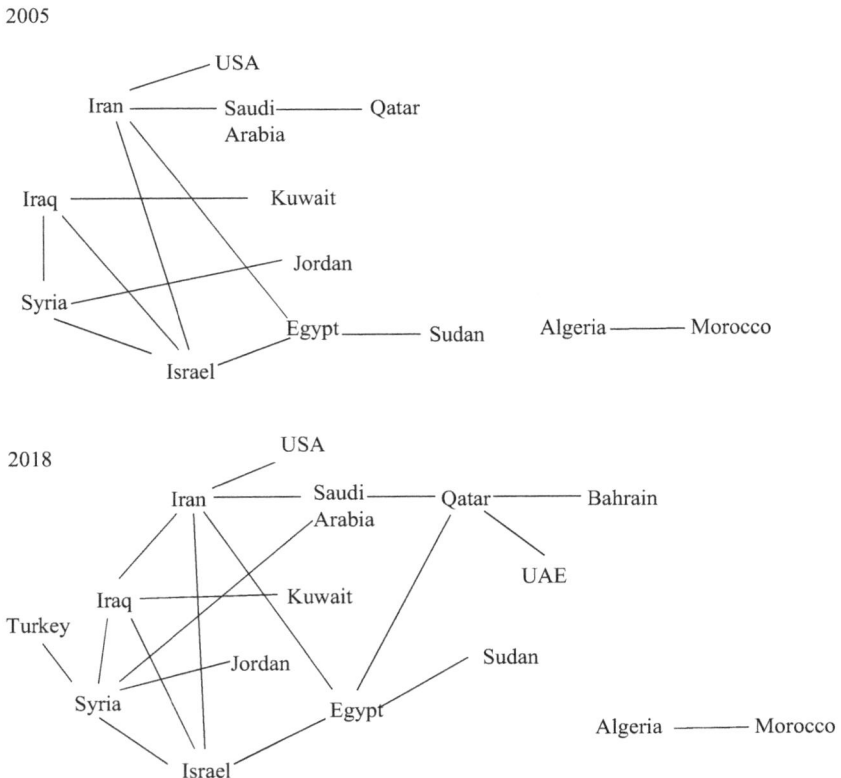

Egypt-Sudan rivalries were not all that visible because both Egypt and Iraq had major internal problems with which to contend. The Algerian-Moroccan rivalry seems to persist without many visible displays of intense hostility as well. By default that leaves the Iranian–Saudi Arabian rivalry standing as the premier manifestation of intense rivalry. The UAE, Saudi, Bahraini, and Egyptian rivalries with Qatar are linked to the Iranian-Saudi polarization even while they are complicated by factors specific to each dyad.[15] The Saudi involvement in the Syrian Civil War is another linkage represented in figure 3.3, but it is itself closely linked to the Iran-Saudi contest given the Iranian support for Bashar al-Assad as an ally and the Saudi opposition to the survival of the Assad regime.

More or less simultaneously, the Gulf subsystem became more complex. The central rivalries between the United States and Saudi Arabia, on one side, and Iran, on the other, continued. Added to the conflict axis was a fracture within the Gulf Cooperation Council (GCC) states involving Saudi Arabia and the United Arab Emirates against the nonconformity of Qatar.

Scanning across all three figures (1949–2018), we can say that the MENA rivalry field has evolved in two ways. It has fluctuated in complexity as the number of rivalries wax and wane. Some of the older major competitors have been bought off, defanged, or eliminated. New major competitors have been few in number and have demonstrated little staying power. Yet some of the complexity is returning in more recent years.

The rivalry field has also shifted its central foci from an anti-Israel coalition and the inter-Arab cold war between monarchs and more revolutionary regimes that had dethroned their monarchs and wanted to see more monarchs dethroned to what is shaping up to be a Saudi-Iranian cold war that combines Sunni-Shi'a overtones with an assault on and defense of the regional status quo.[16] Egypt was the champion of change in the first cold war. Iran has become the change champion in the second cold war. The antagonism toward Israel persists, but it seems less likely to be an issue worth going to war about, barring a major Israeli attack on Palestinians. Whether Saudi-Iranian issues are deemed worth going to war over directly remains to be seen, while there is little question that their antagonism plays itself out in several proxy combats in Yemen, Lebanon, and Syria.

Volgy et al. (2018) argue for a linear relationship between regional hierarchy and conflict. The stronger the hierarchy, the less is the conflict because a dominant regional power can impose an order on the region. While they find empirical support for their argument, it is most relevant here because the MENA lacks a coherent hierarchy.[17] Many of the earlier inter-Arab rivalries, and now the Iran-Saudi rivalry, reflect the persistent absence of a dominant regional power. Instead, the MENA has experienced several claimants for regional leadership. Part of the problem is that no single state has amassed enough capabilities to subordinate the other challengers, although Egypt came closest to doing so between 1956 and 1967. Even so, Egyptian predominance was as much due to Gamal Abdel Nasser's finite charisma and the popular hunger for revising the 1948–49 outcome as it was to the size of the Egyptian population or army.

Another part of the hierarchy problem is that capabilities tend to be deconcentrated in the MENA. The richest states tend to have small populations and armies. The states with the largest populations and armies tend to be poor. Saddam Hussein's grab for Kuwait was neither random nor unrelated to regional leadership ambitions. At times states could bid for leadership based on control of Mecca and Medina, reinforced by large pools of oil. Most unusual by regional standards, the strongest state in the region has always been considered a pariah because of its distinctive religious makeup. Officially isolated, it is definitely in the region but not viewed as fully a part of the region.

Geography also interferes with the probability of constructing a single regional hierarchy. The MENA is a large territory stretching from Morocco in the west to Iran and Turkey in the east. As a region, it can be broken down into three subsystems in which some players operate exclusively and others overlap in one or more of the subsystems. A dominant actor in the Maghreb might have little clout in the Gulf and vice versa. Great distance is something of an equalizer.

Compounding the hierarchy problem is that major players in the region continue to go "on and off line." Egypt was ostracized for years for worrying more about control of the Sinai than continuing the fight for the Palestinian cause after Anwar Sadat agreed to a US-sanctioned deal with Israel. Iraq was defeated and occupied by foreign troops for years. Syria has been tied down in a devastating civil war for years. Hierarchy is unlikely to have much effect if many of the major players are effectively off the board for substantial periods.

Nonlocal major players are likely to interfere with regional hierarchical effects as well. In the twentieth century the MENA was first penetrated considerably by the British and French mandates. Their legacy was a host of boundaries and countries that did not always make much sense. One could easily argue that the states left behind when the British and French withdrew defied the likelihood that a regional hierarchy would or could emerge.

The second half of that century saw the United States and the Soviet Union vie for influence until the USSR disintegrated. With some states allied to one or the other and a number trying to avoid alignment, a single regional hierarchy was less likely to emerge. In the "unipolar moment," the United States had little major power competition and could do things that had not been possible when local actors were aligned with two opposed global powers. But what US decision-makers chose to do did not work out quite as planned. Among other outcomes Baghdad was taken out of play for a time and perhaps transformed into an Iranian ally. Iran watched two of its rivals (Iraq and the Afghani Taliban) be taken out of contention, thereby inadvertently improving Iran's immediate and long-term threat environment, other things being equal.[18]

Of course, all these considerations underscore the absence of a strong hierarchy in the MENA. Paired with the consistently high levels of conflict in the region, the Volgy et al. argument finds definite support in the MENA. Unfortunately, the argument does not tell us what to expect in terms of rivalry. The absence of a strong hierarchy has been virtually constant and should imply consistently high numbers of rivalries (as manifestations of conflict), but that is not what we find. Perhaps the problem is that conflict can be manifested in different ways. Rivalries could decline in number while civil wars increase, leading to consistently high levels of conflict of one type or another.

The Humpty Dumpty MENA rivalry field has undergone significant change in the last seventy years. As with most Humpty Dumpties, it seems unlikely that anyone, let alone all the king's men, will be able to restore the original and once fairly stable rivalry field that seemed a hallmark of MENA politics. That there have been fewer strategic rivalries at times than there once were is probably beneficial in the sense that fewer rivalries should mean a lesser probability of interstate war. Yet the temporary movement toward fewer rivalries does not mean that the MENA is becoming a more pacific place as it did in Western Europe or South America. Temporary fluctuations in the number of rivalries reflect an increased absorption with domestic problems and turmoil or shifting issue areas of contention.

Figure 3.4 is suggestive along these lines. The figure plots MENA rivalry density (number of rivalries divided by number of possible dyadic relationships) against the proportion of MENA states with internal warfare (as identified by the PRIO-Uppsala conflict database, which requires specific conflicts to have at least twenty-five battle deaths).[19] When the regional rivalry density was greatest at the beginning of the two series, internal warfare was least and vice versa. Toward the last decade of the series, internal warfare has climbed to new proportional levels, while rivalry density has decreased to its lowest levels. It cannot be claimed that figure 3.4 represents a causal relationship between the two indicators, but it does seem logical to anticipate overall less interstate conflict when

Figure 3.4. Internal war and rivalry density in the Middle East, 1946–2015

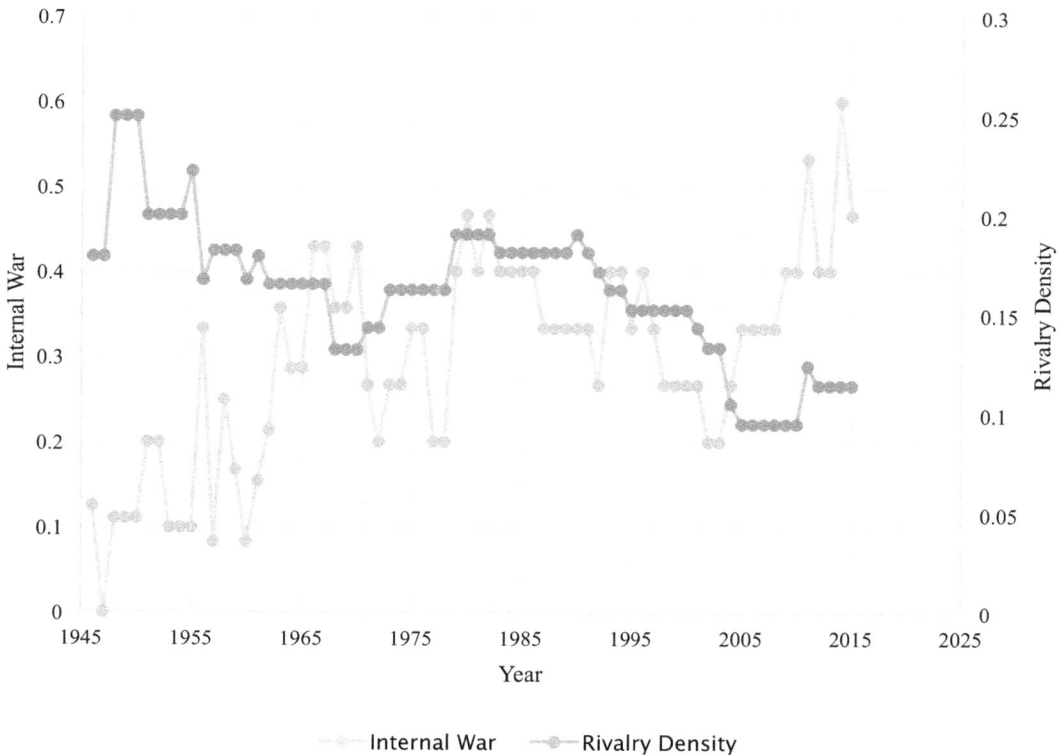

decision-makers are absorbed by more intrastate conflict. If that holds true, one might see some movement toward greater interstate conflict to the extent that the domestic conflicts are resolved in some fashion. But it may also be that the genie is out of the bottle and the salience of domestic conflict has become or is becoming supreme.[20]

The salience of domestic conflict would encompass the ascendancy of non-state groups as major conflict actors. Once upon a time, Fatah was the main non-state group in the MENA. Since then a profusion of groups have risen to prominence and have even taken on states (e.g., the Kurdistan Workers' Party [PKK] versus Turkey, Hezbollah versus Israel in Lebanon, and ISIL versus a rather extensive list of state opponents). The non-state groups have not been able to decisively defeat their state foes, but one possible outcome of their struggles is the fragmentation of many of the actors that were once major players in the MENA rivalry field. At some point Iraq could devolve into three or more states (Kurdish, Sunni, and Shi'ite); Syria could easily become much smaller in size with various rebel warlords ruling in the periphery. Yemen might split again along north-south lines. Libya has some potential for breaking down into three or more subregionally based states as well. Sudan has finally split along its north-south axis. There is no reason to assume that Saudi Arabia will remain intact for all time to come. All of this possible fragmentation could multiply the number of MENA states considerably, but these new states could also lack the capability to engage in much interstate rivalry. That alone would reduce the rivalry density in the MENA even more, if only mathematically.

At the same time, there is no reason to lament the fall of the Humpty Dumpty rivalry field in the MENA. Rivalry fields are subject to change—they are likely to evolve. In some places they have vanished completely. In others they become more complex. In the MENA they have moved back and forth, without vanishing completely. To the extent that the field has been transformed, rivalries should have become somewhat less interdependent. A prime example is that Saudi Arabia apparently can no longer count absolutely on Egypt to back Saudi opposition to Iran (Ahmadian 2016; Trofimov 2016). Such a development would have been far less probable in past decades when Egyptian decision-makers felt that they had to thwart Iranian positional gains lest the gains come at Egyptian expense.

One caveat is that states increasingly have to contend with powerful non-state groups within a renewed regional cold war pitting Iran and its coalition against Saudi Arabia and its coalition. The non-state groups do not appear because the networks that have been sketched here are restricted to interstate disputes. A network tracing non-state group rivalries with states and other non-state groups would be a far more complex undertaking. But perhaps it would offer a more realistic map of current tensions. The new cold war, on the other hand, is still emerging and at the same time is very much embedded in the non-state group network.

Embedded networks have always characterized the MENA. Global feuds overlay regional feuds that overlay local feuds. It looks also as if one dimension of the global network in the guise of the US-Russian rivalry is back as well. How that will play out remains to be seen. The MENA rivalry field has always been layered, but the external major power layer fluctuates in intensity just as the local interstate layer has. What we do not know is how much these differential fluctuations matter, if in fact they do matter.

CONCLUSION

Rivalries have been fairly common in MENA international relations. Focusing on them will not tell us everything we might want to know about what has transpired or is transpiring in the region. In contrast, not giving them any systematic attention at all seems a clear waste of a promising opportunity. As a form of interstate behavior, they have structure and processes that we should get to know better. Why do they begin? What maintains them? How do they escalate or de-escalate in hostility? Why do they terminate? What difference do they make? Do they help us make sense of MENA politics?

At the beginning of this chapter, two well-known MENA specialists were quoted. One said that the Arab uprisings had so far (writing in 2013) not dramatically changed anything about alignments in regional international relations. The other one suggested that there was a tendency to adopt one of two extreme positions when major upheavals occurred—either everything or nothing changed as a consequence. Ottaway (2013) is probably right if the stress is placed on dramatic changes. She runs through a list of issues and actors that have not budged after the Arab Spring events. Yet changes can be found in the rivalry field. The Syrian-Turkish rivalry was renewed, the Iraqi-Syrian rivalry seems to have ended, and Saudi Arabia became more active in the struggle against the Assad regime. Gulf politics have become more complex given the feud between Qatar and Saudi Arabia, the UAE, and Bahrain. None of these shifts represent dramatic changes, but they do appear to be significant changes and realignments.

Halliday (2002) is also right to warn against exaggerating the effects of upheavals. Yet shocks constitute the prime mechanism for opening opportunities for rivalry field adjustments. Every shock will not lead to an impact. Some shocks will have several impacts. They possess variable potential for contributing to the overcoming of the very strong inertia found in most international relations. A series of sufficiently strong shocks, therefore, is likely to lead to changes in rivalry fields. Presumably, a rivalry field could remain constant over a long period only if there were no or few shocks, whether endogenous or exogenous in origin. Since shocks have not been rare in MENA politics, its rivalry field has undergone substantial modification over the past seventy years.[21]

Evolutionary processes tend to lead to greater complexity, but not always. In the MENA the regional rivalry field has demonstrated that it can be simplified over time (even if not necessarily permanently). Why that is the case is open to debate. Presumably, it is not the absence of an overarching hierarchy, because that has been pretty much a constant. It may have something to do with increasing domestic violence that leaves less time and fewer resources for interstate hostilities. Knocking out, restraining, or diverting the usual suspects in Arab leadership contests (Baghdad, Damascus, and Cairo) may also have something to do with this outcome.

Nevertheless, the MENA rivalry field outcome is still in flux. Further simplification in the field structure could lead to the end of interstate rivalries in the MENA, as has taken place in other regions. If their place is taken by endemic civil warfare, one type of conflict will have been substituted for another. On the other hand, if the region is in a transitional phase, a return to the days of a fairly dense rivalry field cannot be ruled out. Thus, unlike most other regions in the world system, rivalries remain quite prominent in the international relations of the Middle East and North Africa.

NOTES

First epigraph: Ottaway (2013, 2).
Second epigraph: Halliday (2002, 235).

1. Nor is interstate conflict. Volgy et al. (2018) list the Middle East as the most conflictual region in terms of militarized interstate disputes (MIDs) in most decades since World War II with the exception of the 2000s, in which it still claimed the largest number of MIDs but not on a per capita (or per state) basis.

2. Asymmetrical rivalries are not ruled out, they are simply less likely. Of course, a statement like this one hinges on how one views asymmetry. One or another side may have more tanks or fighter jets, but the question is whether they are both minor or major powers. Asymmetry in this context refers to rivalries in which major powers confront minor powers.

3. There are a few exceptions. Analysis of MENA rivalries is featured in the following works: Barnett (1992), Lieberman (1995), Maoz (1995), Leng (2000), Rasler (2001), Maoz and Mor (2002), and Lebovic and Thompson (2006).

4. The regional subsystem term follows usage established in Thompson (1973). More recent applications can be found in Noble (2008) and Maddy-Weitzman (2012).

5. The principal members of the Middle East and North Africa are Morocco, Algeria, Tunisia, Libya, Sudan, Egypt, Jordan, Syria, Israel, Lebanon, Iraq, Kuwait, Bahrain, Qatar, UAE, Oman, and Yemen. Some states, such as Iran and Turkey, have moved in and out of the region depending on their foreign policy orientations. Some of the North African states have southern interests that lead them to become involved, sometimes only intermittently, with African states and subsystems in the Sahara and Northeast Africa.

6. Libya and Sudan are the main offenders given their participation in Northeast African politics. These rivalries include Chad-Libya, Chad-Sudan I and II, Eritrea-Sudan, Ethiopia-Sudan, Kenya-Sudan, Sudan-Uganda I and II, and most recently, Sudan-Southern Sudan. The older Egypt-Ethiopian case (1868–82) is also not listed. For more details on these African rivalries, see Thompson and Dreyer (2011). The case of Turkey and Iran is another omission that may puzzle readers. Historically, they were certainly once quite prominent strategic rivals, with Ottoman Turkey oscillating between Russian and Persian hostility for centuries. In the more contemporary era, they have been competitors and even cultural and commercial rivals in Southwest and Central Asia, but it is not clear that there is sufficient evidence that they see each other as strategic rivals as yet. See, for instance, Akbarzadeh and Barry (2016). Such categorizations are surely subjective and sometimes must be made on incomplete information. For a different take on Iran and Turkey, see chapter 7 in this volume.

7. However, there are good reasons to believe that Iraq's rivalries with Syria, Kuwait, and Saudi Arabia (but not Iran) continued after 2003.

8. But as noted earlier, that does not mean that both sides must view the other side in exactly the same way. For instance, Qatari decision-makers may worry about a Saudi military invasion without our insisting that Saudi decision-makers must be equally worried about a Qatari military invasion to qualify as a strategic rivalry. Saudis need only perceive a threat from Qatar in terms of its support for the Muslim Brotherhood or for different factions in Syria or Libya to satisfy a definitional requirement that rivals see themselves as threatening enemies.

9. Earlier I had resisted acknowledging an Iranian-US rivalry owing to the tendency for major-minor pairings not to be characterized by rivalry, but I have had to concede that I have been wrong because the evidence seems to suggest otherwise.

10. Diehl and Goertz (2000, 222) refer to shocks as windows of opportunity that make change possible and, as such, "necessary conditions for dramatic changes in what are normally stable relationships." Shocks themselves can be complicated events that require interpretation within layers of deeper etiologies. Sayigh (2016), for instance, argues that the official reaction to Arab Spring protests varied from country to country and that subsequent violence tended to be linked to coercive responses by authoritarian regimes. Arab Spring protests, in turn, stemmed from decades of authoritarian rule that had grossly undelivered public goods.

11. Sometimes the Iran-Iraq War is referred to as the First Gulf War, and in that context one can trace a thread linking all three Gulf wars as highly interdependent phenomena. Thus, the statement stands regardless of how Gulf wars are enumerated.

12. Hazbun (2012) advances an interesting interpretation of American motivation in the Bush administration that saw American moves in Iraq as a step toward transformation of the entire region so that the MENA (a) was a less dangerous zone for breeding instability and (b) could better fit into a globalizing world. These views hinged on regarding processes in the MENA as working differently than elsewhere in the world. How much of this argument was post hoc rhetoric as opposed to genuine motivation is open for discussion. However, the Trump administration also seems likely to view the MENA in equally exceptionalist terms but without the interest in transformation. More exogenous shocks can be anticipated as a consequence.

13. See Thompson (2003) and Rasler and Thompson (2014) for an argument that changes in several rivalry fields contributed considerably to the outbreak of World War I in 1914.

14. One could do something similar with alliance linkages and membership in international organizations to sketch a region's cooperative structure.

15. For instance, it is possible to argue that some of these rivalries date back to tribal conflict (involving tribes located in what are now Bahrain, Abu Dhabi, and Qatar) over possession of Qatar in 1867.

16. The standard reference on the first Arab cold war, of course, is Kerr (1971). For the second one, see Bank and Valbjorn (2012), Ryan (2012), Gause (2014), Grunet (2015), Esfandiary and Tabatabai (2016).

17. Ironically, this author began his publication career trying to decipher the MENA regional hierarchy (Thompson 1970).

18. Needless to say, other things were not equal given threats from various sources to remove its nuclear plants in a coercive manner. American occupation of adjacent Iraq was perceived by Iranian policymakers as a matter of exponentially increased threat in the short term (Kamrava 2011, 191).

19. See Sorli, Gleditsch, and Strand (2005) for an earlier application of this internal warfare index to MENA conflict.

20. Cammack et al. (2017) argue that geopolitical tensions are a function of the collapse of multiple domestic authoritarian bargains, along with an increase in failed states, new technology, climate change, and dependency on oil revenues and falling prices for petroleum.

21. If someone ever enumerates the number of shocks experienced by all regions in the contemporary era, it would be surprising if any region has experienced more shocks than the contemporary MENA.

4

The Saudi-Iran Strategic Rivalry

"Like Fire and Dynamite"

John Calabrese

> Iran and us [Saudi Arabia] are like fire and dynamite. We are the rowdies
> who could bring the whole house down.—Jamal Kashoggi

Since 2015 the Saudi Arabia–Iran strategic rivalry has intensified, punctuated by a string of incidents reminiscent of the immediate aftermath of the 1979 Iranian Revolution. However, recent events have been taking place in a fundamentally different and fluid context—one in which the Arab regional order has collapsed and the US commitment to regional security and stability is being seriously questioned. There is a possibility that a mishap or miscalculation could result in escalation to outright war. But even if Saudi Arabia and Iran do not stumble into a direct military conflict, the intensity of their competition risks pulling the region into even more destructive and protracted turmoil.

What set this rivalry in motion? What can explain its persistence? What can account for variations in its intensity? And are the short- and medium-term prospects for a de-escalation, if not termination, of this rivalry as grim as they seem? This chapter addresses these questions by tracing the evolution of the Saudi-Iran rivalry from its inception, shedding light on how political shocks have been responsible for triggering, as well as inflaming and dampening, the rivalry dynamic and highlighting the role that extra-dyadic actors can play—and that the United States *has* played, in this case—both in containing and sustaining the rivalry.

CONCEPTUALIZING ENDURING STRATEGIC RIVALRIES AND POLITICAL SHOCKS

The literature on Saudi-Iranian relations falls roughly into studies that focus on the balance of power between the two states (Wehrey et al. 2009; Haseeb 1998; Al-Saud 2003, 10), on their religious and ideological differences (Keddie and Matthee 2002), and on the personalities of leaders and the structure of foreign policy decision-making (Korany and Fattah 2008; Ramazani 1992). The treatment of Iran-Saudi relations in this chapter as an enduring rivalry is not intended as an alternative to any or all of these approaches. Rather, it seeks to highlight the interplay between these several dimensions in order to gain a fuller understanding of how the Saudi-Iran relationship has evolved and where it might be heading.

In this chapter the Saudi-Iran rivalry is depicted as being a "strategic" (Thompson 2001), "positional" (Thompson 1995), and "enduring" one (Goertz and Diehl 1995b). It is "strategic" in the sense that each side identifies the other as an enemy and an explicit threat. It is positional, as opposed to spatial, in that the rivalry is rooted in a contest over *relative status* rather than over the exclusive control of *territory* (Thompson 1995). And it is enduring in that "severe and repeated conflicts" between the two sides have persisted "for an extended period of time" (Goertz and Diehl 1995b).[1] Casting the Saudi-Iran rivalry as an enduring rivalry helps focus attention on its longitudinal and dynamic aspects, that is, on how the rivalry has developed (Goertz and Diehl 1995b).

Diehl and Goertz claim that a political shock—at the system or state level—is a "virtual necessary condition" for initiating a rivalry (Goertz and Diehl 1995a, 228; Diehl and Goertz 2000, 138), the idea being that shocks set the stage for rapid changes in relationships and that rivalries, once they "lock in," become hard to dislodge (Goertz, Jones, and Diehl 2005). In contrast, an evolutionary approach postulates that rivalries encompass a "history of hostility"—that is, they are not "born" but rather grow slowly into conflictual relationships (Klein, Goertz, and Diehl 2006, 336; Hensel 1999). An evolutionary approach thereby draws attention to variations in the severity of a rivalry and the potential factors responsible for such oscillations. This chapter adopts a syncretic perspective, one that considers not just the nature of the shock that unleashed the Saudi-Iran rivalry but also the key events and interactions within each phase that have sustained it and contributed to variations in its severity. This approach allows for the possibility that a rivalry might experience multiple shocks as it runs its course as well as multiple shocks "clustered" within a compressed time frame.

An enduring rivalry can be maintained at varying levels of intensity for years, even decades—and without necessarily erupting into a full-scale war. The threat, display, or ever-present possibility of the use of military force to resolve competing claims is a standard tool for prosecuting a rivalry. However, states can and do deploy various other instruments of statecraft, separately or in combination, including proxy warfare, economic pressure, and soft power, for this purpose. Furthermore, the relative priority and allocation of resources to these tools is likely to change over the life span of the rivalry. As will be shown, Saudi Arabia and Iran have employed a wide array of tools within and beyond the Gulf in pursuing their rivalry.

Rivalries are about more than just recurring conflicts and a history of grievances between a pair of adversaries; the involvement of third parties can have the effect of sustaining, even escalating, competition between the focal adversaries (Goertz and Diehl 1997). Some have pointed out that third-party involvement can make rivalry more complex and can also guide how hostile or cooperative the rivalry is (Ganguly and Thompson 2011b, 207). Others have examined third-party involvement in the form of "intersecting rivalries" (Kinsella 1994), whereby the rival countries become "linked" (i.e., through alliance ties, joint disputes, common foes, and shared borders) (Diehl and Goertz 2000, 247; Valeriano and Powers 2016). This chapter looks specifically at the singular role that the United States has played—as an external balancer for the weaker rival (Vasquez 1996; Paul 2005, 2006) (Saudi Arabia) and as post-revolutionary Iran's principal nemesis—in the sustainment of the Saudi-Iran rivalry.[2]

SAUDI-IRAN RELATIONS IN A VOLATILE RIVALRY FIELD: TREMORS AND SHOCKS

Enduring interstate rivalry is one of the defining characteristics of the contemporary Middle East. Over the years such rivalries have been fully on display—including the casualties and costs they have inflicted—in the various dyadic relationships embedded in the Arab-Israeli conflict. Two features of the Middle East have made the region especially prone to enduring rivalries: (1) its unusually high degree of external intervention yet stubborn resistance to subordination and (2) the dense cultural and political ties that transcend state borders (Brown 1984, 3–5; Hinnebusch 2005, 154; 2003, 152). These features have helped shape an environment that is conducive to militarized interstate competition not just over territory or other tangible goods but also over status, influence, and the desired normative order of the regional system (Barnett 1998, 2).

Enduring interstate rivalries are inherently dynamic phenomena, which among other things necessarily implies that they have a beginning. However, it is often difficult to pinpoint the exact date of the inception of a rivalry. In fact, it might be more practical and more realistic to consider the circumstances whereby a relationship *becomes* a rivalry. Accordingly, the first order of business is to provide a brief account of the relationship between Saudi Arabia and Iran prior to when their rivalry can reasonably be said to have commenced.

SAUDI-IRAN RELATIONS: FROM LATENT TO FULL-BLOWN RIVALRY

Saudi Arabia and Iran established diplomatic relations in 1929. However, almost from its very inception, the bilateral relationship was marked by mistrust. The pre-rivalry stage of the relationship can be divided roughly into three phases—the first marked by limited engagement, the second entailing a tenuous partnership, and the third defined by an incipient rivalry.

The first phase (1920s–50s) encompassed the state-building and consolidation processes of the Pahlavis and Al-Sauds and the era of British hegemony in the Gulf. During this initial phase, there were few diplomatic exchanges and very limited commercial ties between Saudi Arabia and Iran. In general, the relationship between the Pahlavis and the Al-Sauds was one of mutual suspicion (Halliday 2000, 118), with Persian territorial ambitions and differences over religious practices—especially as related to the Hajj—serving as sources of friction that waxed and waned throughout the period (Badeeb 1993, 50–51).

British involvement in the Gulf constituted yet another source of friction. Shah Reza deemed the 1927 Treaty of Jeddah signed between the United Kingdom and Ibn Saud to be a direct challenge to Iran's sovereignty as he believed the accord undermined Iranian claims to the Gulf, particularly with respect to Bahrain (Saïd Zahlan 1989, 14). Similarly, during the early Cold War years, the bilateral relationship was strained over Iran's decision to join the Baghdad Pact (Badeeb 1993, 53) and by King Saud's initial attempt to accommodate Gamal Abdel Nasser in light of the wide popularity the latter enjoyed (Vassiliev 1998, 354).

The second phase, the decade of the 1960s, was a period in which Saudi-Iranian relations were arguably the most cordial they had ever been or have been since. During that time Riyadh and Tehran—both facing communist and republican threats and bolstered by the patronage of the United States—forged an uneasy partnership with each other. In fact, it was not until the 1960s that they engaged in close consultations and coordination on regional policies.

The shift toward a more cooperative bilateral relationship was rooted in a heightened concern about the dual threat of the Soviet Union and radical Arab nationalism, as manifested especially by the perceived belligerence of the Abd Al-Karim Qassim regime following its 1958 overthrow of the Iraqi monarchy and the Egyptian intervention in Yemen in 1962 (Fürtig 2007, 628; Stratfor, 2009, 2010; Spindle and Coker 2011).

The Shah's initial outreach to Saudi Arabia was favorably received by King Saud and later reciprocated by King Faisal, who assumed full power in November 1964 (Al-Saud 2003, 9). The fledgling partnership included support for the establishment of the Muslim World League (MWL) and Organization for the Islamic Conference (OIC). Saudi-Iran cooperation progressed on several other fronts as well. In 1969 Faisal sought and obtained military equipment from Iran in order to contain the potentially destabilizing effects of the turmoil in Yemen (Keynoush 2016, 101).

The ways in which the two countries chose to handle their competing territorial claims during this phase, as well as the outcome of their efforts, are instructive. In 1966 and 1968 King Faisal and Shah Mohammad Reza exchanged visits. The elevation in diplomatic relations was directly related to the efforts by both sides to resolve disputes over the two islands of Farsi and Arabi, which they eventually succeeded in doing. Lengthy negotiations between Riyadh and Tehran followed, ultimately producing a bilateral agreement on maritime boundaries as well (Al-Saud 2003, 51). Yet the Shah's reported attempt to find a face-saving formula to settle the dispute over Bahrain was unsuccessful (Al-Saud 2003, 39–41).

These attempts to mend fences are suggestive. First, their timing and context indicate that both Saudi Arabia and Iran viewed progress on territorial issues as being highly salient—as a means to further improve the bilateral relationship, which in turn could serve to ameliorate the security situation given the challenges posed by other actors. Second, these efforts demonstrated the two countries' willingness to seek common ground. Yet at the same time, they highlight an enduring source of mistrust.

The third phase, that of an incipient rivalry, was presaged by the sudden announcement by Prime Minister Harold Wilson in January 1968 that Britain would withdraw all its forces from the Gulf. This announcement was followed six months later by the bloodless coup in Iraq that brought the Ba'ath Party to power and ushered in a decade of uneasy partnership between Saudi Arabia and Iran. Hallmarks of the Saudi Arabia–Iran competitive maneuverings during this period included Saudi Arabia's modernization of its military, Saudi Arabian resistance to Iranian efforts to establish a regional security architecture, both countries' building bilateral ties with their smaller neighbors, competition over supporting Iraq, and different positions over Organization of the Petroleum Exporting Countries (OPEC) price increases (Gause 2009, 37–39).

The British withdrawal ultimately had the effect of redefining the regional order in the Gulf, giving rise to a fragile balance within a tripolar system composed of Iran, Iraq, and Saudi Arabia (Fürtig 2007, 628)—a configuration that prevailed for the next two decades and that the United States sought to shape but was periodically forced to adjust to in order to safeguard its own and Western interests.

From the outset US officials regarded Iran as being militarily more capable of securing Western interests and politically more stable than Saudi Arabia (Hurwitz 1972, 33; Long 1985, 55). In fact, during the 1960s Iran's national power had grown significantly, both in economic and military terms. Oil price increases in 1970 and 1971 further boosted both Iran's and Saudi Arabia's capacities to fund sizable military purchases. As Iranian power increased, so too did the Shah's regional ambitions (Alam 2008, 185). Although he acknowledged that the two states "could become the nucleus for stability and progress in the Persian Gulf," his views about Saudi Arabia were tinged with arrogance and condescension: "Nixon would like to consign us to the level of the most backward countries in the whole Middle East. Why lower us to the standard of the Saudis rather than raising the Saudis to meet us?" (Alam 2008, 281).

With the British presence and influence having receded, the Shah was determined to—and did—follow a more assertive and independent policy in the Gulf (Al-Saud 2003, 24–27). Iran renewed its territorial claims over Bahrain and the Hormuz islands. Likewise, the maritime dispute between Iran and Saudi Arabia became more contentious (Al-Saud 2003, 30–56). Unsurprisingly, Saudi concerns about Iran at the time centered on the latter's attainment of military preeminence in the region and the reassertion of Iranian territorial claims (Al-Saud 2003, 70–77). Moreover, within the Twin Pillars security architecture devised by Washington, Saudi Arabia, though recognizing Iran's military superiority, nonetheless sought to be an equal—not a junior partner (Chubin and Tripp 1996, 9).

Here it is important to note that there was no sudden, definitive break in the relatively cordial relationship that had prevailed in the Saudi-Iranian relationship during the 1960s (Safran 1985, 135; Afkhami 2009, 280–84; Keynoush 2016, 101). While in some instances welcoming the application of Iranian military power and indirectly benefiting from it, the Saudis still found it unsettling. Such was the case with the 1971 Iranian intervention in Dhofar, which, although proving decisive in crushing the rebellion, resulted in the lingering presence of Iranian forces in Oman (Keynoush 2016, 88). Resentful, and perhaps fearful of Iranian dominance, though they were, the Saudis were careful not to risk a direct confrontation. Instead, they "endeavoured to use Iraq to frustrate the

Shah's scheme to institutionalize his hegemonic aspirations through a Gulf collective defense pact, and to use Iran to check Iraq's aspirations to become the center of the Arab countries of the Gulf" (Safran 1985, 265). In a somewhat similar fashion, the Shah sought to compartmentalize the disputes with Saudi Arabia. He dispatched a series of private messages expressing the desire to develop a positive working relationship with Saudi Arabia even while continuing to press Iran's claim to the Tunbs and Abu Musa (Al-Saud 2003, 127–29).

Yet it is important to emphasize that both Saudi Arabia and Iran, certainly until the mid-1970s, were primarily concerned about Iraq rather than about one another. Following the Ba'ath takeover in 1968, Iraq "adopted socialism at home, a stridently anti-Western posture in foreign policy, and a revolutionary rhetoric directed at conservative Gulf and Arab regimes" (Bakhash 2004, 17), as well as a close economic and military relationship with the Soviet Union. In addition, Iraq supported national liberation movements in Iran and Oman, leftists in Yemen, and the Popular Front for the Liberation of the Occupied Arabian Gulf (PFLOAG). For the most part reflecting the shared aim of containing the spread of Iraqi radicalism, Saudi Arabia and Iran appear to have gone to some lengths to limit their competition with each other and to manage their differences (Bakhash 2004, 17). Thus, the interposition of the Iran-Iraq and Saudi-Iraq rivalries seems to have ameliorated the Saudi-Iran rivalry.

SHOCKS AND RIVALRY ONSET: THE IRANIAN REVOLUTION IGNITES THE SAUDI-IRAN RIVALRY

The 1979 Iranian Revolution altered the geopolitical landscape of the region, delivering the seismic shock that ignited the Iran-Saudi rivalry. It marked the beginning of a protracted period pitting a set of transformational actors (Iran, Syria, and Hezbollah) that have sought to limit Western influence and constrain Israel against a set of status quo actors that includes, and has been supported and to a certain extent led by, Saudi Arabia operating under a Western (mainly US) security umbrella (Long 1985, 100–115).

Before the revolution and in spite of their differences, Saudi Arabia had viewed the Shah as a source of stability and as a counterweight to radical states and the influence of the Soviet Union over them (Kéchichian 1999, 232–33; Chubin 1992, 68–69; Al-Alkim 2000). The public face of the Saudi reaction to the initial spasms of revolutionary upheaval in Iran—expressions of hope for stability—masked the fear of possible chaos in Iran and its potential ripple effects (Quandt 1981, 41). However, the overthrow of the Iranian monarchy created great uncertainty in Saudi Arabia regarding the postrevolutionary regime's regional foreign policy approach while simultaneously shaking Saudi confidence in the United States, which had seemed either unwilling or unable to rescue the Shah (Long 1985, 122–23).

With the ascendancy of Ayatollah Khomeini and his followers, all the latent suspicions between Iranians and Saudis were rekindled (Quandt 1981, 39). Each side actively challenged the authority and legitimacy of the other in an ideological competition that ranged across the region and beyond (Korany and Fattah 2008; Ramazani 1992; Marschall

2003). Two competing discourses regarding the regional normative order rapidly evolved. One called openly for religious revolution, while the other demonized Shi'a expansionism (Al-Mani 1996, 159).

Ayatollah Khomeini's declaration that "monarchy is one of the most shameful reactionary manifestations" (Khomeini 1981, 202) and his questioning of the Al-Sauds' Islamic "authenticity" challenged both the regime's domestic legitimacy and an important source of its regional influence. Iran thus became the most dangerous threat because it challenged the basis of Saudi state identity (Wilson and Graham 1994, 104). What most concerned the Saudis was not the possibility of an Iranian territorial grab but political subversion. Kindling these fears were the unprecedented protests staged in the Saudi Shi'ite stronghold of al-Qatif in November 1979 that spread to other Shi'a cities in the Eastern Province as Saudi authorities struggled to respond to the seizure of the Grand Mosque in Mecca (T. C. Jones 2006). Indeed, the clustering of shocks within the span of less than a year—the seizure of the Grand Mosque, the protests in al-Qatif, the Soviet invasion of Afghanistan, and the outbreak of the Iran-Iraq War—magnified the shock effect produced by the Iranian Revolution, heightening Saudi insecurity and inflaming the Saudi-Iran rivalry.

The Iranian Revolution raised the stakes of religio-ideological issues, which in the past had been confined mainly to incidents related to the Hajj—incidents that ultimately had inflicted only limited and temporary damage on Saudi-Iran relations. However, the revolution amplified the importance of such incidents. It set the two states' obligations and aspirations in direct conflict: an Iranian theocracy duty bound as the new spiritual leader of Shi'ism "to foment and assist insurrection wherever Shi'ites were under oppression" (Rich 2012, 472) in opposition to a Saudi hereditary monarchy in control of Mecca and Medina that espoused a deeply conservative Wahhabi doctrine and viewed itself as the natural leader of the Islamic world (Nader 2013, 12). It is therefore not surprising that the issue of the Hajj became highly salient. Whereas the Saudis saw the pilgrimage as strictly religious, the Khomeinists saw it as religio-political (Baktiari 1996, 104; Amiri, Samsu, and Fereidouni 2011, 680; T. C. Jones 2006). The Saudis quickly came to regard the Hajj as a matter of internal security and to view political agitation by Iranian pilgrims not just as an impropriety but as a potential domestic political risk.

Thus, between 1983 and 1986, the annual Hajj became a secondary battlefield in the struggle between Saudi Arabia and Iran. The protests and clashes with Saudi security during the Hajj—often instigated by Iranian official delegates—were exploited to expose Saudi shortcomings in its management. The battle over the Hajj peaked in July 1987, when nearly four hundred Iranian pilgrims who were staging a political protest were killed in clashes with Saudi security forces (T. Jones 2009, 10–11). Unlike the disputes over the Hajj that had occurred during the pre-rivalry period, this incident was followed by the storming of the Saudi embassy in Tehran and culminated several months later in the severing of diplomatic relations for a period of three years (Kifner 1987). It is also important to note that the Hajj riots were sandwiched between the founding of Hezbollah in the Hijaz (Saudi Hezbollah) and the bombing of a gas plant in the Eastern Province for which the group was thought to have been responsible (Hegghammer 2010;

Kéchichian 1999). Thus, from the Saudi vantage point, the Hajj protests and domestic subversion fomented and assisted by Iran were cut from the same cloth.

Revolutionary Iran's bid to transform the regional order also had a geopolitical dimension. The geopolitical code adopted by Iran under Khomeini called for opposition to two hegemonic forces: the global superpowers, especially the United States, on the one hand, and corrupt, oppressive ruling elites, notably the Arab monarchies of the Gulf, on the other. Iran's revolutionaries viewed the Saudi monarchy with disdain—as an outpost of Western imperialism and as a cornerstone of the regional Pax Americana they were determined to resist (Nader 2013, 12). Thus, the role of the United States in the Middle East and the US-Saudi relationship figured prominently in the onset of enduring rivalry between Saudi Arabia and Iran.

With the inability of Iraqi forces to achieve a quick and decisive victory after launching a full-scale invasion of Iran in September 1980, the Iran-Iraq War settled into a prolonged stalemate. Over the next two years Saudi Arabia adopted a number of countermeasures to gird itself against the threat posed by Iran, including the formation of the Gulf Cooperation Council (GCC) but especially the strengthening of its deterrent capabilities, initially through the US Senate–approved Air Enhancement Package (1981) and the request for and receipt in 1984 of a shipment of Stinger missiles and other aid (Ramazani 1986, 10–11). Iranian officials responded to these developments with public allegations and threats, determined to exploit Saudi military reliance on the United States (Ramazani 1986, 11).

The course of the Iran-Iraq War had a strong bearing on the oscillations in intensity of the Saudi-Iran rivalry. When in June 1984, for example, as part of the expanding "tanker war," a Saudi vessel was attacked, a clash ensued between Iranian F-4s and Saudi F-15s that resulted in the shooting down of an Iranian aircraft followed by a brief standoff (Randall 1984; Ramazani 1986, 9). Yet in this instance, Iranian planes withdrew, and remarkably, few other such direct confrontations took place. Furthermore, this incident, rather than set in motion an escalatory dynamic, spurred Saudi attempts, though ultimately unsuccessful, to persuade Iran to agree to a cease-fire (Keynoush 2016, 120–21). Shortly thereafter, in a conciliatory gesture, Riyadh significantly increased the number of Iranian pilgrims granted entry for the annual Hajj. Reciprocal visits by Foreign Ministers Prince Saud (May 1985) and Ali Akbar Velayati (December 1985) occurred, and discussions aimed at expanding bilateral relations were held. Still, these interactions yielded no breakthrough on ending the Iran-Iraq War (Ramazani 1986, 96–100).

Rather than risk a direct military confrontation, Saudi Arabia and Iran both chose instead to prosecute their rivalry by other means. After the war with Iraq broke out, OPEC meetings became arenas in which Saudi Arabia and Iran wrangled over oil price and production quotas and thus played out their rivalry (*Economic and Political Weekly* 1982, 2070; Calabrese 1994, 58–62; Bahgat 2000, 109). Saudi-Iranian competition also extended to new terrain. The cementing of relations with Syria and establishment of Hezbollah in Lebanon in 1982 marked the beginning of postrevolutionary Iran's penetration into the Levant. Iran's presence and influence complicated Saudi efforts to restore peace in Lebanon and to forge under its leadership a pan-Arab approach to settling the Arab-Israeli conflict. Meanwhile, however, Saudi Arabia sought to reclaim its position as Islam's chief defender while redirecting the energy of Sunni Islamic extremism outward and thereby diminishing the threat to the kingdom through funding the Afghan jihad against the Soviet Union. Thus, the shock produced by the Iranian Revolution, whose reverberations were felt throughout the region and beyond, sparked a strategic rivalry between Saudi Arabia and Iran that has endured to this very day.

SHOCK CLUSTERS AND RIVALRY DYNAMICS: SAUDI-IRAN RELATIONS TRANSITION TO AN UNSTABLE DÉTENTE

Shocks can consist of a single potent blow or of a series of them occurring in rapid succession. They can originate from within the domestic, regional, or extra-regional environments. And they can spur the inflammation or the tempering of a rivalry. Between 1988 and 1991 the Saudi-Iran rivalry was subjected to multiple shocks. Having largely exhausted its military capabilities, Iran swallowed the bitter pill of accepting a UN-brokered cease-fire that ended the eight-year conflict with Iraq. The cessation of hostilities paved the way for the transition to a new political elite in Tehran, which occurred at roughly the same time as the emergence of new leadership in Riyadh. These parallel domestic developments converged with the ebbing of the Cold War and demise of the Soviet Union. The cumulative effect of this shock cluster was a de-escalation of tension between Saudi Arabia and Iran that ushered in an extended period of détente (Bahgat 2000, 108–15; Okruhlik 2003). However, as the following passages will demonstrate, Saudi-Iranian détente—spanning the Ali Akbar Hashemi Rafsanjani–Mohammad Khatami presidencies and the latter part of King Fahd's reign and emergence of Crown Prince Abdullah—was slow to develop, marked by uneven progress, and gradually gave way to renewed rivalry.

Fürtig (2002, 69, 103) notes that Saudi-Iran relations improved when, as a result of the Iran-Iraq War, the regional balance of power changed in favor of Iraq and Saddam was perceived as dangerous to and by both Riyadh and Tehran. Yet as important as this development undoubtedly was, it captures only part of the picture. On the domestic front, leadership changes and consequential policy shifts were also highly conducive. The death of Ayatollah Khomeini in June 1989 removed from the scene Iran's leading proponent of an activist foreign policy. There followed a more pragmatic approach spearheaded by President Rafsanjani. This policy adjustment, which reflected the country's exhaustion and the realization of the costs of isolation, made economic reconstruction the top policy priority and included a cautious rapprochement with Saudi Arabia (Bahgat 2000; M. M. Milani 1994; Mahdavi 2011, 96–97).

In regional affairs a certain climate of mutual accommodation and restraint prevailed during this period. Tehran appeared to make no effort to sabotage the 1989 Ta'if Agreement, which was engineered by Saudi Arabia, if only because the structure of the accord did not require the disarming of Hezbollah (Keynoush 2016, 125). Iran's "active neutrality" (M. M. Milani 1992) in the 1991 Gulf War was well received in Riyadh (Keynoush 2016, 126–29). Indeed, within less than a month of the end of the war, Riyadh and Tehran restored diplomatic ties.

Saudi-Iran détente also included some softening on the secondary battlefields, that is, with respect to the Hajj and OPEC production and pricing policy. Regarding the Hajj Saudi Arabia revised upward the quota for Iranian participants and, while insisting that no literature be disseminated by them, nonetheless loosened restrictions on low-key demonstrations (Amiri, Samsu, and Fereidouni 2011, 683–84). Thus the Hajj became not just an arena of contention but also a "venue for smoothing over differences" (Wehrey et al. 2009, 42; Amiri, Samsu, and Fereidouni 2011, 680).

Saudi-Iranian détente was also marked by periods of cooperation on oil production and pricing. For example, between March and July 1991, Tehran and Riyadh struck a compromise in an effort aimed at preventing an anticipated oil price collapse. However, within just a few months, the doves-hawks battle within OPEC resumed, as Saudi Arabia sought to eradicate the existing quota system while Iran resisted the pressure to do so even at the risk of damaging relations with Riyadh. In a meeting with the ruling clergy in September 1991, Minister of Petroleum Gholam Aghazadeh underscored the importance of oil to the fulfilment of the country's regional aspirations: "If the Islamic Republic is to maintain its regional preeminence, it must improve its economy by increasing its [oil] production" (Gillespie and Henry 1995, 209). In September 1993 a personal intervention by President Rafsanjani in the form of a telephone call to King Fahd (Chubin and Tripp 1996, 67–70) reportedly led to another agreement, which boosted Iran's quota. Several months later, however, Saudi Arabia resisted pressure to cut production, with the result that prices dropped to five-year lows, leading to public recriminations by Iranian officials, who painted Saudi Arabia as a lackey of the United States (Salehi-Isfahani 1995). Thus, throughout the 1990s one can observe a pattern of brief periods of goodwill and cooperation, punctuated by short-lived agreements on oil production and pricing.

Saudi-Iranian détente continued and in some ways matured during the Khatami presidency. With the ascendancy of the Reformists came a more conciliatory tone toward Saudi Arabia. Meanwhile, Crown Prince (later King) Abdullah, who assumed governing duties of the kingdom in 1995, believed constructive engagement might strengthen Iranian moderates and thus embarked on a steady but cautious effort to improve relations with Tehran (Eilts 2006, 239–40). In 1997 direct flights between the two countries resumed. Détente reached its peak in May 1999 with President Khatami's trip to Saudi Arabia—the first visit by an Iranian president since the revolution. The Saudi-Iranian rapprochement also produced two key agreements: the Cooperation Agreement (1998) and the Security Accord (2001). The Saudi-Iranian Economic Commission was established, and trade exhibitions were held (Altoraifi 2012, 208–20). In 1999 King Fahd urged other Arab Gulf states to follow Saudi Arabia's lead and seek to improve relations with Iran (BBC 1999).

Nevertheless, attempts to further improve Saudi-Iran relations ran up against skepticism and opposition on both sides (M. M. Milani 1994, 338). In Tehran there was pushback from within the Majlis and a harsh press campaign. In Riyadh most senior officials agreed that Iran represented a concrete challenge to Saudi Arabia's own regional aspirations (Kéchichian 2001, 120). A flare-up over the Tunbs and Bahrain in 1992 had reinforced these sentiments. Persistent mistrust stemmed also from divergent views about post–Gulf War Iraq. For the Saudis a weakened Ba'athist regime, even with Saddam in charge, was thought preferable to the creation of a pro-Iranian Islamic Republic of Iraq (Halliday 1996).

But the divergence in views between Saudi Arabia and Iran concerning US involvement in the region was even more pronounced. Following the Iran-Iraq War, Washington's strategy was predicated on fortifying Saudi Arabia as a counterweight against both Iran and Iraq (M. M. Milani 1994, 336). Throughout the 1990s the role of the United States was both a source and a symptom of Saudi-Iranian rivalry. Tehran continued to insist that the security problems of the Gulf should be solved without external involvement, and in particular without the involvement of the United States. This position clashed with those of Saudi Arabia (and Kuwait), whose security policies rested on a US guarantee (Halliday 1996; Amirahmadi 1994, 123).

Beginning in May 1993, the United States had followed a policy of "dual containment" in the Gulf (Lenczowski 1994, 52; A. Lake 1994, 1). In fact, by 1996 the United States had all but declared war against Iran, imposing comprehensive trade sanctions and launching a covert action program. These efforts were matched by aggressive Iranian efforts to derail the Arab-Israeli peace process and to undermine the US position in the Gulf. The hostility between the United States and Iran intersected with disturbances in the Gulf region, notably the uprisings that took place in Bahrain (1994–96), which occurred primarily in Shi'a villages and towns. To help quell the unrest, Saudi officials deployed security forces and advisers. However, they stopped short of publicly endorsing the Bahraini leadership's allegation that Iran had instigated the uprisings (Alsultan and Saied 2017, chap. 5).

With the Khobar Towers bombing on June 25, 1996, the Iranian security threat manifested within Saudi Arabia itself. Unconvinced that the United States would respond militarily and uncertain whether, even if such action were taken, it would deter Tehran rather than invite retaliation, the Saudis withheld information definitively linking the Iranians to the attack (Clarke 2004, 117; Pollack 2004, 280–86; Riedel 2015). The Saudi decision to keep Washington in the dark was, therefore, a precautionary measure—and clearly not a sign of abiding trust in Iran. Meanwhile, Iran, for its part, took its own precautions to avoid provoking a confrontation with Saudi Arabia. Those few attacks bearing Iranian fingerprints that were conducted on Saudi soil targeted American personnel and facilities, and not Saudi Arabia per se. Furthermore, Iran appears to have reined in Hezbollah al-Hijaz, as between 1989 and 1996, no attacks were attributed to the group (Matthiesen 2010, 197). Saudi attention shifted focus to domestic terrorist threats sponsored by radical Sunni groups, which between 2003 and 2006 were responsible for dozens of attacks in the kingdom. They included the coordinated truck bomb attacks that took place near Western housing facilities in Riyadh on May 12, 2003, and that were reportedly staged by members of Al Qaeda living in Iran, allegedly with Iranian complicity (S. G. Jones 2012; Bergen 2013). Thus, a favorable admixture of domestic and international shocks—developments that occurred in rapid succession (i.e., a cluster) between 1988 and 1991—led to a period of Saudi-Iran détente, albeit brief and unstable.

THE 2003 IRAQ WAR: SHOCK AND RIVALRY ESCALATION

The fall of the Ba'athist regime in Iraq in 2003 administered yet another shock—one that ultimately elevated the intensity of the Saudi-Iran rivalry and widened its geographic scope. The US-led invasion, by shattering the Iraqi state, unleashed Kurdish nationalism and paved the way for Shiʻa ascendancy, in turn provoking Sunni resistance and the onset of sectarian conflict. The destruction of Saddam's regime had the salutary effect of shielding the GCC countries against the possibility of another Iraqi invasion. At the same time, however, the war transformed Iraq from a counterweight to Iran to the latter's weaker ally—a dramatic shift in the Gulf balance of power.

The growth of Iranian activism and influence in post-Saddam Iraq raised concerns among Sunni leaders in the Gulf and beyond. King Abdullah of Jordan anxiously warned about the emergence of an ideological "Shiʻite crescent" from Beirut to the Persian Gulf—shorthand for the expansion of Iran's regional role and power. Though dismissed by some at the time as "alarmist," "mythical," or "self-serving" and by others as "a common anti-Iranian trope," the specter of a Shiʻa "rise" nonetheless resonated, especially with some Arab leaders. At a September 2005 Council on Foreign Relations (CFR) meeting in New York, Saudi foreign minister Saud al-Faisal expressed his deep frustration: "We [Saudi Arabia and the United States] fought a war together to keep Iran from occupying Iraq after Iraq was driven out of Kuwait. Now we are handing the whole country over to Iran without reason" (CFR 2005). Compounding Saudi misgivings about Iran's growing influence in Iraq were their apprehensions about its clandestine nuclear activities.[3] A nuclear-armed Iran would, at minimum, provide Iran with decisive leverage and possibly unleash aggressive tendencies in its regional foreign policy.

Here it is important to note that the fall of Saddam coincided with the end of the "moderate" era in Iranian foreign policy and its replacement by a conservative-populist alliance.[4] The Iranian reformists were soon supplanted by a conservative-populist alliance in the election in 2005 of President Mahmoud Ahmadinejad, an individual whose temperament and politics were reminiscent of the radical phase of the revolution. Saudi-Iranian relations did not turn instantly and unremittingly hostile. The Saudis offered their congratulations to Ahmadinejad upon his accession to the presidency and received assurances from Iran's Supreme Leader Ali Khamenei that the rapprochement process would continue to move forward.

Nevertheless, an important outcome of the 2005 Iranian election was the realignment of the institutions of the state, and more specifically, the militarization of politics. The latter was marked by the ascendance of the Islamic Revolutionary Guard Corps (IRGC) (Kamrava 2010, 403–4) and a corresponding increase in the IRGC Quds Force's support for non-state armed groups (NSAGs) in Iraq and elsewhere in the region (Gresh 2006; Knights 2010; Smith 2007; Filkins 2013).

The 2006 war between Hezbollah and Israel confirmed Iran's position as a major actor in the Arab-Israeli conflict and overall growing strategic influence in the region. From Riyadh's vantage point, the war, in conjunction with ongoing Sunni-Shi'ite violence in Iraq, "represented an almost seismic shift in the regional balance of power in Iran's favor" (Wehrey et al. 2009, 81). During the war the Saudi objective was to sideline Iran in Lebanon in order to break or at least weaken Tehran's alliance with Damascus, enabling Riyadh to advance its peace plan and thereby gain leverage in relations with Washington. Meanwhile, Iran did its best to exploit fissures in Saudi-Qatar relations, using Qatar to block or circumvent Riyadh on issues pertaining to Syria and Lebanon (Keynoush 2016, 209–15).

The Lebanon War reverberated in Saudi Arabia itself. Hezbollah's performance during the war inspired an emerging radical faction within the Shi'a community. In addition, it spurred a counterreaction by popular Salafi clerics and their supporters, who, calling into question the national loyalty of Saudi Shi'a, unleashed a campaign of anti-Shi'a, anti-Iranian statements and Internet postings calling for sectarian repression (Wehrey 2014, 115, 127).

The Lebanon War also spurred Saudi Arabia to be more proactive in regional affairs so as to counterbalance Iran. In November 2006 King Abdullah visited Turkey (the first visit by a Saudi monarch in forty years) in an effort to coordinate a policy of containment against Iran. In February 2007 he attempted to construct a unity government between rival factions Hamas and Fatah, and at the Arab Summit that same year, he reintroduced the peace plan that Saudi Arabia had initiated five years earlier.

In addition, the Lebanon War supplied additional motivation for Saudi Arabia to strengthen its conventional military capabilities—a buildup undertaken largely in response to Iran's deepening involvement in Iraq and the dispute over the Iranian nuclear program. In fact, since the mid-2000s Saudi Arabia and the other GCC states have spent lavishly on defense, investing in newer, more sophisticated technology and weaponry (Cordesman 2015; IHS Markit 2015). Between 2006 and 2015 Saudi military spending doubled, reaching an estimated $87.2 billion in 2015 (Perlo-Freeman et al. 2016, 5). During the Ahmadinejad years Iran's military expenditures also increased (Ehteshami 2013). However, since 2007 Saudi Arabia has spent four to five times as much as Iran (Cordesman 2015). Furthermore, the conventional military gap between Saudi Arabia and Iran is not just a matter of spending but of access to advanced American and European arms, US intelligence, and battle management technology.

Iran, therefore, has had to contend with a conventional military imbalance increasingly in favor of Saudi Arabia and the other Gulf Arab states, when combined with US military assets in the region and over the horizon. Decades of sanctions have prevented Tehran from effectively upgrading its arms and military equipment and have made it difficult to obtain spare parts. Thus, Iran has come to greatly rely on asymmetric maritime capabilities and irregular warfare. With respect to the latter, Iran acquired valuable experience in Iraq, where the Quds Force supplied arms and instruction to numerous insurgent factions (Sahimi 2011). Especially given Iran's conventional military limitations, the survival and stability of its network of allies and proxies remains a priority—enabling Tehran to project power and to prosecute its rivalry with Saudi Arabia well beyond its own borders.

To be sure, over the past decade Saudi Arabia and Iran have, at times, sought to temper their rivalry. Despite their sharp differences they held consultations behind the scenes in an apparent effort to mediate the conflict between Hezbollah and other parties in Lebanon, as they did in 2007 in an attempt to improve security in Baghdad (Keynoush 2016, 170–75). However, neither effort bore fruit. A March 2007 meeting between Iranian president Mahmoud Ahmadinejad and the late King Abdullah intended to explore the potential for a positive turn in relations likewise yielded no tangible results. In fact, King Abdullah reportedly declared during the meeting that Iran "should stop interfering in Arab affairs and should not underestimate the US military threat" (Koch 2007). In essence, there was not unremitting, continuous high-intensity hostility between the two countries. There were some attempts to defuse tension; these efforts, however, proved futile. The Saudis and Emiratis in particular seemed—or became—convinced of Iran's perfidy. Whether it was Iran's nuclear program or posturing that hardened their views is debatable, since it was less of a concern than Iran's regional activities. Saudi Arabia saw the nuclear issue as Washington's top priority and tried to capitalize on that to press the United States to opt for military action that would undercut Iran's ability to persist in mischief making throughout the region.

Regarding the nuclear issue, Iran reached out to Riyadh and the other Gulf states ostensibly in order to assuage their concerns (Keynoush 2016, 165). However, such reassurances fell on deaf ears. According to a US diplomatic cable released by Wikileaks and reported by *The Guardian*, Saudi as well as UAE and Egyptian leaders referred to Iran as "evil" and as an "existential threat." The cable also revealed that King Abdullah "frequently exhorted the US to attack Iran to put an end to its nuclear weapons programme." The same cable reads, "The King, Foreign Minister, Prince Muqrin, and Prince Nayif all agreed that the Kingdom needs to cooperate with the US on resisting and rolling back Iranian influence and subversion in Iraq" (*Guardian* 2008; Black and Tisdall 2010). In a March 15, 2009, meeting with US officials, King Abdullah referred to the conversation he had had with visiting Iranian foreign minister Manouchehr Mottaki earlier that day as a "heated exchange" and concluded by saying, "We have had correct relations over the years, but the bottom line is that they cannot be trusted" (*Guardian* 2009).

SHOCK ABSORPTION AND DIFFUSION: THE ARAB SPRING AND THE GLOBALIZATION OF SAUDI-IRAN RIVALRY

The 2011 Arab Spring uprisings administered a shock leading to generalized disorder across the Middle East that included partial or complete state failure in six Arab countries, intensified regional competition and proxy warfare, and the creation of ungoverned space that enabled the resurgence of Al Qaeda and the formation and spread of the so-called Islamic State of Iraq and the Levant (ISIL). The Arab Spring revolts and their cascading effects also caused the escalatory dynamics of the Saudi-Iran rivalry to persist, with both sides marshaling an array of tools and deploying them regionally as well as globally. The popular uprisings that swept across the Arab world in 2011 engendered in Riyadh a fear of a region-wide contagion—of the possible destabilization of the Gulf monarchies and of an imminent Iranian strategic victory (Ibrahim 2013). The protest movement that emerged mainly in Saudi Arabia's Eastern Province accentuated these concerns (Matthiesen 2012, 628–37). At the same time, though, Riyadh saw the Arab Spring uprisings as an opportunity to pursue regime change in Damascus, where the government of Bashar al-Assad was closely aligned with Tehran, and to seek to rally the smaller Gulf Arab states to its side in an effort to counter Iranian influence regionally. Thus, Saudi Arabia viewed the Arab Spring with a mixture of dread and opportunism. Meanwhile, Iran, which initially had greeted the uprisings with optimism, grew increasingly concerned about and determined to defend its strategic position in the Levant.

In terms of the discourse, Riyadh and Tehran have been engaged in an ongoing war of words. Senior officials have repeatedly traded accusations, as in the dueling op-eds penned by Iranian foreign minister Mohammad Javad Zarif and his Saudi counterpart Adel Al-Jubeir, which appeared nine days apart in January 2016 in the *New York Times* (Zarif 2016; Al-Jubeir 2016). They have spared no effort to paint each other as "overtly hostile" (Mousavian 2016), "clear enemies" (Karami 2016), perpetrators of "nefarious activities" (McDowall 2016a), and the like;[5] and they have issued vague threats and disparaging personal attacks (Hashem 2015; Cullinane 2015). Yet at the same time, there have been attempts to turn down the heat, as in Foreign Minister Zarif's comments at the February 2016 Munich Security Conference: "We need to work together. We have enough challenges in order to move forward. And we are prepared to work with Saudi Arabia" (*Globalist* 2016).

Still, the intensification of Saudi-Iranian rivalry goes well beyond a war of words, encompassing regional and international diplomacy, soft power inducements and economic pressure, proxy warfare, and the instrumental use of sectarianism, along with a continuing military buildup. Since King Salman's accession to power in 2015, Saudi Arabia has gone on the diplomatic offensive in an effort to contain and counter Iran. Saudi tactics include reported overtures to Israel (Graham 2015), successful efforts within the GCC and Arab League to formally designate Hezbollah a terrorist organization (Al-Arabiya 2016a) and strong lobbying of Europeans to do the same (Riedel 2016), creation of the Islamic Coalition against Terror but without inviting Iran to join, the extension of "soft power" competition to Africa (e.g., aid to Djibouti, Sudan, and Somalia) (McDowall 2016b), and efforts to pull Turkey and Egypt into an anti-Iran Sunni bloc (Tastekin 2015).

Saudi Arabia has also used economic inducements and pressure. Pressure has come in the form of attempts to block Iranian investment and disrupt commercial links with the Gulf Arab states. As a result of these efforts, Iranian nationals have had difficulty renewing business licenses and obtaining residency in Dubai. And Iranian ships carrying crude oil have been prohibited from entering Saudi and Bahraini waters (Nasseri and Carey

2016). Another form of pressure is reducing or suspending financial support to those governments that have failed to join ranks against Iran, as in the reduction of security assistance to Lebanon in response to the latter's refusal to condemn Iran after attacks on Saudi diplomatic missions (Reuters 2016). Yet another form of pressure has been Saudi Arabia's unrelenting effort to drive down and sustain low oil prices.

Saudi Arabia and Iran have latched on to natural allies in their struggle for influence and primacy in Lebanon. While Iran has supported the March 8 Alliance—which includes Hezbollah, Amal, and Michel Aoun's Free Patriotic Movement—Saudi Arabia has found a partner in the rival pro–Saad Hariri coalition, the March 14 Alliance (Wehrey et al. 2009, 79).[6] In Syria and Iraq, in conjunction with seeking and supporting natural allies and proxies, Saudi Arabia and Iran have instrumentalized sectarianism (Karagiannis 2016; Hanna and Kaye 2015). Tehran has mobilized Shi'a communities throughout the region for the protection of the Assad regime—recruiting a significant number of Afghan and Pakistani Shi'a to fight in Syria (Dehghanpisheh 2015; Heistein and West 2015). However, it is in Yemen where the Saudi-Iran rivalry is arguably the most pronounced and its consequences most lethal. The takeover of Sanaa by an alliance of Zaydi Shi'ite Houthi rebels and former president Ali Abdullah Saleh in September 2014, followed by increased though limited support by Tehran for the insurgents (Juneau 2016), coincided with the succession of King Salman and his appointment of Prince Mohammed bin Salman as defense minister—two figures seemingly determined to confront Iran rather than to experiment with détente. To bolster Saudi efforts, King Salman extracted a pledge from the United States to expedite the delivery of weapons and equipment and a free hand to use them in Yemen (Fahim and Cunning-Bruce 2016).

Three recent events perhaps best illustrate, and have undoubtedly reinforced, the unusually high degree of tension in the bilateral relationship that has led some observers to worry that Saudi Arabia and Iran are "now standing closer to open war than ever before" (Rich 2012). The first was the human stampede in Mina on September 24, 2015—the deadliest disaster in the history of the Hajj, in which hundreds of lives were lost, including more than 464 Iranian pilgrims (Gladstone 2015).

In response to the tragedy at Mina, Ayatollah Khamenei and other senior Iranian officials threatened "harsh and tough" retaliation, decried Saudi mismanagement of Hajj affairs, called on Muslim nations to challenge Saudi custodianship of the holy places, and harshly criticized Saudi policies in Yemen (Al-Hatlani 2015). Following months of negotiations over visa issuance and security measures, in May 2016 Iran suspended participation in the Hajj (Schemm 2016). Since then the Hajj has remained a highly contentious issue, as on the eve of the 2016 pilgrimage season when thousands took to the streets in Tehran to protest against Saudi Arabia (Radio Free Europe / Radio Liberty 2016) while Iranian supreme leader Khamenei appeared to raise the stakes, rather than seek to defuse the tension, by accusing Saudi officials of "murdering" pilgrims (Associated Press 2016).

The second event was Saudi Arabia's execution of the dissident Shi'a cleric Nimr al-Nimr on January 2, 2016, which was followed by a flurry of escalatory actions, including attacks on Saudi diplomatic missions in Tehran and Mashhad (Hubbard 2016b), an alleged Saudi airstrike on the Iranian embassy in Yemen (Al Omran and Fitch 2016), the severing of diplomatic relations (Hubbard 2016a), and public promises of retaliation by senior officials from both countries.

The third event was Prince Turki al-Faisal's participation and remarks in the July 2016 annual rally in Paris of the exiled Iranian opposition group Mojahedin-e Khalq (MeK) (Asharq Al-Awsat 2016). The message that Prince Turki al-Faisal delivered at the Paris rally was rather surprising given that in his capacity as the Kingdom's ambassador to the United States a decade ago, he—unlike other senior Saudi figures—had reportedly advised US national security officials to engage in direct talks with Iran (De Borchgrave 2016).[7] Prince Turki applauded MeK for seeking to rid Iran of the "Khomeinist cancer" (Black 2016). These public remarks occurred at the very time when clashes had resumed— the first in almost two decades—between the Democratic Party of Iranian Kurdistan (PDKI) *peshmerga* and IRGC forces (Erdbrink 2016; Salih 2016), triggering Iranian allegations of Saudi incitement (Dehghanpisheh 2016).

Saudi Arabia's predisposition to interpret, or at least to portray, Iran as being behind every adverse development has included the attribution of at least partial responsibility for the Arab Spring uprisings in 2011 (especially in Bahrain) and the strife elsewhere in the region (e.g., in Yemen) to Iranian machinations. The Saudis' apparently unshakable assumption that Iran is determined to and capable of destabilizing the region (Alhasan 2011) has combined with their uncertainty about the resoluteness of US commitments and the efficacy of American Middle East policies. Unlike for the Saudis, for Tehran— whose regional security policy "is largely determined by the role and position of the United States in what Iran considers to be its rightful sphere of influence" (Kamrava 2009)—the prospect of US retrenchment represents a potential strategic opportunity.

The launching of a massive air campaign in Yemen in March 2015 revealed the extent of Saudi apprehension regarding the perceived expansion of Iran's regional influence. The Saudi-led intervention was followed four months later by the Joint Comprehensive Plan of Action (JCPOA), which, though forestalling the risk of catastrophic conflict, did not ameliorate the Saudi-Iran rivalry. On the contrary, the nuclear deal extenuated it. The JCPOA had the unintended consequence of stoking Saudi Arabia's fear of abandonment by its main patron, intensifying its concerns about Tehran's regional objectives and reinforcing its determination to assume greater responsibility for its own security. Whereas the JCPOA freed Iran to seek to consolidate its regional strategic gains, it reinforced Saudi Arabia's determination to reverse them.

PROSPECTS FOR SAUDI-IRAN RIVALRY DE-ESCALATION OR TERMINATION

Rivalries are neither predetermined nor irreversible. This raises the question of what circumstances might result in the termination of a rivalry or its de-escalation (Bennett 1997b, 1998; Goertz and Diehl 1995b). One pathway to such an outcome becomes available when either or both disputants lose their competitive status (Rasler, Thompson, and Ganguly 2013, 6–7). The main alternative pathway results from the downscaling of enemy threat perception (Rasler, Thompson, and Ganguly 2013, 9). However, there is no guarantee that either negotiations or shifts in domestic priorities, leadership, or regime will lead to rivalry termination (Cox 2010; Rasler, Thompson, and Ganguly 2013, 10–11).

The path that the Saudi-Iranian rivalry will follow in the coming months and years is hugely consequential both for the two countries and for the surrounding region. The future of the Middle East is currently being forged in Syria and Iraq. When and how the conflicts in those countries are settled depends to a significant degree on the rivalry dynamics between Iran and Saudi Arabia. The history of that rivalry has shown that détente, albeit limited in scope and transitory, is indeed possible. Indeed, as discussed previously, Saudi Arabia and Iran have in the past demonstrated an ability to manage their threat perceptions and to find ways to temper their rivalry.

In addition, disunity and diversity within the GCC have, at times, acted as a brake on the deterioration of Saudi-Iranian relations. There have also been occasions when Riyadh and Tehran have set aside or compartmentalized sharp differences over one issue in the interest of holding open the possibility of cooperation on others (Bahgat 2000, 111–12). And even in the overheated climate of the past couple of years, senior officials have not ruled out the possibility of a de-escalation of tension, as when Saudi foreign minister Adel Al-Jubeir declared, "Iran has been a neighbor for millennia, and will continue to be a neighbor for millennia. We have no issue with seeking to develop the best terms we can with Iran." Yet Al-Jubeir then went on to list all of the many Iranian actions deemed "destabilizing" and concluded by saying, "It's really up to them to change their behavior" (Shafy and Zand 2016). A similar hopeful, though fleeting, positive gesture was the reaction to the July 4, 2016, terrorist attacks in Riyadh by Al-Jubeir's counterpart, Mohammad Javad Zarif, who tweeted his commiserations: "There are no more red lines left for terrorists to cross. Both Sunnis and Shias will both remain victims unless we stand united as one" (Ensor 2016).

Nevertheless, the prospects for accommodation seem quite low. The two sides are far from exhausted. Their extensive domestic and regional commitments combined with the depressed price of oil have strained but not severely depleted their financial resources. They remain captives of deep-seated mistrust of one another and of zero-sum thinking. And they remain fundamentally dissatisfied with the status quo, though they define it differently: Saudi Arabia is bent on reversing the gains that Iran has made in Iraq and the Levant, which Tehran is determined to preserve; Iran is unwavering in its opposition to continued US involvement in the Gulf, on which Riyadh still depends for its security.

Indeed, as 2017 drew to a close, the animosity between the two countries appeared to reach new heights. With military offensives having swept ISIL from the territory it had seized, Iran emerged in the ascendancy both in Syria and in Iraq. In responding to these unwelcome developments, Saudi Crown Prince Mohammed bin Salman appeared determined not to rely exclusively on surrogates and financial largesse but to challenge Iran more directly. This newly aggressive Saudi approach included mounting a campaign to isolate Qatar, partly over differences regarding policy toward Iran; intervening in Lebanese domestic politics in an effort to contain Hezbollah's influence, and by extension that of its patron, Iran; and taking steps to rebuild ties with Baghdad and thus regain leverage against Iran (Abdoh 2017; E. Solomon 2017; Perry and Bassam 2017; Chulov 2017).

Two ballistic missile attacks launched from Yemen in December but intercepted before striking the Saudi capital ignited a fierce war of words between Riyadh and Tehran (Hubbard and Cumming-Bruce 2017).

The fact that Saudi Arabia can claim few successes from their recent efforts to increase the pressure on Iran has not had a restraining or moderating effect on its behavior. On the contrary, the Saudi-led coalition continued to conduct intensive airstrikes in Yemen against the Houthis (Middle East Monitor 2018). Meanwhile, Iranian officials, facing protests rooted in economic grievances that quickly spread to various cities, attributed the unrest to "foreign agents" and closed ranks (Borzorgmehr 2018). On the regional front Iranian proxies have continued their advance into rebel-held enclaves in Syria and their efforts to establish a permanent military presence in the country.

Since early 2016 there have been numerous attempts by third parties to reduce tension (Al Bawaba News 2016). Following the GCC Summit in Bahrain in December 2016, the Emir of Kuwait hand-carried a letter to Iran on the necessity of improving relations (Hashem 2017). However, the Emir's outreach and subsequent efforts by GCC officials to thaw the ice came to naught (Mamouri 2017). Meanwhile, US withdrawal from the JCPOA and reinstatement of sanctions against Iran, the Trump administration's having "officially placed Iran on notice" in reaction to an Iranian missile test, the pledge to rebuild traditional alliances, and anti-Iranian statements and measures (Torbati 2017; *Economist* 2017) have, if anything, bolstered Saudi expectations of renewed and vigorous US efforts to contain Iran (Nareim 2017; Middle East Media Research Institute 2017).

President Donald Trump's confrontational approach toward Iran and strong support for Saudi Arabia has, if anything, further fueled the Saudi-Iran rivalry (White House 2017). Only two weeks after the president's visit in May 2017, Saudi Arabia launched the blockade of Qatar that distracted and divided the GCC. The Saudi move in Lebanon came just a few days after a visit by Trump's son-in-law and close adviser, Jared Kushner, to the kingdom. While having emboldened Riyadh, US hostility to Iran has provided the latter's powerful hard-liners with an opportunity to weaken domestic rivals.

There was a slim reed of hope that the series of discussions that produced the Saudi decision to permit Iranian pilgrims to participate in the 2016 Hajj might lead to further de-escalatory steps (Hubbard 2017). Yet the accumulated mistrust and negative momentum of the past several years have been difficult to counteract. After all, with Saudi Arabia and Iran having spawned and supported groups that they can no longer necessarily fully control and with the region itself polarized, the two rivals appear locked in a contest neither can win outright: each of them too strong to be defeated by the other, and both of them too vulnerable, too deeply invested, and perhaps too ambitious to back away from their respective hardened positions.

If there is a silver lining to this otherwise bleak situation, it lies with three constraining factors. The first is that both sides appear to have long recognized the prohibitive costs of a direct military confrontation and, even at the peak periods of their rivalry, have succeeded in avoiding it. The second is that their capabilities are not boundless. Iran has spread itself thin cultivating and protecting its various allies and proxies, while the depth and durability of the anti-Iran Sunni solidarity forged by Riyadh likely has a limited shelf life. And the third is the fact that neither Saudi Arabia nor Iran can hope to achieve the strategic objective of maximizing its regional influence while at the same time containing domestic security risks by being, or being perceived as, a sectarian actor.

CONCLUSIONS

Although Saudi Arabia and Iran are not contiguous states, their relations nonetheless have been marred by maritime and territorial disputes. Yet it is argued here that their long-standing feud is predominantly a "positional" rivalry—a contest for regional influence whereby each side is attempting to maximize its ability to impose its agenda by means of issuing threats and through indirect confrontation.

The Saudi-Iran relationship has experienced major shocks at three points in its contemporary history. The 1979 revolution, which culminated in the establishment of the Islamic Republic of Iran, was the definitive shock that triggered the onset of an enduring strategic rivalry between the two sides. With both the Saudi and Iranian leaderships contending that their societies and polities are based on true Islamic normative values and that their regimes govern in accordance with them, a certain level of hostility and tension has become embedded in their respective state's identity and nation's domestic politics (McLaughlin Mitchell and Prins 2004; Hensel 1999, 83). As a result, the Saudi-Iranian rivalry has become exceedingly difficult to dislodge.

Having persisted for nearly four decades, the Saudi-Iranian rivalry has been marked by waxing and waning periods of hostility, reflecting the rivals' respective preferences (Mansour 2008, 957–58). Twice since 1979 the Saudi-Iran rivalry has been subjected to multiple shocks, or shock clusters, delivered within a highly compressed time frame, which have conditioned those preferences. In both instances the trajectory of the Saudi-Iran rivalry has intersected with, and has been influenced by, key developments, notably involving Iraq, within the wider regional rivalry field. Whereas Iraq's defeat in the 1991 Gulf War had a dampening effect on the rivalry, the 2003 US-led invasion and occupation inflamed it.

During its lifespan the Saudi-Iran rivalry has not simply absorbed shocks but has also redirected and diffused them. The geographic ambit of the Saudi-Iran rivalry has expanded over the past decade and especially since the Arab Spring uprisings. So too has the repertoire of tools that Riyadh and Tehran have used to prosecute their rivalry, such that today the Saudi-Iranian rivalry consists of two armed camps, with each side lining up allies, fueling sectarianism, and exploiting the region's weak states in a series of proxy wars that stretch from Iraq to Lebanon. In this sense the Saudi-Iran rivalry has reverberated widely across the region.

Furthermore, the record shows the Saudi-Iran rivalry to be quite resilient, possessing not just the capacity to absorb and diffuse shocks but also the capacity for renewal. With the progressive expansion of the Saudi-Iran battlespace and the intensification of their rivalry since 2015, the involvement and impact of external actors in the region, specifically the United States, cannot be overestimated. Saudi Arabia has demonstrated a distinct, consistent preference for an external, non-regional balancer or security guarantor.

That role continues to be borne, however reluctantly and seemingly equivocally, by the United States. Iran remains steadfastly opposed to an American military presence in the region (M. M. Milani 1994, 331). Thus, the United States, which can be said to have played a major role in containing the Saudi-Iranian rivalry, has also unwittingly contributed to sustaining it.

As of the close of 2018, the Saudi-Iranian proxy struggles in Syria and Yemen appear to have dealt severe blows to Riyadh's efforts to roll back Iranian influence while preserving, if not fortifying, Tehran's regional position. Yet this combination of apparent strategic setbacks for Saudi Arabia and strategic gains for Iran has not markedly improved the prospects for rivalry de-escalation or termination. On the contrary, it has fostered a rapprochement between Saudi Arabia and Israel that is likely to be further strengthened in the wake of the US decision to withdraw its forces from Syria and in the context of the escalation of American pressure on Iran following Washington's withdrawal from the JCPOA and reinstatement of economic sanctions. This third-party intrusion runs the risk, if anything, of sustaining the rivalry rather than tempering or ending it.

Both Israel and the United States joined the rest of the world in condemning the murder of journalist Jamal Khashoggi, but neither is prepared to sever its strategic partnership with Riyadh over the killing. For Iran, this strategic axis represents nothing less than an existential threat to the survival of the regime that requires and indeed justifies its continuing efforts to consolidate its influence in the Levant and maintain it in the Arabian Peninsula—at Saudi Arabia's expense.

NOTES

Epigraph: Koelbl, Shafy, and Zand (2016).

1. Note that the rule of thumb Goertz and Diehl have used, namely, that an "enduring" rivalry requires a minimum of six or more militarized disputes between the same two states for a period lasting at least twenty years, has been subject to debate.

2. Contra Vasquez (1996), who argues that power parity is necessary to sustain rivalry over the long term, Paul (2005, 2006) contends that the ostensibly weaker party can, and often does, find ways to bolster its position (e.g., through strategy, tactics, and alliances); therefore, a rivalrous relationship can be both asymmetric and enduring.

3. In 2002 US intelligence confirmed the existence and activities at two clandestine facilities alleged to be producing fissile nuclear material.

4. The student protests in July 1999 in Iran, which had spiraled into widespread public unrest, had been followed by a crackdown on reformists and reform policy.

5. IRGC commander Brig. Gen. Mohammad Ali Jafari used the description "clear enemies" in a July 2016 speech. Saudi foreign minister Adel Al-Jubeir referenced Iran's "nefarious activities" in an interview with Reuters, January 16, 2016.

6. Wehrey et al. (2009) call into question the notion that the face-off between these two alliances is essentially a surrogate confrontation between Iran and Saudi Arabia. Drawing on their research, they suggest that external involvement is often used as a convenient pretext by local factions to avoid any compromise.

7. Prince Bandar, the Kingdom's national security chief; King Abdullah; Defense Minister Sultan; and Interior Minister Naif bin Abd al-Aziz had become convinced that nothing short of military action would prevent Iran from becoming a nuclear power.

5

Rethinking Rivalry Fluctuation

Iranian Rivalry Behavior and the Domestic Level of Analysis

Thomas Keith Wilson

The objective of this chapter is to explore conflict and cooperation dynamics in Iran's strategic rivalry with Saudi Arabia. The Iranian-Saudi dyad has been one of the most consequential relationships in the region since the founding of the Islamic Republic in 1979 (Thompson 2001, 521). Events following Iran's revolution triggered a titanic shift in relations between the two, with Iran asserting itself as a leading defender of Islamic interests, calling for uprisings across the Muslim world and directly criticizing Saudi Arabia for its failure to stand against abuses of power.[1] Informed by long-standing cultural and religious differences, the desired prizes in this contest include regional geopolitical and religious primacy.[2] While these ends have been regularly contested, the life of this strategic rivalry has included extended periods of harmony, extended periods of hostility, and even some points at which the two behaviors operated simultaneously.

This chapter will examine some of the most intense points of conflict and cooperation in the rivalry from 1979 to 2015, with specific attention to Iranian behavior. Over the period of this study, certain event types tend to routinely precede notable increases in conflict or cooperation in the rivalry. Changes to America's role in the region, international pressure surrounding Iran's nuclear program, the annual Hajj pilgrimage to Mecca, changes to the status of militarized conflict in the region, and internal elections are the most prominent of these event types. While a full survey of the rivalry relationship across its thirty-six years and all its many dispute areas is beyond the scope of this chapter, I select several event types to illustrate the fluctuation present in Iran's relationship with Saudi Arabia. In particular, pressure from third-party actors and feuding over the treatment of Iranian-backed Hajj pilgrims were dominant sources of hostility over the first ten years of the rivalry. Yet from roughly 1991 to 2010, these patterns were less consistent and at times even reversed. US-driven pressures were met with an Iranian state intent on cooperating with Saudi Arabia, and Hajj disputes were minimized. The period also includes points of intense cooperation that appear to lack a decisive external trigger.

What explains the different responses Iran provides following what appear to be similar types of triggers? Does domestic politics have any role in accounting for this variance?

These are the questions this chapter seeks to answer. The next section will examine the grounds for a domestic approach to decision-making as it pertains to strategic rivalry and Iran. I follow by offering a political institutional framework in which rivalry outcomes are the product of environmental triggers, but only following internal bargaining processes between actors within distinct governing structures. Emphasis on one state of an interactive rivalry limits the claims I can make about the dyad overall but offers tremendous opportunity to probe domestic mechanisms and the plausibility of this approach. The subsequent section applies this framework to Iran's strategic rivalry with Saudi Arabia from 1979 to 2015. Using a political institutional model proposed here, I will illustrate that the presence of third-party pressure and religious pilgrimage produced different relational outcomes over time owing in significant part to shifts in "who" was in power and what influence they maintained.

DOMESTIC POLITICS AND IRANIAN
FOREIGN POLICY AFTER 1979

Previous work on rivalry fluctuation called for attention to political systems in which competing elite factions are present in order to test the influence of two-level games. In this context internal and external considerations interact to produce behavior (Ganguly and Thompson 2011a, 10–12). It is argued that a system in which greater domestic contestation is present would be ideal to exploring whether and perhaps even to what extent domestic conditions matter in understanding conflict and cooperation between rivals. Iran serves as just this environment and is therefore a "most likely" case for exploring the role of internal politics. First, the Islamic Republic has gone to great lengths since its revolution in 1979 to erect protections against external influences and has at times appeared impervious to outside pressures.[3] Examples include Iran's revolutionary economy (featuring the pursuit of food, petrol, and steel production independence), internal military research and development capability, and a state-run intranet (Salami and Naeini 2014; Radio Free Europe 2017; Hormozgan Steel Company 2012; Vasilogambros 2016; Faramarzi et al. 2010, 1417; Takeyh and Maloney 2011, 1297–1312). In the face of international pressure regarding, for example, its nuclear program and human rights, Iran has often chosen to resist more vehemently, even when doing so has presented clear and present disadvantages to its security and economic conditions. Iran may have succeeded in achieving some level of insulation, but this has been contingent on a precarious domestic balance of actors and preferences. Leaders must have agreed to or at least have had clear incentive not to oppose resistance policy even when disadvantages to doing so were present. Consensus under such circumstances might have been difficult to maintain; therefore, such an approach might well have made the regime susceptible to domestic pressures.

Second, domestic politics within Iran operate within the confines of a complex regime structure. Instead of a centrally controlled power structure, Iran is composed of loosely connected and competitive entities. Rather than resting with a single ruler, power is somewhat diffused (Hunter 2010, 20–22; Buchta 2000, 6–10; Rakel 2008). In this sense, the Islamic Republic defies traditional definitions of "state" in that its design somewhat inherently discourages unity of effort. Iran's complicated institutional arrangements and constitutional divisions of authority, instead, make it a fertile setting for domestic contestation.[4] The Iranian political system features tight controls over which actors compete for power yet simultaneously allows considerable space for contestation among elites provided individuals do not outwardly challenge the principle of *velayat-e faqih* (rule by a distinguished Islamic jurist) or directly challenge the sitting supreme leader. While the Iranian constitution emphasizes the oversight responsibilities of the supreme leader and assigns him tasks that place him squarely at the center of most foreign policy decisions, he is not alone. The Iranian president is popularly elected only following considerable vetting by institutions sponsored by the supreme leader. Though the president is overseen by the supreme leader, the relationship is still one of power sharing, as the former wields considerable influence in executing foreign policy matters. Further, the Iranian president has operated at times quite contrary to the stated desires of the supreme leader, highlighting the risks any ruler faces when employing power sharing. Third, the Islamic Revolutionary Guard Corps (IRGC) reports directly to the supreme leader, yet its constitutionally mandated tasks and heightened security concerns throughout the early postrevolution period have resulted in considerable operational autonomy. Liberties afforded the IRGC early allowed it to produce a sprawling domestic-national security network within Iran featuring loyalties and patronage relations at times quite independent of the supreme leader (Harris 2016, 97–118). The IRGC, like the president, exercises distinct capacity to execute foreign policy, sometimes at the behest of the supreme leader and sometimes not. These are merely some of the entities within Iran that have the capacity to execute, let alone influence, foreign policy.[5]

Contestation occurs across and within republican institutions and is driven by a range of competing ideologies among the Iranian political elite. Divisions largely exist over matters of social and economic issues as well as the extent to which Iran should partake in the Western-governed international system (Ramazani 2013, 114–23). The traditional Right includes current supreme leader Ali Khamenei and emphasizes Islamic-theocratic values and economic privatization. The new Right derives much of its support from certain elements of the IRGC and favors a strong centralized economy, emphasizes social justice dimensions of the revolution, is quite conservative on social and cultural matters, and also offers the most fervent support for the campaign to export revolutionary ideology (Maloney 2015, 320–23). The political center of the current elite features a mixture of both technocrats and pragmatists, includes President Hassan Rouhani, favors economic privatization, and is generally more liberal on social and cultural issues compared with the traditional Right. Finally, the Left features more socially liberal elements, generally favors a more globally engaging foreign policy, and includes Mohammad Reza Aref, former president Mohammad Khatami's first vice president and current reformist parliamentary leader (Buchta 2000, 121–30; Rakel 2008).

Elite infighting in accordance with these factional divisions has long been manifest across Iran's domestic political structure. For example, the supreme leader and president have often been at direct odds, particularly following the death of the Islamic Republic's first supreme leader, Ruhollah Khomeini, in 1989. Shortly after, President Ali Akbar Raf-sanjani attempted to engage in rapprochement with the United States only to be thwarted by Khamenei. Years later Rafsanjani extended a development contract to American oil and gas giant Conoco against the will of the supreme leader, suggesting the ability of Rafsanjani to either soften Khamenei's stance or operate in defiance of him (Maloney 2015, 215–18). Rafsanjani later sought to modify the constitution to allow for a third presidential term and was denied by the supreme leader. He responded by aggressively working to undermine Khamenei's preferred successor to the presidency in favor of Kha-tami.[6] Also, direct contestation between the president and supreme leader was evident late in the administration of Mahmoud Ahmadinejad. In fact, Khamenei openly dis-cussed the elimination of the presidency given his opposition to Ahmadinejad's streak of independence (Maloney 2015, 360–62).

At other times the Iranian security apparatus, often with the endorsement of the supreme leader, has been in direct competition with the president. This dynamic was no more evident than in relations between the IRGC and Khatami. The latter's election to the presidency in 1997 came as a surprise to the political Right in Iran, as the supreme leader had gone out of his way to pave the way for his close ally Ali Nateq-Nuri (Wells 1999, 27–39). IRGC commander Mohsen Reza'i asserted himself a supporter of Nateq-Nuri during the election process, actively rallying against Khatami. Upon being elected, Khatami demanded Reza'i's removal from office given the latter's betrayal of constitu-tionally mandated neutrality requirements for security officials. Given enormous pres-sure from the president, Khamenei succumbed and replaced Reza'i, clearly against his preferences. Backlash from the IRGC included assassinations of reformist leaders, lead-ing to an official inquiry by Khatami into the actions of the country's security services, some of which were constitutionally under his control. Findings from this process led to an admission of responsibility by the intelligence ministry, whose leadership reports to the supreme leader (Buchta 2000, 156–73).

Disputes between the Iranian president and the country's security services also extended to foreign policy. As Iran sought to repair its economy following war with Iraq, Rafsan-jani engaged Europe only to be undermined by IRGC-sponsored assassinations against former officers of the Shah in Europe (Hunter 2010, 83). Khatami's efforts at bridging dif-ferences with the United States appeared to progress following a period of Iranian coop-eration in support of American intervention in Afghanistan after the September 11, 2001, attacks; however, the IRGC is suspected to have offered refuge to Al Qaeda members leaving Afghanistan and engaging in large-scale shipments of weapons to Hezbollah at this time. Talk of potential rapprochement with the United States following sanctions on Iran due to its nuclear program resulted in further strife between the executive branch and security apparatus. In addition to the supreme leader's aversion to relations with the United States, the IRGC benefited financially from sanctions and therefore had further reason to actively oppose rapprochement. The departure of foreign investment due to sanctions resulted in an economy in which self-sufficiency was emphasized. This agenda opened enormous opportunity for the IRGC, as its mission and purpose following war with Iraq shifted to managing much of the national defense industry.[7]

The supreme leader has not always sided with the security apparatus, however. The decision to end war operations against Iraq is a point at which the supreme leader and the president joined forces in opposing the preferences of the IRGC. In 1989 Khamenei and Khomeini engaged in a painful cost-benefit analysis related to continuing Iran's efforts against Iraq, and each came away convinced that pathways to victory had largely been exhausted. The IRGC, alternatively, was unconvinced and pursued a redoubling of Iran's commitment to war. The decision to cease war operations was considered a betrayal by IRGC commanders and led to tensions between the supreme leader and security forces (Maloney 2015, 189–91). Divisions were also evidenced by contradictory foreign policy behavior during an effort by Iranian officials to strike a grand bargain with the United States in 2003. Khatami and Khamenei allegedly partnered to engage Washington, but IRGC-sponsored activities in Iraq and the Palestinian territories largely undermined this effort (Hunter 2010, 59–62).

Other developments since Iran's revolution further illustrate shifts of influence across the political system, including a decrease in clerics and a parallel increase in technocrats and security professionals in government (Arjomand 2009, 112–20; Maloney 2015, 199; Safshekan and Sabet 2010, 543–58). This realignment was neither designed by the supreme leader himself nor entirely beneficial to his ultimate interests, particularly given the degree to which the IRGC appears capable of independent action. At times the IRGC openly feuded with Khamenei's candidate-vetting institution, the Guardian Council, over individuals it preferred be allowed to run for office. While not a consistent division, the IRGC appeared to have assumed a level of autonomy potentially threatening to the supreme leader by Ahmadinejad's second term (Harris 2015, 417–47).

These accounts highlight the existence of multiple centers of influence in Iran and offer initial evidence that levels of centralization and power sharing have been far from consistent. Figure 5.1 further illustrates that levels of domestic contestation within Iran have shifted over the lifetime of the regime. I assume that modifications to institutional bargaining space depicted here are the result of change sanctioned by the supreme leader, who maintains the role of primary gatekeeper to levers of power in Iran. Higher levels account for periods of greater contestation, during which space exists for more divergence of opinion, variance in outcomes, and potential for deviation from entrenched, status quo behavior. Taken from the Varieties of Democracy project, "horizontal accountability" and "elite consultation" each account for different elements of what might reasonably be considered measurements of institutional bargaining space in which domestic contestation can occur (Coppedge et al. 2016).

Horizontal accountability tracks the extent of checks and balances across the system or the degree to which power is shared across institutions. A positive score reflects a greater amount of institutional space for different actors to operate without being pressured by the more powerful members of the regime. A negative score, conversely, represents a higher level of encroachment on the authority of institutions of government by these dominant actors. Varieties of Democracy data measure the Islamic Republic of Iran's horizontal accountability first in 1980, a year following revolution. The score it achieves in 1980 remains relatively stable until 1992, several years following the death

Figure 5.1. Institutional bargaining space in Iran

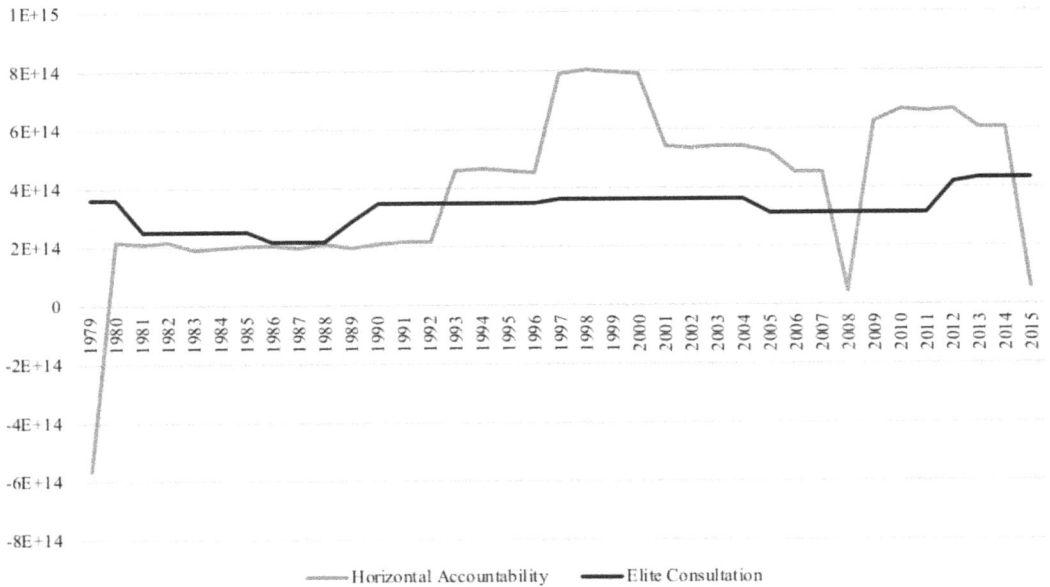

of Khomeini. It appears that more space is afforded to checks and balances within the Iranian system shortly after this point, coinciding with a surge in authority granted to Rafsanjani following the aversion of a succession-related crisis involving new supreme leader Khamenei.[8] Horizontal accountability increases in 1997, likely owing to the arrival of Khatami and his reform-minded administration. This Khatami boost lasts only four years, as levels gradually decrease from 2001 through 2007. Scores indicate a horizontal accountability crash in 2008 and a sudden return to levels experienced during the Khatami administration in 2009. These levels continue until 2014, at which point horizontal accountability in Iran again plummets.

A second measure for institutional bargaining space as offered by the Varieties of Democracy project is "elite consultation." This score is taken from an index evaluating the range of consultation at elite levels when important policy changes are being considered. I contend that high levels of consultation reflect greater openness and space for competition within an institutional structure, while low levels indicate the reverse to be true. Consultation between elites appears to gradually decrease from the 1979 revolution to 1986, and it remains at its lowest point until 1988—the end of Iran's war with Iraq. Levels rise again after this and achieve a score in 1990 that remains stable until 1997. A slight uptick in elite consultation occurs after this, coinciding with the election of Khatami. Consultation between elites appears to decrease in 2004 and then plateaus in 2005 with the arrival of the Ahmadinejad administration. Levels then rise again in 2012 and reach their peak in 2013 at the point Hassan Rouhani is elected president. Elite consultation appears then to shift in large part with the arrival of new presidents in Iran. Overall, each measure supports the notion that presidential change is related to shifts in institutional bargaining space. How then does this impact rivalry fluctuation?

POLITICAL INSTITUTIONAL FRAMEWORK

The previous section should make at least two things clear: individual actors in Iran have the capacity to influence outcomes, and the institutional space within which such actors operate changes over time. A political institutional approach incorporates both these elements, as it assumes that leaders are distinct in their capacity to influence outcomes and that decision-making processes involving such actors operate within defined institutional parameters.[9] In contrast to unitary rational state actor models, political institutionalism allows for the possibility that state decisions are sometimes the result of a complex intersection of small group dynamics, domestic political forces, and personal characteristics of individuals.[10] Outcomes under such conditions are therefore sometimes uncoordinated or accidental, the product of competing actors generating behavior simultaneously, or even the result of inertia rooted in standard operating procedures of organizations.[11] The framework employed here suggests contestation between elites or even autonomous behavior by actors with the capacity to influence foreign policy risks, complicating the ability of rivals to interpret signals coming from a rival state. Finally, power-sharing patterns may be associated with domestic circumstances, insomuch as foreign policy behavior may be the result of perceptions of internal threats (Svolik 2012, 2).

My study accounts for rivalry behavior by way of events, varying in the extent to which conflict or cooperation is promoted. The model I employ (fig. 5.2) assumes these events do not occur automatically but rather are the result of actors and processes operating within institutions, either deliberately or not. I emphasize that certain environmental triggers may cause elevated opportunity for change in the degree of conflict or

Figure 5.2. Rivalry conflict-cooperation events

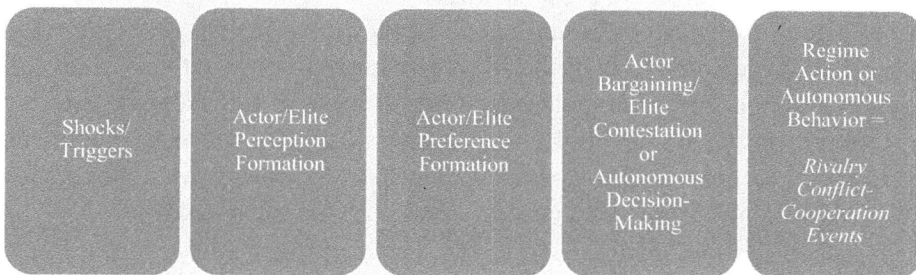

cooperation between rivals. These events effectively shock the political system in that they challenge leaders, prevailing preferences, and standard operating procedures by introducing new information to the decision-making process, often resulting in a heightened level of uncertainty as the effects of these events are absorbed and processed. The absorption and processing of shocks occurs by way of distinct domestic processes that serve as the mechanisms behind rivalry outcomes.

Shocks or Triggers

I define shocks as potential sources of instability that can lead to fluctuation in or modification of structural equilibrium (Rasler 2000, 699–720; Acemoglu, Akcigit, and Kerr 2015). General consensus exists around the notion that institutions and policy produced by them are relatively static in nature and quite slow to change. Significant change may come about through disruptions to these periods of stability. The fluctuation or modification shocks produce tends to be transitory and temporary, as status quo conditions are briefly reconsidered before new equilibrium is achieved (Goertz and Diehl 1995a, 31–32; Laitin 1998; Rasler 2000, 699–720; Acemoglu, Akcigit, and Kerr 2015). Following shocks, actors are empowered with a uniquely higher capacity to make change owing to the openings produced by this disruption to structural inertia (Goertz and Diehl 1995a, 31–32; Laitin 1998). Shocks may trigger shifts in leadership as well as modify interpretations, understandings, and expectations (Rasler, Thompson, and Ganguly 2013, 20–24). In this sense, shocks have the capacity to interact directly with the model's first institutional filter—causing change to who is in power and what they think. Further, shocks may occur either within a state or external to it (Goertz and Diehl 1995a). Common sources of exogenous shock include but are not limited to interstate war, economic crises, sanctions, and significant technological advances. Endogenous shocks, alternatively, include such events as national independence, elections, and civil war.

Meanwhile, shocks do not produce rivalry behavior in and of themselves; rather, they trigger processes internal to the state that in turn determine the resulting effect. To this point, while not sufficient to explain outcomes, shocks or trigger events are entirely necessary to this model. Not every event produces a change in rivalry levels, but levels do not shift in substantive ways without a shock. In addition, some events expected to serve as triggers for change do nothing of the sort. Predicting which event will shock the existing system is an imperfect, probabilistic exercise. The extent to which an event is shocking is entirely predicated on how it is responded to, suggesting wide variance in effect. To this point, much can be learned from non-events or negative results. When ordinarily shocking events do not produce an expected outcome, we must ask why.

Actor or Elite Perception Formation

Shocks enter states by way of actors, though the presence and significance of actors is determined in large part by institutions, each with a distinct configuration and composition. These factors effectively determine who has power in a regime and what influence these actors maintain. The resulting collection of actors within a state has varying capacity to steer outcomes. Owing to this potential influence, it is important to note points at which the collection of actors may be modified. Leader change may itself be a shocking political event. Additionally, other forms of shocks may in turn produce changes to the composition of a regime. Defeat in war, for example, may trigger an uprising within the governing elite, forcing a change in leadership. Whatever set of leaders is in place following a shock, each actor undertakes a process by which he or she evaluates the new information presented by the shock and forms initial perceptions. In doing so, elites consider what this new information tells them in light of any number of factors, including personal interests, their institutional role, and their beliefs in terms of state interests relative to relationships with other states, the region, and the international system. Additionally, actors account for the history of the relationship in evaluating how the trigger event should be interpreted. Likewise, regime insiders weigh their personal ideology and dominant narratives against this incoming information. Each individual undertakes this process to the extent new information affects them.

The significance of perceptions to this model is rooted in an assumption that the decisions of individuals are of primary importance to global politics. The concept of perception refers to activity involving the apprehension, recognition, and interpretation of what is processed (Stein 2013). Rather than anticipate a perfectly accurate cost-benefit analysis, interchangeable between actors in the same position, I assume that individuals are unique in how they receive and process information or perceive their environment (Jervis 1976; Simon 1985, 292–304). Backgrounds, heuristics, operational codes, and cognitive filters vary between actors, suggesting the potential for perceptual differences even when information is constant and even when actors are constrained by shared institutional considerations and environmental pressures (Stein 2013). I attend quite minimally to the more abstract matter of what determines the perceptions of actors at different points. While interesting to other theoretical questions, I regard the professed differences in perceptions according to actors themselves important on their own to the matter of rivalry fluctuation, particularly as variance in perception informs preferences for action.

Actor or Elite Preference Formation

An individual's inclination toward taking one action versus another does not arise on its own. Instead, actors routinely analyze events around them and determine both the extent to which these events affect them as well as interpret any new information these events feature. This assumption is somewhat the product of previous attention in literature paid to the concept of strategic choice, defined as systematic analysis of the strategic setting, involving interaction across levels of analysis.[12] This analytic process does not insist on a particular level of skill, amount of time, or degree of attention. Instead, analysis of one's strategic setting can be done quite haphazardly, without perfect information, in short time, and without dedicated focus—the terms of rather bounded rationality (Simon 1991, 125–30). To this extent, my notion of preference formation also borrows from rational models of decision-making in which strategies are selected to maximize values and goals (Levy and Thompson 2010, 130–31). Rationalist, coalition-based decision-making models in particular account for the assumption that individuals are rational, bounded as their rationalism may be, and strategic in their preference formation, while states as collectives are often not unitary in their rationality (Snyder 1991).

My model holds that if enough actors perceive new information to be significant, an event can be said retroactively to be shocking. Once perceptions are formed, however, much more remains before rivalry relationships are influenced. Elites next take their interpretation of the new information from the preceding trigger and determine their preference for how this new information should be treated. In doing so, individuals identify how their perceptions interact with a range of considerations across all potential levels of analysis, including personal, bureaucratic, domestic, state, region, and system. This step potentially includes preferences for behavior such as diversion, threat inflation, and outbidding (Colaresi 2005, 25–34; Ganguly and Thompson 2011a, 14–16). The fact that one actor may prefer to use a diversionary strategy in response to a shock, however, does not mean the regime will indeed employ a diversionary approach. Instead, the tactics used and the collection of behavior observed by a rival is contingent on the next step in this model.

Actor Bargaining and Elite Contestation or Autonomous Decision-Making

While each actor affected by new information goes through a process by which perceptions are made into preferences, not all preferences contribute to state behavior. Instead, preferences are filtered through a regime's institutional configuration, which defines how much bargaining space is available, who is included in this bargaining, and whether elites have the capacity to act autonomously. This space may change as a direct result of a shock. Bargaining space may be increased or decreased owing to a range of dynamics, to include a trigger event such as the arrival of new leadership or existing leadership reacting to environmental threats. In this sense then, shocks affect bargaining activities within a regime only indirectly, through both the formation of actor perceptions and influence on institutional configuration.

The concept of bargaining has long been considered important to research on war and peace, though work on international politics has more traditionally applied it to matters of interstate behavior (Maoz 2012). Early game theory interested in problems particular to Cold War decision-making observed that relations between states typically involve varying levels of cooperation and conflict, representing a bargaining situation where there is a point at which it is better for all sides to agree on something rather than walk away with nothing at all. Such bargaining involves the communication of commitments, threats, and promises across a series of strategic moves (Schelling 1966, 1–2). Putnam's two-level game proposition addressed criticisms of interstate game theory by deconstructing the assumption of a unitary state. Instead, iterative bargaining occurs both at the inter- and intrastate level, the latter including discussions across domestic groups about how to behave internationally (Putnam 1988, 435–53). Lateral pressure theory extends this concept of bargaining to include the interaction of political behavior across levels of analysis in which individuals bargain, leverage, and form coalitions to secure their interests within their physical and social environments (Choucri and North 1989, 289–91). These individual interests compete and are manifest in state behavior. Strategic choice theory additionally develops the applicability of bargaining to international relations, suggesting that domestic political institutions deeply affect bargaining insomuch as different structural arrangements generate unique sets of pressures and influences on decision-makers (Morrow 1999, 77–114). Streich and Levy (2016) suggest psychological, cultural, and political factors can influence the assessment of individuals during the bargaining process, directly influencing state decision-making.

The extent of bargaining space in a system may fluctuate over the life of a regime. In nondemocratic settings, bargaining space is largely influenced by the degree of control a regime's central actor maintains at a given point. New information from a trigger event, such as unanticipated election results, may shake the incumbent set of leaders to the point at which a level of control is lost, and bargaining space may be made available as a result. This new space may be maintained owing to the modified alignment of elites or may instead be closed once enough control is reestablished. In such conditions, opportunities for entrepreneurship are high. Alternatively, new information may prompt little to no change of institutional control at all, as might be the case after a military attack. In such conditions the composition of the ruling elite is generally not threatened and space for contributing to policymaking therefore generally does not shift. In addition, elites may have the capacity to act on their own, depending on the degree of control in place. Should bargaining occur, however, a range of additional dynamics has the potential of factoring into this step of the model. Contestation may be reflective of factional politics. Alternatively, this step might feature charismatic or decisive leadership, the effect of which is the tightening of control and dominance of a single viewpoint so to achieve or produce the appearance of consensus among elites.

Regime Action or Autonomous Behavior = Rivalry Conflict-Cooperation Events

The result of the bargaining step is some combination of both well-considered behaviors and uncoordinated, autonomous action. To the research questions at hand, not all resulting events affect or are even intended to affect relations with a rival state. The effect of those outcomes that are in fact directed at a rival state is contingent on the actors of that state in accordance with the steps identified in this model. While I allow for the theoretical utility of a direct shock-to-outcome relationship in certain cases, this model suggests the appearance of automated responses conceals these domestic processes rather than disproves their occurring. The perceptions and preferences of relevant elites in the rival state of which the original behavior is directed are applied to the same process of bargaining in accordance with the distinct institutional logic employed by that regime. This process then determines the aggregate effect one rival's behavior has on another. Short of considering the dynamics undertaken by a second state, the model as applied to one state can at the very least highlight the contribution of that state to the levels of conflict and cooperation present in that rivalry relationship. As two or more states interact, behavior offers feedback that is then considered as part of subsequent iterations of this model—particularly important given the historical dimension to strategic rivalries (Hensel 1994, 281–98). For the purposes of this study, change in the aggregate level of events serves as my dependent variable—the product of domestic processes following a trigger event or, in some cases, multiple shocks.

Methods

I measured and compared observations of conflict-cooperation by way of monthly event counts generated through automated coding of news reports. Events in this sense are actions or statements by members of the regime with foreign policy ramifications. I used the Computation Event Data System (CEDS) in support of activity from April 1979 through 1997. News events of interest during this period were identified using the World Event/Interaction Survey (WEIS) coding criteria (McClelland 1999). Each event included was assigned a positively or negatively scaled score that reflected its anticipated impact. For events from 1998 on, I used event data from Conflict and Mediation Event Observations (CAMEO), a coding scheme that expands the number of categories incorporated by CEDS, often resulting in a larger number of total events.[13] The scale of event scoring applied by CAMEO was consistent with that of WEIS, as were the event types that represent the two ends of this scale. I normalized results across data sets by measuring variance observed from the standard deviation of each set.

In conducting this research, I separated data into conflict-only and cooperation-only events. I did this given the potential for high levels of conflict and cooperation events to combine for an otherwise difficult-to-detect aggregate event level. Failure to do so risked missing quite dynamic periods of a relationship, mistaking such points as inconsequential. A second distinction in my approach was the inclusion of negative observations in the form of both dynamic negatives, in which conflict and cooperation events combine to produce directional inconsistency, and non-events, or points at which negligible activity outcomes occur, contrasting with what might otherwise be expected given theory or prior history. The addition of each further supported the need to test propositions in conditions both in which outcomes of interest occur as well as those in which they do not.

I next applied content analysis to event data from months in which rivalry outcomes deviated substantively from previous levels. This step involved verifying quantitative results and probing the stated perceptions and preferences of Iranian elites so as to explore in greater detail mechanisms that lead to conflict or cooperation changes. Interpretation was sometimes necessary in the examination of event data, suggesting the need for additional work to ensure robustness of findings. Thus, I also employed primary and academic source material to validate observations from event count data. This step was applied to gain more contextual depth of the mechanisms included in my model as well as to test for alternative explanations. While not definitive or assuredly transferable to other cases, close focus on context fosters more sound conclusions that can then be tested elsewhere.

IRAN-SAUDI RIVALRY FLUCTUATION

Figures 5.3–5.5 present Iranian conflict and cooperation levels toward Saudi Arabia from 1979 to 2015, normalized across data sets. The two strongest outliers in my data—August 1987 and October 2011—are removed in figures 5.6–5.7 to better illustrate this fluctuation. Several findings are evident from this comprehensive event data. First, four relatively distinct periods of rivalry behavior appear to exist in which Iran's output toward Saudi Arabia is somewhat consistent: 1979–90 (negative), 1991–96 (restrained), 1997–2007 (positive), and 2008–15 (dynamic). I acknowledge a level of subjectivity in determining the beginning and end to each of these periods and proceed with greater confidence that there are four periods than that these periods have clear temporal bounds. Each reflects a shift in the basic rivalry level for a generally sustained period, and each is preceded by an event that meets traditional definitions of a shock. Negative and positive periods include a general consistency of behavioral directionality, while the restrained period features notably less overall activity. The dynamic period, meanwhile, lacks the consistency of these other three in that it entails alternating positive and negative results as well as the presence of both higher levels of positive and negative behavior at the same time. Such behavior includes a high level of overall activity, and the competing direction-ality of output suggests institutional space for a higher number of actors. The general lack of actor consensus reflected in dynamic behavior further suggests the likely presence of both considerable bargaining and decision-makers empowered with acting independent of the bargaining process. The overall inconsistency within dynamic behavior then contributes less coherent state output to the rivalry relationship.

Second, these periods do not combine to reflect a clear behavioral trajectory, indicating that reactions to environmental pressures are not sustained in a consistent fashion. Thus, escalation or de-escalation patterns fail to manifest owing in large part to the turbulence often present within and across periods, with various levels of conflict and cooperation often present simultaneously.

A comparison of patterns evident in conflict-cooperation levels (figs. 5.3–5.7) to those of institutional bargaining space (fig. 5.1) appears to highlight an association. Institutional bargaining space is lowest according to both measures during the negative period. Analysis reflects that Khomeini maintained centralized control during this period and rivalry relations were at their worst. Bargaining space appears to increase in conjunction with the restrained period. Change between periods reflects the space afforded by Khomeini's death, ultimately resulting in an opening for Rafsanjani's attempts at engagement. Bargaining space then increases near the beginning of the positive period, coinciding with Khatami's presidency and his sharply different approach to rivalry relations. Institutional bargaining per the horizontal accountability measure remains high throughout the rest of this study, except for the period 2007–9, which coincides with a high degree

Figure 5.3. Iranian rivalry behavior (normalized, 1979–2015)

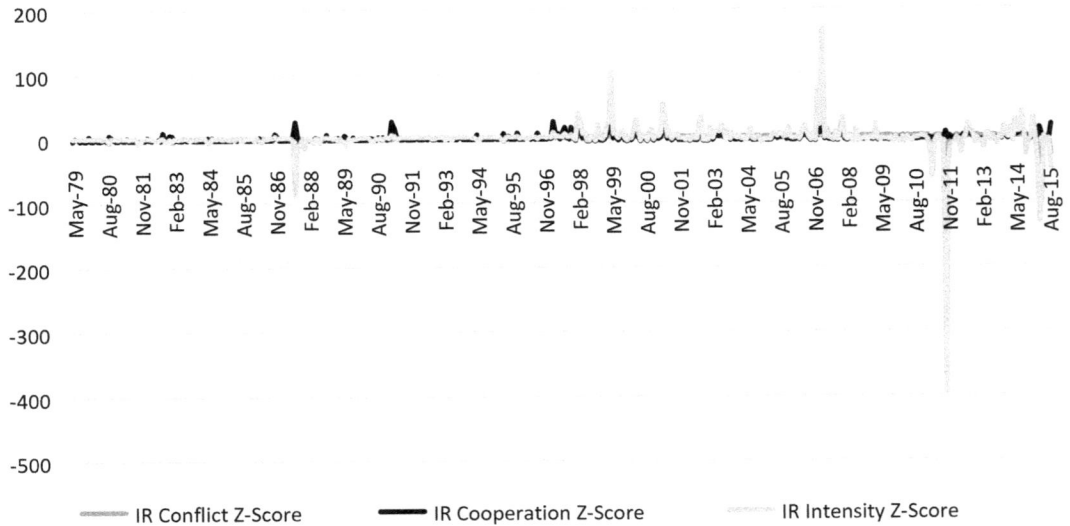

of hostility and a parallel sidelining of Ahmadinejad. From this we can see that less bargaining space appears associated with more hostility.

The return to higher levels from 2010 to 2013 features the return of cooperation alongside sustained hostility in quite dynamic, interactive levels. Institutional bargaining, per the elite consultation measure, remains high through roughly 2004 and falls to moderate levels until roughly 2011. While not significant enough to reflect a rivalry-level

Figure 5.4. Iranian rivalry behavior (normalized, 1979–97)

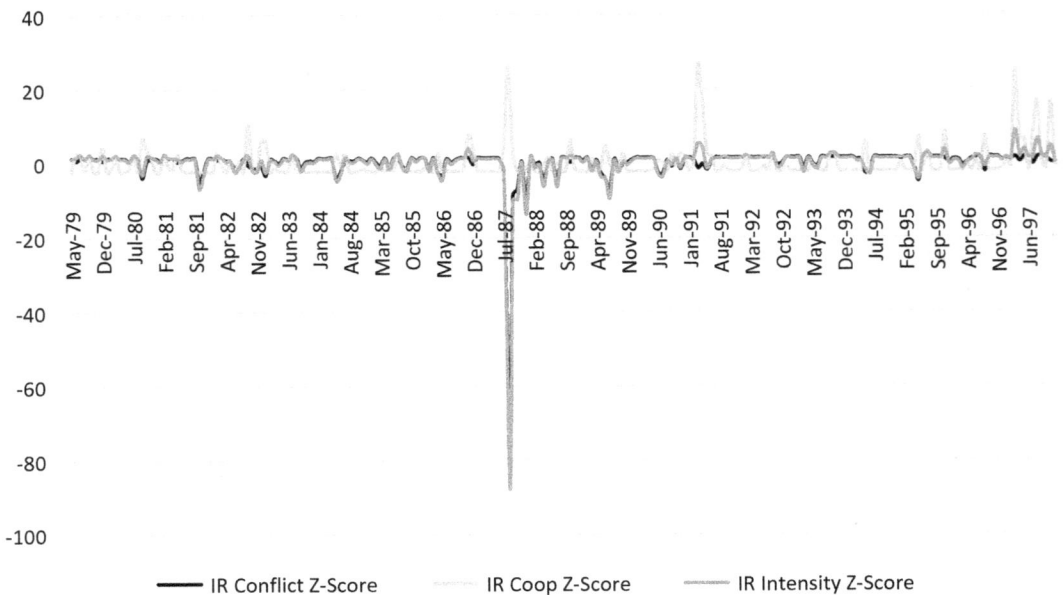

Figure 5.5. Iranian rivalry behavior (normalized, 1998–2015)

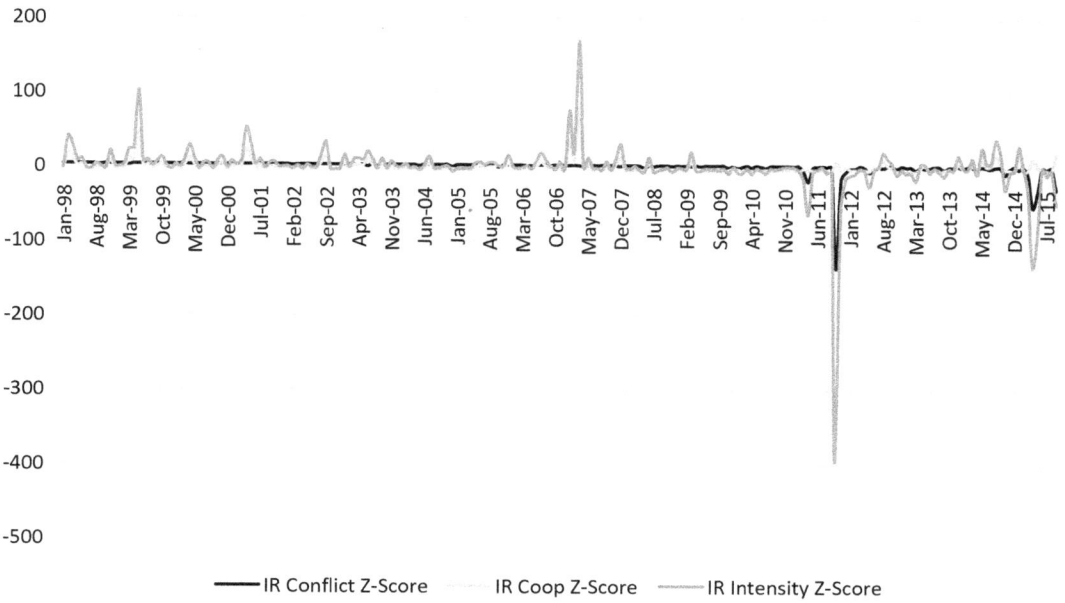

shift, this coincides with a relative rise in hostility levels, as evident in significant dynamic negatives over this time frame, finally culminating in the rupturing of consensus over how to behave toward Saudi Arabia. Elite consultation levels climb to their highest in 2012 and remain there through 2015. This rise coincides eventually with the arrival of greater levels of cooperation following a brief period of consensus on hostility. From these findings, it generally appears that increased bargaining space is associated with more cooperation and less hostility, whereas less bargaining space is associated with less cooperation and more hostility. In addition, modifications to the composition of regime elites appear directly related to levels of bargaining space. This finding is consistent with the

Figure 5.6. Iranian rivalry behavior (normalized, no outliers, 1979–97)

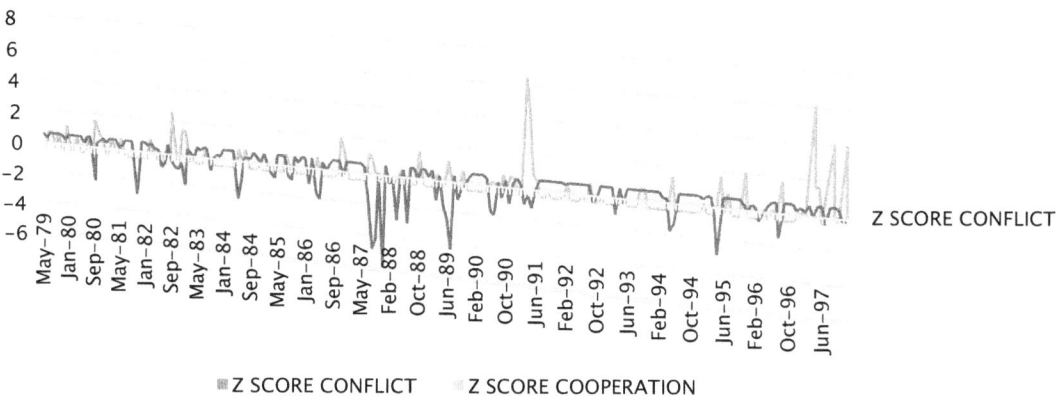

Figure 5.7. Iranian rivalry behavior (normalized, no outliers, 1998–2015)

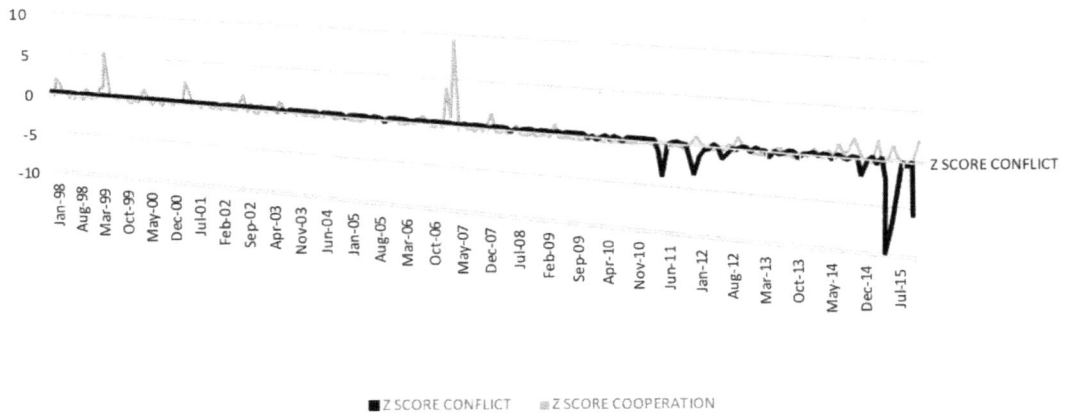

political institutional model applied here in which leaders, each with a distinct set of perceptions and preferences, interact within institutions to produce outcomes.

Content analysis of event data used for this study reveals the consistent occurrence of certain incident types before large shifts in cooperation or conflict. In particular, the annual Hajj pilgrimage, substantive changes to America's role in the region, the introduction of international pressures, conflict in the region, and transitions in leadership routinely precede some of the more prominent outlier points in the figures. Reactions to these environmental triggers, however, vary over the course of my study, as evidenced by the fact these pressures appear routinely throughout different periods. To understand this variance in its entirety requires more space than is available. I seek in the remainder of this chapter only to demonstrate the utility of a political institutional approach by comparing observations following several of these trigger types across periods.

Third-Party Pressure and Change in America's Role in the Region

Following Iran's revolution in 1979, relations with Saudi Arabia were lukewarm, oscillating between periods of relative inactivity and points of minimal cooperation. Riyadh appears to have taken a wait-and-see approach to developments in Iran, despite early signs of prospective difficulties.[14] With minimal cooperation present, Iranian behavior toward Saudi Arabia experienced a dramatic sevenfold increase in negativity in September 1980. Content analysis offers clear evidence that Iran responded during this episode to Saudi Arabia's decision to openly profess support for Iraq in Baghdad's war against the Islamic Republic, which began that month (BBC 1980). Iran viewed itself as the victim of Iraqi aggression and considered Riyadh's position an unjustified provocation. Despite considerable domestic turbulence in the face of ongoing consolidation by Khomeini's supporters, Iran's response to Saudi Arabia's decision to become a party to war is consistent with what would reasonably be expected following an external threat.[15] Thus, the domestic level of analysis does not appear theoretically necessary to this episode.

Saudi Arabia's relationship with the United States, meanwhile, serves as a consistent trigger for conflict throughout Iran's war with Iraq. The association between third-party pressure and conflict propensity is well established and appears to operate consistently with expectations early in this study (Brecher and Wilkenfeld 1997; Colaresi, Rasler, and Thompson 2007, 189–239). Iran's disposition toward Saudi Arabia following its announcement of support for Iraq oscillated between mild levels of hostility and cooperation until October 1981, at which point Iran reacted to the United States inserting itself into the brewing regional conflict. A US announcement that it would not allow a takeover of Saudi Arabia by Iran was followed by a pledge to sell sensitive reconnaissance aircraft to the kingdom (Strout 1981, 1). The rivalry went from bad to worse in August 1987, with conflict figures experiencing their most rapid decline of the period. Military initiative was gained and lost three times in the preceding several years, producing stalemate on the ground. Iranian gross domestic product plummeted, losing roughly 10 percent over the year (World Bank, n.d.). Recognizing its need to seize leverage elsewhere, Iran escalated its threatening behavior in the Strait of Hormuz to include mine laying by IRGC forces, conventional naval maneuvers, and attacks on shipping vessels (Plommer 1987).

The United States answered by entering the Persian Gulf to protect shipping interests in what would be known as the "tanker war," capturing Iranian mine-laying ships and destroying IRGC speedboats.[16] In response, Rafsanjani expressed opposition from within the Iranian parliament, declaring Iran's readiness to respond militarily to continued provocations from Saudi Arabia and Arab states (H. Anderson et al. 1987, 24). Additionally, Khamenei and naval leaders indicated Iran's intention to strike US vessels in the Gulf (*Guardian* 1987). Relations again worsened in April 1988. War between Iran and Iraq had taken enormous tolls on the populations and economies of both countries, and neither side had demonstrated the capacity to maintain military advantage. Further, the introduction of US naval forces negated Iran's advantages over Arab supporters of Iraq at sea. Under these conditions Iraq launched a surprise attack on Iranian forces in which nerve and mustard gases were employed. Baghdad continued the use of chemical weapons, later dropping cyanide bombs on Iranian villages, resulting in substantial civilian casualties. This development coincided with both an increase in US offensive naval tactics in the Gulf as well as Saudi Arabia's decision to break all diplomatic relations with Tehran. Collectively, these efforts facilitated Iran's agreement to finally end the war. Matters became increasingly dire in July, when the United States mistook an Iranian commercial airliner carrying 290 passengers for a military target, killing all aboard (Wilson 1988).

None of these episodes demonstrates clear evidence as to the role of internal politics. A nation at war, Iran responded to the role of the United States throughout this period reciprocally. Although Iran was consolidating power domestically, little evidence exists that its frustration with Washington's stated role was diversionary or inflated. Instead,

Iran responded to US actions as an increase in hostility of the US-Saudi partnership against it and an attempt to further modify balance of power in the region. While analysis indicates that multiple actors by this point maintained the capacity to influence foreign policy outcomes, little evidence exists to indicate less than a consensus perception of these trigger events within Iran.

Reaction to third-party pressure is less decisively external in nature in subsequent periods. Khomeini passed away in June 1989, shortly after appointing his longtime ally Ali Khamenei his successor, despite the latter's relative lack of charisma and religious authority.[17] Meanwhile, Rafsanjani became the nation's next president, calling for better relations with Arab neighbors other than Saudi Arabia. Conflict levels increased in May 1990 and remained elevated until September. Analysis reflects that this episode was driven by Iran's negative reaction to Saudi Arabia's role in hosting US military forces in their war against Iraq (Haeri 1990, 10). The post-Khomeini configuration of Iranian elites viewed this by way of the continued US-Saudi partnership, and some suggested Saudi hospitality as a means of further weakening Iran's place in the region. Similarly, hostility levels climbed again in May 1995 owing to the role of the US. Washington announced a prohibition of Iranian oil, and Iran lashed out at Saudi Arabia and other Organization of the Petroleum Exporting Countries (OPEC) members, warning them not to take advantage of the US trade ban against it. Khamenei and his Friday prayer leaders in Qom and Tehran rebuked Saudi Arabia for its relationship with America (BBC 1995). Again, the third-party Saudi relationship with Washington suggests that an act harmful to the interests of Iran by the United States skews the region's balance of power toward Saudi Arabia. Thus, it might reasonably be expected that Iran respond negatively toward Riyadh during these episodes. As opposed to previous responses and reflecting an opening of elite bargaining space, however, Rafsanjani also produced levels of cooperation, calling for Riyadh to engage in partnership with Iran as opposed to relying on Washington (BBC 1998).

While Rafsanjani's outreach was a notable break from the past, the capacity of leaders to shift Iran's response to American pressure became most recognizable during the period reflected by the August 1997 arrival of Mohammad Khatami's presidency. Khatami ushered in an unforeseen level of cooperation, with even Iranian-Saudi military cooperation advancing. Rivalry levels further improved in February 1998, with Iranian leaders from across the spectrum praising Saudi Arabia's decision not to allow the United States to engage Iraq from its bases in support of Operation Desert Fox. Riyadh's decision to rebuff the US request to utilize its bases to launch strikes signaled to Iranian leadership that its efforts toward repairing relations might well directly correlate with its objective to minimize America's presence in the region. In this sense Iran's response appears at least partially reciprocal to the policy decision announced by its rival. Considerable levels of cooperation, however, remain directly correlated with the strength of Khatami's administration vis-à-vis other actors in the system, particularly as evidence appears to suggest Iran's engagement strategy was paying dividends. Much of the growth in cooperation during this episode is the result of previous outreach efforts, a continued consequence of the presidential election of 1997, which left conservative forces reeling.

The power of Khatami to alter the course of Iran's rivalry with Saudi Arabia following pressure from America, however, is most evident as the United States threatened Iran over its nuclear program. Modest increases in cooperation occurred in August 2002, January 2003, and June 2003—each related to US statements reflecting the potential of action against Iran. President George W. Bush's address to the United Nations demanding action against Iran, statements from Washington regarding the imminence of war, and Iran's being rebuffed in its attempt to strike a grand bargain with the United States each might previously have led to escalated hostility toward Saudi Arabia (Abrahamian 2004, 95–108). Under Khatami, the opposite is true, as conflict from Washington triggered more outreach from Tehran toward Riyadh. Rafsanjani and then Khatami demonstrated that leaders bring different perceptions and preferences to office. Depending on the level of institutional space available for entrepreneurs to operate (per fig. 5.1), this variance can result in different outcomes in the face of theoretically similar trigger events.

The Hajj Pilgrimage

To engage in the Hajj pilgrimage to Mecca at least once during a lifetime is considered an enduring religious duty of all Muslims (Balyuzi 1976, 149–58). Khomeini established strong views as to how the Hajj should be treated by Muslims long before he secured power in Iran, including the duty to protest against injustices (Khomeini 1981, 130–31, 195–99, 237–38, 257–77, 300–306). These ideas were translated into policy shortly after Iran's revolution, policy that was enacted under the cloud of war with Iraq. The second most significant increase in hostility over the life of the Iran-Saudi strategic rivalry occurred in October 1981. In addition to the entrance of the United States into the conflict in support of Riyadh, analysis reveals the relationship declined owing to Saudi Arabia's reaction to Iran's Hajj activities (Mahmoud 1981). On the surface there is no reason to expect Iran to respond angrily to Saudi Arabia's attempt to enforce rule and order during the Hajj. The decision to lash out against the crackdown on Iranian protestors was not automatic; rather, it featured a policy shift in which a new ideology regarding the purpose of Hajj activities was implemented. The formation of this ideology and resulting policy action did not occur on its own but rather came courtesy of Khomeini.[18] Desire for regional hegemony, leadership over all oppressed and all Muslims, and regime consolidation at home are all domestic considerations that extend from Khomeini, and all contribute to the role of Hajj policy. Khomeini oversaw a regime with little potential for contestation and near singlehandedly determined the dominant narrative. Thus, this episode is early evidence of his ideology and preferences being implemented as policy.

Clashes over Iran's export of revolutionary ideology caused a shift toward a more consistently negative basic rivalry level. Conflict figures remained high through the September 1982–January 1983 period owing to frustration at Saudi Arabia over the treatment of Iranian pilgrims. Iran summoned pilgrims to its diplomatic mission in Medina, leading to subsequent arrests by Saudi security forces. Khomeini led the charge in expressing outrage at this development, which was echoed by prayer leaders across the country as well as members of Parliament (Mahmoud 1982). Iran's insistence on rallying in Saudi

Arabia and challenging Riyadh's decision to squelch protests is rooted in the institutionalization of Khomeini's ideology. Had there been no charismatic leader operationalizing a new narrative in which Iranians possessed a duty to rally at the Hajj, the Saudi response to what it regarded as a matter of law and order involving Iranians within its borders might reasonably be suspected not to have led to such backlash. Increases in hostility again in September 1983 and August 1985 followed Saudi crackdowns on Iranian Hajj protests—the product of institutionalized policy (BBC 1983). The process of feuding over Hajj pilgrim quotas with Saudi Arabia, Riyadh's warning Iran not to protest, Iranians' protesting anyways, and Saudi authorities' intervening to stop what was perceived as disorderly conduct became by this point routinized, taking on somewhat procedural character.

Khomeini doubled down on the role of the annual Hajj as a means of protesting injustice in July 1987, inciting Arab leaders by encouraging rallies against their oppressive rule (BBC 1987b). Shortly thereafter, Saudi Arabia cracked down on protestors, killing over four hundred Iranians in the process (Hussain 1987, 25). As a result, Khomeini broke diplomatic relations with Riyadh, Rafsanjani called for death to Saudi Arabia and demanded Iran "avenge the martyrs of Saudi sabotage," and Khamenei accused Saudi Arabia of colluding with other Arab governments to murder Iranians (BBC 1987a). Meanwhile, a subtle undercurrent within the Iranian regime attempted to cool tensions despite the evidence of overwhelming institutional pressure to escalate hostility. Foreign Minister Ali Akbar Velayati called for discussions with Riyadh over the Hajj incident and expressed his desire to find common ground. This related set of cooperative gestures was not enough to cloud the overwhelming negativity of this episode but represents one of the earliest points of evidence that institutional bargaining space within the Iranian system was increasing. Domestic politics was present in the form of Khomeini's continued ideological commitment to utilizing the Hajj for political gain and the strength of his personal leadership in operationalizing this policy. To some extent, Khomeini's decision to recommit to Hajj protests during this episode is reflective of rally-around-the-flag logic in which he sought to refocus an increasingly war-wearied Iranian population on its common purpose.

Iranian behavior toward Saudi Arabia in the summer of 1989 oscillated between mild and moderate levels of hostility and included intermittent signs of cooperation as well. Domestically, Iran committed considerable effort to suppressing dissent of its wartime policies and struggled to address its failing economy. GDP plummeted another 6 percent over the prior year, and the future leadership of Iran appeared in doubt. Khomeini's deteriorating health exacerbated this dynamic, as Iran faced a potential leader succession crisis. Khomeini passed away in June 1989, shortly after appointing Khamenei his successor. Iran's new leadership came into power just as the annual Hajj season was occurring, and Tehran decided to boycott sending pilgrims to the holy sites in response to Saudi Arabia's continued restrictions over Iran's activities while visiting.

Institutionalization of Iran's approach to the Hajj produced continuity in policy following Khomeini's death. Starting in May 1989, there was a steady rise in hostility toward Saudi Arabia, five times the level in April and doubling even this level by July.

Saudi Arabia's announcement of additional Hajj limitations on Iran triggered this pattern and culminated in July (the actual Hajj month), during which an explosion in Mecca injured sixteen people (Mahmoud 1989). Khamenei responded by calling Saudi Arabia an un-Islamic terrorist state and directed the IRGC to prepare for action against the kingdom. Majlis leadership argued Iran should free the holy sites from Saudi rule. Newly elected president Rafsanjani scolded Saudi Arabia for its relationship with the United States and blamed it for the bombings in Mecca (BBC 1989).

As discussed earlier, Khomeini's ideological preferences toward the Hajj were established and operationalized into policy within several years of revolution. His dominant position within Iran drove these preferences toward becoming institutionalized, suggesting elites were hardly reevaluating their positions as part of Saudi limitations; rather, they were responding in accordance with standard operating procedures. The fact that the most significant change of leadership in the Islamic Republic's history took place during this period of Hajj disputes further highlights the extent to which Khomeini's ideology had been institutionalized. Few leaders in the system passed up the opportunity to scold Saudi Arabia for its restrictions and later piled blame on Riyadh for the attack in Mecca. In addition, the Hajj served as a diversion from ongoing domestic squabbles over leader succession, allowing new leadership to point to a common foe and highlight its intent for continuity.

Iran's response to the Hajj continued unchanged over the following years. For example, Tehran responded with outrage in June 1990 following Saudi Arabia's handling of a tunnel collapse in Mecca (Associated Press 1990). Iranian leaders capitalized on the disaster by emphasizing the state's long-preferred policy of shared maintenance of the holy sites due to Riyadh's unfitness for the task. Hostility levels increased again in May 1991 after Saudi Arabia's decision to move its protestors to a secluded space (*Independent* 1991, 12). Similar upticks in conflict occurred in response to Hajj episodes in 1993–95, demonstrating continued routinization of policy toward pilgrimage-related triggers.

As institutional space increased, however, Hajj policy changed. In February 1998 cooperation from Iran toward Saudi Arabia rose, while negative output was minimal. Outreach initiatives fostered by the Rafsanjani and Khatami administrations came to fruition at this point. The former Iranian president visited Saudi Arabia to meet with King Fahd. The result of the meeting included an increased quota on Iranian pilgrims for the upcoming Hajj (BBC 1998). For the first time since the early 1980s, Iranian pilgrims took part in Hajj festivities in Saudi Arabia in April 1998 without incident. Little to no rivalry behavior is evident during this month, highlighting further evidence of the influence of domestic politics on conflict and cooperation patterns. Rafsanjani had secured an increased quota from Saudi Arabia during his visit with King Fahd; however, this alone was not responsible for Iran's calm. As opposed to nearly every other year since Iran's revolution, there was minimal call for Iranians to protest while in the holy cities and very few warnings by Saudi Arabia to Iranian pilgrims. Institutionalized preferences courtesy of the centralized leadership by Khomeini years earlier were overcome this month in favor of the more cooperative approach emphasized in Rafsanjani's later years and the initial months of Khatami's administration. Traditional forces within the regime remained on their heels given threats from reform-minded elites. Thus, it might be argued that Khatami's approach was loosely consolidated within the regime at this point given the permissiveness of the other regime elites, whose preferences had appeared directionally different in the past.

The pattern of provocation surrounding Saudi Arabia's management of the holy cities also ended during Khatami's administration. When the annual "stoning of the Devil" ritual was carried out near Mecca in March 2001, at least thirty-five pilgrims died after being overrun by a stampede. Saudi authorities accepted responsibility, citing lack of organization (Agence France Press 2001). Such an incident would have earlier provoked outrage from Iran, even following Saudi acknowledgment of its own responsibility for the disaster. Yet Iran levied little to no criticism. Instead, Iran exercised restraint and largely emphasized remorse for the victims. This outcome essentially institutionalized Iran's new approach to the Hajj season, in light of its commitment to rapprochement with Saudi Arabia—the result of a modification to the dominant strategic logic governing the relationship courtesy of the different set of actors present and the institutional space afforded these elites to operate. Illustrative of this point, a stampede in February 2004 killing 244 pilgrims resulted in little from Iranian officials besides an expression of concern for those who suffered from the incident (Rageh 2004).

Détente toward Iranian concerns over the Hajj continued beyond Khatami into the early stages of the Ahmadinejad presidency. Iranians cast their ballots for the populist leader in October 2005, and Ahmadinejad was soon faced with the question of responding to a Hajj-related incident. The annual "stoning of the Devil" Hajj ritual ended badly in January 2006, when a stampede resulted in the death of 364 people (Nasrawi 2006). Whereas Iran might have seized this opportunity to lash out at Riyadh under Khomeini, Iranian elites remained relatively silent over the matter, demonstrating a continued commitment to no longer exploiting Hajj disasters through the call for an end to Saudi oversight of the holy sites. This commitment remained despite a new configuration of Iranian elites and the escalating level of concern expressed from Riyadh regarding Iran's regional behavior. Rather than an automatic or natural outcome, the fact that Iran remained silent was a choice made by the new configuration of leadership. The influence of Iran's composition of elites was further evident in November–December 2007, as Ahmadinejad near singlehandedly improved relations with Saudi Arabia. The Iranian president participated in the Hajj, traveling to Saudi Arabia and delivering a call to pilgrims for Iran and Saudi Arabia to work together in resisting US pressures (Agence France Press 2007). Despite different factional allegiances, Ahmadinejad's position was the culmination of Rafsanjani's work decades earlier, itself a departure from the preferences of Khomeini and initial inclinations of Khamenei.

Internal elite consensus over policy toward Saudi Arabia and the Hajj ended in November 2009, just as institutional space for domestic bargaining appears to increase (see fig. 5.1). This represents a tipping point in the relationship, with negative levels outpacing cooperation for the first time in over fifteen years. Levels remained dynamic in that positive output was present as well, but hostility from Iran accounted for more events for this and several proceeding months as well. Reports circulated about the harassment of Iranian pilgrims by Salafi and Wahhabi fundamentalists during annual Hajj festivities, drawing condemnation by Iranian officials. More notably, Nimr Baqir al-Nimr, a popular Shi'i cleric in Saudi Arabia, expressed allegiance to Iran, threatening to undermine Saudi domestic stability and only increasing the level of suspicion Riyadh had of Iran's revolutionary ideology (Abu-Nasr 2009). The perception that Iran's pilgrims continued to be mistreated by Saudi authorities as well as Saudi statements condemning al-Nimr precipitated Khamenei's reversal of standing quietist policy regarding the Hajj (*Daily Star* 2010). Al-Nimr was executed by the Saudi government for alleged terrorism offenses in January 2016, drawing strong condemnation from Iran. Khamenei instructed Hajj pilgrims to display firm resolve against attempts to damage unity and progress, warning them not to ignore events taking place in the Muslim world (*Edmonton Journal* 2009). This call for repoliticizing the Hajj sparked outrage within Saudi channels and prompted a warning to Iran not to pursue a return to aggressive protests and demonstrations. Angered by the treatment of minority Shi'i in Saudi Arabia, Iran simultaneously increased its confrontation of Riyadh regarding its nuclear program. While Rafsanjani and the foreign ministry continued outwardly emphasizing cooperation, Khamenei's representatives expressed outrage (Zaanoun 2009).

The varied approaches to Saudi Arabia during this episode were informed by a range of ongoing inter- and intrastate events in which actors empowered to engage in foreign policy formed preferences, interacted, and produced sometimes contradictory outcomes. Religious tensions during this time operated alongside disputes over Iran's nuclear program and insurgency in Yemen, not to mention internal instability following a contested summer 2009 presidential election. For Khamenei, a reversal of Hajj policy might have served as a diversionary tactic to rally Iranians behind a common purpose in the face of uncertainty caused by these other issue areas. The confluence of criticism regarding Iran's alleged support for Houthi rebels in Yemen and its nuclear program might rather have demonstrated to Khamenei that the Hajj détente policy in place was no longer paying dividends (Voice of America News 2009). Irrespective, the fact that this modification of preference took place as cooperation continued to be present suggests a high degree of contestation within the regime, resulting in high activity levels in which contradictory messages were sent. As with third-party pressure triggers, therefore, outcomes varied in conjunction with changes to internal bargaining space, which allowed political entrepreneurs to modify rivalry outcomes (Zarif 2014, 49–59).

CONCLUSION

The aim of this study has been to examine and account for fluctuation in conflict and cooperation levels present in the rivalry between Iran and Saudi Arabia, with the former isolated to allow for a more extensive probe. An approach employing event data, content analysis, and process tracing to validate initial event data was proposed. This strategy was applied in studying variance in outcomes to theoretically similar environmental triggers across a thirty-six-year period in which four relatively distinct periods of rivalry levels are evident. In doing so, I sought to determine the extent to which political factors internal to the state influence rivalry fluctuation.

The model offered in this study features rivalry outcomes generated by a bargaining process between elites following the formation of individual perceptions and preferences in response to environmental triggers. Elite composition and contestation are instrumental to this model, reflecting the interaction between decision-maker and structure. In addition to illustrating the viability of this model using descriptive data, I demonstrated this relationship through an exploration of Iran's behavior toward Saudi Arabia following several common types of triggers in particular—changes to US policy in the region and the annual Hajj pilgrimage. A natural next step to this work would be an exploration of Saudi behavior toward Iran, followed by the weaving together of domestic factors within each state as part of a more dynamically interactive relationship. While not dynamic in the strictest sense, this chapter is not devoid of interaction either, as Saudi behavior routinely triggers an Iranian response and is qualitatively accounted for.

Results from the first decade of the Islamic Republic, in which the nation was at war and a strong, centralized leader was in place, cast some doubt on how important internal factors are. An opening of bargaining space within Iran's governing system following this period, however, highlighted variance in outcomes according to which actors were in power and challenged the notion that anything about this first period was automatic. Moving from this first decade, similar events stimulated behavior opposite from that which was evident earlier and, in some cases, produced directionally contrary behavior simultaneously or even no activity at all. It was determined that this variance was largely contingent on modified capacity for political entrepreneurship within Iran's institutional arrangement. When actors were afforded space to bargain over policy outcomes, variance in results tended to occur. In terms of the Iran-Saudi dyad, greater institutional space generated the capacity to deviate from status quo forces aggressively challenging Saudi Arabia present during Khomeini's rule. This change occurred first by resorting to calm, then to a period of assertive outreach, and then, finally, to a period of dynamic interaction between actors promoting both positive and negative output. Rarely did behavior shift without the presence of external-interstate dynamics, suggesting the presence usually of an interaction across levels of analysis. Iran, however, encountered the consistent presence of regional conflict, a hostile Washington-Riyadh partnership, international pressure, economic distress, and cultural and religious differences with the Saudi kingdom throughout most of this study, yet considerable fluctuation occurred. While external-interstate factors were present, therefore, actors and institutions instead accounted for a considerable amount of variance in conflict and cooperation behavior between these two states.

NOTES

1. For a comprehensive treatment of the Iranian Revolution, see Kurzman (2004) and Arjomand (1988).

2. For a thorough examination of Islam and the Sunni-Shi'i split within, see Hodgson (1974a, 1974b, 1974c).

3. For a full account of Iranian resistance, see Hunter (2010), Buchta (2000), and Pollack (2004).

4. This contestation contributes to regime maintenance, as accounted for by Keshavarzian (2005). For a comprehensive treatment of Iran's institutional configuration, see Buchta (2000). To best understand its origins, see Moslem (2002).

5. Iran's political order includes both formal and official institutions as well as institutions unofficially, or informally, linked to the regime. For more on this distinction, reference Buchta (2000) as well as Kamrava and Hassan-Yari (2004). For an example of informal institutions, see Saeidi (2004). While difficult to measure, I contend Iran's informal political structure very likely influences rivalry relations with Saudi Arabia and therefore strengthens my central argument. Owing to the methods employed, however, this chapter focuses on Iran's formal, official institutions.

6. For more on the factionalism that helped drive Khatami's rise, see Wells (1999), Tazmini (2013), and Arjomand (2009).

7. For a fuller account of these episodes, see Maloney (2015).

8. For more information pertaining to internal instability surrounding the succession of Khomeini by Khamenei, see Arjomand (2009) and Ehteshami (1995).

9. For a comprehensive account of political institutionalism, see Schedler (2013).

10. Unitary state models are common academic shortcuts taken to evaluate international behavior. An example of this approach is perhaps best portrayed by Waltz (1979). For further illustration of non-unitary decision-making in Iran in particular, see Keshavarzian (2005).

11. This refers to the organizational politics model of foreign policy as described in such places as Halperin, Clapp, and Kantor (1974) and Hudson (2014).

12. For more on strategic choice, see D. A. Lake and Powell (1999).

13. Both CEDS and CAMEO data sets are hosted by Parus Analytical Systems and publicly available at http://eventdata.parusanalytics.com/.

14. For a comprehensive treatment of Khomeini's vision for Islamic government in Iran and its intended influence on Muslims elsewhere, see Khomeini (1981).

15. Beyond examining news reports utilized for event data, I explored academic historical accounts of this period, including but not limited to those referenced in this study's section on Iranian foreign policy. For episodes beyond 1998, I cross-referenced these accounts with coverage from Iranian newspapers and, starting in 2002, statements and speeches available on the websites of Iranian elites.

16. For a full account of the tanker war, see Zatarain (2010).

17. For more on Iran's succession crisis of 1989, see Arjomand (2009) and Buchta (2000).

18. For more on Khomeini's preferences regarding the Hajj, see his message to pilgrims before the Iranian Revolution in Khomeini (1981).

6

Iran-Iraq-Syria

Shocks and Rivalries in a Triadic Pattern

Marwan J. Kabalan

Since the emergence of the modern state system in the Middle East in the aftermath of World War I, but particularly in the post–World War II era, rivalry has been a central feature in the relationships among Iran, Iraq, and Syria. Reasons for these intersecting rivalries varied and included the rivalry structure of the international system (especially during the Cold War), which sometimes overlay regional relations, and in the process shifted regional alignments and balances of power, and at other times had a more modest influence on regional politics; historical and colonial legacies, such as territorial disputes and disputes over natural resources; and last, positional drivers between different governments and their contests for regional leadership or hegemony.

This chapter examines the rivalries among Iran, Iraq, and Syria since the mid-twentieth century. It seeks to explain the fluctuating patterns embedded in this complex rivalry and draws conclusions on how triadic rivalries operate. Over the past six decades, relations among these three states have varied quite widely, shifting from one extreme (antagonism) to another (alliance) and vice versa and at times witnessing accommodation. In most cases, however, the nature of the relationship (amity or enmity) between any two of these actors has been largely defined by their relationship with the third. Importantly, change in this triadic relationship most often came as a result of shocks, which act here as the independent variable par excellence.

Over the past six decades shocks have included internal strife, social revolution, military coup, or foreign intervention. They either toppled governments or posed serious threat to a sitting government and hence affected rivalry dynamics in fundamental ways. From 1958 to 2011 the three countries witnessed a series of changes in leadership: in Iraq changes occurred in 1958, 1963, 1968, 1979, and 2003; in Syria they occurred in 1963, 1966, and 1970, with the possibility for change after the 2011 uprising; and in Iran change occurred in 1979. This chapter, however, explores the effects of four main shocks, in the form of a change of government, revolution, or foreign invasion: Iraq in 1958 and 2003, Iran in 1979, and Syria in 2011.

Investigating these relations offers empirical and theoretical insights. The notion of "triadic rivalry" or "strategic triangle" has not been widely applied in Middle Eastern contexts. It has been examined more commonly with reference to the relationships among the United States, China, and the Soviet Union at the beginning of the Sino-American rapprochement in the early 1970s (Dittmer 1981). Indeed, Stephen Walt (1987) and Malcom Kerr (1971) did address the formation of alliances in the Middle East as well as delineate motives for regional rivalries, but they have not examined them in triadic contexts, that is, the way the relationship between two countries could affect relations with a third. Jubin M. Goodarzi (2008) touched on the Iran-Iraq-Syria triadic relationship but only marginally as his study focused almost exclusively on the Syrian-Iranian alliance.

ORIGINS OF THE IRAN-IRAQ-SYRIA RIVALRIES

Like most neighboring states in the Middle East, Iran and Iraq have had difficult relations throughout modern history. Indeed, Iran as a larger regional power has always tried to dominate Iraq.[1] An ideological driver of this relationship occurred with the conversion of Iran into a Shi'ite state following the Safavid takeover in 1501. Shi'ite holy sites in Iraq became a matter of interest for the new rulers of Persia. Merely seven years later Baghdad was conquered by Safavids (W. Spencer 2000, 51). From a geopolitical perspective, Iran has always regarded Mesopotamia as a sphere of influence. Its rich natural resources (water and fertile land) have captured the imagination of Iran's rulers since antiquity, given the mountainous and arid nature of Persia. Iraq was also a transit route to the Mediterranean for most Persian dynasties.

For almost four centuries the Sunni Ottoman Empire acted as a main bulwark against Shi'ite Persian ambitions in Iraq. The Ottomans forced the exit of the Persians from Iraq in 1534 and ruled the country unchallenged (except for a short period, 1628–34) until World War I. When the Ottomans lost Iraq to the British army in 1917, Iran was weak and under British influence.

In Syria, Ottoman rule ended in 1918. King Faisal I, son of Sharif Hussein, who led the Arab rebellion against the Ottomans during World War I, established the first Arab government in Damascus in October 1918. Less than two years into his reign, however, he was deposed, and Syria fell under French mandate, in accordance with the Sykes-Picot Agreement, which divided the possessions of the Ottoman Empire in the Levant between the Western allies (Fromkin 1989). Faisal was made king of Iraq by the British as a compensation, but he always regarded Syria as part of his greater Arab kingdom. Uniting the Fertile Crescent under its leadership remained the ultimate goal of the Hashemite dynasty in Iraq until it was deposed in 1958 (Hinnebusch 2014, 9). From a geopolitical perspective, Iraq's quasi-landlocked geography makes Syria of vital importance. Iraq's oil export through Syria to the Mediterranean made Iraq almost always inclined to intervene in Syria's internal politics in the postindependence era, naturally favoring friendly governments in Damascus.

With the collapse of the Ottoman Empire and the emergence of the modern Middle East state system, new rivalries were created and old ones revived. In the interwar period, borders between countries of the region were drawn by the European colonial powers. Because the borders were drawn arbitrarily, border disputes between neighbors became commonplace. Importantly, the Shatt el-Arab waterway became a key bone of contention between Iran and Iraq.[2] Yet British influence in the two countries, which continued after World War II, helped Iran and Iraq sign a treaty in 1937 that settled the long-standing dispute, which dated back to the Ottoman-Persian wars of the sixteenth and seventeenth centuries over the control of Iraq. In 1938 Iran and Iraq joined the Saadabad Treaty, a nonaggression pact signed also by Turkey and Afghanistan (Bakhash 2004, 11). The treaty survived the Second World War. With the beginning of the Cold War, Iraq and Iran found themselves part of the Western strategies to contain communism.

To contain the Soviet Union and prevent it from reaching the strategically important oil resources of the Gulf, the United States tried to establish pro-Western regional security systems. Different schemes were contemplated to construct a "northern tier" alliance to isolate the Soviet Union (Rustow 1956, 280–81).[3] Attempts were made to establish a Middle East command—a British idea—to encircle the Soviet Union (Acheson 1969, 562–68). The plan was abandoned in favor of another scheme: the Middle East Defense Organization (Saunders 1996, 23–24). Later efforts resulted in the establishment of the Baghdad Pact.

Iran and Iraq joined the Baghdad Pact, alongside Turkey and Pakistan, to prevent communist infiltration into the Middle East. Syria, which began to associate itself closely with the Soviet Union after the establishment of the state of Israel in 1948, and particularly after the collapse of the pro-West military regime of Col. Adib Shishakli in 1954, stood against the Baghdad Pact and joined Egypt in a Soviet-backed effort to undermine it. Sandwiched between two Baghdad Pact members (Iraq and Turkey) and with an increasingly belligerent Israel, vulnerable Syria turned to Egypt for support. Syrian-Egyptian unity was declared in February 1958, and the United Arab Republic (UAR) was established, turning the heat on the Baghdad Pact (Seale 1965, 186–237). Fearing the ramifications of Syrian-Egyptian unity, King Faisal II of Iraq visited Tehran to strengthen ties with his ally in the Baghdad Pact (Goodarzi 2008, 14). Yet a few months later, leftists and pan-Arab nationalist officers, led by Gen. Abdulkarim Qassim, inspired by Nasser's Egypt and emboldened by the Syria-Egypt unity, overthrew the Iraqi monarchy and pulled Iraq out of the Baghdad Pact.

THE FIRST SHOCK: THE 1958 IRAQI REVOLUTION

The July 1958 revolution marked the first major shock with significant impact on the Iraq-Iran-Syria triangle. It deposed the pro-West conservative monarchy in Baghdad and set the stage for several subsequent military governments that ruled Iraq until 2003, with diverse impacts on the triadic relationship. The 1958 revolution took Iraq out of the Western camp and placed it in the Soviet bloc; moreover, it ended the alliance with Iran and brought Iraq closer to Syria's anti-Western stand.[4] When Iraq changed its Cold War alignments, territorial disputes, ideological differences, and cultural dissimilarities surfaced between it and Iran. In their rivalry the two countries supported Kurdish separatists against one another.

In Syria (at the time part of the UAR under Nasser's leadership), the 1958 revolution was initially hailed as a victory against the West and its security schemes. Yet relations with the government of General Qassim deteriorated shortly afterward. Ideological antipathy between Nasser's Pan-Arabism and Qassim's pro-communist polices was key to the conflict. Competition for Arab leadership also resumed between Cairo and Baghdad after a short thaw following the fall of the Iraqi monarchy.

The conflict with Israel was always of paramount importance for Syria. To alleviate its security dilemma, between the establishment of the state of Israel in 1948 and the 1979 Iranian Revolution, Syria sought alliance with either Egypt or Iraq. Vacillating between Egypt and Iraq was Syria's strategy to ward off Israel's threat; it also reflected a balancing act between two regional powers vying to control Syria and win Arab leadership (Seale 1965).

Following the collapse of the Qassim government in Iraq and the ascendance of the pro-Nasser officers to power in 1963, relations between Syria and Iraq improved again. Yet they turned particularly sour when the Ba'ath Party assumed power in Baghdad in 1968. It had already been ruling Syria since 1963.

The 1968 coup was the latest episode in a series of coups that ripped through the Iraqi military after it had seized power in 1958. The 1968 coup deposed the pro-Nasser government (the Aref brothers) and brought to power Ba'athist officers, establishing a three-decade-long Iraqi rivalry with Syria. Although the coup did not change Iraq's international alignment, ideological enmity with the Ba'ath regime in Damascus (another ally of the Soviet Union) led to increasing tension between Syria and Iraq. The two governments, each claiming to be representing the authentic Ba'ath ideology, sought to unseat and destabilize one another. Hence, Syria supported Kurdish forces in the north of Iraq against the central government in Baghdad, whereas Iraq backed the Muslim Brotherhood's attempt to overthrow the Syrian regime, starting from the mid-1970s until the defeat of the group in Hama, Syria, in early 1982. Iraq also opposed Syria's military intervention in Lebanon's civil war, which started in 1975 (Kienle 1991).

Similarly, the 1968 seizure of power in Iraq by Ba'athist officers led to further deterioration in the relationship with Iran, as the Ba'ath leadership was eager to demonstrate its pan-Arab identity. Given the development of socialism at home, anti-Western positions in foreign policy, a revolutionary rhetoric directed against the pro-US regimes in the region, and a close military and economic relationship with the Soviet Union, Ba'athist Iraq became a source of great concern for Iran (Marr 2012, 144–46).

Following the British withdrawal from the Gulf in 1971 and the signing of the Iraqi-Soviet Treaty of Friendship in April 1972, security of the Gulf became a major concern for the United States (Smolansky and Smolansky 1991, 16–18). Overwhelmed by the Vietnam War, the United States adopted the "Twin Pillar" policy, wherein it assigned Iran and Saudi Arabia the task of maintaining security in the Gulf (Middle East Research and

Information Project 1972, 3–8; Acharya 1989). Although the rivalry relationship between Iran and Saudi Arabia was a part of regional dynamics, Iraq's revolutionary rhetoric brought Iran closer to the conservative Arab Gulf monarchies in line with the Cold War divide (Fürtig 2007).

Following Iran's declaration that the 1937 treaty regarding the rights of access along the Shatt el-Arab waterway must be renegotiated on the basis of the thalweg principle (the median, deepwater line), the first serious crisis between Iraq and Iran broke out in early 1969. Baghdad informed Tehran that, since the Shatt el-Arab waterway was Iraqi territory, Iranian ships must lower their flags and Iranian naval personnel on board must leave the ships during their passage through the waterway (Bakhash 2004, 13).

A second crisis erupted over Iran's claim to the three Gulf islands: the two Tunbs and Abu Musa. The islands were also claimed, respectively, by Ras al-Khaimah and Sharjah (two of the seven emirates that form the United Arab Emirates today). Considering the islands critical for securing the Strait of Hormuz, through which all shipping to Iran's main commercial and oil ports pass, a more assertive Iran started to press its claims strongly when the British announced their intention to withdraw from the Gulf in 1968. Before the British military withdrawal was completed in 1971, Iran seized the islands (Al-Mazrouei 2015, 1–3). Since the occupation of the islands would put Iran in full control of the Strait of Hormuz, through which Iraq exported a sizable amount of its oil, Iraq opposed the Iranian move. Therefore, the Iraqi government broke diplomatic relations with both Iran and Britain and revived the claim to Khuzestan. The Iraqi government lent support to a front fighting for the liberation of Khuzestan (a predominantly Arab-populated region in southwestern Iran). In response, Iran backed an attempted coup to overthrow the regime of Iraq's president Ahmad Hassan al-Bakr. Iraq expelled the Iranian ambassador in retaliation, closed Iranian consulates in three cities and deported thousands of Iranians (Bakhash 2004, 22). Iraq also allowed Islamic and leftist opponents of the Shah to operate from Iraqi soil, accusing Iran of supporting Iraqi Kurds (M. M. Milani 2006, 566).

Following the 1958 revolution, the Kurdish issue became a key factor in the rivalry relationship between Iran and Iraq. The growing Kurdish aspirations for autonomy and statehood following the fall of the monarchy started to pose a serious challenge for the Iraqi government. Iran took advantage and began aiding Iraqi Kurds. Both the Iranian government and Iraqi Kurds were alarmed by the Iraqi-Syrian-Egyptian unity talks in 1965 (Gibson 2013, 149). Therefore, Tehran increased its military support for Mustafa Barzani, leader of the Iraqi Kurds. Following the failure of the 1970 autonomy agreement between the central government in Baghdad and Barzani, Iran, alongside Israel and the United States, increased financial and military assistance for the Iraqi Kurds (Bakhash 2004, 24).

By 1975 the Iraqi government concluded that the Kurdish war for independence and Iranian involvement posed serious threats to its survival and decided to neutralize Iran. Negotiations between the two countries finally concluded with an agreement that was signed by the Shah of Iran and Iraq's vice president, Saddam Hussein, in Algiers in March 1975 (Abdulghani 2011, 152). The agreement gave Iran what it had long sought: half of the Shatt el-Arab waterway. In return Iran agreed to end support for the Kurdish insurgency (Marr 2012, 152–57). The Kurdish rebellion collapsed soon afterward, and rivalry halted between Iran and Iraq. The Algiers Agreement led to a period of cooperation between the two countries. Saddam Hussein visited Tehran, and the two countries signed several agreements to improve commercial and cultural ties. Alongside the establishment of direct flights between Baghdad and Tehran, the two countries also coordinated their oil policies in Organization of the Petroleum Exporting Countries (OPEC), which favored higher oil prices (M. M. Milani 2006, 569).

Syria was not happy with these developments, however. The Algiers Agreement gave the rival Iraqi government breathing space at the same time that the Shah's relations with Israel were evolving. In addition, the thaw between Iraq and Iran had direct impacts on the Syrian economy. Having secured its access to the Gulf, Iraq informed Syria that it would cease to use the trans-Syria pipeline to export its oil—a decision that brought huge financial losses to Syria. Syria, in response, decided to aid the opposition to the Iraqi government. In fact, after the Algiers Agreement, Syria replaced Iran as the main backer of the Kurdish rebellion in northern Iraq (Charbel 1998, 14).

The deteriorating relationship with Iraq prompted Syria's president, Hafez al-Assad, to undertake his first state visit to Iran in December 1975. He tried to halt the steady improvement in the relationship between Iran and Iraq and establish better ties with the Shah, notwithstanding their different regional and international alignments (Keynoush 2016, 92). Clearly, regional rivalry in this three-way relationship superseded international alignments and hence marginalized the structural constraints of the international system, that is, the Cold War divide. Assad's efforts did not pay dividends, however. The Shah decided to respect the Algiers accord and continued to develop relations with Iraq. The Shah also refused a Syrian request to convince the United States to adopt a comprehensive approach toward resolving the Arab-Israeli conflict instead of supporting a unilateral peace treaty between Egypt and Israel (Goodarzi 2008, 16). Assad's failed endeavors with the Shah prompted him to host Iranian dissidents opposed to the Shah, including Kurdish separatists and anti-Shah Shi'ite clerics. The Iran-Iraq détente prompted Damascus to step up its support for the Iraqi and Iranian opposition. Syria, meanwhile, aligned with Jordan to balance against Israel as Egypt was drifting away from the Arab camp.

Relations between Iraq and Iran continued to develop as the Shah's regime was threatened by a popular revolutionary movement in 1978. When Ayatollah Khomeini, residing in the holy Shi'ite Iraqi city of Najaf, emerged as the leader of the revolutionary movement, the Shah requested his deportation (Goodarzi 2008, 16). Syria was one of the few countries that offered to grant Khomeini asylum when Saddam Hussein expelled him from Iraq in October 1978 (von Maltzahn 2013, 25). Yet four months after his deportation, Khomeini returned to Iran, deposed the Shah, and established an Islamic republic against which Saddam Hussein would in September 1980 start a war that would last for eight years (Karsh 2002, 6–10).

Toward the end of this period, it was clear that the 1958 revolution, the removal of the monarchy, and the establishment of the Iraqi republic had profoundly altered the

Iran-Iraq-Syria relationship. It changed Iraq's international alignment in the Cold War and affected its relationship with its neighbors too. Initially, the revolution brought Iraq closer to pro-Soviet Syria and away from pro-US Iran. At a later stage, however, the opposite happened. One can in fact recognize two phases in this period: 1958–68 and 1968–79. In the first phase, Iran-Iraq rivalry increased, reaching a fever pitch toward the beginning of the second phase, and Syria-Iraq relations improved. In the second phase, by contrast, the Syria-Iraq rivalry increased with the ascendance of the Ba'ath Party to power in Iraq, whereas relations between Iraq and Iran hugely improved toward the end of this period.

It is also important to note that while Iraq's relations with both Syria and Iran were greatly affected by the 1958 revolution, relations between Iran and Syria remained largely unchanged until the 1979 Iranian Revolution. Except for a short thaw in 1975, when Hafez al-Assad tried to slow the pace of rapprochement between Iraq and Iran following the Algiers Agreement, relations between Syria and Iran remained cold.

THE SECOND SHOCK: THE 1979 IRAN REVOLUTION

After more than a year of civil strife and street protests, Shah Mohammad Reza Pahlavi left Iran for exile in January 1979. Less than a month later Ayatollah Khomeini arrived in Tehran, abolished the monarchy, and declared an Islamic republic. Raising "Neither East, nor West" as a slogan of the new regime, the Iranian Revolution changed Iran's international alignment and took the country out of the Cold War divide. The revolution also affected Iran's relationship with the other two parties of the triadic rivalry. Taking place at focal regional and international contexts, the Iranian Revolution contributed to changing the political landscape of the Middle East and its alignments.

In 1978 Egypt signed the Camp David Accords with Israel, ending three decades of hostility. Fearing being left alone to face Israel's superior military power, Syria turned eastward and sought rapprochement with rival Iraq. An Arab summit was held in Baghdad to isolate Egypt's unilateral move, and negotiations to unite the two branches of the Ba'ath Party in Syria and Iraq commenced soon afterward. In October 1978 a joint national memorandum of action was signed, paving the way for military and eventually political unity. In June 1979 Syrian president Hafez al-Assad and Iraqi president Ahmad Hassan al-Bakr agreed to establish one leadership to rule the two countries. Yet unity efforts were shelved as a result of internal discord within the Iraqi leadership. This discord led to the ouster of Iraqi president al-Bakr and the ascendance of his vice president, Saddam Hussein. Saddam accused Hafez al-Assad of conspiring to overthrow the regime in Baghdad and therefore cut diplomatic ties with Damascus. As tension was building between Iraq and Syria, the Iranian Revolution presented an alternative partnership for Syria, which had already started to explore avenues for cooperation with the new regime in Tehran.

Unlike Iraq, Syria welcomed the fall of the Shah and was the first country in the region and the third globally, after the Soviet Union and Pakistan, to recognize the new Iranian government. The 1979 Iranian Revolution had in fact canceled the impact of the

Egyptian-Israeli peace agreement on Syria-Iraq relations, returning them to square one. The Iranian Revolution was instrumental in reshaping the rivalry relationship between these three countries. It presented Syria with an opportunity to redress the balance of power vis-à-vis both Israel after the exit of Egypt from the Arab camp and Iraq after the failed unity attempt. The Iranian Revolution may have even made Syria less desperate to repair relations with Iraq after the Egyptian-Israeli peace treaty.

Given the failed Iraq-Syria unity attempt and Iraq's open opposition to the Iranian Revolution, animosity toward Iraq became the key factor that brought Syria and Iran closer together, thus cementing the most enduring regional alliance in the modern history of the Middle East. Indeed, "since full diplomatic relations were established in 1946, a striking and recurrent feature of modern Syrian-Iranian relations has been that the tightening or loosening of bilateral ties depends largely on the state at the time of Syria-Iraqi and Iranian-Iraqi relations" (Goodarzi 2008, 14). Hence, rapprochement between Syria and Iran was accompanied with marked deterioration in Iran and Syria's relationship with Iraq. While Iran encouraged Iraqi Shi'ites to defy the government in Baghdad, Iraq encouraged forces, particularly Arab and Kurdish minorities in Iran, to rise against the new regime in Tehran (Karsh 2002, 13).

In the final years of the Shah regime, relations between Iraq and Iran markedly improved, whereas Iraq's and Iran's relations with Syria deteriorated. In late 1978 Iraq became increasingly concerned about the opposition movement in Iran having assumed a religious character; the ruling Ba'ath Party was wary of the prospect of a Shi'ite revival and its implications for Iraq's Shi'ite population. Iraq also saw the regime change in Iran as a major threat to its security that could spark domestic unrest and destabilize the Gulf region. Syria, by contrast, regarded the Islamic Republic of Iran as a potential ally against both Israel and Iraq.

Indeed, over the past half century Iran was a key factor in defining the relationship between Syria and Iraq. It can even be argued that the failure of the 1979 Syrian-Iraqi attempt at unity can be partially attributed to the success of the Iranian Revolution. Syria saw post-Shah Iran as an alternative should unity with Iraq fail. From this angle the Iranian Revolution may have directly contributed to the failure of rapprochement between Syria and Iraq. The exit of Egypt from the Arab camp brought Syria closer to Iraq while the Iranian Revolution pulled Syria away from Iraq. This is how regional dynamics operated at the time.

Ideology played no role in this triadic relationship. Just like its sister Iraqi Ba'ath regime, the Syrian regime was secular, pan-Arab, and socialist and opposed Islamic tendencies in general. Iran, in contrast, was a revolutionary, pan-Islamic Shi'ite theocracy with mild Persian nationalistic views. In fact, ideological affinity produced exactly the opposite effect (Walt 1987, 181–85). Since the two wings of the Ba'ath Party ascended to power in Syria and in Iraq in 1963 and 1968, respectively, rivalry had become the norm between the two Arab countries. Although the two Ba'athist regimes viewed Iran under the Shah more or less from the same prism—an enemy or a friend of the enemy—Syria was not unhappy to see Iran's relations with Iraq deteriorate in the late 1960s. When Iraqi-Iranian relations improved after the 1975 Algiers Agreement, Syrian-Iranian relations deteriorated over the same period. In the 1970s Syria provided safe haven for the Shah's opponents, while Iraq expelled the Shah's opponents. Assad welcomed the Shi'ite awakening in the Middle East after the Iranian Revolution; Baghdad feared that Iran would incite the restive Shi'ite population in southern Iraq to rebel against it.

Fearing that the new regime in Tehran would take an "export the revolution" approach that could affect Iraq's sizable Shi'ite population, Iraq took advantage of the postrevolution internal conflict and chaos in Iran and declared war in September 1980. Syria denounced the Iraqi decision and expressed solidarity with Tehran. It was the only Arab country that declared its backing for Iran's war effort against Iraq (followed later by Libya). Furthermore, Syria helped circumvent the American-led arms embargo against Tehran and served as a conduit for arms shipments to Iran from different sources (M. M. Milani 2013, 80).

Throughout the eight-year war Syria was an exceptionally valuable ally for the embattled Iranian regime. Relations with Syria, from an Iranian perspective, were extremely important to prevent the Iraq-Iran War from turning into an Arab-Persian conflict or a Sunni-Shi'ite war. It indeed made it difficult for the Arab League to take any sort of collective action against Iran. Syria closed the Iraqi Kirkuk-Banyas oil pipeline, depriving Saddam Hussein of an important financial resource at a time of war. As a result, the Arab Gulf states, which supported Iraq, cut aid to Syria. Despite the war and sanctions, Iran was willing to compensate. It provided Syria with crude oil shipments for most of the first half of the 1980s (M. M. Milani 2013, 80).

Indeed, rivalry with Iraq was a key—but not the only—factor in cementing the Syria-Iran alliance, which endured for decades despite major ideological and political differences. Israel's increasing belligerence after securing its southern borders with Egypt, following the signing of the 1979 peace treaty, was a major concern for Syria too (Seale 1989, 353). It climaxed with the Israeli invasion of Lebanon and the occupation of Beirut in 1982. Syria tried to get Iran to compensate for the absence of Egypt, help redress the balance of power, and deter Israel from taking further hostile actions. Following the Israeli invasion, Iran sent a brigade of its Iranian Revolutionary Guard Corps (IRGC) to Lebanon to support the Syrian army stationed there since 1976. Syria and Iran also cooperated in forcing the US-led multinational forces to withdraw from Lebanon following the bombing of the US Marine headquarters in Beirut in 1983 (M. M. Milani 2013, 81). Iran also proved helpful in strengthening Syria's hand among Lebanese Shi'ite, whose role was on the rise. The support of the religiously oriented Iranian regime in the confrontation between the Syrian government and the Muslim Brotherhood in the early 1980s was also important. Syria was being viewed by Iran as a primary partner in the Arab-Israeli conflict, offering Iran a symbolic but important political role in the central cause of the region.

Between 1985 and 1988 Syria-Iran relations faced some difficulties when Iran tried to pursue certain policies in Lebanon that countered Syrian interests. Yet these problems did not lead to the breakup of the alliance but to a new understanding, wherein "Syrian interests took precedence in the Arab-Israeli arena, while in the Gulf region, Damascus would defer to Tehran" (Goodarzi 2013, 36). The end of the Iran-Iraq War in 1988 did not also decrease the need for the Syria-Iran alliance; to the contrary, it strengthened it. In fact, Iraq emerged from its war with Iran more ambitious to play a leading regional role than it had been before. Syria and Iran recognized the need to contain and tame these ambitions.

When Iraq invaded Kuwait in 1990, Syria supported the American-led coalition to expel Iraq from Kuwait. Iran did not cooperate with Washington but was not unhappy to see Iraq defeated in the 1991 Gulf War. Following the expulsion of Iraq from Kuwait, Iraq and Iran became subject to the "dual containment" policy, devised by the Clinton administration to keep the two countries at bay and away from disrupting the American agenda, which focused almost exclusively on establishing a Pax Americana in the Middle East through an Arab-Israeli peace agreement.[5]

As for Syria, which had lost its Cold War patron (the Soviet Union), the Iraqi invasion of Kuwait presented an opportunity to change its international alignments without having to pay a big price, as the Eastern European countries had. It joined the US-led coalition and sent troops to Saudi Arabia to take part in Operation Desert Storm to expel Iraq from Kuwait. Syria also participated in the American-sponsored Madrid Peace Conference. Having accepted American hegemony, Syria saw its need for an alliance with Iran decrease but not vanish. Syria established stronger ties with pro-American allies, particularly Egypt and Saudi Arabia, but kept strong ties with Iran too. Iran also tried to improve its ties with its Gulf neighbors.

Syria's need for an alliance with Iran was reduced with the defeat and containment of Iraq following the 1991 war and the American-sponsored Middle East peace process, which alleviated the Israeli threat. Despite two Israeli offensives against Hezbollah in 1993 and 1996, the situation remained unchanged. Syria continued to believe in the American-sponsored peace process until the ascendance of the Israeli Right to power in 1996. As a sign of frustration with American-led peace efforts to recover its occupied territories, Syria turned to Iraq, and so a slow rapprochement process began with Baghdad toward the end of the 1990s. Syria and Iran also reinvigorated their alliance in response to the 1996 Turkish-Israeli military alliance, which tried to isolate Iran and "cow Syria into submission" (Wallish 2013, 112).

Toward the end of this period, the nature of the relationship among the three countries shifted away from where it started at the beginning of the second shock—the Iranian Revolution. Syria's relations with Iraq changed from conflict in the early 1980s to cooperation in late 1990s, and the relationship between Iran and Iraq moved from amity before the Iranian Revolution to full-fledged enmity after it.

It is important to note also that unlike the 1958 revolution in Iraq, which affected Iraq's relations with both Syria and Iran but left no real impact on the Syria-Iran relationship, the 1979 Iranian Revolution transformed the nature of the triadic relationship, leading to the establishment of the Syria-Iran alliance. Relations between Iraq and Iran, on the other hand, turned from amity under the Shah's regime to enmity under the Islamic Republic. The Syrian-Iraq relationship remained one of rivalry and tension. Toward the end of this period, however, Syria's disillusionment with the American-led peace process and the lack of tangible economic rewards made it rethink its regional alignments. It took the unusual step and turned toward rival Iraq.

THE THIRD SHOCK: THE 2003 INVASION OF IRAQ

The failure of the US-sponsored peace talks in ending the state of war with Israel, coupled with increasing economic difficulties, led Damascus to explore new avenues with Iraq. Starting in 1997, relations between the two countries began to improve, but it was the departure of Hafez al-Assad and the ascendance of his son Bashar in 2000 that accelerated the process. Lacking the personal and ideological animosity of his father toward Saddam Hussein, Bashar was more open to mending fences with Iraq. Syria ignored UN sanctions on Iraq and resumed economic cooperation with the besieged Iraqi government (Aljabiri 2007, 18). These policies generated popularity for the new Syrian leader, who sought to establish legitimacy apart from his father's policies and alignments (International Crisis Group [ICG] 2004, 18). In this regard, Bashar showed more hostility toward American policies than his father ever did, and his appreciation of the importance of the relationship with Iran was more modest too. The 2003 American invasion of Iraq revealed a deep schism between the two long-standing allies. Iran supported American efforts to remove the regime of Iraqi president Saddam Hussein, whereas Syria opposed the American invasion and was accused by the George W. Bush administration of supporting Iraq's war efforts (*Guardian* 2003). From 2003 to 2010 Syria backed the Sunni opposition to the American occupation of Iraq and the Iran-backed Shi'ite government in Baghdad.

The US invasion of Iraq was a major shock to the Iran-Iraq-Syria relationship. It led to reshuffling the alignments and shifting the policies of the three countries. In a repetition of the different views and interests that prevailed at the time of the removal of the Shah's regime in 1979, Syria and Iran saw the US invasion of Iraq differently. For Iran, the US invasion was an opportunity to remove a major foe with whom it had fought an eight-year war. Iran was, in fact, the major beneficiary from the US military intervention in Iraq. With the fall of the Iraqi regime, the Iran-based Shi'ite opposition groups, acting on instruction from Tehran, rushed to fill the vacuum. Iran became, therefore, the major power broker in Iraq. Its newly empowered Shi'ite allies, some of whom had pledged allegiance to the supreme leader in Tehran, moved quickly to replace the secular pan-Arab nationalist regime of Saddam Hussein.

By contrast, Syria, which had established better relations with Iraq in the last few years of Saddam's regime, saw its removal as a major loss. It also regarded the US invasion of Iraq as a major threat to its security and economic interests. Hence, unlike its position in 1991, when it supported the American-led war to liberate Kuwait from Iraq, Syria opposed the US invasion of Iraq. In early April 2003 Syrian president Bashar al-Assad expressed hopes that the invasion of Iraq would fail and that "popular resistance" would ensue and prevent the United States from controlling the country (*As-Safir* 2003; ICG 2004, 18). As for the choice Syria would make, then–foreign minister Farouk al-Shara' told the Syrian parliament that his country had chosen to stand with "the Iraqi people and international legitimacy," which the United States and Britain discredited by invading Iraq without a UN mandate (Kabalan 2009, 32). Syria went a step further when its Grand Mufti, Ahmad Kaftaru, acting on government instructions, issued a statement calling on all Muslims to perform jihad against the American invasion of Iraq (Macfarquhar 2003).

Syria's position on the American invasion of Iraq was dictated by economic and geopolitical terms directly related to its security dilemma. The ascendance of Benjamin Netanyahu to power in Israel in 1996 put an end to Syria's endeavors to recover the occupied Golan Heights through negotiations. Protracted economic crises—as Arab financial aid dried up and international oil prices plummeted—also contributed to Syria's vulnerability. As a result, Syria started looking for other ways to pursue its interests, and Iraq was an option. By 1997 Syria and Iraq had started to see cooperation, rather than conflict, as a means to serve their interests. Syrian president Hafez al-Assad started cautiously developing relations with his lifelong rival, Saddam Hussein. Syria used the UN-authorized Oil-for-Food Program to develop ties and normalize relations with Iraq. The ascendance of Assad's son Bashar to power in 2000 hastened this process. Bashar tried to develop political and economic ties with Iraq but was careful not to provoke the United States. The September 11 attacks provided Syria with an opportunity to proceed with a quid pro quo policy: Damascus cooperated in the war on terrorism and supplied information about Islamic activists, hoping that Washington would in return condone the smuggling of Iraqi oil through Syria. This tacit understanding did not last long as the Taliban regime crumbled quickly in Afghanistan and Iraq became the focus of American policy in the region (ICG 2004, 2–3).

From Syrian political and strategic perspectives, an American-backed government in Baghdad would place Damascus between two hostile powers: Israel and a pro-US Iraq. Bashar al-Assad also feared that he could be next on America's hit list, and Washington made no effort to assure Damascus to the contrary (ICG 2004, 5). Moreover, Syria was profiting economically from relations with Iraq. Between October 2000 and November 2002, Syria received 200,000 barrels of Iraqi oil daily at reduced prices; this allowed Syria to increase its share in the oil market and generate $1 billion annually of a much-needed hard currency (ICG 2004, 16). Right after the fall of Baghdad in 2003, the American army cut oil supplies to Syria; the advent of an unfriendly regime in Iraq deprived Syria of an important economic privilege at a time when it was most needed (ABC News 2003).

The Syrian government could not challenge a near national consensus in opposition to the American invasion of Iraq, which was seen as an imperial crusade to control Arab resources that had nothing to do with alleged Iraqi acquisition of weapons of mass destruction (ICG 2004, 17–18). Syria not only opposed the American invasion but also aided armed opposition to it. Syria's support for the Sunni insurgency and efforts to shelter elements of the former Iraqi regime made relations with the post-Saddam Iraqi regime tense right from the start. The pro-Iran Iraqi government repeatedly accused Damascus of supporting the Sunni insurgency and condoning the transit of foreign fighters into Iraq to target the US Army and Iraqi security forces. The Shi'ite-dominated Iraqi government was also unhappy with Syria's pressure to reconsider the de-Ba'athification law, which excluded major Sunni opposition powers and elements from the former regime from the political process. Syria was clearly unhappy with the rise of pro-Iran, Shi'ite religious parties. It sought to include secular Sunni forces in the political process so that it could balance Iran's rising influence in Iraq (Hinnebusch 2014, 20).

As American pressure mounted, Syria started to show signs of flexibility toward the Iraqi government. In the autumn of 2005 Syria decided to reinforce its military presence on the Iraqi borders, deploying extra troops to stop would-be infiltrators from entering Iraq and joining the anti-American insurgency (Prados 2006, 8). In addition, Damascus allowed Iraqi candidates for the 2005 legislative elections to campaign among the 2 million Syria-based Iraqis (Katzman 2005). This was a clear departure from Syria's original policy, which opposed the American invasion and its effects. In 2006 Syria recognized the new Iraqi government and reestablished diplomatic relations with Baghdad (Tavernise 2006).

Syria's regional status was seriously damaged when it was forced to end its three-decade-old military presence in Lebanon following the assassination of former Lebanese prime minister Rafiq al-Hariri in February 2005. In addition to American pressure on Syria to tighten control over its permeable borders with Iraq, France, which regarded Hariri's assassination as a personal loss, joined the effort to destabilize the regime in Damascus. Syria was subject to a barrage of UN Security Council resolutions that almost put it in total isolation. The European Union froze the Association Agreement (which was initiated in October 2004 and went through six years of difficult negotiations). Moreover, except for the American-based Marathon Petroleum Company, most Western oil companies either were discouraged from investing in Syria's oil sector or—out fear of possible sanctions—sold their assets and left the country (*Al Hayat* 2005; Kabalan 2013, 35). Syria's reliance on Iran increased as a result.

The ascendance of the hard-liner Mahmoud Ahmadinejad to power in Tehran in the summer of 2005 was hence a welcome development in Damascus. Ahmadinejad's ascendance can be partially attributed to antagonistic American policies toward Iran. Following the September 11 attacks, Iran backed American efforts to overthrow the Taliban regime in Afghanistan. Instead of getting rewarded, Iran was made part of the "axis of evil," alongside Iraq and North Korea. Disillusionment about American policies, hence, contributed to the election loss of the reformers and the ascendance of the hard-liners, led by Ahmadinejad.

American animosity toward Syria and Iran brought the old couple back together. Ahmadinejad's supportive statements also compensated Syria for the lack of sympathy in the Arab world. Bashar al-Assad was the first foreign leader to visit Ahmadinejad in Tehran in August 2005—just a few days after he assumed power; Ahmadinejad returned the visit, making Damascus his first foreign destination in January 2006. Political, economic, military, and other agreements were signed between the two countries, and Iranian investments in Syria increased (von Maltzahn 2013, 50).

Under Ahmadinejad, Syrian-Iranian relations gained strategic importance, but that was mainly due to increasing Western pressure to "change the behavior" of the two regimes. Indeed, the Syrian-Iranian alliance was purely defensive and sought to minimize risks and maximize gains in an inhospitable regional environment. Yet while Syria's regional standing was improving, Iran's influence was on the rise, at times taking advantage of Syria's own relative weakness and vulnerability. In Lebanon, for example, Iran took advantage of the Syrian withdrawal in 2005 to enhance its position in that country. For Iran, the Syrian army was the only military power that could, theoretically at least, disarm its ally—Hezbollah—should Damascus's interest deem that necessary. Iran thought that this possibility might increase in the event of a peace treaty between Syria and Israel. In fact, following the withdrawal of the Syrian army, Iran replaced Syria as the major power broker in Lebanon; Iran's Lebanese ally, Hezbollah, became the major military and political powerhouse in the country. The July 2006 Israel-Hezbollah confrontation signified the importance of this alliance and Iran's increasing weight in Middle East politics. The war contributed to strengthening Iran's influence in Lebanon and throughout the region, and Hezbollah became an important element in the military balance of power between Iran and Israel.

In Iraq too, following the American invasion, Syria watched Iran's influence growing at a time when Syria's role in Iraq was diminishing. Apart from their common interests in preventing the establishment of a Kurdish state in northern Iraq and keeping the United States busy fighting the Iraqi insurgency so that it did not turn against them, Syria and Iran had little in common in that country. They supported different political and sectarian factions and developed contrasting views about the future of Iraq.

Syria's concerns about Iran's rising influence from both its eastern and western flanks prompted it to strengthen relations with Turkey. Given the historic competition between Tehran and Ankara for regional influence, strengthening ties with Turkey was an important tool for Syria's balancing act (ICG 2009, 5–7). Given Turkey's position as a major regional Sunni power, Syria-Turkey relations were also instrumental in warding off domestic criticism that the regime in Damascus had become part of a Shi'ite axis that stretched from Tehran to South Lebanon.

In addition, Turkey played an important role in reviving the Syria-Israel peace talks, something Iran strongly opposed. When the Bush administration called for the Middle East peace meeting in Annapolis in November 2007, Iran was not invited. Iran attacked the meeting and urged Syria not to attend. In a Friday sermon the supreme leader, Ali Khamenei, predicted that conferences such as the one in Annapolis "are destined to failure even before they start." He expressed regret that so many countries in the region had decided to attend the conference. "What results could they obtain from such conferences in the last 60 years that they want to repeat it now?" Khamenei concluded (Kabalan 2007). Iran went a step further in its opposition to the Annapolis meeting. It proposed a rival conference that would bring together all the anti-American actors in the region and form a united resistance front against Washington's policies. The plan did not work out for the Iranians, however. Palestinian rejectionist groups—most of them based in Damascus—shunned the Iranian invitation, under instruction from Damascus, which had already accepted an American invitation to attend the meeting in Annapolis (Kabalan 2007).

Despite differences on several issues, Syria remained committed to its alliance with Iran given the uncertain prospects of its relations with the United States and the Arab world. At this stage Syria was acting as a junior partner in the alliance relationship with Iran. It therefore sought to manage its foreign relations so that it could keep its independence via-à-vis an increasingly powerful Iranian partner—by balancing with Turkey, on one hand, while trying to fend off threats to its national security by keeping close relations with Iran, on the other hand (ICG 2009, 5–7).

While the American invasion of Iraq brought Iran and Iraq into a full-fledged alliance, Syria's relationship with Iraq deteriorated markedly. Syria opposed the post-invasion Iraqi regime and supported the Sunni opposition. It was extremely difficult for Syria to cope with the economic loss and the strategic shift resulting from the invasion of Iraq, which made the United States a neighboring Middle East power. Syria's relations with Iraq remained difficult almost until the outbreak of the Syrian uprising / civil war in early 2011.

Syria's relations with Iran were also affected by the 2003 American invasion. Around that time clear divergence could be noted in the interests of Syria and Iran on a number of issues, including Iraq, Lebanon, and the Middle East peace process. Yet American pressure and its weakening regional position pushed Syria back into Iran's arms, this time as junior partner. To preserve its independence vis-à-vis Iran's rising regional power, Syria opted for developing its political and economic ties with Turkey.

In sum, we can delineate four phases in the Syrian-Iranian alliance relationship. In the first phase, which lasted throughout the Iran-Iraq War (1980–88), Syria had the upper hand whereas Iran was isolated and vulnerable. During the second phase (1988–2003), the two allies were more or less on an equal footing. In the third phase (2003–11), Syria became the junior partner in this alliance. In the last phase, which started in 2011, Syria almost lost independence and became completely dependent on Iran for survival.

THE FOURTH SHOCK: THE 2011 SYRIAN UPRISING / CIVIL WAR

Starting in 2011, Syria, Iran, and Iraq—for the first time since the emergence of the modern state system in the Middle East following World War I—forged a tripartite regional alliance. The main reason for this unique development was the breakout of the Syrian revolt against the regime of President Bashar al-Assad. The changing regional dynamics resulting mainly from the American withdrawal from Iraq, and the ensuing shift in the threat perceptions of the ruling elites in the three countries, led to this new alignment.

For most of the eight-year-long American occupation of Iraq (2003–11), relations between Syria and Iraq were at an all-time low. Iraqi officials persistently accused Syria of working to undermine the stability of post-Saddam Iraq by providing easy access for Al Qaeda sympathizers to enter the country and support the Sunni insurgency. In fact, since day one of the American invasion, Syria had struggled to accommodate itself with the strategic shift, which made the United States a Middle Eastern power. Syria recognized the new regime and resumed diplomatic relations with Iraq only in 2006 but still did not improve bilateral relations, and Damascus did not send an ambassador to Baghdad until the summer of 2008. The Syrian ambassador was withdrawn the following year, however, when Iraqi prime minster Nouri al-Maliki accused Syria of responsibility for a wave of bombs that struck the heart of Baghdad in August 2009 (Arraf 2009). Charging that the Syrian government was harboring Ba'athist officers among the two million Iraqi refugees it hosted who—allegedly—planned the attacks, al-Maliki also called on the UN Security Council to establish an international tribunal to investigate Syria's behavior (Reuters 2009). Interestingly, it was Turkey, not Iran, which offered to mediate between Syria and Iraq on the crisis. Turkish foreign minister Ahmet Davutoğlu shuttled between the two capitals in early September 2009 to ease tension. Iran, which was concerned about the rapprochement between the new Obama administration and Damascus and the possible resumption of peace talks between Syria and Israel, seemed unbothered by blaming Syria for the bombings (Lynch 2009).

Relations between al-Maliki and al-Assad improved only after the 2010 general elections in Iraq. Al-Maliki whose pro-Iranian, Shi'ite-dominated coalition came in second in the elections, after the cross-sectarian coalition of the al-Iraqiya bloc, led by his rival, Iyad Allawi, needed the support of Damascus to form a coalition government with Sunni powers in order to keep the premiership post (Reuters 2010a). Fearing the possibility of Allawi, a close American ally, forming a government in Baghdad, Iran pressured al-Maliki to bury the hatchet with Syria. In October 2010 al-Maliki made a high-profile visit to Damascus: he offered oil and gas deals and a plan to reopen a pipeline linking Iraqi oil fields to a Syrian port on the Mediterranean. Syria agreed to support al-Maliki's bid for power, hence giving Tehran the upper hand over Iraq while leaving Syria with more say over Lebanon (Reuters 2010b).

Despite improvement the Syria-Iraq relationship did not undergo fundamental change and remained marred with suspicions and distrust. It was not until the outbreak of the 2011 Syrian revolt that the dynamic of the relationship radically changed. Fearing an anti-Iran Sunni rule in Syria that would help undermine its influence in Iraq, Iran rushed to support the regime of Bashar al-Assad. Iraq too believed that a victory of the pro-Saudi Sunni opposition forces in Syria would ultimately lead to its demise. Hence, the shock resulting from the Syrian revolt helped bring about a completely new realignment in the region.

Shortly after revolts in Syria broke out in the spring of 2011, Baghdad started to provide a safety net for the increasingly isolated Syrian regime, particularly in the Arab world. Unlike Saudi Arabia, Kuwait, and Qatar, which had called on al-Assad to step down, Nouri al-Maliki rejected calls for al-Assad to give up power. "We believe that Syria will be able to overcome its crisis through reforms," al-Maliki said (Reuters 2011). Iraq also supported the Syrian government in the Arab League, and following the US withdrawal from Iraq at the end of 2011, Iraq acted as a land route that connected the Syrian regime to its solid base of support in Iran (Schmidt and Ghazm 2011). The United States accused the al-Maliki government of allowing Iranian arms to be flown to the al-Assad regime through Iraqi airspace (Risen and Adnan 2012). Iraq also provided financial assistance to the embattled Syrian government. Baghdad hosted several delegations of Syrian officials and businessmen to discuss closer economic ties, including the construction of a gas pipeline that would run from Iran through Iraq to Syria (Warrick 2011).

Al-Maliki feared that a regime change in Damascus would embolden his Sunni opponents, who had openly expressed support for the protest movement in Syria (Spencer 2012). Following the withdrawal of the US troops in December 2011, sectarian tensions ran high in Iraq and were further fueled by the Syrian revolution, which started to take the shape of a Sunni uprising against the pro-Iranian and Alawite-dominated regime of Bashar al-Assad. Al-Maliki was already having trouble with his coalition partners, especially the Sunni political forces. Thus, he concluded that his interests lay with his former foe, Bashar al-Assad (al-Khoei 2013).

As a result of the new alignment, Damascus turned in some of the former Iraqi regime officials who had taken refuge in Syria following the fall of Baghdad in 2003. Al-Maliki had for years been asking for their extradition but to no avail. Others had been asked to leave. The anti-al-Maliki TV station, Al Raai, which had been airing from a location nearby Damascus, was also shut down (Kabalan 2012).

Strangled by Arab and European economic sanctions, Syria received billions of dollars in aid from the al-Maliki government (Schmidt and Ghazm 2011). Syrian exports to Iraq increased and exceeded $20 million daily in December 2011, meaning that Iraq was taking the lion's share of Syria's overall industrial products (Warrick 2011).

As the position of Syrian president Bashar al-Assad became increasingly untenable with the opposition gaining ground, economic and political support turned into military support too. As early as 2012 Iraqi Shi'ite militia started pouring into Syria to fight in support of al-Assad (Reuters 2012). The role of Iraqi militias hugely increased afterward and became, in conjunction with the Lebanese Hezbollah, the major foreign land force fighting in support of the Syrian regime (Hauslohner 2013). Al-Assad returned the favor to al-Maliki when his air force targeted Islamic State in Iraq and the Levant (ISIL) positions inside Iraq after the fall of Mosul in June 2014. In fact, Syria and Iraq acted as if they were fighting the same war against the same enemy (Black 2014).

Iran too threw its weight behind both Syria and Iraq after ISIL took control of huge swaths of Syrian and Iraqi territories in the summer of 2014. Both the IRGC Quds Force (IRGC-QF) and elements of the conventional IRGC Ground Forces (IRGC-GF), as well as several Iranian intelligence organizations, were dispatched to Syria and Iraq to train and advise Syrian and Iraqi forces in the fight against ISIL. In 2016 Iran went a step further and sent troops to support the regime of Bashar al-Assad. It was the first time Iran sent its regular army outside the country since the end of the Iran-Iraq War in 1988 (Qaidaari 2016).

Given the generations-old animosity between Syria and Iraq, and between Iraq and Iran, the new alignment stands in full contrast with the old pattern of the relationships among the three countries. The improved relations between the two Arab neighbors constitute today the cornerstone of a new regional alignment, which began to take shape following the outbreak of the Syrian uprising and the withdrawal of US forces from Iraq. In the new alignment, Damascus and Baghdad found themselves in one camp. Both are strong allies of Tehran. They both suspect that the Sunni Arab Gulf states, some of them in coordination with Turkey, are attempting to bring them down and shift the regional balance of power. In fact, the two Arab neighbors constitute today the cornerstone of the Iran-led axis.

The shock resulting from the Syrian conflict will most probably lead to far-reaching consequences, with more shifts and changes in regional and international alignments expected. The 2015 Russian military intervention in support of Bashar al-Assad; the emergence of an Israel–Arab Gulf states understanding, backed by the Trump administration, to counteract the Iran-led axis; and the Turkish-Russian-Iranian détente that emerged out of opposition to US policies are all likely to play out and produce different regional and international alignments in the coming months and years.

CONCLUSION

The origins of the Iran-Iraq-Syria rivalries date back to the end of World War I. Some of them are much older. Drivers of these rivalries include the rivalry structure of the international system and regional balances of power. Other drivers are bilateral, such as border disputes and disputes over natural resources. Hegemonic motives were also an important aspect of the triadic rivalries, with the larger country aspiring to dominate the smaller one in order from the largest to the smallest (Iran → Iraq → Syria).

These complex relationships, with their different drivers and aspects, provide a prime example of how internal and external shocks affect and shape alignments in a triadic rivalry context. For a variety of external and domestic factors, relations between these three countries have fluctuated sharply over the past half century within a pattern that pits two of them against the third.

A thorough examination of this triadic relationship shows that a shock in one of the countries almost always leads to a new alignment. A change of leadership usually brings new ruling elites with distinct ideological positions and worldviews and different threat perceptions. Yet whereas a shock almost certainly produces new alignments, realignment is not always triggered by a shock. It can also come as a result of a change in the threat perceptions of the ruling elite. The improvement in the relationship between Iran and Iraq after the signing of the Algiers Agreement in 1975 is one example. The rapprochement between Syria and Iraq in the late 1990s is another. These improvements came as a result of changing threat perceptions following the rise of the Israeli right and the failure of the peace process. What is unique about the Iran-Iraq-Syria rivalry relationship, however, is that any change of leadership or policies in one of the three parties will almost certainly affect the relationship with the other two in the three-way relationship. In other words, the nature of the relationship (amity or enmity) between two of the three actors is largely defined by their relationship with the third.

Since the collapse of the Ottoman Empire at the beginning of the twentieth century, the three countries balanced against each other in a triadic mode. The pattern has always been that two sides of the triangle would join forces to balance against the third, for example, Iran and Iraq versus Syria (the UAR) in the 1950s and Iran and Syria versus

Iraq in the 1980s. This tendency remained true as long as the threat was emanating from within the triangle. When the threat originated from outside it, the three powers joined forces and established a three-party alliance. This was the outcome resulting from the shock of the 2011 Syrian uprising, when Iraq and Iran, fearing that the Sunni Arab states and Turkey were attempting to change the balance of power against them, rushed to support the regime of Bashar al-Assad, forming the first alliance ever among the three countries.

Common threat perception led to this unique development in the three-party relationship. One should expect, therefore, that the moment the common external threat ceased to exist, the old dynamics likely would return. The junior party in the triadic relationship would most probably try to retain its independence vis-à-vis the senior ones. One should also expect that any new shock in one of the three countries would certainly lead to new alignment within the triadic relationship.

Finally, one can note that the last two shocks in the triadic relationship (the US invasion of Iraq and the Syrian revolt) have not only led to a change or possible change of leadership in Iraq and in Syria but have also affected the regional structure of the triadic relationship, leading to a completely new alignment. The structural settings, which influenced the dynamic of the Iran-Iraq-Syria relationship for almost half a century, have changed in the last decade and have hence produced different alignments. The Iran-Iraq-Syria axis is the outcome of this structural change. This outcome is likely to endure as long as the changes that produced it remain in place.

NOTES

1. Iran is four times larger than Iraq in terms of area and three times larger in terms of population.

2. Shatt el-Arab is formed by the confluence of the Euphrates and the Tigris in the town of al-Qaunah, south of Iraq. The southern end of the river constitutes the border between Iraq and Iran down to the mouth of the river as it discharges into the Gulf.

3. For more on the US concept of the northern tier security arrangement, see Yesilbursa (2001).

4. Iran responded by improving its ties with the Arab world's archenemy, Israel. As a non-Arab power on the edge of the Arab world, Israel too viewed Iran as a natural ally. After the Six-Day War Iran became Israel's main oil supplier. Iranian-Israeli military relations have also evolved (see Parsi 2006).

5. For US policy toward Iran, see Chubin (1996–97), Gerges (1996–97), and Amuzegar (1997). For US policy on Iraq, see Weller (1999–2000). For the viability of the dual containment policy, see Brzezinski, Scowcroft, and Murphy (1997). For US policy toward both Iraq and Iran, see Khalilzad (1995).

7

Iran-Turkey Relations

Between Rivalry and Competition

Meliha Benli Altunışık

The Iran-Turkey relationship is interesting as, at any given time, it contains elements of cooperation in several issue areas, albeit in varying degrees, and yet it is also characterized by intense competition with historical roots, presenting characteristics of rivalry.[1] A quick review of the literature reflects the ambiguity between rivalry and cooperation in this dyadic relationship (Calabrese 1998; Jenkins 2012; Akbarzadeh and Barry 2016; International Crisis Group 2016). Historically as one of the two biggest empires in the Middle East, then as two nation-states that were never colonized, and recently as two regional powers, they have competed for geostrategic and ideational reasons. Mutual distrust and threat perceptions characterized this relationship. Their identity constructions have been contradictory and indeed antagonistic. Their rivalry has a domestic dimension as it developed its own constituency in both countries. Although the two countries have not engaged in a direct military confrontation in the modern period, they have fought indirect wars. All these characteristics make Iran-Turkey relations an enduring rivalry. However, an interesting element of this rivalry has been that, in the modern period so far, it has not developed into direct military confrontation, and the two countries have also been able to develop multilayered cooperative relations not only in the economic field but also at times in the realm of security. This makes the Iranian-Turkish rivalry a complex one.

How can we account for the coexistence of cooperation and antagonism? How can cooperation coexist with rivalry and threat perceptions? In addressing this issue, the present chapter explores the impact of shocks in effecting the perception of rivalry and cooperation by both sides. It argues that the articulations of two dimensions, namely, the significance of the issue area and the nature of the shocks, determine the variations in relations between cooperation and rivalry.

Therefore, the Iran-Turkey rivalry particularly raises the following significant questions: Why do some long-lasting rivalry relations not turn into a full-fledged militarized confrontation? How and why can rivalry and cooperation coexist? As a corollary, what are the domestic, regional, and global contexts that enable this coexistence and prevent the outbreak of full-fledged conflict? How do shocks affect the Iran-Turkey rivalry? What explains the prevalence and escalation of rivalry as well as its de-escalation?

The first part of the chapter focuses on the historical background of Iran-Turkey relations as a rivalry. The rest of the chapter identifies shocks and their impact on Iran-Turkey relations in the modern period, particularly on the pendulum swing between competition and rivalry. In this regard, seven shocks or clusters of shocks were identified. It is argued that perception of these shocks as well as the importance of relevant issue areas by policymakers determine the swinging of the bilateral relations between rivalry and competition.

THE IMPERIAL RIVALRY

The Iran-Turkey rivalry generally can be traced back to premodern times, namely, to the rivalry between the Ottoman and Persian Empires. Having territorial, geostrategic, and ideological disputes that particularly intensified during the rule of the Safavid dynasty (1486–1722) in Iran, this rivalry involved a series of wars. This epoch is invoked in the current competition or rivalry between the successors of the two empires, Iran and Turkey. The presence of the past in the present demonstrates the historical depth of the current rivalry. The imperial rivalry is connected to the current one and constitutes the temporal component of the rivalry between Iran and Turkey. But it is at the same time separate as the political units that engaged in rivalry are different. This does not, however, prevent the influence of past events on the present as Iran and Turkey were reconstructed and institutionalized in the formation of modern states despite attempts of their contemporary governments to create a rupture with the past.

Shah Ismail established Safavid rule in 1501 and accepted Ithna Ashara (Twelver) Shi'ism as the state religion.[2] The Ottoman Empire, on the other hand, had adopted Sunni Islam (Hanafi interpretation) as the state religion. The adoption of Shi'a Islam by the Safavids was perceived as "a threat to the stability of the Anatolian provinces of the Ottoman Empire, due to the Safavid leadership's inherent ability to use its influence among the population of these regions for the achievement of its political designs" (Allouche 1980, 3).

The rivalry went through several stages and many wars. Although both sides used sectarianism against each other, the rivalry was based mainly on the threat perception of the Sunni Ottomans owing to the political and geostrategic ambitions of the newly established regime in Iran. Istanbul was first and foremost concerned about the possible political and religious influence and attraction of the Safavid rulers, who were also ethnically Turkic, for the Turkmens of Anatolia. At that time in Anatolia there existed heterodox Islamic cultures and Sufi understandings. The geopolitical context in the region further accentuated the rivalry. The complex web of relationships with the Mamluks and the Uzbeks, on the one hand, and the European powers, on the other, provided opportunities for alliances and counter-alliances for the two protagonists (Allouche 1980, 148). The Safavids formed alliances with Sunni Mamluks and to some extent with the Hapsburgs, the two main enemies of the Ottomans. Thus, in the sixteenth century the dual shocks, namely, the emergence of a new regime in Iran and the geopolitical context in the Middle East, led to the intensification of rivalry between Iran and Turkey, which was characterized by a series of wars between the two. Ottoman Sultan Selim I, who launched the campaign of Chaldiran in 1514, defeated the Safavids and captured Syria and Egypt from the Mamluks. The rivalry de-escalated after this campaign, when the Ottomans also once again recaptured Baghdad from Iran after fourteen years. The two sides signed the Treaty of Qasr-i Shirin (Treaty of Zuhab) in 1639. This treaty ended the 150-year history of intermittent wars between them and largely settled the territorial issue. Although the imperial rivalry continued afterward, its intensity decreased. The Ottomans contended with containment of Iran, while focusing more on their struggles in the European territories and the Mediterranean.

The rivalry reemerged in the late nineteenth century, when the Ottomans weakened considerably. The question of boundary resurfaced again in the context of Kurdish tribes that were trespassing the agreed border in their seasonal movements. The Ottomans and the Qajars, another Turkic dynasty then ruling Persia, "competed to gain the tribes' loyalty and to establish patronage over each other's Kurds" (Çetinsaya 2003, 117). The Qajars were also accusing the Ottomans of harboring the rebellious tribes in Iranian Azerbaijan. The tensions mounted and eventually led to a war between the two sides in 1821–23. The rivalry had a larger geopolitical context as the Ottomans were concerned more about Iran's support to its archrival Russia in the eastern frontier. The boundary issue was settled, however, with British and Russian intervention that stipulated an establishment of a mixed commission that conducted a survey, the results of which were confirmed by a convention signed in Istanbul in 1869. The Ottoman concerns about the Qajar dynasty's relations with Russia, on the other hand, were confirmed as Iran supported Russia during its war with the Ottomans in 1877–78. At the Berlin Conference after the Ottoman defeat of Russia, the disputed territory of Kotur (near Van) was given to Iran (Çetinsaya 2003, 117–18). The intensification of imperialist rivalry between Britain and Russia in the region, especially in the second half of the nineteenth century, overshadowed the Iran-Turkey rivalry.

SHOCK ONE: THE TRANSFORMATIONS IN THE MIDDLE EAST AND THE EMERGENCE OF THE MODERN STATES

World War I led to great transformations in the Middle East. The Ottomans entered the war as one of the Axis Powers, and Iran was already divided into British and Russian spheres of influence. The Ottoman Empire collapsed after the war, and eventually, Turkey was established in 1923 as an independent republic. In Iran the Qajar dynasty ended in a coup by Reza Khan, who eventually established the Pahlavi dynasty in 1925. The interwar years thus witnessed the establishment and the consolidation of states in both Iran and Turkey.

During this period the leaders of the two countries, Reza Khan and Mustafa Kemal Atatürk, established good relations as two nationalist, anti-imperialist, and reformist leaders. In 1934 Reza Khan paid an official visit to Turkey, during which he toured different parts of the country to observe firsthand the effects of reforms. Despite general rapprochement, however, the two countries shared a mutual distrust, as Iran was anxious about Turkey's possible irredentism in Iranian Azerbaijan and Turkey continued to harbor suspicions about Tehran's support for Kurdish nationalism. The Kurdish revolts in eastern parts of Turkey in the 1930s increased tensions between the two countries. After Turkey suppressed the revolts, few adjustments in Turkey's favor were made to the border agreement (Mojtahed-Zadeh 2007, 140). The mutual agreement on territorial status quo was reinforced with the founding membership of both countries, together with Afghanistan and Iraq, in the Saadabad Pact of 1937.

Thus, the two countries weathered the storm of great transformations in the Middle East during and after World War I by building and consolidating their independence. In the context of that common aim, they established relatively close relations. As the two regimes were secular, the geopolitical conflict between them did not focus on sectarian identities but rather emerged from their desires to build "nation-states" out of the multiethnic societies that they had inherited from their former empires. Although mutual suspicions remained, the escalation of rivalry was prevented by their pragmatic desires to survive in a volatile environment.

SHOCK TWO: THE RISE OF THE COLD WAR

While Iran could not escape its division into spheres of influence, again by Great Britain and the Soviet Union, during World War II, Turkey managed to stay out of the war without being invaded. In the postwar environment, however, both countries became the earliest theaters of the emerging Cold War between the United States and the Soviet Union. In the new bipolar international system, Iran and Turkey felt threatened by the Soviet Union and turned to the Western camp. Turkey became a member of the North Atlantic Treaty Organization (NATO) in 1952, and Iran developed bilateral relations with the United States. The height of the Cold War in the 1950s–60s put the rivalry between the two countries on the back burner. Their common concern with the Soviet Union and Arab nationalism led to de-escalation of their rivalry. To deal with these threats, the two countries, together with Great Britain, Iraq, and Pakistan, became the members of the Baghdad Pact in 1955.

The waning of the Cold War in the 1970s did not lead to further cooperation. On the contrary, the trajectories of the two countries began to diverge. The oil crisis affected the two countries very differently. Oil-rich Iran increased its military power and became more ambitious in terms of its aim of becoming a regional power. Economically hit by the oil crisis, Turkey, on the other hand, increasingly felt isolated after its military intervention in Cyprus in 1974 and the following US military embargo. Turkey was also suffering from internal strife between leftist and rightist groups, which led to enormous instability in the country.

Thus, in the 1970s the balance of power between the two countries clearly shifted in favor of Iran. Given these circumstances the Shah became concerned about the collapse of the political order in Turkey and tried to convince the US administration to lift the embargo. The Shah, with Washington's consent, even sent some spare parts to Turkey. Iranian military and economic aid to Turkey remained limited, however, as the Shah had concerns about Turkey's ability to pay it back (Kayaoglu 2014, 467–68).

Turkey, on the other hand, resented the rise of Iran as a powerful regional actor and its closer relations with the United States as well as the fact that it could get only a limited amount of aid from Tehran (Çetinkaya 2003, 127). More significant, the Shah's support to Iraq's Kurds in their rebellion against the central government disturbed Ankara. Although the Shah ended his support after Iraq had accepted Iran's demands for redrawing the boundary in the Shatt al-Arab waterway to its favor in the 1975 Algiers Agreement, the policy only reiterated for Iran Turkey's distrust of Iran's policy of using Kurdish nationalism to weaken its neighbors.

Thus, after they had emerged as modern nation-states in the twentieth century, the two countries initially established a more cordial relationship defined informally by warm interpersonal relations between the two leaders, Mustafa Kemal and Shah Reza, as well as shared statist foreign policy positions, such as membership in regional organizations, like the Saadabad Pact (1937) and Baghdad Pact (1955). Nonetheless, Iran and Turkey never developed a close partnership. Even though during the Cold War both of them were in the Western camp and developed close relations with the United States, they did not form an alliance. In addition to domestic turmoil in their countries and diverging geostrategic priorities, mutual distrust prevented the development of a partnership between the two countries (Kayaoglu 2014).

SHOCK THREE: IRANIAN REVOLUTION

The 1979 Islamic Revolution in Iran could have ushered in a new era in Iran-Turkey relations in terms of escalating the dyadic rivalry. Turkey's staunchly secular regime felt threatened by Iran's Islamic revolution and its intention to export that revolution. Furthermore, the direction that the new regime would take in its foreign policy orientation was unclear, which further disturbed Turkey as a NATO member. The newly established regime in Tehran, on the other hand, was clearly seeing in Turkey an ally of the United States, which it denounced as the "Great Satan."

Yet initially, despite expectations to the contrary, bilateral relations between the two countries were cooperative. Turkey became one of the first countries to recognize the new regime and continued its visa-free policy toward Iran. The eight-year Iran-Iraq War, which broke out in 1981, brought pragmatism to both Iran and Turkey. In April 1981 and March 1982, barter agreements were signed according to which Turkey would buy oil from Iran. As a result, the volume of bilateral trade increased from $63 million in 1975 to $2.3 billion in 1985 (Gündogan 2003, 4), and by 1983 Iran had become Turkey's biggest trading partner (Jenkins 2012, 17). For Turkey, the main objectives of its policy were "to prevent Iran from falling into the Soviet sphere of influence" and to enhance economic relations. Iran, on the other hand, aimed to keep Turkey neutral during the war. Furthermore, Turkey had become crucial for Iran's economic links to the outside world (Sinkaya 2005, 2).

During this period, however, the two sides continued to mistrust each other ideologically, and as a result several diplomatic crises erupted owing to ideological conflicts. The late *faqih* Ayatollah Khomeini criticized Turkey's secularism and referred to Atatürk as hostile to Islam (Akbarzadeh and Barry 2016, 3). Iranian leaders during their official visits to Turkey refused to visit Atatürk's mausoleum, contrary to the norms of diplomatic courtesy (Elik 2012, 41).

In terms of the global context, the US position toward the new regime in Iran was quite hostile. The Iranian Revolution, concurrently with the Soviet invasion of Afghanistan, led to a sense of increased Soviet threat toward the Gulf and the flow of oil from there. Turkey, as an ally of the US, shared these threat perceptions yet chose to focus on its short-term economic benefits. As a result, Ankara refused to comply with the US sanctions on Iran. Turkey, like the US, however, did not want any of the protagonists of the Iran-Iraq War to emerge as clearly victorious, nor did it want Iran to fall or be destroyed, as it formed a wall that protected the Arab Gulf states against more direct influences from the Soviet Union.

Overall, in the 1980s economic logic put ideological differences on the back burner and promoted cooperation rather than conflict. The shock of the toppling of the Shah regime through an Islamic revolution affected Iran-Turkey relations. Revolutionary turmoil in Iran meant a need for Turkey as a lifeline, which weakened the threat perception in Turkey; consequently, Turkey clearly felt that it had the upper hand and thus focused on enjoying the economic benefits.

However, the atmosphere began to change dramatically after the end of the Iran-Iraq War. The late 1980s and 1990s saw an intensification of ideological and geopolitical rivalry between the two countries.

SHOCK FOUR: THE END OF THE COLD WAR AS AN "END OF CERTAINTY" AND THE GULF CRISIS

In the late 1980s and early 1990s, there were a cluster of shocks, due to the disintegration of the Soviet Union and the Gulf War of 1990–91, that altered regional politics and the perceptions of policymakers.[3] These developments led to an intensification of geopolitical and ideological rivalry between Iran and Turkey. Furthermore, the rivalry started to become part of domestic political struggle and ideological competition in both states. This led to instrumentalization of bilateral relations domestically and thus made the Iran-Turkey relationship more open to crises.

In geopolitical terms the two countries engaged in intense competition in two regions. First, both Iran and Turkey were eager to increase their influence in the newly independent states in the Caucasus and Central Asia that emerged after the disintegration of the Soviet Union. This region was historically a part of their imperial rivalry, yet both countries had lost their presence and influence after the establishment of the Soviet Union. The intense competition became most visible in "pipeline politics." The transportation routes for oil and gas available in the landlocked countries of the region (Azerbaijan, Kazakhstan, and Turkmenistan) became a highly contentious issue between Iran and

Turkey. Furthermore, the emergence of close relations between Azerbaijan and Turkey especially increased threat perceptions in Tehran about the promotion of Turkish nationalism among Iran's own Azeri Turkish population. In fact, Iran perceived Turkey's interest in the region and the references of Turkish policymakers to a common Turkic past and solidarity as the revival of Pan-Turkism. Similarly, Turkey had concerns about Iran's religious solidarity discourse. This rivalry intensified when the United States also promoted the "Turkish model," as opposed to the "Iranian model," for the newly independent countries.[4] Soon, however, both Iran and Turkey realized their limitations in the region due to not only their own lack of necessary resources but also the return of Russia to the region with its "near abroad" policy. Nevertheless, with the support of the United States, Turkey was able to achieve more successes, such as the realization of the Baku-Tbilisi-Ceyhan oil pipeline, which was built to bring Caspian oil to the Turkish Mediterranean coast. Turkey's interest and activism in Central Asia and the Caucasus "briefly elevated Turkey to an Iranian national security threat in the early 1990s" (Hentov 2011, 29).

Second, the two countries began to compete in the Middle East, especially in Iraq after the 1991 Gulf War. Turkey's military interventions in the de facto autonomous Kurdish region in pursuit of the Kurdistan Workers' Party (PKK) and Turkey's cooperation with the United States over Iraq created a sense of threat in Tehran. The two countries were also drawn into the rivalry between the two Iraqi Kurdish parties, the Kurdistan Democratic Party (KDP) and the Patriotic Union of Kurdistan (PUK): "When fighting broke out between the two factions in May 1994, Turkey and Iran became involved in what was almost a proxy war: with Ankara providing support—including arms—to the KDP, while Tehran backed the PUK, which had in turn aligned itself with the PKK. The factional fighting was not formally ended until September 17, 1998, when the KDP and the PUK signed a U.S.-brokered peace deal" (Jenkins 2012, 21).

Finally, Iran felt threatened by Turkey's alliance with the United States and now also with Israel, Iran's two major enemies. From the Iranian perspective, in the 1990s the United States and Israel were trying to reshape the Middle East, and Turkey was their helper. The United States, which had been seen as a threat since 1979, was now actively engaged in the Gulf, having presence in Iraq and the Gulf Cooperation Council (GCC). Turkey's cooperation with the United States in Iraq was presenting new threats to Iran. To balance that development, Iran was building its own counter-alliance.

The ideological competition, in contrast, centered on secularism versus theocracy. For the secular and pro-Western establishment in Turkey, which was particularly concerned about the rise of the Islamist Welfare Party (Refah Partisi) in the 1990s, the Iranian regime became anathema. The Turkish establishment started to talk openly about an Iranian threat to Turkey. Iran was accused of intervening in Turkey's internal affairs, particularly by providing funding, weapons, and training for Islamist militants in the country. In the early 1990s Tehran was blamed for involvement in the assassination of some prominent secular intellectuals (Jenkins 2012, 20). In addition, the two countries used counternarratives for identity construction during this period. For seculars in Turkey who were feeling threatened by the rise of the Islamist Welfare Party in elections, Iran represented what they did not want Turkey to become. "Turkey is not going to be another Iran" (*Türkiye İran olmayacak*) was their slogan. Similarly, for the Iranian radicals who were trying to revive ideological fervor and consolidate the regime after the devastation of an eight-year war, Turkey represented what was wrong with secularism.[5] The debate about the headscarf ban in Turkey at that time, for instance, was used as an example and widely reported in the Iranian press. Several Iranian officials, probably encouraged by the electoral successes of the Welfare Party, began to argue that the people of Turkey themselves were calling for an Islamic government.

The ideological war of words between the two countries culminated in what became known as the Sincan affair. In January 1997 in Sincan, a town close to Ankara, an Al-Quds Memorial Night was organized. The mayor, who was from the Welfare Party, invited the Iranian ambassador to Turkey, Mohammad Reza Bagheri, who in his speech challenged the Turkish people "not to be afraid of being radical" and called on Turkey to adopt sharia as the basis of its legal system. The whole event, including the ambassador's speech, created an outrage among the seculars. During the crisis, civil and military officials began to openly target Iran. Deputy chief of the General Staff Gen. Çevik Bir called Iran "a registered terrorist state." Similarly, President Süleyman Demirel called on Iran to stop trying to export its revolution to Turkey. The leader of the Center-Right Motherland Party, Mesut Yılmaz, who became prime minister in the government formed after the ouster of the Welfare-led coalition government, identified Iran as "the number one enemy of Turkey" (Olson 2001, 38). The crisis led to the expulsion of Ambassador Bagheri and several Iranian diplomats from Turkey (G. Ozcan 2001, 21). In retaliation Iran expelled Turkey's ambassador, Osman Korutürk, as well as the consul general in Urumiye (Elik 2012). At the meeting of the National Security Council on February 28, 1997, the military presented to Prime Minister Necmettin Erbakan eighteen measures to be implemented to protect secularism in Turkey, which they thought was in grave danger. One of these measures directly referenced Iran and called for "the preparation and implementation of measures against Iran to prevent its destructive and damaging activities without disrupting economic or neighborly relations" (Jenkins 2012, 24). This event constituted the beginning of what is called the February 28 Process, an ouster of the Welfare Party coalition government through pressures from the military that has been dubbed a "postmodern coup." The wording of the warning, however, was yet another example of the ambiguous and complex nature of the relationship between the two countries.

Iran, on the other hand, perceived threats to its domestic regime from Turkey and became openly critical of Ankara. For instance, Tehran accused Turkey of allowing the members of anti-regime groups, such as Mojahedin-e Khalq, to reside in Turkey and even assisting them. More significant, Iran became concerned about any possible influence of Turkey over the sizable Turkish-speaking population in Iran (Sinkaya 2005, 4).

However, the Kurdish issue, given its possible implications for the territorial integrity of both countries, became the most important and at the same time most complex issue in bilateral relations. The two countries felt equally threatened by the rise of armed Kurdish nationalist movements in their own countries and yet unable to cooperate fully against them as they suspected or accused each other of supporting the other's separatist movement. The lack of trust, even in the case of clear mutual interest, sometimes led to the escalation of rivalry between the two, especially in the 1990s. As Sinkaya (2017, 9) argues, Iran accused Turkey of "harboring armed Kurdish groups from Iran" until these groups allegedly left for northern Iraq in the mid-1990s. Yet for most of the 1990s, Turkey blamed Iran for giving logistical support to PKK. The intensification of PKK attacks on the border areas led to several crises between Iran and Turkey during the 1990s. Although Iran rejected Turkey's accusations, Turkey continued to accuse Tehran of encouraging PKK attacks in Turkey. It was widely reported that the Çiller government seriously considered a military attack on what it claimed to be PKK bases inside Iran in May 1995. Another major crisis erupted in April 1996, "when both countries exchanged accusations of espionage and support for terrorism" (Kirişçi 1997). At one point Iranian officials claimed that the Turkish air force had bombed a village in northwest Iran. Turkey countered with claims that members of the Iranian Revolutionary Guard Corp (IRGC) and their alleged allies in Hezbollah—which Turkey accused Iran of forming in Turkey mainly to recruit Islamists among the Kurdish population—were responsible for a series of assassinations of prominent Turkish secularists. In a press conference the Turkish minister of the interior declared that members of radical Islamist organizations underwent months of military and theoretical training in Iranian security installations, traveled with Iranian riyal and forged documents, and participated in attacks on Turkish citizens and also Iranian regime opponents (Sinkaya 2005, 2).

Once again, the Iran-Turkey rivalry became very much a part of the two countries' domestic politics. In Turkey the Islamist Welfare Party, which briefly came to power as a coalition partner, promoted relations with Iran. Its leader, Necmettin Erbakan, took his first trip abroad as prime minister to Tehran, where in August 1996 he signed a twenty-two-year deal—later extended to twenty-five years—to import natural gas from Iran. The seculars, on the other hand, were very much critical of Iran and its policies. As a result, there were efforts to block Erbakan's initiatives with Iran. For instance, Erbakan's plan to sign a defense cooperation agreement with Iran during Iranian president Hashemi Rafsanjani's visit in December 1996 was blocked by the General Staff and Defense Minister Turhan Tayan from the True Path Party (Kirişçi 1997). However, it would be wrong to consider either the Islamists or the seculars as monolithic blocs on relations with Iran. Although some Islamists looked on Iran's revolution with admiration, others were aloof toward the Iranian regime, which they considered "untrustworthy heretics" (Jenkins 2012, 21). Similarly, while most of the seculars were very critical of the Iranian regime, some political leaders called for pragmatism and a moderate approach (Sinkaya 2005, 2).

Similarly, in Iran reformist presidents, namely, Hashemi Rafsanjani and later Mohammad Khatami, tried to improve ties with Turkey. Their efforts, however, generally were blocked by conservative and radical elements. The supreme leader, the IRGC, and the judiciary continued their critical stance against Turkey. These three negatively affected even economic relations between the countries. The IRGC and the conservative elements in the Iranian Majlis were instrumental in calling off Turkcell and TAV contracts in 2004. The contract with Turkcell, a Turkish mobile phone company, was canceled for "security reasons" as it was argued that the deal would allow Turkey, and by extension Israel, Turkey's ally, to eavesdrop on Iranian cell phone calls. The second contract won by Turkish construction company TAV to build Tehran Airport was canceled when IRGC accused the consortium of including Israeli firms. The next day the company's employees had to leave Iran, and an Iranian company built the airport (Elik 2012, 169). Yet the Iranian regime too continued its pragmatism to control the escalation of the rivalry so that it would not develop into a full-blown conflict.

Overall, the twin shocks of the early 1990s led to a perception of both threat and opportunity for Iran and Turkey. The issues involved were mainly related to regime security and territorial integrity. Moreover, the transformation in the two neighboring regions provided both new challenges and opportunities for both countries. This situation intensified the competition and at times led to open rivalry.

SHOCK FIVE: A CLUSTER OF SHOCKS AROUND THE US INVASION OF IRAQ AND DOMESTIC TRANSFORMATIONS

Two developments in Turkey affected bilateral relations. First, the capture of PKK leader Abdullah Öcalan in 1998 ushered in a de facto cessation of hostilities with the PKK. This removed a quite contentious issue from the agenda of Iran-Turkey relations. Second, the coming to power of the Justice and Development Party (Adalet ve Kalkınma Partisi [AKP]) in Turkey in late 2002 further decreased tensions. The AKP's new foreign policy initiatives contributed to the development of cooperation between Iran and Turkey. The slogan "Zero problems with neighbors" and the regime's quest to develop economic relations with neighboring countries facilitated normalization. The frequency of high-level visits between Iran and Turkey went up immediately.

However, one of the most important reasons for this shift was the transforming regional environment after the US invasion of Iraq in 2003, which presented several challenges to both countries. They were both unhappy about the invasion and the US presence in Iraq. The George W. Bush administration had already called Iran a "rogue state" and threatened the country as the next target of US military might. Turkey, on the other hand, was concerned about the territorial integrity of Iraq after the invasion and removed itself from post-invasion Iraqi politics after Iraq's parliament rejected Turkey's participation in the war, a decision that angered the US administration. The deterioration of Turkey-US relations pushed Turkey toward the regional countries, including Iran.

Iran, on the other hand, was happy about AKP efforts to weaken the secularist establishment in Turkey. Furthermore, Tehran needed Turkey's friendship at a time when it was isolated, not only from the region but also globally, owing to the intensification of the nuclear crisis.

Iran also shared Turkey's concern about the possibility of establishing a Kurdish state in the north of Iraq. Furthermore, like the PKK, which had long established a foothold in the Kurdish areas of Iraq, a new organization of Iranian Kurds with ties to the PKK, the Kurdistan Free Life Party (PJAK), was now operating on the border areas. This development coincided with PKK's restarting its war in Turkey in June 2004 (Jenkins 2012, 32). Thus, the two countries began to cooperate against what they saw as a common enemy. During Turkish prime minister Recep Tayyip Erdoğan's visit to Tehran in July 2004, Iran announced that it officially considered PKK to be a terrorist organization. Soon Iran started a crackdown "on PKK activity in Iran, arresting and even extraditing suspected PKK members to Turkey" as well as launching "a major offensive against PJAK and PKK militants in the mountains of southwest Iran, including shelling suspected PJAK camps 10km inside northern Iraq" (International Institute for Strategic Studies 2006, 3).

Therefore, there were both pull and push factors for Iranian-Turkish rivalry during this period. The regional transformations due to the US invasion of Iraq, the fall of the Ba'athist regime, and the emergence of the Kurdistan Regional Government (KRG) provided opportunities and challenges to the neighboring countries of Iran and Turkey and thus intensified rivalry. Domestic changes, especially the coming to power of the AKP, which for domestic and foreign policy reasons adopted a "Zero problems with neighbors" policy, and the presidency of Ahmadinejad, who needed better relations with Turkey again for domestic and foreign policy reasons, led to attempts at cooperation. The two countries also cooperated against PKK and PJAK during this period.

Both ideological and geostrategic rivalry continued, although it was not seen clearly on the surface. Iran felt threatened by the increasing involvement and influence of Turkey in the Arab world. Both aimed to limit each other's influence in the region and engaged in soft balancing in Iraq, Syria, Lebanon, and Palestinian territories. Turkey's close relations with the KRG in Iraq and the Bashar regime in Syria were seen as limiting Iran's influence. In fact, the AKP believed that if "Turkey could disentangle Syria from Iran's influence and thereby remove Tehran's strategic entry point to the Levant," this would be a significant achievement (Stein and Bleek 2012, 139). Similarly, Erdoğan's active involvement in the Palestinian issue and his popularity due to taking strong positions against Israel meant the decline of Iran's popularity in the region. The two countries started to compete for the leadership of the Islamic world. Tehran, which used to see the staunchly secular regime in Ankara as a threat, now started to see AKP, which represented "moderate Islam" also as a challenge to its interests. The AKP government, facilitating Turkey's "return" to the Middle East, wanted to limit Iran's influence in the region. Its policies had become popular in the Arab world, and its version of "moderate Islamism" was seen as much more attractive (Altunışık 2014). In this context, even Turkey's attempts to mediate the nuclear crisis, starting in 2006 and ending with the nuclear swap deal together with Brazil in 2010, were considered in Tehran as a way for Ankara to increase its clout in the West. Soon Iran was angered by Turkey's decision to allow NATO to install a missile defense shield on its soil, close to the Iranian border, as Tehran considered this development a threat to its security (Jenkins 2012, 42).

Thus, in 2009–11 Iran's and Turkey's immediate interests seemed to align, and this led to claims in the US media and think tank circles about an Iran-Turkey alliance and

Turkey's "axis shift." Yet Iran and Turkey continue to soft balance each other in regional politics while trying to expand their influence. They also engaged in efforts to limit each other.

SHOCK SIX: THE ARAB UPRISINGS

The Arab Spring further complicated an already complex and multilayered relationship. Turkish officials considered the transformations in the Arab world an opportunity to increase Turkey's influence in the region. It was hoped that the new regimes would be closer to the AKP government and would consider Turkey's blend of "moderate Islamism," democracy, and market economy an "inspiration." Iran, on the other hand, claimed that the uprisings were inspired by the Iranian Revolution and should be considered the "Islamic awakening."

However, it was the spread of the Arab Spring to Syria that created an important rift between Iran and Turkey. At the beginning both Iran and Turkey tried to convince their allies that Bashar needed to respond to popular demands by introducing some reforms (Stein and Bleek 2012, 145). When this did not happen, the positions of Ankara and Tehran diverged completely. Iran supported the Bashar regime, whereas Turkey called on Bashar to step down and lent its support to the opposition. The narratives on each side about the meaning of what was happening in Syria were totally opposite. For Ankara, what was happening in Syria was a continuation of the Arab Spring and violent oppression of the population by a dictator. Tehran, on the other hand, characterized the events in Syria as a regime change effort by outside powers: the United States and its allies, including regional countries, like Israel and increasingly Turkey and Saudi Arabia. After the rise of radical organizations and especially the Islamic State of Iraq and the Levant (ISIL), Iran presented its position together with its allies, the Syrian regime, and Russia, as a fight against radicalism (Hokayem 2014, 83–84).

As the uprising turned into a civil war and the war continued to drag on, these diametrically opposed positions and consequent involvements in Syria increased the rift between the two countries. In the course of the war, Iran's military commitment to support the Syrian regime meant the involvement of the IRGC, as well as Hezbollah, in the fighting on the ground. Turkey, on the other hand, was involved in the war indirectly for the most part by actively supporting the opposition groups, such as the so-called Free Syrian Army, providing training, bases, and arms to them. Thus, in a way, the two countries faced each other indirectly on the ground.

At the beginning Iran and Turkey were able to compartmentalize their relations, meaning they agreed to disagree on Syria and did not allow the Syrian issue to poison the rest of their relations, especially the economic ones. Although this policy worked for some time, it became highly unsustainable as the war became more complicated and the stakes for both sides became higher. Ankara, for instance, threatened to seize Iranian shipments to Syria if they entered Turkish airspace. Iran, for its part, increasingly saw Turkey's support for the opposition as a significant factor in the opposition groups' success in controlling parts of Syria. Turkey's support to the opposition became more problematic with the rise of ISIL in 2013. Turkey started to be called "the 'jihadist highway', referring to its policy of keeping the Syrian border open to allow militants to cross into the conflict zone" (Akbarzadeh and Barry 2016, 985). The Iranian media also began to openly accuse Ankara of supporting and even training ISIL members (Press TV 2015a). Even though Turkey started to crack down on ISIL members in Turkey, tightly control its borders, and actively support the anti-ISIL coalition starting in late 2013—because of not only ISIL attacks in Turkey but also domestic and international pressures—Iran continued its accusations. At the same time, Turkish pro-government media became highly critical of Iran. Tehran was blamed for restarting its support to the PKK. Deputy Prime Minister Bülent Arınç, who argued that intelligence "pointed to Iran with regard to (the) escalation in PKK violence," echoed this argument (Ünver 2012, 107).

Soon the rivalry between Iran and Turkey widened to include Iraq. Disturbed by Turkey's close relations with the KRG in Iraq and its support for anti-Assad groups, the Baghdad government, an ally of Iran, started to problematize Turkey's military presence at the Bashiqa base near Mosul. In December 2017 Baghdad and Tehran accused Turkey of further building up its military presence there. Iran declared that such a move would result in "chaos and intensification," while Iraq considered it as "a hostile act" (Press TV 2015b). In the meantime, Erdoğan became openly critical of what he characterized as "Iranian domination of the region" (Pamuk 2015). In October 2016, after the meeting of GCC foreign ministers that Turkey's foreign minister, Mevlüt Çavuşoğlu, attended as an observer, the GCC and Turkey adopted a joint declaration in which they called on Iran "to stop its sectarian interferences in the region" (Al-Arabiya 2016b). The Iranian foreign ministry responded: "Countries whose irresponsible interferences in the affairs of other states has led to the spread of insecurity, war and terrorism and who have violated the national sovereignty of their neighbors are not in a position to advise others not to interfere in regional affairs" (Press TV 2016).

Although, for the most part, the two sides refrained from invoking each other's sectarian identities despite the rise of sectarian politics in the region, at times the politicians used identity politics in their criticism of each other's policies. For instance, Erdoğan accused Iran of "Persian nationalism," while Foreign Minister Çavuşoğlu claimed that Iran was pursuing not only nationalist but also sectarian aims in the region (İdiz 2017). Iran, for its part, indirectly constructed Turkey's "Sunni identity" by associating the ruling AKP government with ISIL and takfiri groups.[6]

Iran also invoked ideational discourse to criticize Turkey's ambitions in the region. Tehran accused Turkey of having "neo-Ottoman" designs in the Middle East, especially after the Syrian crisis. Thus, "neo-Ottomanism began to be interpreted as a threat as it was seen to be encroaching on Iranian interests in the region and has operated as a means through which Iran can explain Turkey's maneuvering in the region" (Akbarzadeh and Barry 2016, 987). In other words, both countries invoked historical references in their quest to explain and criticize their foreign policy actions.

In short, the Syrian uprising exposed the rivalry between the two countries. As the uprising turned into a civil war, their consequent involvements in Syria increased the rift. Initially, they were able to compartmentalize their relations and continued cooperation, especially in the energy and economic fields, even while taking increasingly confrontational positions in Syria. In the last two years of the war, Iran and Turkey engaged in a war of words, with Turkey accusing Iran of aiming to dominate the Middle East, and Iran criticizing Turkey for its support to the opposition in Syria.

SHOCK SEVEN: BUILDING POST-ISIL SYRIA

With the effective defeat of ISIL, all the actors involved (global, regional, and local) began to make their moves to strengthen their positions and spoil the game for the others. This entailed not only diplomatic processes (like Geneva and Astana) but also the support of local combatants and groups with money and arms. The Iran-Turkey rivalry clearly has been affected by these developments. Although theoretically their positions continued to remain a zero-sum game, the strategies and policies of external powers and Iran and Turkey's relationship with them ultimately have influenced their rivalry. Iran from the beginning was allied with Russia, whereas Turkey's position has been precarious.

The United States at the beginning of the Syrian crisis supported the overthrow of the Assad regime and acted together with its allies, including Turkey, to this end. Soon Washington also started a diplomatic process through Geneva meetings. Yet the Obama administration did not see Syria as a major interest for the United States and refrained from direct intervention to achieve its objectives. With the rise of ISIL, however, the Obama administration opted for a military intervention to defeat it. Yet it aimed to limit its military intervention by relying on local forces. This meant US reliance on the Turkey-backed Free Syrian Army groups and the Kurdish groups, the Peoples' Democratic Party (PYD) and its armed wing, People's Protection Units (YPG). For several reasons, including the divisions within the Free Syrian Army and the effectiveness of the more secular YPG on the ground, the United States mostly relied on the YPG in its fight against ISIL. Disturbed by the rise of the PKK-affiliated PYD/YPG and its developing relations with the United States, Turkey in 2016 launched a military operation inside Syria to fight ISIL, to stop the advancement of PYD/YPG, and to demonstrate to the United States that it was a reliable ally.

For such a military move Turkey had to mend fences with Russia. This opened the way for the general improvement of Russia-Turkey relations vis-à-vis Syria. Russia also wanted to develop its relations with Turkey, not only to deepen the wedge between Turkey and the United States but also to control its allies in Syria, namely, Iran and the Assad regime (Friedman 2017, 3).

In the meantime, the post-ISIL strategy of the Trump administration also became clearer. A State Department official told the Senate Foreign Relations Committee that the United States must stay in Syria and that its military role in Syria will be focused on Iranian activities (Kheel 2018). For that, like the previous administration, the Trump administration has decided to continue to rely on the PYD/YPG. Despite the claims that Washington's relations with PYD/YPG are tactical rather than strategic, the United

States has continued to arm the PYD/YPG with weapons, including heavy arms and artillery.

Thus, the positions of both Iran and Turkey have been affected by the policies of the two major external actors. With the coming to power of the Trump administration, Iran has started to feel more threatened by the United States, which has now openly challenged the nuclear agreement and has based its policy in Syria (and even in the Middle East) on limiting Iran's influence. As to its alliance with Russia over Syria, Tehran also diverges from Russia on some issues (such as on the relations with Syrian Kurds, the activities of Hezbollah, and in general the future role of Iran in Syria), as the time has come for a political settlement in the country. Improving relations with Turkey under these circumstances probably seems logical to Tehran. In any case, Russia in a way forced Iran to work with Turkey through the Astana process.

Turkey, on the other hand, has been experiencing problems in relations with its US ally and feels threatened by US policies in Syria. American support for the PKK-affiliated PYD/YPG is considered a threat to Turkey's territorial integrity. The AKP government is also quite disturbed by what it sees as US support to Fethullah Gülen, the accused mastermind behind the failed coup attempt against the government on July 15, 2016. These developments have pushed Ankara toward Russia and to some extent toward Iran.

Thus, recently there has been an improvement in Iran-Turkey relations. Iranian support after the failed coup and Iranian foreign minister Javad Zarif's visit to Ankara in August 2016 seemed to open up a new chapter in the relationship (Jafari 2016). Similarly, when riots broke out in different parts of Iran in January 2018, the AKP lent its support to the regime. However, the fragility of this rapprochement in Syria was exposed when Turkey decided to militarily intervene in Afrin to stop what Ankara considered as a threat posed by the PYD/YPG military presence on its border.

CONCLUSIONS

Competition is a part of relations between states and is generally situational. Thus, competition can easily coexist with cooperation. Rivalries, on the other hand, are positional and historical. Rivalries are classified according to the type of competition and scope (Thompson 1995; Colaresi, Rasler, and Thompson 2007). Competition can be spatial, positional, or ideological. The Iran-Turkey rivalry historically had all these components. The Ottoman-Safavid (and later Qajari) rivalry was spatial, positional, and ideological. Yet the territorial aspect of this rivalry was largely resolved with the 1639 Treaty of Qasr-i Shirin (Treaty of Zuhab). This agreement has remained intact in the modern period except for some mutually agreed minor adjustments in the border area in the early state formation process. Yet the imperial rivalry continued after the resolution of territoriality and even in the modern period. The geopolitical and ideational elements of the imperial rivalry continued to affect Iran-Turkey relations despite significant changes in the territorial boundaries of the modern states, their shifting ideologies, and the context. The positional element also continued to be an important part of this rivalry. Iran and Turkey have been competing to enhance their relative positions in the dyadic relationship as well as in different regions. They generally perceive their positions to be in a zero-sum game. I would argue that the cessation of the spatial element in this dyadic rivalry largely explains lack of direct military confrontation (Dreyer 2012).

The second dimension of rivalry, scope or location, refers to where the rivalry is contested. In the case of the Iran-Turkey rivalry, it has been contested dyadically as well as regionally. As two contending regional powers, both countries competed for status and influence in their neighborhoods, namely, the Middle East, Central Asia, and the South Caucasus. The rivalry in the latter two regions emerged with the collapse of the Soviet Union yet remained limited as the opportunities for extending influence proved to be limited with Russia's return and relative stability in the regional countries. In the Middle East, however, the rivalry intensified especially in the 2000s, with the post-2003 environment presenting opportunities for both. For the regional rivals, not only are the characteristics of the regional context crucial but so are the forms of engagement of the extra-regional Great Powers with the regional system in determining the evolution of dyadic rivalries. The relations of the rivals with Great Powers affect their mutual relationship. Whenever one of the rivals establishes closer relations with a Great Power, that affects the balance of power between them and as such de-escalates the rivalry.

The other two elements are ideological/identity competition and domestic/regime security. Ideology and identity have been an important part of this rivalry. This entails securitization of Sunni and Shi'ite identities (Malmvig 2015) as well as secularism versus theocracy or moderate Islam versus theocracy. These identities and ideologies are embedded in the structure of the rivalry and thus not only continue to affect the relationship but also are continuously reinvented. The second element of Iran-Turkey rivalry is about concerns over domestic and regime security. "Political Islamism," "Pan-Turkism," "Neo-Ottomanism," "Persian nationalism," or "sectarianism" have all been considered a threat to their regime security by the parties at different times. This perception has prevented them from establishing a strategic partnership even on issues where their interests coincided. The Kurdish issue is a prime example of this phenomenon. Although rising Kurdish nationalism has been considered as a common threat, mutual distrust has prevented cooperation in the long haul.

This study showed that a fourth element—domestic politics—is also important in the rivalry relationship. The more rivalry issues become part of domestic power struggles, as happened in the 1990s between Iran and Turkey, the more chances for rivalry escalation. However, in general, the existence of division among political actors as to how to deal with threats emanating in the rivalry relationship can be seen as a factor of de-escalation as pragmatic political actors may prevent hard-liners from pursuing escalation.

Finally, the escalation or de-escalation of the Iran-Turkey rivalry has been a function of shocks or a cluster of shocks emanating from the domestic, regional, and global contexts in which the parties redefine their interests. In the domestic contexts, the Iranian Revolution, the coming to power of the AKP in Turkey, and the struggles between reformists and conservatives in Iran and seculars and Islamists in Turkey have been significant. In the regional context, the transformations in the region after the Gulf War, the US invasion of Iraq, and finally, the Arab Spring have all had an impact. Globally, the Cold War, the end of bipolarity, the unipolarity, and finally the new US form of engagement with the Middle East as well as Russia's global ambitions have also affected the Iran-Turkey rivalry.

The resolution of the territorial dispute early on decreased the probability of direct military confrontation. Similarly, when the interests of the two sides aligned, they managed to cooperate even though they continued to harbor suspicions against each other. However, when the policymakers perceived a challenge to their state's territorial integrity or regime security, the rivalry escalated. Similarly, when the parties perceived that they had equal chances to advance their positions in the regional or international environment, then the rivalry also escalated. On the other hand, domestic actors are an intervening variable here as the worldviews, ideologies, relations with different societal actors, and political positions affected policymakers' perception of shocks and thus their decision to manage, escalate, or de-escalate the rivalry.

NOTES

1. In bilateral relations, although it is normal to have cooperation and competition at the same time, having rivalry and cooperation is rare. In comparison, Syria-Turkey relations, for instance, have been characterized by rivalry except for a brief period, in the early 2000s, of intense cooperation.

2. Shah Ismail mandated that all regions under Safavid rule convert to Shi'ism. Before that, although there were significant Shi'ite communities in Iran, the land was also an important stronghold for Sunni Islam and one of its intellectual centers. The bringing of religious uniformity in the sixteenth and seventieth centuries by the Safavids was largely successful (Abisaab 2004).

3. The description in the subhead regarding "End of Certainty" belongs to David Campbell (1998). Disintegration of the Soviet Union weakened its allies, like Syria, forcing it to engage with the United States and with the peace process. It also made the Gulf War possible, to mention a few effects. The perception was that the regional countries lost their ability to use one superpower against the other.

4. According to this view, while the "Turkish model" was a secular, democratic, and pro-Western democracy with a free market economy, the "Iranian model" was undemocratic and anti-Western theocracy with a command economy.

5. It is often noted that Iran after the war with Iraq sought regional improvement of relations, especially under Rafsanjani and given the retreat in the role of the Pasdaran, to allow it to recover. Rafsanjani also tried to improve relations with Turkey. However, like secularists in Turkey, conservatives in Iran were mainly using Turkey as a negative example. Pasdaran, the judiciary, and Khamanei continued to promote radicalism. There were covert operations, for instance, against dissidents, including in Turkey.

6. See, for instance, *Iran Daily* (2016a and 2016b).

8

Dangerous Entanglements

The Rivalry Effects of the Iran and Israel Narratives

Imad Mansour

This chapter explores rivalry dynamics through a comparison of the Israeli and Iranian cases in order to make two main arguments. The first demonstrates the explanatory power of societal narratives in rivalry analysis. Such an explanation is particularly important given the fact that some states become rivals and engage in exchanges of threatening messages and acts when there "appears" to not be a strategic ("objective") reason for them to be rivals or pose threats to each other. Leaders of these states must perceive and assess the other to be a threat; this chapter demonstrates how ideas explain such hostile relations. Narratives, as ideational structures, highlight why and how mistrust, threat perception, and goal incompatibility derive from complex histories in which state leaders are socialized, thus influencing interactions with the world and designation of rivals. Narratives play an important, and understudied, role in shaping rivalries, even if they are not exclusively responsible for either onset or termination, and transforming the relationship over time. The impact of the nonsubstantive nature of such rivalries is exemplified by the rivalry between Iran and Israel—two noncontiguous states.

The second argument traces how shocks impact a dyadic rivalry by acting on narratives. Shocks influence a rivalry (or any other relationship) because what they imply for the state is given meaning by narratives. Consequently, narratives also shape the constellation of options that the decision-makers can or should pursue in reacting to shocks; narratives make some options more desirable than others and even create blind spots (i.e., some possibilities are not even contemplated as options). The chapter pursues these two goals with the study of the persistent rivalry between the Islamic Republic of Iran and the state of Israel.

Studying the Iran-Israel rivalry allows for an added explanation to existing scholarship as to what goal incompatibility means and where it could be rooted, as well as how ideational structures influence rivalry dynamics. Studying rivalry among noncontiguous nonmajor powers allows for a magnification of how ideas are important since these states have opted to deploy their capabilities to target one another. This means that they are intent on being rivals, and studying narratives helps us understand why.

The chapter analyzes how three shocks, of different natures, have affected the rivalry. The first shock was the Iranian Revolution, which prompted the rivalry; the second shock was the publicized information on Iran pursuing a nuclear program (uranium enrichments and technical advances), which added hostility to the rivalry, manifesting itself in multiple violent exchanges; the third shock was Iran's 2015 nuclear energy agreement, which added pragmatism to both states' strategies and thus made the rivalry more stable in a predictable way.

The chapter proceeds by highlighting the importance of studying narratives in rivalry analysis. It then presents a reading of the narratives of both states, after which the chapter analyzes the interaction effects of these narratives and maps the effects of the three shocks on the rivalry. A concluding section reflects on the main strengths of using narratives in rivalry analysis and suggests ideas for future research.

POSITIONING NARRATIVES IN RIVALRY STUDIES

States become rivals when a government (or both governments) designates another state as a rival because it sees in that state's actions or rhetoric some form of threat (Colaresi, Rasler, and Thompson 2007, 25). The onset of a dyadic rivalry can be triggered by many proximate causes. States become involved in a rivalry to defend their position in situations where an inherent goal incompatibility exists and where a designated rival poses a threat; a rivalry persists if these dynamics do (Thompson 2001, 559). Incompatible goals can emerge over spatial issues, such as natural resources or border claims, or positional issues, such as regional dominance or clashing ideologies. Because of the threat posed by the other, branding a rival is a decision made regardless of the regime type or military capabilities (relative or absolute) of either state, since though material disparities might make a rivalry less likely, they do not prevent it from occurring.

Rivalries are partly "psychological relationships" in which decision-makers' perceptions matter significantly in designating rivals and sustaining the competition (Mor 2004, 310; Colaresi and Thompson 2002, 263). It would make sense therefore to look for goal incompatibility in decision-makers' ideas, perceptions, or images of the other. Moreover, and critically, since rivalries are not "one-time events" but extend over significant time frames during which leaders are very likely to change, there must be factors responsible for this continuous competition that go beyond individual leaders' whims or ideological idiosyncrasies.

Widely held societal ideas about the other matter in a rivalry, regardless of regime type: "If the public is mistrustful of an adversary, as in the case of many rivalries, public pressure may support escalation rather than de-escalation" (Colaresi, Rasler, and Thompson 2007, 110). Narratives can help provide an insight into societally shared intersubjective understandings as to why a rival constitutes a threat, how much of a threat, and what policy options are viable and acceptable in dealing with them. Thus, the more accurate our reading of shared meanings, the more we are able to understand what the differences might be and hence better understand the underlying bases for goal incompatibilities and how these bases are shared among different decision-makers over time. Importantly, this approach also allows us to better explain why noncontiguous dyadic competitions over positional issues can become so fierce. Action, for rivalry onset and persistence, starts with narratives.

HOW NARRATIVES INFLUENCE RIVALRIES

As ideational structures, narratives are stable but remain open to contestation and change. Building on earlier work (Mansour 2016) in which I address how narratives affect contemporary state building, I contend that a state should be thought of as having a central narrative, one that is not simply the worldview of the ruling elite or a collection of random stories by members of the society. Rather, a state's narrative is larger than the sum of its members' ideas and worldviews; it is consolidated at independence, which is a moment of formal birth allowing rulers and the public to act in the contemporary Westphalian order. Narrative formation happens most frequently through acts associated with Westphalian statehood, such as the establishment of police forces, universities and hospitals, post offices, and a national anthem and a flag. Ideas constituting narratives are not the property of any one government, person, or subgroup; rather, they are part of a larger imaginary and historical repertoire, meaning that they are open to contestation and change. Change in narratives comes from many sources. They can be a function of generational shifts in ideas, catastrophe facing the group, or the emergence of a figure who mobilizes material and moral capital around an idea and is able to have it included or discarded from a narrative. While not fixed then, narratives are nevertheless stable and often change slowly (see Barnett 1999).

The central function of a narrative is to explain the world outside a group, among its members, and over time. In so doing, it stabilizes the world, which allows ruling elites or governments to act. Narratives relate states to their own histories and include ideas about their past, present, and potential future interactions with the world (Shih 1992). Narratives socialize decision-makers in intersubjective societal understandings of themselves, others, and the world. This means that narratives give meaning to the world and the state's history and influence decision-makers' perceptions of available policy options and what legitimate and acceptable action would and would not be.

Particularly salient under rivalry conditions, narratives help governments identify where threats facing the core values of their state come from. The government places its national interest against this canvas, locates threats, determines options for action, and acts; in this process, narratives help governments discern friends from foes, including who a rival is and why. Narratives help shape a government's set of policy options (Barnett 1999) and influence the choice of foreign policy, including strategies and objectives (war, alliances, and trade relations), because they indicate what actions are acceptable. When a government encounters an external situation or action by some state that demands a reaction, the narrative helps contextualize the situation, filter actions of others as hostile or not, forecast potential implications for the state, identify a range of responses, and decide on an action (Shih 1992).

Importantly, individual or governmental leadership influence over narratives indicates that there is an important element of agency pertinent to understanding narratives and their influence on rivalry dynamics. While in a rivalry policy goals reflect present concerns, these are tied to historical interactions with rivals. In such a context, if an individual or a group believes that an action that violates the narrative is nevertheless strategically advantageous, they have to secure collective agreement, take the action, and deal with political or other consequences. Alternatively, as is often the case during attempts to transition out of rivalry or conflict, individuals or governments may attempt an incremental change in narratives. This last action is undertaken by framing the idea in a manner that explains its potential fit with the narrative. Hence, a government's ability to successfully implement its goals depends on its talent for framing policies within an accepted narrative (Barnett 1999). Importantly, framing is not the same as a narrative. Narratives are necessary to the way that groups exist in the world, whereas framing is a conscious action that is undertaken by governments in order to legitimate actions or induce political change. Framing events within a narrative allows government to "make sense of what is going on" (Trevino 2003, 20). It also ensures that policies are consistent with dominant narratives and explains why government policies are vital and measured reactions to a given event. Governments recognize the existence and relevance of narratives as well as the importance of situating and relating policy decisions directly to narratives (Scheff 2005, 374). The approach to narrative analysis in this chapter subsumes economic and political dimensions into what it considers as dominant narratives for Iran and Israel.

Finally, while individuals and groups in any society have their own understanding of what their past and present look like and how to act in the world, this chapter seeks to unpack a dominant societal narrative, that is, the narrative that is shared by a majority in society. Thus, reference to a societal narrative is effectively to the dominant narrative unless otherwise indicated. Furthermore, the chapter presents *a* reading of the dominant Israeli and Iranian narratives for the period under study. It focuses on continuities and changes in dominant narratives and identifies and analyzes broad historical patterns of narrative changes rather than their contents at particular moments.

What are the narratives of Israel and the Islamic Republic of Iran? Importantly, how have these narratives influenced the onset and persistence of their rivalry? In the following section, I draw on my previous work on Israeli and Iranian narratives, which drew on various historical sources, in order to describe the contents of both Israel and Iranian narratives. This brief review will allow informed inferences on the relationship between narratives and rivalry dynamics.

ISRAEL'S NARRATIVES AND THE WORLD

Drawing on a general Jewish narrative, Israel's dominant narrative was crafted upon independence and remains largely similar in its general contours to this day. The Israeli narrative emphasized negative experiences in a world hostile to Jews, one in which foreign powers, even allies, are unreliable to alleviate existential threats facing the group (Brecher 1972). The survival of the state is therefore a core value and political concern. These ideas were not born with the state in 1948 (i.e., created out of nothing) but were there long before independence, most significantly vocalized by Ze'ev Jabotinsky, who died in 1940, a time when a state was not a certainty for the Zionist movement. This narrative explained what Jews faced in the world over millennia: destruction and destitution (e.g., the destruction of the Temple and the Holocaust), moments of resistance and self-reliance (e.g., the Maccabis and the Bar-Cochva Revolt), and the ways Jews worked together to ensure their survival and integrity (Mansour 2016, 66–69). In essence, the dominant sense of Jewish history is a "history of negatives," or one defined mostly by negative experiences.

From these core ideas Zionists crafted a dominant narrative for the state of Israel, whose creation was seen as the epitome of Jewish existence: Israel would be the guardian of the Jewish people, of the historically beleaguered group. The main task of decision-makers (and all Israelis and Jews) would be to ensure that the creation of the state of Israel did not become a historical anomaly, that is, to ensure that Israel would not be destroyed. One of David Ben-Gurion's long-lasting imprints on the state, which still dominates Israeli decision-making circles and the public alike, is that Israeli foreign policy, in both its military and its politico-diplomatic dimensions, is derivative of its security policy (Mor 2004), and that its security policy in turn is derivative of a narrative of loss and historical dispossession. To face negative experiences, Israelis need to remain united with their leadership, and they need to rely on themselves to face existential threats (Ben-Gurion 1958). This narrative advocates that Israeli governments engage in a continual process to devise policies to guard state survival, before anything else, but also to look at the well-being of the group (Sofer 1998).

While this is the dominant narrative, disagreements in interpreting lessons from history and the best way to protect the state were present upon independence and have remained since. Disagreements have also been present and remain around what the nature of the state should be. Specifically, the idea of creating a modern Westphalian manifestation of the biblical idea of Eretz Israel, which does not coincide with the present territory of the state of Israel, is a part of the Jewish narrative—one that was and remains contested. Related to these ideational disagreements have been the commitments incumbent on modern state institutions to materialize and sustain territorial expansion.

Grounded in this dominant narrative, Israel needs to pursue policies that demonstrate, through verbal rhetoric or military acts, that costs on enemies would be so high that they would be deterred from even contemplating aggressive actions. Moreover, given what Israelis (and in general Jews) agree on as the challenges and threats that have traumatized them throughout history, they need to ensure that the state of Israel remains able to defend itself—no matter what the cost, and regardless of who supports it and who does not (Tal 2000). Therefore, Israel needs to constantly maintain the balance of power in the Middle East in its favor—as military power is the main means of ensuring survival and protecting against contingencies. For the state of Israel, the thinking of the Iron Wall doctrine told ruling governments that they should constantly teach enemies, such as the Islamic Republic of Iran, lessons about who should hold superior power and punish anyone who threatens it, even verbally (Harkabi 1970). Such ideas about why and how to protect Israel were shared among the decision-making elite that oversaw independence and have since remained dominant. Israeli governments since independence have embraced the essence of a narrative of negatives that advocated the creation of a strong state that can withstand threats.

IRAN'S NARRATIVES AND THE WORLD

Central to the Iranian narrative is an idea that withstood the 1979 Revolution, namely, that modern-day Iran descends from Persia, a society with a long-established historic place in the world. Persia was an empire that radiated knowledge and power across a wide geographic area; it also was a center of scientific discovery and artistic production. Both the dominant narrative of the pre-1979 monarchy and the post-1979 Islamic republic hold that this historic greatness was undermined in great part by external pressures, especially from other global powers. These pressures made Iran the target of several military invasions and occupations over the past millennium, especially in the twentieth century; these came from actors acting independently or in concert and were conducted with material capacities significantly greater than Iran's, thus reducing its ability to fight back (Ward 2009, chap. 10).

Under the monarchy in the twentieth century, Iran aspired to revive its once-held status of greatness in the world and to be a leader in its immediate region; the narrative of Persia's historic greatness was espoused by the Shah, a wide circle of decision-making elites, and a large public (Ramazani 1972). Importantly, the Shah thought that Persia would become respected among the Great Powers of the day—an empire that deserves its place in the sun. Persia, however, was occupied and divided by Britain and the Soviet Union (USSR) and denied a possibility to revive its long-held image of glory and empire by the United States and USSR (Kiastevan 1978). Therefore, Iran in the twentieth century, like the Persian Empire historically, was not able to credibly defend what it perceived was a *legitimate* status (see Fatemi 1980). Moreover, Iran was instrumentally supported by the Great Powers of the twentieth century. This meant that from a narrative perspective, if the policies of the major powers and regional neighboring states toward monarchic Iran were instrumental in supporting its independence, it is because they perceived it as a buffer against the Soviet Union. In the narrative framing, moreover, the United States invested in Iran's royal military personnel and capabilities as a regional policeman, not as a major power in its own right. More powerful states intervened in 1953 and then again in 1979 to violate Iran's independence, even if the purposes and means driving such interventions were very different.

The Islamic Republic of Iran emerged with significant changes in the shape and functions of state institutions, state structures, and narrative. Though there were important changes in ideas, there was also some continuity with the past. The Islamic Republic's dominant narrative inherited ideas of suffering from hostile regional and international environments—and in the dominant narrative that emerged with the revolution were ideas infused from the Shi'ite religious narrative (Khomeini 1980). Central to Shi'ite understandings of history are ideas of victimhood and their historical persecution by groups that perceived their religious practices and convictions as heretical; such challenges came from many Sunni clerical and political quarters who self-defined as the orthodoxy. Shi'ite liturgy is laden with grief and iterations of the need for the group to unite to face external threats to its integrity. Central to the narrative of the Islamic Republic are memories of Shi'ites as an oppressed and disinherited minority. However, in many ways, as in the Israeli narrative, there are also overtones of the ability of Shi'ites throughout history to resist oppression and work to empower the disinherited with social and political liberation as a central goal. These ideas form the ideational core of Iran's dominant narrative, with interpretations differing among clerical schools (Fadlallah 1997).

The Shi'ite narrative that was elevated by the clergy to a dominant status in Iran after the revolution is founded on negative experiences (Fadlallah 1997). It is laden with stories of martyrdom, suppression, and consistent interventions to wrestle political power away from Shi'ites and undermine them as a legitimate segment of Islam. From centuries of Shi'ite relations with the environment, the Iranian narrative sees the world around it as being composed of two systems. The first system is defined by goodness and justice and is built around Islamic principles (Dar al-Islam), while the other system is unjust, oppressive, and dominated by evil (Dar al-Harb) (Mozaffari 1999). The two worlds do not meet and are irreconcilable; this binary perspective, in theory, is shared in the Shi'ism dominant in Iran and less so among various other Islamic bodies of thought. Iran believes in the just world and the necessity of the struggle to achieve it, and it does so by supporting the disinherited and the meek on the earth, who are locked in a constant struggle with forces of arrogance.

Given the prominent political and social status of religious ideas, clerical agency has been important in crafting Iran's dominant narrative, in which *narrating* history becomes driven by attention to religious symbols, "divine" interventions, and the idea that "right is on our side." Furthermore, confirming the distinctness of this narrative has been an almost persistent and widespread framing of Shiism as contra to the Sunni orthodoxy. That the world order is one that is at odds with Iran has been reinforced since 1979, when the Islamic Republic was immediately branded as a challenger to the world order and physically attacked by an Iraq that was aided by many regional states and major powers. Moreover, Iran has been under attack because it challenges a world order that, at least since 1990, has been set by the United States. For example, as punishment for its principled position, Iran has been under a series of diplomatic and economic embargoes and branded as part of an axis of evil.

IRAN AND ISRAEL BEFORE RIVALSHIP

Iran and Israel have not always been rivals nor have they always framed each other as threats. Before 1979 Iran was among a group of states that voted against UN General Assembly Resolution 181, which called for the partition of Mandate Palestine and the creation of the Israeli state. This position (which could at best be termed cold) toward Israel ended with the Shah regaining full control over government by 1953, which occurred by purging opposing persons and ideas. Under the Shah, and until 1979, Israel-Iran relations changed markedly toward improvement. Throughout the pre-1979 period, both governments considered the other as assets in pursuit of respective goals in regional politics. Israel saw in Iran a natural ally by virtue of both states' tensions with Arab neighbors. In the 1950s Israel proposed that Iran join the Periphery Pact, together with Turkey, to resist pressures from the Soviet presence as well as potential Arab collaboration (Mansour 2016, 64–67).

Moreover, pre-1979 Iran-Israel relations included cooperation on a range of regional issues of common interest, taking the form of intelligence sharing and provision of material support to third actors. For example, in viewing Iraq as a common threat, Israel and Iran supported Kurdish military groups in their struggle against the Iraqi government (Kaye, Nader, and Roshan 2011, 10). Geopolitical interests, therefore, have been influential in bringing the two states together. Convergence in strategic interests, however, was premised on non-oppositional narratives. This means that in the pre-1979 period, the dominant narrative in policymaking circles in Iran (in addition to general, though not necessarily total, acceptance socially) did not frame Israel as hostile; the same was the case in Israel.

SHOCK ONE: IRANIAN REVOLUTIONARIES REFRAMING THE STATE NARRATIVE

As a shock (consistent with the definition in chapter 1), the 1979 revolution in Iran significantly interrupted the existing ideational status quo; it introduced significant change to the ideational infrastructure in Iranian government and society, and not simply a passing change in individual decision-makers' perceptions. Specifically, fundamental to the revolution was the rise to power of a religiously motivated group that held different ideas about what the dominant Iranian narrative should look like. Their ideas were widely shared in Iranian society, and this group was therefore able to incrementally introduce these ideas into the dominant narrative. For example, while the importance of Iran's historic status and mission in the world was retained from the previous 1979 monarchy, how to achieve it was reinterpreted; so too was the status of religion in the public and political spheres. In this new ideational context, Israel was reframed as an enemy and threat; exactly how and when it was to be countered became decisions to be made in conjunction with a range of other considerations.

The revolution changed Iran's foreign policy when it brought into government people who championed ideas that emphasized the necessity of acting in the world against oppressors (of Iran and others) and violators of human rights principles, such as self-determination. It was not one event during this period per se that brought about the rivalry with Israel but rather the slow moving of the revolution into the hands of a select group of revolutionaries. Specifically, the narrative of the Islamic Republic emphasized a distinctly religious interpretation of Iran's history; holders of this interpretation overpowered a large collection of actors who had made the revolution possible after consistent and forceful public protesting. Actors who had rallied against the Shah included women's movements, labor, student groups, and leftist parties, among others; collectively, and in general, these groups had not joined the revolution to bring to power a religious government or to frame a postrevolutionary Iran in almost exclusively religious terms. These actors were purged soon after the ousting of the monarchy.

In the few months between late 1979 and early 1980, a pro-Khomeini revolutionary group consolidated control over state and society, particularly by purging the opposition. In formulating the narrative for the future Islamic Republic, this group heightened the importance of ideas that positioned Iran as responsible for leading the global fight against injustice and oppression. The policy implications of such ideas were that it was incumbent on the government to find the means and resources to undertake this mission. The Islamic Republic's foreign policy has since emphasized the centrality of acting to "resist oppression and arrogance" in its immediate region and globally and itself as a champion of the meek whose role is to rally together excluded parties.

Thus, it was not the revolution per se, as an act to alter the domestic political structure, that birthed the rivalry, but the change in revolutionary leadership that brought about a specific interpretation of the revolution's purpose. More specifically, and from an ideational perspective, it was the "new" narrative that brought about the rivalry. A series of Iranian government policies and discourses positioned Israel in an anti-Iranian camp. Israel belonged to Dar al-Harb, especially given that its statist project negated the Palestinian cause and it associated with global oppressors such as the United States. Iran's government associated the creation of Israel with the plight of the Palestinians from a principled human rights perspective and framed this plight as an Islamic concern given the importance of Jerusalem. These two principled positions, publicly announced in speeches, effectively brought about the rivalry with Israel.

Taken together, these events related to the Islamic Revolution constituted the shock that engendered the rivalry with Israel. Since the Israeli-Iranian rivalry began, relative material capabilities have put Iran and Israel "in the same league," with some asymmetry (Thompson 2001, 561; Colaresi, Rasler, and Thompson 2007, table 2.1).

Since 1980, therefore, Iranian decision-makers' discourses frequently reference the illegitimacy of the "Zionist entity" as a colonial creation while also highlighting how Israel is an abusive state built on the abolition of Palestinian rights. These ideas have endured in the foreign policy of the Iranian political establishment. For example, in the discourses of Iran's highest political figure after Khomeini, Ayatollah Khamenei, the Israel-Palestine conflict featured most prominently, regardless of its limited impact on the daily lives of Iranians (Sadjadpour 2009, 19).

That Israeli governments have framed Iran as a threat should be expected given that its very existence and right to exist are questioned by Iran. At the ideational level, Iran's narrative poses a threat because it denies Israel's narrative and calls for resources to be mobilized to reverse the creation of the state. Recall that an important pillar of the Israeli narrative is that the state should not be a historical anomaly, that is, that it should strive to maintain itself. Hence, from the Israeli perspective, Iran necessarily became a rival post-1979. Israel has since sought to mobilize global and regional energies to counter Iran, framing its policies as threats to peace given its support for "global terrorism."

Dueling Narratives and Rivalry Dynamics

It is important to qualify the intensity of the rivalry since fierce Iran-Israel rivaling did not really start in 1979, even if the two states were set for rivalry at the level of narratives. Despite not sharing a border and not engaging in direct militarized confrontations, both states confronted each other in multiple theaters, especially through proxy warfare in Lebanon. They also led covert operations, including the assassination of scientists; engaged in clandestine technological warfare; and launched an unrelenting war of rhetoric.

With a rights-based foreign policy emerging from its narrative, Iran sought allies with shared interests in resisting oppression, such as Hezbollah and later Hamas. Iran aided its allies with military hardware, personnel, and training as well as economic support, such as oil exports at reduced prices. Such material capabilities were framed as important to counter Israeli (and American) intransigence. Israeli and American policies resemble a pincer around Iran, thus confirming the perception of Iranians that the world is a hostile place.

During the 1980s Iran was more preoccupied with the immediate physical threat from Iraq and from the support it was receiving from Gulf states, especially Iran's other rival, Saudi Arabia. Soon after Kuwait was liberated, Iraq's capabilities were seriously diminished, and thus the level of threat toward Iran also decreased. It was then that the first Palestinian intifada propelled the rise of a novel indigenous Islamic movement in Palestine, while a strengthening Hezbollah emerged in Lebanon; both intensified the Iran-Israel rivalry (Kaye, Nader, and Roshan 2011, 65–67). Though the absence of shared borders reduced the chances of a militarized confrontation between Israel and Iran, it did not prevent them from engaging in a positional struggle in intense and violent ways. Since the 1990s Iran and Israel have periodically renewed their rhetorical attack that the other is "motivated by evil," as well as their promise to inflict harm on each other, and have used violence and force, but never in a direct militarized exchange. Intent to harm was demonstrated in proxy confrontations, especially over Lebanon's territory through Hezbollah.

Over time a diversity of positions among Iranian intellectual elites, civic movements, and political activists developed over how best to govern and interact with the outside world; these ideas importantly made their way into government via elections. Foreign policy in general was affected by such ideas, including toward Israel. Unlike the tendency to select confrontational positions in the immediate post-1979 environment, which Iran's government framed as reactions to external threats and invasions, more moderate positions have been advocated in recent years. Perhaps the most well-known shift in policy alternatives occurred during the rule of President Khatami (1997–2005). His ideas about the need for a "dialogue among civilizations" were shared by a wide cross section of Iranians (Sariolghalam 2002). In essence, he recognized the centrality of fear in the Iranian narrative but proposed his own interpretation about acceptable and appropriate action. Thus, his policy position was that dialogue was best to secure Iran, not clashing with the world. In tandem with such a policy position, indirect confrontations with Israel, especially verbally, continued with Iranian support of proxies; rivaling centered mainly over Palestinian rights as well as Israel's occupation of Lebanon. Israel's contemplation of a lasting resolution to the Palestine question that had occurred in the early 1990s under Yitzhak Rabin did hold potential to dampen the threat from Iran (or others) since it would have demonstrated a clear Israeli intent to help advance the right of the Palestinians for self-determination. This ended with the collapse of the peace process in the early 2000s; Israel's exit from Lebanon, meanwhile, reduced but did not eliminate the opportunity for friction with Hezbollah.

Moreover, the United States branded Iran as part of the axis of evil at a time when Iran had tried to help in the Afghanistan war with intelligence and had not been implicated with the 2001 attacks on the United States. In the face of renewed and direct American intervention in Iraq in 2003, as well as growing Israeli calls for intervention in Iran, Iranian fears of a hostile world were heightened rather than attenuated. They therefore expected a government that would confront threatening actors.

SHOCK TWO: IRAN'S NUCLEAR PROGRAM PUBLICIZED

In 2002 Mojahedin-e Khalq (an anti-Iranian government political-military group) released information about Iran developing a clandestine uranium enrichment program, information that was later confirmed in a 2003 International Atomic Energy Agency (IAEA) report. Around 2004–5 Iranian leaders made public their intent to develop a nuclear program geared toward energy production and other civilian needs. Against a backdrop of goal incompatibilities emerging from their narratives, hostility in the Iran-Israel rivalry was set on an ascendancy track. Tensions fluctuated but rose consistently, ranging from clandestine operations to open hostilities.

For monarchic Iran, a nuclear program promised to place it in the club of modern states (even if the state did not have the necessary militarization program), which was a right for Iran under the terms of existing nonproliferation rules around the mid-1970s. From the perspective of the Shah's interpretation of the dominant narrative, a nuclear program was "the symbol of progress and power" (A. Milani 2010). On more technical matters, a nuclear program would allow Iran to export its oil rather than burn it and thus accrue rent well into the future to spend on expansive state-building programs (Sabet 2017, 3). Similar to the hesitation that the United States leveled against the Israeli nuclear program, Washington was reserved about Iran's pursuing such a program without thorough oversight by international bodies. Historical documents (see A. Milani 2010) demonstrate that the Shah claimed Iran's right to nuclear power while simultaneously trying to affirm it did not want the bomb. Therefore, Iran's government at the time assessed that resistance to its nuclear rights came from others that deemed it somehow "unworthy" of such status and thus acted to hinder its program (Mansour 2016,

198–99). An important outcome by the end of the 1970s was "Iranian nuclear leadership's growing resentment toward the United States and nuclear suppliers" (Sabet 2017, 7). This resentment took different shapes in the later decades, driven by similar interactions with global powers.

The Islamic Republic of Iran initially halted work on the nuclear program, owing to differing clerical interpretations of how such capabilities complied with religious dictums. However, the nuclear program was relaunched in the mid-1980s with the help of Russian and Chinese technology, under intense objections from many global actors, especially the United States. Such objections ended up pushing Beijing to withdraw support for Iran in the 1990s; for the Iranian narrative, American and other pressure confirmed the global hostility vis-à-vis Iran and its rights since nuclear energy was framed by the Iranian government in these terms. An important conclusion to be drawn from the Iranian-global interaction over the nuclear file in the twenty-first century is that "Iranian officials express little confidence in the international community" (Bahgat 2006, 311). In their view the world surrounding Iran, in which Israel is leading an anti-Iran campaign with the help of the United States, still remains defined by mistrust concerning Iranian intentions or, at the very least, lacks the ability to understand Iranian strategic objectives. Moreover, vested interests continue to "manufacture" information in order to vilify Iranian policies (Porter 2014). Therefore, the United States and its allies, including Israel, acted in ways consistent with what the narrative expects. Iran, therefore, reacted to guard against another round of international hostilities, in which Israel spearheaded several means to undermine its nuclear ambition.

Israel had stakes in undermining Iran's nuclear ambitions. Israel had itself sought nuclear capabilities to protect against a surrounding environment that does not accept its existence; the memory of the 1948 war by Arab armies combined with their collective material capabilities make them a formidable foe (Cohen 1998, 12). This image of hostility, of course, did not align with the reality of Arab states having no unified or coherent strategy to counter Israel's own nuclear ambition. Nevertheless, the nuclear bomb, for Israel, was supposed to deter the Arabs and other potential threats and was worth the many confrontations with major powers during the Cold War over the process of normalizing its nuclear program.

Iran's development of a nuclear program is problematic for Israel because Israel has been able to protect itself in a hostile region (and world) by having nuclear exclusivity. A nuclear Iran means that Israel loses nuclear exclusivity in the region and thus would likely have to compromise more frequently with regional states and major powers—a position it would prefer to avoid. More important, however, Israel was able to deflect attention from its program by shrouding it in official "opacity" (a policy it incrementally fell into, not strategically thought out). As Cohen (1998, 343) notes, opacity has come to be an integral part of Israel's understanding of its security and the way it should relate to the world around it. Therefore, a nuclear Iran, even if in the civilian sector, carries the potential of forcing Israel to develop a clear deterrent posture, which means abandoning the opacity that has served it, and comforted it despite internal doubts, for decades.

Rivalry Tensions over Nuclear Matters

Cyber war has arguably been a valuable means of rivaling between Iran and Israel. With news emerging of Iranian efforts toward a nuclear program, reports surfaced documenting Israel's responses. It is often reported that relative to Israel, Iran's technological capacities in a largely internet-based confrontation appear to be limited, thus affecting their reach (Anderson and Sadjadpour 2018, chap. 3). In 2009, for example, a news report cited intelligence experts describing Israeli electronic efforts to undermine Iranian research capacities (Sherwell 2009). Then in 2010 the Stuxnet computer virus, allegedly attributed to Israel and the United States, hit Iran's computer systems, targeting in particular its nuclear facilities in Natanz and Bushehr (Savage 2016). Israel is widely suspected to have infected the Iranian facilities with the virus, and according to a German computer specialist, "This was nearly as effective as a military strike, but even better since there are no fatalities and no full-blown war. From a military perspective, this was a huge success" (Katz 2010). Crucially, then, rather than avoiding direct physical contact, virtual combat actually enabled new forms of direct physical confrontation. In addition to the disabling of Iranian nuclear facilities in Iran, confrontation has also taken the form of operations to assassinate top scientists, such as an attack on an Iranian expert in 2007 (Sherwell 2009).

Other forms of attacks have also occurred alongside cyber warfare and assassinations. The American invasion of Iraq left more space for Iran to expand its influence regionally. A series of critical American mistakes in Iraq allowed Iran to consolidate relations with allies and sympathizers inside Iraq (and elsewhere). The situation in Iraq also enabled Iran to strengthen its relation to Syria and Hezbollah. Israel countered by developing its own regional outreach. Reports emerged detailing Israel's development of tactical and strategic regional relations that would allow it to encircle Iran as part of a coordinated military attack. For instance, Israel strengthened military ties with Central Asian allies, such as Azerbaijan (Macintyre 2012), and some reports went so far as to suggest the development of an Israeli–Saudi Arabian alliance to coordinate attacks against Iran (*Haaretz* 2013). While such reports have received a combination of official denial and indifference, they have also fed intense media speculations. More recently, official Israeli statements have lent credence to such speculation, particularly when in 2012 outgoing Home Front Defense Minister Matan Vilnai announced Israeli plans to attack Iran that would see a direct military attack follow a cyberattack on relevant Iranian infrastructure (BBC 2012). In addition to this public declaration, a recording was leaked in 2015 of former Israel defense minister Ehud Barak detailing plans for strikes against Iran (Brumfield 2015).

Confrontations have also heated via proxies, especially Hezbollah in Lebanon and in the ongoing internal Syrian conflict. In this context of rivalry and incompatible narratives, Iran's alliances with actors across the region, such as Hezbollah, the Assad government in Syria, and Hamas, have all made the Iranian threat physically contiguous to Israel. This remains the case even though no signs exist that Iran has or would provide these allies advanced military systems with capabilities to threaten the existence of any considerable entity (be it Israel or any other actor). Israel has fought several proxy confrontations against Iran, especially with Hezbollah in Lebanon and with Iran's main regional ally, Syria. Iranian interventions have been central to enhance the capabilities of both Hezbollah and Syria. The driving force behind maintaining these two alliances can be found in the Iranian narrative of resisting imperial and colonial policies, such as those of Israel. It should be underscored here that Syria and Hezbollah are receptive audiences allowing Iran considerable reach in the Levant (Mansour 2018); this highlights the argument made earlier that narratives help shape policy options, while actual policies are shaped by external reactions and conditions. What is important to highlight, nevertheless, is that Iran's actions and rhetoric confirmed to Israelis that the world is hostile, regardless of how much culpability Israeli leaders have in causing these insecurities (by, for example, not acting more concertedly to create a Palestinian state) or whether other parties were acting in self-defense (e.g., in the occupation of Lebanon).

After protracted negotiations, and under intensive sanctions, in 2015 Iran reached a deal with major powers and international institutions known as the Joint Comprehensive Plan of Action (JCPOA). The world now recognized Iran's right to a nuclear program, albeit a controlled and limited one. This shift in global engagement with Iran, which was embodied in the JCPOA, represented another shock that affected the Iran-Israel rivalry.

SHOCK THREE: INTERNATIONALLY RECOGNIZING IRAN'S RIGHT TO A NUCLEAR PROGRAM

In the midst of concerted international sanctions and restraints, Iran nevertheless proceeded with its nuclear energy program and managed to achieve international recognition, including by the United States, of its right to nuclear energy. The JCPOA signaled a significant change in the international stance vis-à-vis Iran, since a consortium of international actors was ready to end or at least decrease decades-old sanctions, a good part of which were placed by the United States with direct Israeli support. Moreover, the agreement also relaxed international pressures on Iran, promising greater space to focus on economic growth and development to counter the effects of decades of sanctions. Thus, from Iran's narrative perspective, the JCPOA was a shock inasmuch as it was an abrupt change to what the narrative had assumed to be an enduringly hostile status quo: it delivered recognition of rights-based claims, therefore weakening claims that Iran was a threat to global and regional peace.

The JCPOA placed operational controls and inspections on Iran, which eased but did not eliminate Israeli anxieties. Importantly, the agreement normalized the idea of Iranian nuclear capabilities. In so doing, the JCPOA's shock effect on Israel was that it highlighted Iran's ambitious, calculating, and ultimately successful foreign policy strategy to obtain nuclear capabilities. Particularly unnerving to Israeli leaders has been Iranian restraint and perseverance in achieving goals that emerge from their narrative and reflect their ambition (Allison 2016). Israel's political process continues to produce several, often times contradictory, interpretations of Iran's threat, as well as how to deal with it. Some frame Iran's nuclear ambition as an existential threat, while others envision Israel as a state that should be more confident given that it has come a long way since (at least) the Holocaust to protect its community (see Kaye, Nader, and Roshan 2011, chap. 3). Still others worry more about the threat to Israel from Iran's strategic, regionally expanding circles of alliances (Inskeep 2015). Observers note that the nuclear agreement is symptomatic of a more serious "reality" for Israel, namely, a regionally ascendant Iran (Ahren 2015). Manifestations of Iran's ambitions are not restricted to a nuclear program but include Iran's extended and sustained influence globally, such as its relations with China and with the European Union, which it has cultivated through active diplomacy. Iranian ambition, in effect, has entrapped Israel, a dynamic that Israel has not faced, at least not at the same intensity, from other regional actors. This means that the JCPOA also shocked Israel in the sense of forcing it to confront the serious reality of an Iran with long-term strategizing capabilities, an Iran that understands the necessity of pragmatism to navigating world politics and knows how to obtain remarkable international recognition on issues of global import, such as its nuclear programs.

Nuclear Recognition Stabilizing the Rivalry

The JCPOA confirmed Iran's need for pragmatism in pursuit of national protection in a hostile world, not because its narrative appreciates it but because its narrative appreciates strategic planning and, under the constant pressure of sanctions, new approaches are necessary to contemplate. The agreement also motivated Israeli policy pragmatism (despite internal differences) in pursuit of its strategic national interests regionally (see Avishai 2017). The shock effect of the JCPOA added a measure of cautious stability to the rivalry, which is likely to endure. This effect derives from both rivaling narratives valuing pragmatism as an appropriate strategy in dealing with what they view as a perseverant and strategic rival. Shocks, as noted in the introduction of this volume, take varied forms and carry variable impacts. In the case of the JCPOA, the effects of this third shock have been underappreciated and continue to unfold. So far, the following reactions in behaviors can be observed.

Israel and Iran have so far backed down when necessary, especially in their confrontations in Syria. There have been frequent reports about Israeli targeted strikes on Iranian material supplies to the Syrian government and on Iranian military personnel in Syria, signaling Israel's concern about the expanded influence of Iranian national forces as well as those of Hezbollah. These confrontations have escalated as the Syrian government has gained the upper hand in the conflict with direct support from Iran; it is this direct Iranian intervention that has incrementally increased Iran's control of zones bordering Israel and Israel's confrontational behavior. Despite this escalation, the history of Iranian-Israeli confrontation in Lebanon demonstrates that both states prefer a policy of controlled escalation (Mansour 2018). It is therefore reasonable to expect that both parties will continue to intervene in Syria in ways that guard the gains they made in the 2015 agreement through predictable foreign policy.

In sum, before and after the nuclear deal, the internecine exchanges over Iran's nuclear program have exposed how Iran and Israel act in ways more similar than they perhaps care to admit. For one, Israel shrouds its nuclear agenda with opacity and secrecy, as Iran has done. Israel also fought Soviet interventions to stop its nuclear project and French resistance to developing its capabilities, much as Iran has done in the face of American, Israeli, and other regional opposition to its nuclear program.

FINAL COMMENTS AND PRELIMINARY OBSERVATIONS ON NARRATIVES IN RIVALRY ANALYSIS

Looking at the region from the outside, Iran and Israel would not seem to an observer to be each other's logical rivals. They are not contiguous, they do not really need to get in each other's way, they do not share resources; and they are both actually threatened by others nearby, such as the Palestinians, Syria, Saudi Arabia, and Iraq. So what can account for the fact that they did become such important rivals? This is where analyzing narratives and shocks allows for understanding of this rivalry and its regional implications.

The narratives of Iran and Israel share many ideas concerning their environment. Both narratives place emphasis on the fears provoked by living in an unforgiving world. Central to this fear is the sense of having been a historical victim to broader events over which neither group had much effective control. At varied points in the twentieth century, both Iran and Israel held strong fears that their existence as a political project was exposed to threats coming from major powers and from surrounding states. Given how major powers and regional states acted toward Iran and Israel, their narratives underscore the belief that they will always be challenged because they do not fit into many others' version of history. In both the Iranian and Israeli narrative, they are positioned as states that others in the region perceive as a threat—threats that provoke constant efforts at containment and intervention (Tal 2000). This view has elicited declarations from both Iranian and Israeli decision-makers about the need to redress the global injustices done to them at varied points in time. Therefore, both states' point of departure for action to counter threats has been similar.

Narratives of negatives such as those of Iran and Israel predispose societies to a certain hypersensitivity to world politics, making their governments especially attentive to what could potentially be interpreted as hostile acts. These states are not necessarily prone to fight militarily, but they tend to have an in-built tendency to mistrust, thus laying the ideational foundation for rivalry. Such negative ideational structures also incentivize these states to hold a noncompromising position vis-à-vis the world given the threat of constant adversity. While states with such negative narratives have an ideational infrastructure that predisposes them to be wary of others, these foundations do not necessarily position everyone or anyone as a threat. The onset of a rivalry between two states that hold such narratives is caused by multiple factors, an important one of which, as I have argued, is the occurrence of shocks, as in the case of the Israel-Iran rivalry.

This relationship was delicate exactly because both states shared the sense of being encircled and under stress from the world, which encouraged strategic planning to safeguard the group or state. This demand for rationality and strategy can help shed light on how we evaluate shocks and their impact. For example, while the first shock studied here, the 1979 Iranian Revolution, started both states down the rivalry path, the subsequent shocks, Iran's nuclear program and international recognition of this program, showcase how the rivalry developed. By 2015 Israel had a well-established nuclear opacity or ambiguity posture regarding nuclear capabilities—a position that has allowed it to pursue a wide range of relations with enemies and allies while (largely successfully) dampening provocations of confrontation or retaliation.

So why pragmatism in this rivalry? Pragmatism is not built-in in a narrative of negatives; rather, a noncompromising position is built-in in such a narrative. Both states ended up reverting to pragmatism and valuing it given interactions with external realities. In effect, perhaps supporting the idea that sanctions do work, Iran became pragmatic when it realized that it needed to negotiate rather than fight to get its right, whereas Israel became pragmatic when it realized that Iran had outmaneuvered it diplomatically and now it had to contend with an Iran with some nuclear capabilities and with international support. The magnitude of the shock in 2015 can be appreciated only if we understand how it was profoundly problematic for Israel to see Iran succeed in the same game of survival by resorting to strategy and calculated diplomacy; it was a shock for Iran because the international recognition meant that society now, perhaps, has to think of a world that might be changing its position on Iran. Of course, these are ongoing overtures with uncertain outcomes. They are, therefore, worth further analysis.

Moreover, the domestic audience positively interacts with its leadership insofar as rhetoric and action conforms to general narrative contents. Shocks, such as the ones analyzed in this chapter, can cause changes in narratives, as ideas can be disproven and new ones, say, concerning the means of resistance or survival, make their way to being collectively accepted. Thus, while narratives do foreclose possibilities from becoming policy options, they can change, and new policy options can become feasible.

In sum, Iran's and Israel's respective abilities to develop material capabilities to protect themselves were not *caused* by their narrative. Governments were the ones that made sense of these narratives in terms of what would be acceptable and what would not; they also chose from a constellation of options for international alliances, policies in war and peacemaking, and relations with major powers as well as political and economic governance policies. Nevertheless, what should be emphasized is that Israel and Iran's need and willingness to pursue the development of said capabilities and deploy a wide range of them in their rivalry were if not caused then certainly driven by their respective dominant narratives.

9

Revolution and Rivalry Onset

The Emergence of the Egyptian-Saudi (1955–70) and Iranian-Saudi (1979–2018) Rivalries

Karen Rasler

Scholars have long noted the consequences of revolutions for changing domestic political, economic, and social structures. Yet we have devoted less time to analyzing how revolutions affect international politics. Although international relations (IR) scholars have demonstrated that revolutionary states tend to be highly conflict prone (Armstrong 1993; Goldstone 1997; Gurr 1988; Maoz 1996; Skocpol 1979; Walt 1996), we have spent less time theorizing about how and why their leaders increase their state's propensity for instigating conflict with other countries. In an effort to rectify this issue, Colgan (2013, 23) argues that revolutionary leaders who emerge through internal revolution are more risk tolerant and politically ambitious than nonrevolutionary leaders. Having taken office outside the regularized political process, revolutionary leaders have learned to be risk tolerant, to persevere in the face of failure, and to be ready to eliminate internal rivals to consolidate their political control. Moreover, revolutionary politics will select leaders who are ambitious to change the status quo. Hence, revolutions pose dangerous problems for leaders in neighboring states who are likely to perceive that revolutionists will have political goals that transcend domestic boundaries into the international system. Inevitably, new rivalries are likely to develop.

This chapter presents a theoretical argument that links revolutions with rivalries as a consequence of conflicts between states over clashing political ideologies. How and why revolutions led to new rivalries between Egypt and Saudi Arabia in the 1950s and 1960s and between Iran and Saudi Arabia in the post-1979 era are the subjects of this paper. The case will be made that leaders who emerged in the aftermath of an internal revolution pursued radical foreign policies on the basis of their political revolutionary ideologies. Moreover, these ideologies were closely linked to the rise of new definitions of Pan-Arabism in the 1950s and 1960s and pan-Arab Islamism in the 1980s.

By focusing explicitly on the role that revolutions played in generating new rivalries, the following discussion slices into a section of history on Middle East politics since 1945 without covering all aspects of the political dynamics that came before or after the Egyptian and Iranian Revolutions. The discussion is more about how new ideologies gave rise to Saudi Arabia's rivalry relationships with Egypt and Iran and how they affected regional cleavages from a regional, rather than a global, perspective.

THEORETICAL ARGUMENT

The emergence of the rivalries between Egypt and Saudi Arabia in 1955 and between Saudi Arabia and Iran in 1979 occurred in the aftermath of revolutions in both Egypt and Iran.[1] The 1952 Egyptian Revolution ushered in a revolutionary leadership under Gamal Abdel Nasser, who attempted to promote Egypt's regional status to hegemony. In the aftermath of the 1979 Iranian Revolution and the overthrow of a pro-American autocrat, Mohammad Reza Pahlavi (the Shah), a radical Islamic government under the leadership of Ayatollah Khomeini also sought regional hegemony. Both of these cases illustrate Diehl and Goertz's (2000) theoretical and empirical arguments that 90 percent of the birth or commencement of rivalries is associated with internal or external shocks. While external shocks are connected to wars, changes in territorial control, and rapid shifts in the distribution of capabilities among states, internal shocks are independence, civil war, and changes in regimes. In the cases of Egypt and Iran, revolutions not only brought about significant changes in the domestic politics of these nation-states but also had dramatic impacts on the regional politics of the Middle East by generating new rivalries that altered the pattern of regional alignments, cast doubt on existing agreements and norms, and introduced new security competition. Revolutions bring about these developments largely as a result of the rise of new entrepreneurial leaders who bring novel ideologies to their foreign policies that essentially clash with the prevailing views in the region. Figure 9.1 illustrates the theoretical argument about how and why revolutions generate new strategic rivalries that in turn affect regional competition and

Figure 9.1. Relationships among revolution, rivalries, and regional conflict

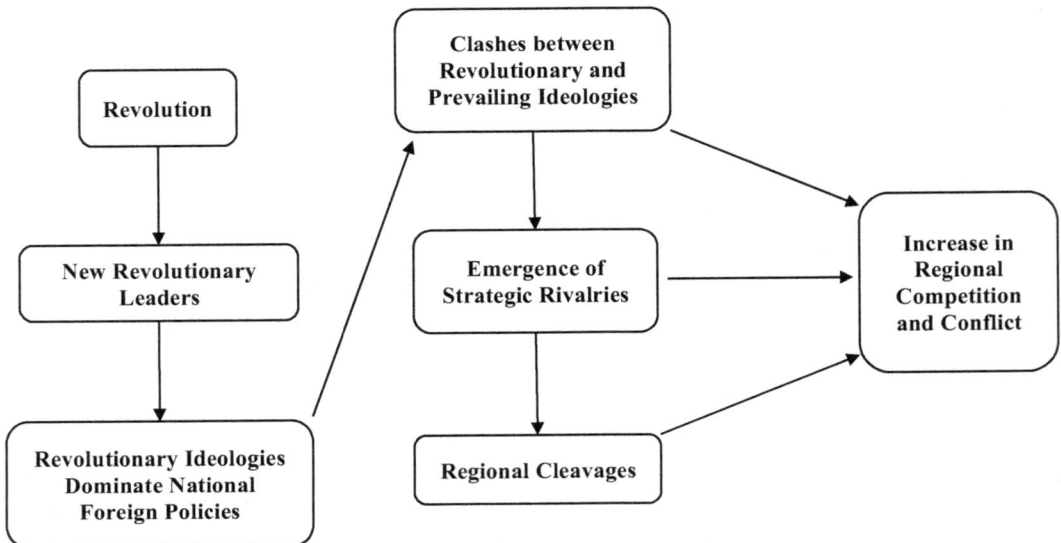

conflict. This framework will be applied to two rivalries: the Egypt–Saudi Arabia case (1955–67) and the ongoing Iran–Saudi Arabia case (1979–). But key concepts and theoretical relationships need to be explained more precisely before the analysis can proceed.

First, what do the terms "revolution" and "revolutionary leaders" mean? A revolution brings about the destruction of an existing state by members of its own society and a new political, economic, and social order (Walt 1996, 12). Revolutions are distinguished from insurrections, rebellions, revolts, coups, and wars of independence (Huntington 1968, 264). Revolutionary leaders are those who are central to a revolution and who obtain control of the state's postrevolutionary government (Colgan 2013, 21). As a result of their struggle to topple an incumbent regime successfully, these leaders will have a high degree of risk tolerance and be politically ambitious. They are risk tolerant in that they are willing to achieve payoffs through risky gambles, which means they are likely to settle disputes through armed conflict. Meanwhile, revolutionary leaders also have ambitious goals that transcend domestic boundaries and spill over to their foreign policies. They will seek changes both inside and outside their revolutionary state, which increases conflict with their neighbors, but the perceived benefits of this conflict will exceed its costs (Colgan 2013, 25).

Second, what is a "strategic rivalry"? Strategic rivalry is essentially about the core conflicts of interest between two states over territory, influence and status, and ideology (Thompson 2001). These actors must regard each other as (a) competitors, (b) the source of threats that pose some possibility of becoming militarized, and (c) enemies. All three of these criteria must be present to create a strategic rivalry. Thompson's (2001) definition of strategic rivalry stresses a perceptual perspective in that each side expects hostile behavior from the other and both sides deal with each other with that expectation in mind. Over time these expectations become more rigid and even reinforced by domestic constituencies who lobby for maintaining the rivalry. The combination of expectations of threat, cognitive rigidities, and domestic political processes reinforce substantial barriers to cooperation and conflict de-escalation between the participants. Hence, some level of conflict and distrust becomes the norm (Colaresi, Rasler, and Thompson 2007, 28).

Next, why is a strategic rivalry likely to emerge in the aftermath of a revolution? Revolutions create strategic rivalries because they bring forth revolutionary leaders who challenge the prevailing status quo and consequently heighten the threat perceptions held by their regional neighbors. Revolutionary leaders, who have successfully toppled their government, are likely to challenge not only its domestic policies but its foreign policies as well. And since they are likely to have ideologies that portray their regional neighbors in harsh and uncompromising terms, these leaders create conflicts of interests with other states, especially those that were allies of the old government. Meanwhile, leaders in neighboring states are likely to be insecure about the possibility of the revolution spreading to their own territories (Walt 1996).

Revolutionary foreign policies are the direct result of the ideology of the revolutionary movement that toppled the old regime. This ideology shapes both the preference of the new regime and its perceptions of the external environment. Most revolutionary ideologies contain ideas, themes, and symbols that challenge the status quo. In the context of these ideologies, revolutionary leaders are likely to adopt uncompromising views that their neighbors are intrinsically evil and incapable of internal reform. They also believe that the principles of their own revolution are "universal" and relevant for other societies and should not be confined within the boundaries of a single state. In short, revolutionary leaders are not constrained by the norms of sovereignty and nonintervention (Walt 1996). These ideologies are likely to clash with the prevailing norms and agreements established by regional governments. As revolutionary leaders adopt different regional foreign policies that alter the status quo, they magnify the perceptions of threat held by neighboring leaders, especially when they combine their policies and ideologies together in an attempt to secure regional hegemony. In that event a key strategic rivalry relationship will emerge.

Finally, what is the connection between rivalry onset, the emergence of a regional cleavage, and conflict? The strategic rivalry will define the main regional cleavage that results. In other words, the regional rivalry will reflect the confrontation between a coalition of revolutionary states ideologically aligned together and opposed by a coalition of conservative states that aim to protect the status quo both internally and externally. One can also expect that extra-regional actors will also partner with one of these coalitions. But the strategic rivalry is at the heart of these two opposing coalitions, and it will influence foreign policy conflicts in the region. The attempt by rivals to manipulate their domestic publics as well as the domestic publics in other states will reflect this conflict as well.

THE ROLE OF REVOLUTIONARY IDEOLOGIES
IN THE EMERGENCE OF THE EGYPT–SAUDI ARABIA RIVALRY

Although the Egyptian Revolution occurred in 1952, Nasser and his military colleagues focused initially on reforming the Egyptian political system rather than directing their attention to the regional politics of the Middle East. The extent of their revolutionary ideology was "primitive and general" and centered on ending corruption, social oppression, and imperialism (Kerr 1967, 8). Until 1955 Nasser concentrated on bringing about reforms that would produce an independent state with a strong army, an advanced economy, and a modernizing society—all in preparation for Egypt to play a major international role, especially in the Middle East (Sela 2004, 182).[2]

By 1955 Nasser had shifted his attention to regional Arab politics. Before the Egyptian Revolution in 1952, Egypt's foreign policy had been based on the principles of balancing inter-Arab relations rather than on dominating them and opposing any revisionist plans for regional unification. Yet Nasser deviated from these principles by promoting Egypt's regional status to hegemony. He challenged the inter-Arab status quo and the rules and norms of the Arab League, in which Arab states agreed to respect each other's independence and sovereignty (Sela 2004, 188). Nasser's foreign policy was based on ensuring the liberation of the region from Western influence, promoting Arab national unity as an existential necessity against imperialism, and securing worldwide stature as a leading force for decolonization and support for national liberation movements everywhere (Sela 2004, 182).

These goals were an extension of Nasser's ideology of Pan-Arabism, which was fundamentally revolutionary because it challenged other regional states' understanding of Arab nationalism. According to Valbjorn and Bank (2012, 8), there are three variants of Arab nationalism. As an overarching framework, Arab nationalism itself is based on the "idea that special bonds exist between people speaking Arabic as they belong to the same distinct Arab nation based on common language, history, culture and tradition" (Valbjorn and Bank 2012, 8). While cultural Arabism is one type of Arab nationalism, the other variants—"political Arabism" and "Pan-Arabism"—are more important because eventually they will account for the ideological clashes that will emerge between Egypt and some of its regional neighbors, especially Saudi Arabia. Political Arabism was based on the understanding that the Middle East regional context was anarchic in the sense that it lacked centralized authority, but it was also marked by a strong sense of a supra-state community. More precisely, the Arab states were only to be considered as territorial states, while their national constitutions declared that they were part of the "Arab nation." Hence, it was understood that membership in the Arab nation involved solidarity among Arabs and a commitment to Arab "core issues," with the defense of Palestine as the most prominent (Valbjorn and Bank 2012, 10–11). This understanding of Arab nationalism dominated the views of the conservative Middle East states such as Saudi Arabia.

Meanwhile, Pan-Arabism is based on the understanding that the Arab world constitutes a "pan-system" (Valbjorn and Bank 2012, 9)—a notion that supports the goal of territorial unity in terms of a merger of "artificial Arab territorial states" into a "true" Arab nation-state. Until that merger occurs, Arab interests and security concerns should always take precedence over a narrow definition of national interest, including state sovereignty. Nasser declared through radio broadcasts throughout the Middle East that since Arab nationalism was the primary ideological and emotional identification of every Arab, then Egypt had not just the right but the duty to intrude into the affairs of other countries that were not conducting themselves in accordance with Arab nationalist principles. Moreover, Egypt had a revolutionary mission to promote a unified Arab future and would refrain from extending cooperation with other Arab states should it adversely affect the "people's movement" (Dawisha 2016, 151–53). In short, Egypt "as a revolution" would not observe the same territorial boundaries as Egypt "as a state" (James 2006, 53).

Nasser's efforts to monopolize the meaning of the "Arab interest" while discrediting his adversary's Arab credentials were opposed by conservative, pro-Western monarchies, such as Jordan, Iraq (until 1958), and Saudi Arabia, which subscribed to a weak political Arabism. Their understanding of the role of Arab nationalism was similar to the ideas formulated in the Arab League charter, which endorsed interstate cooperation between sovereign Arab states within an Arab framework of "brotherhood, solidarity and coordination" (Valbjorn and Bank 2012, 11).

Unfortunately, from the viewpoint of the conservative monarchs, Nasser's understanding of Arab nationalism won widespread support around the entire Arab world, fueled by the Voice of the Arab radio broadcasts throughout the region. When Nasser announced a major Czech arms deal with the Soviet bloc in 1955, to great public acclaim across the region, he introduced an Arab cold war with local alliances split into two blocs and linked to extra-regional states, such as the United States and the Soviet Union.

According to Lynch (2013), the Arab cold war was a battle of ideas with intense polarization between the views of Pan-Arabism and political Arabism. Crucial issues about whether an Arab government should be a republic or a monarchy, or whether it should be oriented toward the West or the Soviet Union, or whether it should be nationalistic or pan-Arabic were fought out across the region through radio broadcasts. Lynch (2013) maintains that those states that were unable to control the flow of ideas and popular mobilization within their own borders became the arenas for regional competition, while states that had relatively closed political systems gained strength.

Lynch (2013, 60) also argues that a decisive turning point in the regional politics of Arab nationalism occurred with the military intervention in the Suez by Britain, France, and Israel. The eventual Western withdrawal from the Suez (due to Eisenhower's intervention) boosted Nasser's pan-Arab ideology throughout the region. Taking advantage of his widespread popularity, Nasser moved more aggressively to bid for regional hegemony.

As a consequence of Egypt's intrusion into the interstate relations of Iraq, Syria, Lebanon, and Jordan, other ambitious Arab states saw Egypt as a competitor, while weaker states feared the threat that Egypt constituted to their political independence. Nasser's practice of directly calling on the Arab masses' allegiance and mobilization for action against their regimes constituted a threat to the other Arab states' sovereign rulers. Nasser's secular, radical vision of Arab nationalism contrasted sharply with conservative, pro-Western Arab leaders, including Saudi king Faisal and Jordanian king Hussein. As head of this conservative coalition, Saudi Arabia sought to counter Nasser's pro-Soviet alliance of Egypt, Syria, Algeria, and the Yemen Arab Republic. In 1957, after a visit to the United States, King Saud gave his support to the Eisenhower Doctrine. He believed that a strong US role in the Middle East, coupled with the provisions of military and economic assistance to friendly regimes, would constitute a means for keeping the area secure from the threat of communism (Holden and Johns 1981, 190–91). At this point, any remaining cooperative relationship with Nasser was over. Over the next decade a bitter confrontation raged between the Egyptian and Saudi regimes as both competed for building strong relationships among the Arab states (Sharnoff 2011).

Despite his promotion of revolutionary ideals, Nasser's primary ambition was to achieve predominance in the Arab world—and to a lesser extent, throughout the Middle East and Africa. This aspiration constituted the most persistent attribute of Egyptian foreign policy under Nasser (Ferris 2013, 4). Nasser transformed Egypt's military into a preeminent regional power, largely as a result of his ability to negotiate advanced weapons and cheap development credits from the Soviet Union as well as plenty of economic aid from the United States. His success was based on his ability to manage the superpower competition between the United States and the USSR.

In addition to Egypt's transformation, Nasser led a successful campaign against the Baghdad Pact in 1955; emerged triumphant against the British, the French, and the Israelis in the Suez War of 1956; and announced a union between Egypt and Syria (the United Arab Republic) in 1958. All of these developments—Nasser's revolutionary zeal, the buildup of Egypt's military capabilities, and his regional popularity among the Arab populace—threatened the conservative status quo countries (Ferris 2013, 9).

THE APEX OF THE EGYPT–SAUDI ARABIA RIVALRY, REGIONAL CLEAVAGES, AND CONFLICT

Between 1955 and 1967 the central axis of regional politics was the inter-Arab conflict between Egypt and Saudi Arabia. Between 1955 and 1967 the "Arab cold war" split the Arab world in two alignments: the Egyptian-led revolutionary military regimes backed by the Soviet Union versus the Saudi-led conservative monarchies supported by the United States and Great Britain (Ferris 2013, 2). In the early phases of the rivalry the Arab cold war consisted mostly of propaganda and subversive attempts to undermine rival governments and their allies, but in September 1962 the rivalry became intense as a result of a coup d'etat in Yemen in which a coterie of military officers succeeded in overthrowing the Imamate, a dynastic institution of religious leaders. The Egyptian government backed the revolutionaries, and within days its troops arrived in Yemen to support them. In reaction the Saudis gave refuge to the deposed Yemeni imam Badr and provided his followers with military and financial assistance, declaring their support for the Yemeni royalists.

From October 1962 until December 1967 Egypt and Saudi Arabia were locked in a bloody struggle to control the outcome of the Yemen Civil War, which would shape the political future of the Middle East. The eventual outcome of Egypt's five-year campaign had major consequences for the participants and the region as a whole: the decline of Egypt and the rise of Saudi Arabia, the twilight of Arab nationalism, and the dawn of political Islam (Ferris 2013, 3).

Egypt's intervention in Yemen proved to be very costly. The war was not coming to a successful close quickly enough. In fact, the Yemen republic required the protection of nearly one-third of the Egyptian armed forces, which were mired in guerrilla war with no end in sight (Ferris 2013, 216). Although exact figures are hard to come by, Ferris (2013, 198) asserts that the war was a substantial burden on the Egyptian budget at a time of deep economic crisis. The drain of approximately $100 million per year in the mid-1960s was a serious problem while Egypt was running a current account deficit of approximately $250 million. Ferris (2013, 198) also suggests that the annual expenditure on the war equaled at least 2 percent of Egypt's gross domestic product (GDP) and consumed more than 20 percent of the entire budget for national security. Some Egyptian officials contended that the price tag for the war was in the vicinity of $1 billion, of which at least $500 million constituted debt to the USSR, which canceled it in 1965.

However, Ferris (2013, 199) argues that the far greater indirect costs to Egypt were incurred in its financial and political relations with the Great Powers. The availability of foreign resources for domestic development depended on Egypt's international behavior. In terms of its relationship with the USSR, Egypt's intervention generated enormous debt to the USSR, and with the Soviet Union's forgiveness of that debt, Egypt paid a political price in terms of its loss of independence. Equally important, after 1965 the United States halted its aid to Egypt, largely as a result of Egypt's unwillingness to withdraw from Yemen. Consequently, the Egyptian government had to spend more than $100 million annually in scarce and increasingly expensive foreign exchange to purchase food abroad—while continuing to spend a roughly equal amount directly on Yemen (Ferris 2013, 199).

In addition to the economic costs of the Yemen War, Nasser faced growing discontent among the Egyptian populace over the costs of the war and the growing shortages of basic foodstuffs. From mid-1963 onward Nasser realized that the growing economic burden of the war required him to negotiate with Saudi Arabia in order to end the conflict. As a result, the first Arab summit meeting between the region's heads of state was held in Cairo in January 1964. There Nasser initiated negotiations with the Saudis over Yemen. The summit produced a Saudi-Egyptian rapprochement shortly afterward, but differences over the Saudis' unwillingness to recognize the new Yemen government and Egypt's unwillingness to militarily withdraw from the Yemen republic unless its survival was guaranteed emerged as obstacles that would not be resolved until after the Six-Day War in June 1967 (Ferris 2013, 216–18).

In the aftermath of the devastating results of the June 1967 war, Nasser revised his overall regional strategy. In addition to the massive destruction of arms and combat units, the loss of the main sources of revenues in foreign currency—the Suez Canal, Sinai oil, and tourism—were especially destructive for Egypt's economy. Consequently, Nasser opted for a new realism (Sela 2004, 197). At the Khartoum summit Nasser abandoned his revolutionary slogans and assertive inter-Arab policies and accepted diplomacy as the best strategy for dealing with Israel. He called for the use of Arab oil to realize the Arab goal of forcing Israel's withdrawal to prewar 1967 borders. He suggested that recovering Egypt's lost territories was a higher priority than the Palestinian issue. Although he had become more pragmatic, Nasser also reassured Arab militants associated with the Palestine Liberation Organization, Syria, and Algeria that he was still committed to Palestinian liberation.

Also at Khartoum, Nasser confronted the necessity of unilaterally withdrawing his military forces from Yemen. The key bargain that Nasser struck with the Saudis was the full military withdrawal of his forces from Yemen in return for Saudi financial aid for a weak Egyptian economy. The Saudis refused to negotiate any precise plans on the future of the new government in Yemen until Egypt had withdrawn completely. In return, the Saudis along with Kuwait and Libya offered Egypt an annual economic aid package of 95 million pounds, which was roughly equivalent to the revenues lost in the closure of the Suez Canal (Ferris 2013, 291).

In conclusion, Egypt's retreat from Yemen brought about a fundamental shift in the regional balance of power, the decline of Egypt, and the rise of Saudi Arabia. After Nasser's death Egypt became increasingly preoccupied with internal challenges and eventually lost its regional preeminence. The oil-rich Saudis, in contrast, became the "kingmakers of Arab politics." The withdrawal of Egypt's armies from Yemen ended the existential threat to Saudi Arabia for a generation. According to Ferris (2013, 298), Egypt's setbacks in Yemen and the June 1967 war signaled the decline of the resource-poor Levant—once the central axis of Arab politics—and the rise of the oil-rich Gulf as the primary arena of geostrategic competition in the Middle East.

The Egyptian-Saudi rivalry was primarily a struggle for political influence and a competition for legitimacy between contending political orders. In the context of the regional Arab cold war, the rivalry was at the heart of the contest between the "secular-socialist model of nationalist republicanism," which was imported from Europe, and a model of monarchic conservatism that was grounded in the Islamic tradition of government. Egypt's venture into Yemen played a significant role in the decline of Egypt's leadership role in the Middle East as well as the decline of Nasser's understanding of Pan-Arabism and the revival of Islam (Ferris 2013, 299).

THE ROLE OF IRAN'S REVOLUTIONARY IDEOLOGY IN THE EMERGENCE OF THE IRANIAN-SAUDI RIVALRY

In the aftermath of the Iranian Revolution, between 1979 and 1982, Ayatollah Khomeini consolidated his political control over the country through the elimination of rival factions and the defeat of local internal rebellions in outlying regions of the country. The central element of Khomeini's revolutionary program was that the Iranian government was to be based on Islamic law with the clergy as its most powerful political actor to ensure that the political system adhered to Islamic principles. Since the 1979 revolution Iran's foreign policy and outreach in the Middle East has been based on Khomeini's revolutionary vision, which stressed two core beliefs. First, Khomeini regarded all other forms of government to be illegitimate because they were not based on Islam. He was especially critical of the West, the US, and the USSR, and their allies. He accused Western states of deliberately keeping the Arab world backward by conspiring to undermine the unity of Islam and the Muslim world and by exploiting its wealth and natural resources. He was especially suspicious of the US, whose support for the Shah qualified it as the "Great Satan," but the USSR and other major powers were seen as equally hostile. Khomeini was deeply insecure about efforts by the United States and the West to subvert the revolution through foreign intervention (Walt 1996, 196). In addition to the United States and the USSR, Khomeini held a great deal of hostility toward Israel, naming it an enemy of Islam. He asserted that the creation of the Zionist state was a crime against Islam as it transgressed on Islam's sacred domain. He called on his Islamic followers to donate a portion of their religious taxes to the Palestinian cause, long before Iran began supporting Hezbollah and Palestinian terrorist organizations (Takeyh 2009, 20–21).

A second core belief was based on the principle that the existing borders of the Middle East nation-states were created by Islam's enemies and hence were illegitimate. Khomeini emphasized that Muslims are part of the same *umma* (or community). He also attributed other Muslim countries' acceptance of these borders as adherence to a form of "American Islam," which reflected a lack of commitment to true Islam, as embodied in the Islamic government in Iran (Unver Nois 2013, 94). He called for active efforts to spread the Islamic revolution for the purpose of overthrowing "treacherous, corrupt, oppressive and criminal regimes" (Walt 1996, 196). This latter principle reflected Khomeini's objective to reorganize the international order in the image and spirit of Iran's own revolution. Iran would become not only the defender of Muslim rights but also the liberator of oppressed Muslims through the export of its revolutionary ideals (Unver Nois 2013, 94). Khomeini asserted that Iran would be the epicenter of a new Islamic order, seeking allies among Muslims regardless of sectarian division or ethnic differences. In other words, the Iranian Revolution reflected a "revolution without borders" whose appeal would be universal to all Muslims. The purpose of the revolution was to "liberate the discontented masses of Muslims, whether they live in the independent states of Egypt, Saudi Arabia, and Morocco or under non-Islamic government," declared Khomeini. Khomeini sought a leading regional role on the basis that the revolt in Iran was for an Islamic goal, not for Iran alone. Iran was merely the starting point (Takeyh 2009, 19–21).

Khomeini targeted Saudi Arabia as a focal point to spread the revolution. He directly challenged Saudi Arabia, calling it an American lackey, an unpopular and corrupt dictatorship that could be easily overthrown. On several occasions Khomeini used the annual Hajj to stage protests with the aim of fomenting trouble in the kingdom as well as spreading revolutionary messages among the Muslim faithful from around the world. One such instance occurred in July 1987, when clashes between Iranian pilgrims and Saudi security forces left 402 people dead. Meanwhile, Iranian revolutionaries encouraged the Shi'ite minority in Saudi Arabia (between 10 and 15 percent of the population) to organize and demand political change (Nasr 2006).

In addition to targeting Saudi Arabia as an illegitimate regime and a puppet of the United States, the Khomeini revolutionists co-opted the Palestinian cause, challenging Saudi Arabia's leadership on the Israeli-Palestinian issue. By financially supporting Hamas and the Palestinian Islamic Jihad after 2000, Iran has tried to reduce its isolation in the region and to demonstrate that it is more than a sectarian actor in the Middle East (Wehrey et al. 2009, 21–22).

Over time Iranian rhetoric about a pan-Islam identity gained considerable traction and influence in the region, particularly in the aftermath of the 2006 Lebanon War. During the 2006 war Hezbollah, an Iranian ally, clashed successfully with Israeli forces for thirty-four days. While conservative regimes such as Saudi Arabia, Egypt, and Jordan criticized Hezbollah for "irresponsible adventurism" that would drag the region into needless conflict, the mass populace in the region expressed unqualified support for Hezbollah's role, especially among Sunni leaders and news outlets. The Lebanese conflict revealed a cleavage between the mass publics supporting Hezbollah and their conservative governments that opposed it. Moreover, at the societal level the predominant framing of the conflict was rooted in an Arab nationalist narrative based on Arab solidarity, resistance to occupation, and the liberation of Palestine. According to Valbjorn and Bank (2012, 9), Hezbollah was popularly perceived as more of an Arab than a Shi'ite movement, and Hassan Nasrallah, as secretary general of Hezbollah, was viewed as the "only true Arab leader" of the day. At the same time, Iranian president Mahmoud Ahmadinejad came in second after Nasrallah as the most important leader in the region. The Lebanon War revived the sense of "Arab nationalism," not unlike the Pan-Arabism of Nasser's era, and Iran's belief that it could draw support from Arab publics encouraged it to be more aggressive toward the Saudis (Wehrey et al. 2009, 23).

Saudi Arabia's Response to the Iranian Revolution

Throughout the 1960s the Saudis had resisted the idea of Arab nationalism and survived the days of Nasserism and Ba'athism by branding them as atheistic. Saudi Arabia relied on its Wahhabi identity to stave off secular nationalism at home and across the Middle East. After the Iranian Revolution in 1979, the Saudis began to export Wahhabi Islamism aggressively around the Islamic world through financial donation to Islamic colleges, centers, mosques, and schools. The Saudi monarchy maintains its domestic legitimacy by portraying itself as the leader of the Islamic faith. It also balances the competing Islamic forces within Saudi Arabia with its need to outmaneuver competing Islamic trends in the region. In particular, the Saudis have a deep hostility to Iran and Shi'ism and aim not only to protect their monarchical rule but also increase their sphere of influence around the Middle East against alternative Islamic models (Unver Nois 2013, 94–95).

In the immediate aftermath of the Iranian Revolution, the Saudis perceived a direct threat to their own domestic stability, especially from their Shi'ite populace in the Eastern Province, where long-term discriminatory policies against the Shi'ites would find a receptive audience. Khomeini revolutionists did indeed attempt to promote internal conflict through the export of leaflets, radio broadcasts, and tape cassettes castigating the Saudi government as corrupt and oppressive. Saudi insecurities were reinforced by an upsurge of protests and demonstrations among Shi'ites against Saudi authorities in towns and cities between 1978 and 1980. In February 1980 violent demonstrations erupted when Shi'ite protesters attacked banks and vehicles while holding placards with Khomeini's image. The Saudi government responded with a mix of coercion and co-optation, arresting leading Shi'ite activists while committing to more infrastructure projects for electricity, schools, hospitals, and improved sewage disposal. The strategy worked, and further outbreaks of Shi'ite protests declined significantly (Commins 2006, 171).

In an effort to contain Iran's influence in the Middle East region, the Saudis played the sectarian card by emphasizing Khomeini's Shi'ite identity as well as the divide between Shi'ism and Sunnis in order to undercut any Sunnis who might accept Khomeini as an Islamic leader. The Soviet Union's invasion of Afghanistan in 1979 presented an opportunity for the Saudis to reaffirm their Islamic legitimacy in the face of the challenges posed by Khomeini. In an effort to appeal to both international and domestic audiences, the Saudis began subsidizing the recruitment, travel, and training of foreign jihadist volunteers to Afghanistan. They also sponsored the production of anti-Shi'ite and anti-Iranian tracts designed to highlight the narrow ethnic and sectarian aspirations of the Iranian regime in order to slow its universal appeal throughout the region (Wehrey et al.

2009, 14). Saudi Arabia pursued this strategy by also working with Wahhabi ulama to build a network of religious and education institutions including activists, writers, journalists, preachers, and academics to highlight militant Wahhabism and create cleavages between Sunnis and Shi'ites. One of Saudi Arabia's aims was to support Sunni radicalism from Pakistan, to Afghanistan, and into Central Asia—all in an effort to contain Iran's growing influence (Nasr 2006). By the mid-1990s, according to Nasr (2006), Iranian financial support for Shi'a activism had dried up because the Iranians could not compete with the scale of Sunni militancy that Saudi patrons had bankrolled with millions of dollars.

From the late 1980s to the early 2000s, Khomeini's dream of spreading the Islamic Revolution throughout the Muslim world, starting in the Middle East, had failed, largely owing to Saudi efforts to contain it. Instead, Iran began engaging in more normal state-to-state diplomacy in the region, improving its relationships with the Gulf Cooperation Council (GCC) states, Turkey, and Egypt. If Iran's regional moderation was partly the result of a lack of opportunities to spread its influence, the US invasion in Iraq in 2003 opened up new possibilities considering the majority Shi'ite population in Iraq. Meanwhile, the election of President Mahmoud Ahmadinejad in 2005 brought to power a domestic Iranian faction that was more committed to the revolutionary rhetoric of Ayatollah Khomeini and to spreading Iranian influence to the domestic politics of other states. After 2003 Iran reached a new position of influence and power in the eastern Arab world. By the mid-2000s Iran was a leading, if not the leading, foreign influence in Lebanon, Syria, and Iraq (Gause 2014, 12).

THE IMPACT OF THE IRANIAN–SAUDI ARABIA RIVALRY ON REGIONAL CLEAVAGES AND CONFLICT

The emergence of an Islamic state in Iran after its 1979 revolution disrupted the Middle East regional order and eventually eroded the alliances of moderate forces in the area (Ehteshami 2002). Iran's ideological competition with Saudi Arabia played out in two key areas of the region: the Gulf and the Levant (Mabon 2013). In the Gulf area three wars drove the competition between these rivals: the Iran-Iraq wars in the 1980s; the Second Gulf War in 1990, after Hussein invaded Kuwait; and the Third Gulf War with the US invasion of Iraq in 2003. In the aftermath of Iraq's defeat in 1991, US military presence in the area increased substantially, and this issue was a source of friction between the Saudis, who welcomed the US presence for protection, and the Iranians, who perceived the US presence to be an obstacle to its regional dominance (Mabon 2013, 55–62). However, it was the 2003 US invasion and subsequent occupation of Iraq that fundamentally altered inter-Arab alignments and the geopolitics of the region. Since 2003 relations between the Iranians and the Saudis had worsened every year, but the trigger for a more active regional policy by the Saudis occurred when Prime Minister Nouri al-Maliki, sponsored by Iran, emerged in Iraq in 2005. At this point the Saudis overtly rejected the new Baghdad government. In addition, Iran's nuclear program also escalated the conflict. The Saudis feared that Iran would acquire nuclear weapons and the United States would be too conciliatory and might accept Iranian regional supremacy in return for concessions on its nuclear program (Steinberg 2014, 13).

As for the Levant, the competition between Iran and Saudi Arabia has been no less intense than in the Gulf area. According to Gause's (2014, 8) analysis of regional politics in the Middle East, the Iranian-Saudi rivalry is better understood as a competition that is not based on testing each other on the military battleground as the Egyptian-Saudi rivalry was in the Yemen Civil War. Rather, the rivalry is based on the efforts of the two adversaries' ability to promote the success of their non-state clients in weak states that face domestic instability. The Iranians and the Saudis have worked to expand their regional influence through their political connections with subnational actors in order to blunt or contain the influence of the other. They were most effective in states whose governments were unable to co-opt, control, and repress their populations effectively. For instance, in Lebanon in the 1980s, Iran was able to support the creation of Hezbollah after Israel's invasion of 1982. Eventually, Hezbollah became the most important actor in the country despite the Saudis' support for their own Lebanese clients. In the Palestinian Authority, an example of a weak pseudo-state, Iran supported Hamas and Islamic Jihad, and in 2007, Hamas gained control over Gaza at the expense of Fatah, which maintained its influence in the West Bank. Meanwhile, the Saudis have maintained their support for Fatah in the West Bank. In Yemen, another example of a weak central government, Saudi Arabia built relationships with tribal sheikhs, Islamist leaders, regional factions, and ambitious politicians in order to contain the Houthis, a Zaidi Shi'ite movement that developed in the early 2000s (Gause 2014, 13–14).

The upheavals of the 2011–12 Arab Spring have intensified the rivalry significantly. The loss of Hosni Mubarak in Egypt was especially worrisome since it was yet another setback in the Saudis' efforts to confront Iranian influence (Gause 2014, 15). At this point the Saudis pursued very aggressive policies to protect the allied monarchies in the region and blunt growing Iranian influence (Salloukh 2013, 40). First, they extended financial assistance to Morocco and Jordan against mounting domestic calls for reform in the form of $5 billion worth of development funds via the GCC (Salloukh 2013, 40; Steinberg 2014, 16). The Saudis also extended $20 billion of financial aid to Bahrain and Oman through the GCC (Steinberg 2014, 15). In Egypt the Saudis openly approved the July 2013 military coup against Egyptian president Muhammad Morsi, and in 2014, they declared the Muslim Brotherhood a terrorist organization. Next, the Saudis intervened militarily when protests by Shi'ites in Bahrain threatened the stability of the government. The Saudis justified the intervention by characterizing the Bahrain uprising as the work of Iran's Shi'ite agents in the area.

The Syrian uprising in 2011 started as a peaceful protest movement, but by 2012 Syria was in the throes of a sectarian civil war instigated primarily by its regime. Saudi Arabia used the uprising to end Iran's alliance with the regime of Bashar al-Assad (Salloukh 2013, 40; Steinberg 2014, 15) and sever its links to Hezbollah. In their view, control over a post-Ba'ath Sunni-dominated Syria was fair compensation for the Saudi loss of a Sunni-ruled Iraq to Iran (Salloukh 2013, 41). Consequently, Saudi Arabia supported an alliance consisting of Turkey and Qatar, along with the United States and France, against Iran, Hezbollah, and Russia with the sole aim of replacing the Iyad Allawi regime with a Sunni protégé. By 2012 the Saudis supported the more secular Free Syrian Army, while Turkey and Qatar backed Islamist groups in northern Syria. As the Free Syrian Army forces made little progress, the Saudis refocused their support toward Islamist, and particularly Salafi, opposition groups, other than Islamic State in Iraq and the Levant (ISIL) and Al Qaeda–affiliated Jabhat al-Nusra (Gause 2014, 15).

As of now, the competition between Iran and Saudi Arabia has expanded significantly beyond the Levant and the Gulf area. In the 2000s it included new terrain in Yemen, Egypt, Sudan, Pakistan, and Afghanistan. In addition, Iran's and Saudi Arabia's commitments to their client states and non-state actors in the Middle East have polarized the region between the Houthis (Yemen), the pro–Bashar al-Assad forces in Syria, and pro-Shi'ite Iraqis behind the Iranians and the Gulf states, anti-Assad Syrian rebels, anti-Houthis, and Iraqi Sunnis behind the Saudis (Bin Huwaidin 2015).

CONCLUSION

This chapter uses "rivalry" as a conceptual lens to understand the Egyptian-Saudi and the Iranian-Saudi competition in the Middle East. These rivalries emerged in the context of domestic environmental shocks associated with the Free Officers Egyptian Revolution in 1952 and the Iranian Revolution in 1979. In general, revolutions bring about tremendous domestic changes in the economic, political, and social structures of the societies in which they occur. But revolutions do more than bring about domestic change; they also alter the foreign policy relationships both on a regional and an international level. Once new revolutionary leaders consolidate their political control at home, they pursue new foreign policies vis-à-vis their traditional ones, usually policies that upend the old policies of the ancien régime. In particular, new revolutionary leaders are ideologically dogmatic and eager to export their revolution to other groups and states nearby. Consequently, revolutionists threaten the domestic stability of their neighbors, usually labeling their governments as corrupt and illegitimate. Neighboring states develop a heightened perception of threat and mobilize their resources to fend off these revolutionary challenges. The consequence is the emergence of a new rivalry. In both the Egypt–Saudi Arabia and Iran–Saudi Arabia cases, revolutions in Egypt and Iran brought new leaders with radical ideas that threatened domestic and regional stability. As new revolutionary states, Egypt and Iran embarked on aggressive policies to establish their regional dominance largely through their attempts to suborn other conservative governments, build new alliances with like-minded leaders or groups, and appropriate leadership over important symbolic issues of the day.

Other scholars have also noted that both of these rivalries were central to the rise of two distinct Middle East cold wars that share dramatic similarities. Eschewing the notion that today's Middle East politics is fundamentally different from that of earlier historical periods, Valbjorn and Bank (2012) argue that Malcolm Kerr's (1971) description of the Arab cold war of the 1950s and 1960s had important regional dynamics that also characterize the new Arab cold war. The central theme linking the old and new Arab cold wars is the role of Arab nationalism. In the aftermath of the Egyptian Revolution, Nasser invoked Pan-Arabism as a new ideology that would unite the Arab world under the leadership of Egypt. Likewise, in the aftermath of the Iranian Revolution, Khomeini advocated a pan-Arabic Islamic order that would also unite the Arab world (disregarding sectarian differences between Shi'ites and Sunnis) under Iran's leadership. Both revolutionary ideologies were disseminated to mass publics through transnational media outlets: in Egypt, radio broadcasts; in Iran, Al-Jazeera. Contrary to the Old Arab cold war, which was waged largely between Arab states on regional and domestic levels, today's cold war has a stronger regime-society dimension, in which the "radical" block is dominated by societal actors (Hezbollah, Hamas, and Islamic Jihad led by Islamists) advocating an Arab-Islamic order that resonates with the Arab publics. Yet in both cold war periods, anti-Western imperialism and support for the Palestinian cause were central elements in the ideological frameworks of their times. In both cold war eras, regional cleavages were centered on radical versus conservative or status quo axes that defined political competition and conflict over regional leadership. And in both eras revolutionary leaders, espousing new Arab narratives, were politically ambitious with designs for regional dominance. They did so by monopolizing the meaning of the "common Arab interest" and discrediting their adversary's Arab credentials (Valbjorn and Bank 2012, 16). In short, the role of revolutionary ideals rooted in Arab nationalism was important in the emergence of new rivals and their subsequent political competition.

NOTES

1. The date of the Egypt–Saudi Arabia rivalry is derived from Thompson and Dreyer (2011, 153).

2. These reforms included economic reforms (e.g., the nationalization of banking and commercial corporations, land redistribution laws, the development of new industries), education reforms (e.g., expansion of primary and secondary schools), and social welfare reforms (e.g., health care services, food and clothing subsidies, rent control, and low-cost housing) (Danielson 2007, 31–52). Egypt's military budget was expanded substantially: in 1958 Egypt spent $211 million on defense, and by 1968 the budget increased to $506.9 million, significantly more than any other country in the region (Dawisha 1976, 87).

10

The Algerian-Moroccan Rivalry

Constructing the Imagined Enemy

Yahia H. Zoubir

With the notable exception of the period 1989–91, and a brief one following the Arab Uprisings that began in 2011, Algerian-Moroccan relations have always been antagonistic or marked with suspicions, despite the seeming occasional cordiality. True, when facing major threats as they did in the late 1980s (the rise of radical Islamism) and in 2010–12 (the Arab Spring), the two countries seek rapprochement; however, once the threats recede, the long-established competition resumes in a more pronounced way than before (Zoubir 2012). The two countries engaged in a fateful short war in 1963 and were on the brink of major war from the mid-1970s to the early 1980s. Although the two countries are central to the construction of the Maghreb, their rivalry has prevented that long-standing aspiration from materializing. Moreover, despite its existence since 1989, the Arab Maghreb Union (UMA) cannot function without the effective cooperation and the concomitant lessening of conflict between Morocco and Algeria.

Akin to a cold war, Algeria and Morocco's strained relations are not solely the result of the Western Sahara conflict; they derive from a historical evolution of which the Western Sahara is only one aspect, albeit one that has occupied a predominant place in that relationship since 1975 and has structured the foreign policies of these two states. The UMA has failed to serve as the framework within which the parties can solve the conflict owing in great part to the inability of the two countries to settle the issue on their own. The rivalry between Algeria and Morocco, including negative perceptions of each other, has not only endured but has intensified in recent years. This rivalry is visible in their relations with other states and on several issues, such as the fight against terrorism, mediation diplomacy, policy toward Africa, and relations with major powers. Given that the two sides reckon that war would result in a lose-lose outcome and "compromise the future" (Anonymous senior official, interview by the author, Algiers, August 3, 2011), they have pursued their rivalry through tit-for-tat actions meant to counteract the moves of the other.

In this chapter I will argue that the image of the other that each state has painted dates from the pre-independence period, and negative perceptions have resulted in increasingly antagonistic relations that have persisted and consolidated to this day. The chapter will look at how the policymakers in the two states have constructed the image of the other throughout the evolution of this long-standing rivalry. Studies of rivalry are interested in factors that cause rivalry to develop. In attending to those causes, this chapter argues that history, national identity, psychological motivations, state and nation building, border issues, attitudes toward the outside world, and ideological differences have all contributed to the Algeria-Morocco strategic rivalry. However, I contend that while all the factors were latent, two shocks played defining moments in initiating and intensifying the development of this interstate rivalry via construction of a hostile image of the other: the Sands War (1963) and the inception of the Western Sahara conflict (1975–76). I will also advance the argument that the Western Sahara conflict has occupied a central position in the strategic rivalry and has structured the two countries' foreign policies, particularly that of Morocco, which has elevated it to an existential and survival question. The Western Sahara is also important because of the support that France, the former colonial power, has offered Morocco since the beginning of the conflict. In sum, foreign interferences have exacerbated the ideological and provided the ammunition for each side to lambast the other.

This chapter attempts to provide an in-depth analysis of the Algeria-Morocco strategic rivalry, especially since serious research on Algerian-Moroccan competitive relations from the rivalry perspective is scant (Conesa 2011, 62). Thus, this chapter will seek to fill at least part of this gap. The endeavor is challenging because neither country represents a military threat to the other despite perceptions to the contrary; indeed, there is a "gap between the [Moroccan] discourse that builds the menace and reality" (Mekki 2016). The challenge is, of course, to understand the underlying reasons behind the construction of the enemy. Undoubtedly, the colonial legacy, historical memory, psychology, (mis)perceptions, postcolonial border issues, and foreign alignments and interference (an important dimension) have all played a role in shaping the images and sustained the rivalry. Therefore, it is important at the onset to discuss the shaping of perceptions in Algerian-Moroccan relations and their impact on the strategic rivalry.

PERCEPTIONS IN THE STRATEGIC RIVALRY

In the Algerian-Moroccan rivalry, perceptions have played a consequential role. Decision-makers in the two states tend to see the other state as more hostile than it is. "They fit incoming information into the existing theories and images" that they have developed about the other, and they are unwilling to change their views in the face of conflicting information (Jervis 1968, 455). The actions one side takes are often interpreted by the other side as an attempt to harm its interests. Moreover, whenever one actor seeks to convince the other of its good intentions, the other actor perceives it as confirmation of bad faith. This type of interaction obviously prevents the establishment of rational dialogue among the parties. Unsurprisingly, the two rivals "are competing over largely unresolved, distinctive goal incompatibilities. Both sides want things that the other side denies them and they have not devised a way to compromise. . . . This stream of conflict alters the way objective events are perceived, increasing the escalatory potential of even pre-sumably innocuous events. Adversaries believe that they have ample reason to mistrust the opposite side" (Colaresi, Rasler, and Thompson 2007, 25). This mistrust has been the hallmark of the Algeria-Morocco rivalry. Until the 1990s Algeria's defense policy rested on defense against potential aggression from Morocco (high-level defense official, inter-view by the author, Algiers, September 28, 2011). This policy has shifted owing to domes-tic terrorism and the threat of global terrorist groups at its borders with Libya, Mali, Niger, and Tunisia. Morocco's defense policy, for its part, is articulated around the threat from its neighbors, primarily, Algeria. "The main component of this threat [to Morocco] is associated with Algeria whose military confrontation with Morocco dates back to the 'sand war' in October 1963 shortly after Algeria's independence, and following Moroc-co's claims over a Saharan area included in the limits attributed to Algeria" (Saïdy 2009–10, 124). After 1975 Morocco's defense concentrated an important component of its troops in Western Sahara. While neither country fears a military attack from the other, the two countries exemplify the concept of "security dilemma." The substantial arms purchases that Algeria began making as of 2000 were justified by the obsolescence of its equipment and lack of financing in the 1990s, when the country was near bankruptcy; however, Morocco did not trust the reassurances coming from the decision-makers in Algiers that those purchases were not aimed at any nation. Outsiders amplified this per-ception, suggesting an arms race when, objectively, Algeria's rearmament did not aim at Morocco.[1]

The construction of Algeria as an enemy, coupled with the mutual misperceptions between the two protagonists, has been relatively easy because Algeria does not have a positive image in Morocco, especially since the media have carried out an all-out cam-paign on behalf of the Moroccan political elite (Dekkar 2016). The interesting element is that this image is also prevalent among academics, who may provide an image similar to the representation that the decision-makers and the media convey about Algeria. For instance, a Moroccan academic argues that a "military junta" that conceals its weight in the political system by focusing on external events, namely, on Western Sahara, rules Algeria. The existence of such a military-dominated regime explains, in this view, the protracted nature of the conflict in Western Sahara (El-Maslouhi 2011, 12). In fact, the media in Morocco refer to the regime in Algeria as "the regime of the generals," which has a negative connotation. Most Moroccan analysts, with few exceptions, hold the view that the Western Sahara conflict is the Algerian regime's creation aimed at erecting a pup-pet state in order to weaken its eastern neighbor (Berramdane 1992, 344). This view sup-ports the image of Morocco that King Hassan (and later Mohamed VI) and Moroccan diplomats have sought to project around the world, especially in the West: one of a pro-Western, stable kingdom. This alignment with the West has not only contributed to the divergent identities of the two states but also exacerbated the strategic rivalry to this day. Indeed, until the early 1980s Algeria pursued a radical foreign policy (support for national liberation movements, unconditional support to the Palestinians, and opposi-tion to apartheid), and though nonaligned, it maintained closer military and political relations with the Soviet Union and China than with Western countries. This was because the USSR, China, and Yugoslavia had supported it during its war of liberation. Unlike republican, revolutionary Algeria, Morocco is a conservative monarchy opposed to socialist ideology. And despite the pragmatism and abandonment of radical rhetoric, Algeria maintains a foreign policy that embraces many of the principles that bring it at loggerheads with Morocco (Zoubir 2004).

Furthermore, the Western Sahara question "has been instrumental in forming Moroccan national identity" and "has also played a crucial role in the survival and further legitimization of the Moroccan monarchy" (Messari 2001, 48). Before dealing with the events and the shocks that initiated the strategic rivalry, it is important to establish first the context in which this rivalry emerged.

ALGERIA, MOROCCO, AND THE MAGHREB SUBSYSTEM

One can safely describe the Maghreb as a regional system (Hurrell 1995); therefore, the strategic rivalry between Algeria and Morocco occurs in the context of a subsystem or subregion (Colaresi, Rasler, and Thompson 2007, 79). "System" means the existence of observable patterns of interactions and relationships and of boundaries separating the system from its external environment. One can also assume that, in their foreign relations, the units of the system constitute mutually interrelated entities. In the Maghreb the characteristics common to all units underscore this premise. More specifically, the core units (here understood as Algeria, Morocco, and Tunisia, with Mauritania and Libya later included in the Maghreb) display different patterns. Algeria, Morocco, and Tunisia (a.k.a Central Maghreb) share elements of identity, such as common language (including a common dialect), an ethnically homogeneous population (Arab-Berber), an Islamic religion and a common Islamic rite (*Maleki*), an identical historical experience (such as French colonialism and resistance against it), and a similar culture. More important, those characteristics are a major component of Maghrebi consciousness and identity. Elites and masses in the region equally share this consciousness and sense of belonging (Abed-Jabri 1985). Yet despite the strong similarities that characterize the Maghreb states and the deep-seated aspirations toward regional unity, the Maghreb has suffered the same intra-systemic conflicts that have plagued other regions of Africa. Thus, to understand Algerian-Moroccan relationships, it is important to identify first the major causes and sources of conflict and the states' management of issues concerning borders (boundaries), sovereignty, and national security, or rather securitization (Balzacq 2010).

As in other parts of Africa, power politics dominate postcolonial interstate relations: nation-states behave in a way that would preserve their territorial integrity, ensure their sovereignty, and guarantee their survival (Ojo, Orwa, and Utete 1985). Short of war, Maghrebi states responded to a perception of a threat to those values by entering alliances—albeit short-lived—to preserve the balance of power, thereby deterring any attempt by one unit to dominate the system. The Maghrebi balance of power involved states still in the process of national construction and consolidation. In other words, the process of building the nation-state constitutes one of the major sources of interstate conflicts. The intensification of the nationalist feelings in Algeria and Morocco soon after their independence in 1962 and 1956, respectively, resulted in the differentiation between the two states and the development of otherness, whereby the other can hardly question the moral superiority of the self (Shapiro 1988, 102). A Moroccan analyst captured this reality accurately when he said, "In the name of nationalism, the inhabitants of border regions of Morocco and Algeria, who are of the same ethnic and cultural makeup, are summoned to ignore each other. In the name of nationalism, they maintain big defense budgets at the expense of the vital needs of the population. In the name of nationalism, people are placed under the tutelage of security services that stretch their tentacles into the fields of politics and mass media, in the service of their interests, through manipulation, disinformation and intimidation" (Aourid 2013). As we shall see, this process has intensified since the conflict erupted over Western Sahara. Moroccan decision-makers, the monarchy in particular, have disseminated the view that had it not been for Algeria, the question of Western Sahara would not have existed, portraying Algeria as the evil because it has prevented Morocco from completing the recovery of its territory (Messari 2001, 53).

What distinguishes the Maghreb from other African regions is the existence of a unifying Maghrebi ideology that favors interstate cooperation and helps mediate conflict. In addition, the perception of external and internal threats to the region and incumbent regimes strengthens Maghrebi interstate cooperation. Although definite similarities exist between the Maghrebi states, considerable differences of political, economic, and ideological nature also persist. The nature of French colonial rule in Algeria, Morocco, and Tunisia fostered these differences. The implantation of the colonial system in northwestern Africa proceeded through the destruction of existing interactions between the different entities. The unfolding of colonial rule sped up a process of national differentiation that had already begun before European colonization. However, by introducing the European concept of territorial and geographic boundaries, rather than religious and ethnic ones, France helped, in the end, to shape the nature of the future Maghrebi units (Hermassi 1972). The different paths that the nationalist movements in the Maghreb undertook helped to reinforce this process. At independence the three countries adopted distinct ideological, political, and economic systems. Morocco remained a monarchy with a quasi-liberal economic system, while Algeria chose a socialist, militant orientation. The nature of the colonial experience in Algeria, as well as the violent and bloody character of the war of national liberation, had a lasting impact on Algeria's political, economic, and ideological system quite different from the one in place in Morocco. Those differences too constituted a source of conflict in the relations between the two states and resulted in ideological rivalry in the economic and political realms.

RIVALRY IN CONTEXT

The strategic rivalry between Algeria and Morocco has been one of the most enduring between two neighbors. The rivalry predates the independence of both countries from colonial France. However, the shock that provoked the rivalry occurred immediately following Algeria's independence in July 1962, when Morocco reasserted irredentist claims over Algerian territory and invaded the country in October 1963, resulting in the so-called Sands War. The second shock occurred in 1975, which resulted in two military skirmishes in January and February 1976, respectively. Despite the absence of war since then, the rivalry has continued unabated to this day. The rivalry is evident in animosity, suspicions, competition in international arenas, and endless arms purchases, which the concept of security dilemma alone cannot explain without reference to the long-term rivalry since 1963.

The definition of rivalry used in this chapter is "Rivalry is a process; it is a situation that develops through time due to reactions in response to context and stimuli. . . . Rivalries begin due to both events and responses to events" (Valeriano 2013, 11). Moreover, "rivalry is by no means necessary for conflict to occur, but conflicts associated with rivalry processes erupt with a great deal more historical, identity, and psychological baggage than is likely in the absence of rivalry" (Colaresi and Thompson 2002, 263). Several reasons account for the mistrust that exists between the two Maghrebi countries, but historical, identity, and psychological reasons are among the most important.[2] Vasquez (1993, 75–76) defines rivalry as "a relationship characterized by extreme competition, and usually psychological hostility, in which issue positions of contenders are governed primarily by their attitude toward each other." As in other rivalries, Algeria and Morocco "have had time to develop images of their adversaries as threatening opponents with persistent aims to thwart their own objectives" (Colaresi and Thompson 2002, 263). In addition, as Valeriano has put it, "The image of another state as an enemy endures in the relations between the two states and in the minds of the elites and the mass public. Despite any information that may cause reevaluation of the relationship, rivals typically are stuck in the situation because of the traits exhibited by addicts. . . . Denying gains to a rival is a central theme in rivalry" (Valeriano 2013, 13). Undoubtedly, Algerian-Moroccan relations rest on a zero-sum mind-set and reflect such an assessment.

The literature identifies many factors for relationships between states to qualify as rivalry. One approach defines rivalry as "a perceptual categorizing process in which actors identify which states are sufficiently threatening competitors to qualify as enemies" (Thompson 2001, 557). Rivalry between two states exists in situations whereby policymakers as state actors "regard each other as (a) competitors, (b) the source of actual or latent threats that pose some possibility of becoming militarized, and (c) as enemies" (Colaresi, Rasler, and Thompson 2007, 25).

Undoubtedly, and notwithstanding their discourse about their "brotherly relations," Algeria and Morocco have identified each other as primary enemies and have prepared their armies to counter the perceived threat. The divergent Algerian and Moroccan views on the conflict in Western Sahara have intensified the strategic rivalry and perpetuated it; they have calibrated their foreign policies to support their respective positions and to spoil the interests of their rival. This corroborates the approaches on rivalry, which assert that "disputes about territory, influence, status, and ideology . . . are at the core of conflicts of interest at all levels" (Colaresi, Rasler, and Thompson 2007, 24). Therefore, policymakers in the context of rivalry will continuously seek to negate any advantage that their adversary might gain. The conflicts of interests will persist when the rivals have equal capabilities because neither side can impose its will on the other. Decision-makers in this instance will consistently keep the conflict of interests on the front burner, over-stating the contest with their rival—even when it does not exist—to attain their strategic objectives and mobilize their domestic constituencies.

Three points are in order here. First, as shall be seen, rivalry can occur without there being any antagonisms between the two societies and even between societies with more similarities than differences. Second, strategic rivalry does not preclude cooperation.[3] Third, outside interference exacerbates the strategic rivalry, especially when any of the parties enters alliances to weaken the interests of the other party. As articulated in recent research, "during rivalry, relative positions matter, and rivals will fight about anything and everything" (Valeriano 2013, 2). The rivalry between Algeria and Morocco has evolved over a long period and, indeed, the two sides "will fight about anything and everything." Theorists argue that the rivalry operates over "some stake or issue with a high degree of salience, but the issues at stake may vary over time" (Valeriano 2013, 5). In the case of the Algerian-Moroccan rivalry, the border dispute between the two countries was settled and subsided after the eruption of the conflict in Western Sahara, which has taken the central stage. However, the rivalry has evolved in a way whereby other issues constantly emerge, thus indicating that the Western Sahara remains only one of many other issues. The two countries have pursued this rivalry to the detriment of some common interests (e.g., economic integration). Both Algeria and Morocco consider certain issues as vital to their interests. For instance, Morocco has made the annexation of Western Sahara an existential concern, while the right of self-determination is one of fundamental principles of Algeria's foreign policy. Territorial disagreements were initially at the heart of this rivalry; however, even if the two countries had settled their territorial disputes, Algeria's suspicions about Moroccan irredentism have not dissipated in the minds of the policymakers. Thus, that question cannot be dissociated from Morocco's irredentism over Western Sahara. One can argue that once the rivalry began and developed over the years, the two states fought over anything and everything within the context of power politics, with the question of Western Sahara serving as an instrument of disruption of the policy of the other. The next section looks at the genesis of the rivalry and the shocks that have greatly contributed to shaping the perceptions and images of the other.

ALGERIAN PERCEPTIONS OF MOROCCO

In Algerians' collective memory the Moroccan monarchy has never been sincere with Algerians. They believe that Moroccan sultan Abdul-Rahman, who allegedly committed in 1844 to assist the French against Emir Abdelkader, betrayed the first Algerian national hero who opposed resistance to France's occupation from 1832 to 1847. Algerians also believe that during the war of national liberation, in 1956, Prince Hassan II informed on five leaders of the Algerian Revolution, plus another revolutionary, who were on a plane from Morocco to Tunisia. Given this information, the French hijacked the plane and forced it to land in France, which kept the six captive until Algeria's independence in

1962. Furthermore, Algeria's revolutionary leaders were surprised that Morocco did not offer support for Algeria in its war against France until King Mohamed V—quite respected by Algerians to this day—called for Algeria's independence in his speech of September 1956 (Harbi 2010, 429). As early as 1955 in Cairo, Allal El Fassi, leader of the Istiqlal Party in Morocco, produced a map of the Almoravids' Greater Morocco, which ended at the borders of Senegal, a claim adopted by the Istiqlal and published in El Fassi's newspaper, *El Alam*, in 1956. National Liberation Front (FLN) officials were truly astounded when El Fassi declared in 1957 that "the best support provided to our Algerian brothers would be to return to Morocco the territories appended to Algeria" (cited in Harbi 2010, 430). Months later his statements became clearer: "For us, the Saharan land is not simply a territorial boundary. It is an economic entity, a vital source for the prosperity of our country. Our natural borders are delineated by the line that links Saint-Louis of Senegal to Melilla going through Mauritania, Touat, Gourara, as a result of which, Colomb-Béchar and Kenadsa are part our territorial integrity" (cited in Harbi 2010, 430). This vision of Morocco not only encompasses Western Sahara but also includes two Algerian cities, namely, Colomb-Béchar and Kenadsa. El Fassi's statement was worrisome to the wartime FLN, but the concern persists today. The map of Greater Morocco that El Fassi's newspaper published was the first sign of Morocco's irredentism, and many official departments still display this map. Evidently, colonial France also manipulated the border issue by offering Morocco territorial concessions in exchange for Morocco's acquiescence for its policy in Algeria. However, King Mohamed V thought that Morocco should discuss this issue with independent Algeria. This was not the position of his son Hassan II, who succeeded his father after Mohamed V's sudden death in 1961. From the FLN's perspective, other grievances during the war of liberation included France's use of independent Moroccan territory to launch attacks against Algerian fighters and the Moroccan government's mistreatment of Algerian refugees (Harbi 2010, 434, 442–47).

THE FIRST SHOCK: THE MOROCCAN-ALGERIAN BORDER DISPUTE AND THE SANDS WAR

Territorial or boundary disputes have been among the major sources of conflict in the Maghreb system, as discussed earlier. One of the reasons such conflicts have erupted in this region is the colonial legacy and the fact that the building and consolidation of nation-states was still under way in the postcolonial era. Given the territorial nature of independent Africa in general, and in the Maghreb in particular, well-defined boundaries represent one of the essential features of national sovereignty. Although the colonial system did differentiate the component units of the Maghrebi system, territorial divisions among those units responded to, and fulfilled, the needs of the colonial power without regard to the concerns of those units. Consequently, border issues muted under colonial domination erupted once Morocco, and later Algeria, achieved its independence. Hence, following independence in 1956, Morocco began to pressure France to review its border with Algeria—still under French colonial rule—arguing that the French colonial administration had favored its Algerian colony by enlarging its size at the expense of the Moroccan and Tunisian protectorates.

While the colonial past has influenced the Algeria-Morocco rivalry in the postindependence era, the shocks experienced by one of the parties have been a primary determinant of the construction of the image that each has had of the other. The territorial dispute between Algeria and Morocco rests on divergent interpretations of borders. In the Algerian perspective the borders inherited from the colonial period are unchangeable; therefore, any claims by a neighbor are tantamount to an infringement on Algeria's sovereignty and territorial integrity. Moroccan decision-makers hold a different view, arguing that such definition of borders deprives Morocco of some of its territory; thus, the objective is to recoup what it considers to be part of the kingdom. Moroccans argue repeatedly that Morocco will endeavor to complete the repossession of its lost territories. The previous discussion shows that the mistrust between Algeria and Morocco was evident even before Algeria's independence. From the perspective of Algerian policymakers, Morocco's irredentism was among the most important factors in the tense relations between the two countries. During the wartime period, members of the FLN argued, "We think that the Moroccans are letting us down and we shouldn't take gloves with these people who have uncovered their game. They want Ain Sefra and Colomb Béchar [two Algerian regions], and a share of the oil of the Sahara, and they want to take advantage of our predicament to seize them definitively. They have become as colonialist as others have and we need to stop them[—]if not, our revolution will no longer make sense" (cited in Harbi and Meynier 2004, 765).

In 1961 Ferhat Abbas, the president of the provisional government who admitted that a problem existed with respect to the borders, signed a memorandum of understanding with the Moroccan government. The agreement stipulated that the border issue would be resolved through negotiations and that a joint commission would be set up for this purpose once Algeria had gained independence.

The first shock that set the stage for the development of the rivalry occurred in 1963. The buildup of tensions had begun soon after Algeria's independence in July 1962 because of the question of borders between the two countries. Soon after Algeria's independence, King Hassan II began to pressure the new authorities in Algiers to resolve the border issue. In Algeria the new military-backed government of Ahmed Ben Bella refused to negotiate anything regarding the borders inherited from the colonial era. How could it do this when one of the promises of the FLN was to preserve the unity of the territory, in particular to prevent France from separating the Sahara region from the rest of Algeria—a fear that persists to this day.[4] Ben Bella and the leaders of the National Liberation Army (ALN), therefore, were unwilling to hand over any part of the territory, which, as Algerians are keen on saying, was "liberated and irrigated with the blood of one-and-a-half million martyrs."[5] Unsurprisingly, after independence they categorically refused to recognize Morocco's historical or political claims (Lounnas and Messari 2018, 6). Essentially they saw Morocco's repeated territorial demands as an attempt to exert pressure at a time when the country was emerging enfeebled after a horrific war of independence. The refusal to negotiate territorial changes led the Istiqlal Party to renew its earlier territorial claims. In 1962 already, the Royal Armed Forces (FAR) sought to occupy the Algerian city of Tindouf; they withdrew once they realized that the Algerian army had already deployed there. The FAR also briefly settled in the Colomb-Béchar region (Reyner 1963, 317). By summer of 1963 tension was already apparent, even if no one thought that an armed conflict would erupt. Algerians were quite nervous because the best of their troops were concentrated in the Kabylie region, where an armed rebellion, led by one of the wartime leaders, Hocine Aït-Ahmed, had erupted over political divergences regarding the future of the country. On October 8, 1963, the hostilities had begun. The embryonic Algerian army was quickly defeated in the first stages of the war. The war lasted for several weeks and caused many casualties, especially on the Algerian side. From a theoretical perspective, this represented the shock that confirmed the negative perceptions and triggered the enduring effect on the rivalry. This was particularly true for Algerians.[6] Fifty-five years after that short war, a retired high-level Algerian official described the impact of the 1963 war:

> The Sands War was a terrible shock at the level of the Algerian people who felt betrayed by our neighbor, who had given the impression of having supported the Algerian struggle. However, Algerians were grateful to the Moroccan people who have made a sincere and consistent contribution to our struggle for liberation.
>
> Of course, the attitudes of duplicity of the *Makhzen* [monarchy and central government] were known only to the Algerian leaders who had no interest in making them public so as not to weaken the extraordinary drive of the Algerian people in favor of the struggle for independence.
>
> This shock was the driving force behind the popular mobilization and the unity found to face the enemy. The example given by Kabylia is a perfect illustration of this. . . . For some [in the government], Morocco wanted to gain from the fragility of the country drained by seven years of a gory war and dissension at the level of the leaders. . . . Let us address the consequences of this conflict at both the domestic and international levels. There is no doubt that the international community was on the side of Algerians: Egypt, Cuba and so many others. Algeria emerged stronger and with recognized stature despite its postwar situation.
>
> At the domestic level, this situation has allowed serious thinking on national security, the need for national unity and the nature of relations with neighboring countries and at the international level.
>
> Regarding national security, the shock explains the defense policy that the authorities have adopted since then, that is, one based on a solid Army with substantial resources, which explains the links with the USSR and the distrust towards the West, more favorable to the Moroccan regime, which is more malleable than Algeria, which has defeated France.[7]
>
> This desire for power was also a message to other neighbors who also had territorial claims, including Tunisia. Algeria was to adopt a reserved and cautious attitude in its relations with its immediate environment. Strong ties rested primarily on political commitment to freedom and fair socioeconomic relations.
>
> At the national level, this conflict, although a mobilizing one at the popular level, accentuated the mistrust between the leaders of the revolution who split between

revolutionary nationalists and "democratic" nationalists. This mistrust revealed itself at the Constituent Assembly (1963), where two tendencies dominated the debate: those in favor of the single party and a socialist policy and those in favor of an open democracy (Ferhat Abbas).

Subsequent events and the coup of June 1965 consolidated the "revolutionaries" although their motives were also a struggle for power and the control of the country by the military supporters of this power. (Confidential email interview by the author, February 2, 2018)

This 1963 war illustrates the concept of shock in interstate rivalry, which the editors of this volume have discussed in their introduction. In this chapter it is indubitable that "shocks are events that alter the calculations of policymakers about their environments" and that they "can affect states' overall foreign relations, may contribute to rivalry onset or termination, and lead to the escalation/inflammation or de-escalation/dampening of hostilities." This chapter also corroborates the possibility that "shocks essentially are disruptive events that are perceived to significantly alter threat environments in some way and, therefore, encourage responses to the changes." The 1963 episode left an indelible stain on the course of Algerian-Moroccan relations since. As the editors theorized, and as happened in the Algerian case, the 1963 war "saw the emergence of revolutionary fervor for overthrowing the status quo in another state." Morocco interpreted Algeria's refusal to acquiesce to Morocco's demand for a revision of the borders as betrayal by the Algerians (Lounnas and Messari 2018, 6).[8] The position was that "although there was no clear formal agreement between Algeria's independence movement and Morocco about the western part of the Eastern Sahara claimed by Morocco, Moroccans considered that there was an Algerian moral commitment on the issue" (Lounnas and Messari 2018, 14). The consequence of the dispute was that Hassan II had virtually abandoned the relatively neutralist foreign policy of his father. Thus, soon after the Sands War, he shifted Morocco's foreign policy toward a decidedly pro-Western stance, not just because of the Sands War, of course, but also because of Algeria's turn to revolutionary socialist policy (Berramdane 1987, 242). The shift to the West aimed to break the isolation in which Morocco found itself at that time. Accusing Algeria of colluding with nationalist Cairo and communist Havana, Hassan had hoped that he would break his domestic isolation and gain support from the West, which he called to the rescue. "Morocco desired a much stronger attachment with the West, especially the United States, and wanted to join in combating these subversive forces"—that is, revolutionary forces, Algeria included (cited in Torres-Garcia 2013, 328). The subversive forces King Hassan referred to were obviously the leftist forces that Mehdi Ben Barka was leading against the monarchy. Thus, when King Hassan decided to invade Algeria, he did not garner complete support in Morocco. Indeed, "as the conflict developed into war, the Moroccan leftist leader Mehdi Ben Barka denounced the monarchy's maneuvers and called upon Moroccan troops to refuse to fight their Algerian brothers. A similar response came from the leadership of the Moroccan students' union" (Farsoun and Paul 1976, 13). Undoubtedly, King Hassan used the occasion of the conflict and rivalry with Algeria to rally the population around a national cause and save the monarchy. As McGinnis (1990, 112) argued, "'Regime interest' includes the need to maintain sufficient domestic support to preclude establishment of a different political order." The fact that the leftist opposition was sympathetic to the Algerian Revolution and Algeria's postindependence socialist policies, coupled with Hassan's lack of legitimacy during the early years of his rule, provides a plausible explanation for his military intervention in Algeria. Not only that, but as seen previously, the king also sought to exploit the power struggle in Algeria to create a fait accompli through the military invasion that triggered the first shock in the rivalry between Algeria and Morocco. The rivalry between the two states resulted in Morocco's alignment with the West (Willis and Messari 2003); Algeria, though nonaligned, turned to the Soviet Union for its arms supplies (Zoubir 1987).

In 1963 both Algeria and Morocco were experiencing domestic difficulties resulting from the state-building process. The Moroccan monarchy resorted to irredentism to unite the nation behind the throne for its claims against Algeria and Mauritania (Ashford 1962). Furthermore, Morocco, a conservative monarchy, had begun to see Algeria's socialist course as a threat to its own political and ideological orientations. Algerians perceived the Moroccan attack on the Algerian border as a threat to the young republic, thus helping the Ben Bella regime to unify the different factions in the country and to rally the opposition behind him on a national question. The Algerian-Moroccan crisis also helped Ben Bella solidify his personal power. In other words, the crisis helped both regimes domestically but also accentuated the process of differentiation and rivalry. However, it also had a negative impact on the future because the Moroccan attack on Algeria not only created long-term distrust but also widened ideological and psychological differences between the two states. Though genuinely nonaligned, Algeria moved closer to the Soviet bloc (Ottaway and Ottaway 1970)—politically and militarily—while Morocco moved even closer to the Western bloc (Berramdane 1987, 242). These orientations, reflected in the respective foreign policies of the two states, exacerbated the ideological differentiations and security perceptions. The process of nation-state building through a differentiation with the "other" evolved into an inevitable, quasi-permanent interstate conflict, intermittent periods of cooperation notwithstanding. The eventual resolution of the border issue between the two states did not mean the end of the conflict.

The Sands War and Its Aftermath

The cease-fire that followed the Sands War, under the auspices of the Organization of African Unity (OAU), did not solve the border question. Because of their limited capacity and power to change the status quo in the region and because of the lack of well-established conflict-management procedures within the Maghrebi system, the two countries resorted to an extra-regional organization, the OAU, to settle the dispute. The OAU brokered the Bamako Agreement of February 20, 1964, which outlined proposals to definitively solve the dispute between the two states (Touval 1967; Wild 1966). Even though the issue remained unresolved, and at times threatened to resurface, bilateral relations, especially in the economic sphere, resumed and improved considerably in the following years. There was tacit agreement that it was possible to conduct state relations while putting the border question on the back burner. This method proved effective, for there was improvement in bilateral relations, allowing the two countries to sign several accords. In January 1969 Algeria and Morocco signed the Treaty of Good Neighborliness, Fraternity, and Cooperation, also known as the Ifrane Treaty. This treaty paved the way for a negotiated solution of the border dispute. By 1972 the two countries had signed two conventions: one formally demarcating the Algerian-Moroccan border and the other providing for cooperation between the two countries for the economic exploitation of natural resources in the area in question. Although Algeria ratified the border treaty in 1973, it was not until the spring of 1992 that Morocco ratified it. The non-ratification of the border by King Hassan II raised suspicions among Algeria's decision-makers, who doubted Morocco's abandonment of its irredentist claims over Béchar, Tindouf, and Hassi Baïda. The king's foot-dragging in having the border treaty ratified not only intensified fears among Algerian decision-makers that the king had not relinquished Morocco's claims, but it also compelled the former to negate Morocco's irredentism over Western Sahara, Spain's former colony (1884–1976). Although the king's procrastination over the ratification derived from domestic imperatives and other calculations, Moroccan irredentism has not abated. Indeed, claims over parts of Algerian territory reemerge intermittently in the discourse of some leaders of Moroccan political parties, especially the Istiqlal Party, whose secretary general, Hamid Chabat, declared in February 2016, "Everyone knows full well that Algeria has taken control of these Moroccan regions while it was under French colonization. It occupies these regions in the same way as the occupation of Ceuta and Melilla by Spain" (Alaoui 2012).

What is important to understand here is not that the Istiqlal Party and the monarchy's idea of the Greater Morocco is still alive, even though Hassan II had abandoned claims over Algeria in exchange for Algeria's support for his claims on Western Sahara (Lounnas and Messari 2018, 14). However, more fundamentally, the idea of the Greater Maghreb helps in the construction of Algeria as a threat to and enemy of Morocco because Algeria is accused of occupying parts of the mythical Greater Morocco. It also serves as a mobilizing factor inside Morocco; at the same time, it exacerbates the differentiation with Algerians. Statements emanating from Moroccan political leaders tend to corroborate Algerian decision-makers' apprehensions about their western neighbor and its perceived enmity toward Algeria, especially since Algeria's territory is considered sacred. Clearly, while for Moroccans the repossession of allegedly lost territory during colonization and the expansion of the actual borders are paramount, for Algerians, the existing borders are inviolable and thus no one can ever alter them. Undoubtedly, the concept of Greater Morocco has largely defined Algerian-Moroccan relations, based on misgivings and mistrust, as antagonistic. The perception that Algeria seeks to establish regional hegemony and to contravene Morocco's "legitimate territorial claims" has provided the necessary ingredients for the construction of the enemy.

THE SECOND SHOCK: THE WESTERN SAHARA
CONFLICT AND ITS FUNCTION IN THE CONSTRUCTION
OF THE IMAGE OF THE ENEMY

The eruption of the conflict in Western Sahara in 1975–76 provided the opportunity for the protagonists to instrumentalize the conflict to widen their dissimilarity and, in so doing, to construct the enmity and intensify the rivalry that has persisted to this day. Because of the centrality of the Western Sahara conflict in constructing the image of the "enemy," it is thus essential to examine the conflict from this construction.

The rivalry between Algeria and Morocco is not limited to territorial disputes, which Morocco raises occasionally. However, the question of borders does not have any serious incidence beyond confirming the image that Morocco has constructed about Algeria ("the amputation of Moroccan territory"). The Western Sahara conflict, for its part, has reinforced the respective perceptions (and emotions in Morocco) of each state's decision-makers; the dispute has been instrumental in consolidating their internal legitimacy or reaffirming their differentiated identities. The dispute has also structured their foreign policies. Unquestionably, the events leading to the open conflict constituted the background to the second shock for Algerian decision-makers and reinforced Morocco's image of Algeria as its enemy. Before 1975 Algerian and Moroccan officials had secretly discussed the question of Western Sahara. However, the declaration on November 14, 1975, of an illegal trilateral agreement between Spain, Morocco, and Mauritania (which also laid claims on Western Sahara), wherein Spain would relinquish Western Sahara to Morocco and Mauritania, infuriated Algerians. "It was indeed a shock felt as a betrayal, especially a betrayal by Ould Dadah [Mauritania's president at that time]. No contact had taken place to inform us, either from Morocco, or from Mauritania, or from Spain. I personally attended a meeting where Boumedienne said in Arabic, *enrabihoum* [I will educate/discipline them], speaking of Hassan and Ould Dadah" (retired senior Algerian official, interview by the author, February 3, 2018). Algerian policymakers resented the change in the regional balance and the involvement of foreign powers, namely, Spain, in the region. They also were fearful of another Palestine in the Maghreb region and a new diaspora, namely, the Sahrawis. Although relations were still fragile, the Madrid Accords initiated the political shock that intensified the rivalry and made it an enduring one. This corresponds to Diehl and Goertz's (2000) theorizing on how a shock influences the initiation (and termination) of a rivalry. Except for two direct military skirmishes between the two countries in Amgala in January and February 1976, the accords did not result in all-out war between Algeria and Morocco. Morocco entered a war (until the 1991 UN-brokered cease-fire) with Sahrawi nationalist forces, which have enjoyed full, continuous Algerian backing ever since.

The Western Sahara dispute has been the longest conflict that the Maghrebi system has experienced in the postcolonial era. Because of its nature and its stakes, the dispute has affected intra-Maghrebi relations more than any other event in the region. The rise of terrorism in the Maghreb-Sahel since the early 2000s and the collapse of the Libyan state in 2011 have not overshadowed the conflict in Western Sahara in any significant way. The epicenter of the rivalry between the two countries on a variety of issues is Western Sahara (Zunes and Mundy 2011; Zoubir 2010).

Upon its formal withdrawal from the territory in February 1976—under the terms of the November 1975 Madrid Accords with Morocco and Mauritania—Spain ceded illegally its former colony to Morocco, which had already occupied portions of the territory through the so-called Green March in November 1975, and to Mauritania.[9] This occupation of Western Sahara led to tensions in the Maghrebi system. Morocco, which claimed historic sovereignty over the former Spanish colony, faced staunch opposition by Algerian authorities. The latter have supported Sahrawi self-determination not only as a fundamental principle of Algeria's foreign policy but also for fear that absorption of the territory into the Moroccan kingdom would upset the regional balance of power in Morocco's favor, thus threatening Algeria's national security (Zoubir 2015, 2004). As Damis (1985, 139–40) correctly pointed out, "Algerians fear that the absorption of the Sahara by their neighbors would only encourage Moroccan expansionist tendencies and whet the Moroccans' appetite for pursuing their unfulfilled and frequently articulated irredentist claim to territory in western Algeria." From the onset the conflict took a regional dimension and led to bipolarization in the structure of the system. Algerian recognition in March 1976 of the newly created Sahrawi Arab Democratic Republic (SADR) by the Frente Popular para la Liberación de Saguia el Hamra y Rio de Oro (Polisario Front) resulted in Morocco immediately breaking off diplomatic relations with Algeria. Initially, Tunisia sided with Morocco and Mauritania on the issue, thus creating a pole opposed by a coalition made up of Algeria, Libya, and the SADR. Yet only a few isolated military clashes occurred between Algerian and Moroccan troops. Both countries were fully aware that a war between them would be extremely costly, and neither could sustain it because of the logistical difficulties that they would have faced in a desert war (Nezzar 1999, 125). Because it could no longer sustain Polisario attacks, Mauritania withdrew from the conflict under the terms of the 1979 Treaty of Algiers. The failure of either Morocco or Polisario to defeat the other resulted in a military stalemate. Only direct military confrontation between Algeria and Morocco could overturn the stalemate, an option that neither state could afford nor was willing to pursue. Therefore, the only available alternative to Morocco was to build support for its position through de facto military and civilian occupation, diplomatic and political maneuvers, or negotiation of a peaceful settlement while establishing a situation of fait accompli on the ground.

As in the 1963 border war between Algeria and Morocco, domestic factors played a crucial role in King Hassan's decision to invade and occupy Spanish Sahara. In Morocco the question of Western Sahara was elevated to a national priority. Domestic problems had reached critical dimensions during the 1970s, following the two failed coup attempts against the monarchy in 1971 and 1972 and the repression against opposition parties and other mass organizations. Economic problems had also peaked in that period, and inflation reached high levels. The monarchy had hoped to alleviate and solve those problems through the annexation of Western Sahara, a territory extremely rich in phosphates and other minerals. Furthermore, the king had expected the political parties to set their grievances aside and rally around him on the Western Sahara issue by presenting it as a question of national sovereignty and historical right. Whereas King Hassan had little difficulty neutralizing internal opposition and stabilizing his rule, he failed to impose his foreign policy objectives on the region. The perception of Algeria as the enemy could only be strengthened because of its strong diplomatic and military support to the Polisario Front. From a Moroccan perspective, Algeria wished to play the role of subregional hegemon and to isolate Morocco from the rest of Africa. Thus, "establishing a 'puppet' state in the Sahara—as Morocco calls it—would ensure the success of that Algerian objective" (Lounnas and Messari 2018, 14). In fact, "Hassan II stated clearly to the participants in the Green March of November 1975 that Spain was not the enemy, but that 'others'— indirectly referring to Algerians—were the enemy" (Lounnas and Messari 2018, 15).

One can explain Hassan II's failure to impose his foreign policy objectives on the region by examining the power politics of the Maghreb. To counter Moroccan and Mauritanian objectives in Western Sahara, Algeria moved closer to Libya and gave considerable military, logistical, political, and diplomatic support to Polisario. With Mauritania's definitive defection on Western Sahara from the Moroccan side in 1979 and the rapprochement between Tunisia and Algeria, the balance began to tilt against Morocco. Feeling isolated in the region, Morocco sought, as it had done in the 1970s, extra-regional support from the Western allies, primarily France and the United States, and the Gulf sister monarchies. Furthermore, mounting tension between Tunisia and Libya in the late 1970s led to a formal alliance in March 1983 between Tunisia and Algeria, known as the Treaty of Fraternity and Concord, to which Mauritania also adhered in December 1983. In the meantime, Morocco's relations with Libya had warmed up considerably owing to their mutual isolation—Morocco because of Western Sahara, Libya because of its adventure in Chad in support of one of the factions, an involvement that led to a confrontation between Libya and France. This resulted in the unholy alliance between the two countries in August 1984, formalized as the Treaty of Oujda (Mortimer 1993). Such realignments established a new balance of power or new equilibrium in the region. Interestingly, although each alliance aimed to neutralize the power of the other, they both claimed to lay the foundations for Maghrebi unity and regional integration. Ultimately, however, the alliance under Algeria's leadership proved more lasting. The incompatibility between the Moroccan and Libyan regimes—in addition to the opposition to the union by the United States, an important Moroccan ally—meant that the Treaty of Oujda could not survive for more than two years. Algeria, for its part, succeeded in maintaining cohesion within its alliance, and Libya began to express interest in joining following the predictable failure of its pact with Morocco. However, despite the lack of diplomatic relations between Algeria and Morocco and the existence of a bipolar power structure in the Maghreb, channels of communication always remained open between the two countries. There is a clear awareness in the Maghreb that any alliance in the region achieved at the exclusion of any unit in the system would have little chance of success. Unquestionably, the existence of Maghrebi identity and ideology largely facilitated the movement toward reconciliation in 1988–89. Of course, other domestic and extra-regional factors added more impetus to the process.

Morocco's strategy in the late 1980s consisted of de facto annexation of the territory, while still claiming to support a negotiated settlement. However, King Mohamed VI, who succeeded his father in 1999, abandoned any notion of negotiations, opting instead for a policy of consolidation of the colonization of the territory, promoting Morocco's own position on Western Sahara (called the "autonomy offer" since 2007), countering Algeria's diplomacy in Africa, and, more important, raising the level of hostility toward Algeria. For Algeria, the policy since the late 1980s has been to oppose Morocco's moves to create a de facto annexation of Western Sahara. The positive atmosphere and the seeming reconciliation in the late 1980s (reestablishment of diplomatic relations in May 1988, King Hassan's meeting with Polisario leaders in January 1989, and the creation of the Arab Maghreb Union in 1989) were short-lived. The rise of radical Islamism and the bloody civil strife throughout the 1990s did little to improve relations between the two countries. During that period Algerians were convinced that Moroccan decision-makers had taken advantage of the Algerian crisis to advance their interests in the region. Worse still, they accused Moroccans of overlooking arms shipments smuggled through their border to supply antigovernment Islamists in Algeria.[10] Whatever the truth,[11] with or without Moroccan knowledge, arms transited through Morocco into Algeria.[12] These activities strengthened the perception of Morocco as an enemy. However, although there is no doubt that he wished to weaken Algeria, King Hassan did not wish an Islamic republic as a neighbor, despite a public statement in 1993 in which he said that allowing the Islamic Salvation Front (FIS) to come to power would have been "an interesting experience. Algeria would have served as a laboratory" (Achouri 2017).

Obviously, what Hassan hoped to accomplish in that period was to wrest concessions on Western Sahara in exchange for cooperation with Algerian authorities against armed Islamist groups. Morocco's policy has been to regain the diplomatic losses of the 1970s and 1980s and to capitalize on the Algerian crisis to impose its hegemony in the region and win in the zero-sum rivalry. Unlike Algeria, which looked to Africa for backing on Western Sahara, Morocco, which had withdrawn from the OAU in 1984 because the OAU recognized the SADR, continued to seek international support from the West and from the Gulf monarchies, support it has obtained to this day. Morocco positioned itself as the bulwark against radical Islamism in the region. Therefore, Moroccans expected that the West would give them full backing. In many ways, this policy proved successful because France, a staunch opponent of Sahrawi statehood, has granted Morocco overwhelming support on Western Sahara, presumably to avoid destabilizing the kingdom. This, of course, created resentment among Algerian decision-makers toward Morocco; indeed, military and civilian officials interviewed during that period complained that Morocco had taken advantage of the crisis in order to weaken Algeria's position in the Maghreb, with the help of France. In addition to their grievances about Morocco's alleged blackmail—that is, cooperation on terrorism in exchange for Algeria's reduced support for Sahrawis—they reassessed their entire relationship with Morocco since the reestablishment of diplomatic relations in May 1988. Politically, officials felt that while Moroccans talked about the virtues of a Maghreb union, they were advancing their selfish interests at the expense of Algeria, especially where those interests pertained to Western Sahara and to association with the European Union.

By the mid-1990s a turn for the worse had taken place. The criminal attack that four French nationals of Maghrebi origin launched against the Atlas-Asni Hotel in Marrakesh triggered the summer 1994 crisis. Two of the gunmen were French citizens of Algerian origin. In an unusually swift reaction, Moroccan authorities decided to impose visas not only on Algerian citizens but also on foreign nationals of Algerian origin. Algerian authorities reciprocated, albeit "regretfully," by imposing visas on Moroccan subjects wishing to travel to Algeria. Furthermore, in a move that stunned Moroccan officials and citizens, Algerians decided to "temporarily" close the border between the two countries—the land border has remained closed to this day despite Morocco's appeals to Algeria to reopen it. The rough treatment that the Moroccan police and gendarmerie imposed on Algerians after the attack created severe tensions not only between the two states but also between the two peoples.

While the events of 1994 added tensions, the Algeria-Morocco rivalry intensified with the coming to power of both Mohamed VI (who decided to make Western Sahara an existential question—one of survival) and Abdelaziz Bouteflika. Both leaders inherited a complicated past to say the least. To consolidate their respective authority, both had to pursue power politics, their aspirations for normalization notwithstanding. Since then the question of Western Sahara has occupied the center of both countries' diplomacy. During the decade-long diplomatic isolation of Algeria, Morocco used that isolation to its advantage. Therefore, it was not surprising that to revive its diplomacy, Algeria had to reassert its position on that question. In Morocco the consolidation of Mohamed VI's throne rested on the radicalization and intransigence of Morocco's position on Western Sahara, even if gestures for reconciliation with Algeria were visible now and again.

In Algeria the question of Western Sahara is the domain of the government, even if some political parties support the Sahrawi cause in their programs. In spite of some engagement of civil society support groups, society feels rather unconcerned about the question. Self-determination of people is a basic principle of Algeria's foreign policy, even if support for the Sahrawi liberation movement has a strategic dimension because it serves to contain Morocco's irredentism. This is not true in Morocco, where this question has been elevated to a "national cause" and where a Moroccan is either "a patriot or a traitor" on Western Sahara.[13] In Morocco, Western Sahara has important functions. It serves as an instrument of consensus between the monarchy and the nationalist parties. The designation of Algeria as the enemy of the recovery of the "southern provinces" (territorial integrity) cements the relationship between the monarchy and society and mobilizes the society around a "sacred question." This supports the view that "identity and difference are linked in a relationship of opposition of one to the other" (Campbell 1998, 10). The "other" here is Algeria since it opposes Morocco's territorial claims. Pointing to Algeria as the enemy played a role in Morocco's "establishing its identity in opposition to Algeria's" (Messari 2001, 54); it has also helped Morocco conceal the fact that no country in the world, not even Morocco's closest allies, recognizes Morocco's sovereignty over the claimed territory. In this context, in Morocco, the perception is that

Western Sahara is a bilateral question between Algeria and Morocco. A former high-level Moroccan intelligence official told the author, "We are willing to discuss with Algerians access to resources in Western Sahara and other benefits to them; however, this can only happen if they don't question Morocco's sovereignty over Western Sahara. Western Sahara is Moroccan" (interview by the author, April 14, 2017). Clearly, for Moroccans, Algeria is the enemy of Morocco's territorial integrity; that no country recognizes its sovereignty is irrelevant. What matters is its rival's position toward this conflict.

The Expansion of the Rivalry

In the last decade, perhaps owing to Algeria's preoccupation with the various security problems along its southern and eastern borders, Morocco has launched an all-out diplomatic war to counter Algeria's policies in areas where Algeria had built its influence rather successfully. In addition to the conflict in Western Sahara and other bilateral issues dating back to the 1960s and 1970s, geopolitical changes in the Maghreb-Sahel resulted in an intensification of the rivalry (Zoubir 2001). Hernando de Larramendi (2018, 6) points out correctly that "although the security interdependence between the Sahel and Maghreb poses increasingly transnational threats, the asymmetrical perception of this situation by Algeria and Morocco has complicated bilateral cooperation and coordination." Thus, this has made it "difficult for the two countries to collaborate in crisis management, which has turned into another arena of competition for each country to reinforce its status as regional power" (Hernando de Larramendi 2018). Indeed, in the last decade Morocco has initiated a more assertive foreign policy whose main objective is to counter Algeria, not merely on Western Sahara but also in areas where Algeria has been predominant, namely, in mediation diplomacy and in the fight against terrorism. Mediation diplomacy, more than its military power, has been the hallmark of Algeria as a middle power (Zoubir, forthcoming). Undoubtedly, Algerian policymakers have conducted quite successful international mediations since independence, including with the Malian government in the 1960s, 1990s, and since 2013; Iran and Iraq (1975 and 1980s); the United States and Iran (1979–81); and Ethiopia and Eritrea (2000), to name but a few. While an analysis of Algeria's policy in the Sahel is beyond the scope of this chapter (Zoubir 2018), suffice it to say that "Rabat took advantage of the crisis in Mali . . . to reposition itself as a regional actor in the Sahel. It exploited a window of opportunity created by the combination of, first, the vacuum left by the collapse of Libya . . . ; second, Algeria's self-imposed limits on becoming militarily involved outside its borders; and third, the paralysis in Algerian diplomacy due to the worsening health of President Bouteflika" (Hernando de Larramendi 2018, 9).

All these factors created an opportunity that Morocco could not pass on to weaken its regional rival. Algerian policymakers rejected pressure from Western powers to include Morocco, or non-Sahelian states, in the security architecture that they have set up. They reject Morocco's inclusion, not only because Morocco is not a Sahelian state but also because they fear that recognizing Morocco as a Sahelian state would be tantamount to recognizing Morocco's sovereignty over Western Sahara, which borders the

Sahel. For their part, Moroccans have continuously accused Algeria of not cooperating fully on terrorism in the Sahel with the kingdom. For instance, Moroccan foreign minister Nasser Bourita stated during a meeting of the France-backed G5 that the "Sahel is not the preserve of anyone," suggesting that Algeria could not exclude Morocco from being a player in the Sahel (cited in Jaabouk 2018). Undoubtedly, Morocco took advantage of the seeming paralysis of the current regime in Algeria to advance its interests in the Sahel. Unlike Algeria, which refused to go beyond its borders, preferring to provide support to France's intervention, "Morocco quickly joined in the French-led intervention in Mali. By picking up the slack, Morocco was able to gain an advantage in its battle with Algeria for regional clout. Things that were previously unattainable—such as exerting influence and establishing bilateral ties with states in the Sahel without the involvement of Algeria—are now within Morocco's grasp" (Sakthivel 2014). However, Algerian policymakers do not believe that such Moroccan involvement would eclipse Algeria, because they know the limitations of Morocco's power reach into the Sahel, whereas Algeria, with its military might, is contiguous to the Sahel and has a much better grasp of the reality in that area. Nevertheless, the perception in Algiers is that Morocco, with the support of France, seeks to undercut Algeria's efforts in the Sahel. Of course, France's inclusion of Morocco in security operations in the Sahel reinforces Algeria's perception of Morocco as an enemy.

A review of the two rivals' actions in different areas confirms, if need be, the high level of rivalry between the two countries, rivalry that has gone beyond the immediate neighborhood not only to the Sahel but to the entire African continent. Absent from the OAU and its successor, the African Union (AU), until recently, Morocco decided in 2017 to join the AU. It has since sought unsuccessfully to force the SADR, a founding member of the organization in 2002, out of the union (Hernando de Larramendi and Tomé 2017). King Mohamed VI initiated a new African policy with the primary objective of undermining Algeria's gains in the continent. Unlike Algeria's president, who was confined to a wheelchair before he was forced out of office on April 2, 2019, Mohamed VI has been able to travel over the entire continent to promote bilateral relations even with states, such as South Africa, that have been staunch supporters of Sahrawi self-determination and that have diplomatic relations with the SADR.

In addition to the two countries' claiming to be at the forefront of the war on terrorism, they have also competed in mediation diplomacy, particularly since the eruption of the crisis in Libya and its ramifications in Mali. In the area of mediation Algeria boasts a greater deal of experience. Its credentials as an avowed anti-colonialist and anti-imperialist champion, part of its identity, granted Algeria a great deal of credibility, which Morocco has not been able to match. In both the Malian and the Libyan crises, Algeria has displayed more efficiency than Morocco. With respect to the fight against terrorism and violent extremism, Morocco has been more daring than Algeria in going beyond its borders and joining alliances with Western powers, two actions that are antithetical to Algeria's foreign policy principles. Nevertheless, the United States and France express more appreciation to Morocco than to Algeria, although US security officials have a high admiration for Algeria's counterterrorism expertise and cooperation despite the limitations that Algeria has set. In fact, Algerians fear that France and other states seek to use Algeria as proxy in their own fight in the Sahel. They also fear being bogged down in the Sahelian desert, from which France is trying to extricate its five thousand forces that have failed to win the war hitherto. The most important point here is that Morocco not only pursues a policy to counteract and defeat Algeria in its own backyard in the zero-sum game but foreign powers also seem to want to exploit the rivalry to lure one of the contestants to serve their interests. France's actions in the Sahel and the pressure on Algeria to join military arrangements that would include Morocco only exacerbate the rivalry between the two neighbors and increase the animosity that has characterized their relationship for decades.

CONCLUSION

In this chapter the rivalry between Algeria and Morocco is clearly shown to be the result of a long process, in which history, contexts, perceptions, and international events have been key factors in accelerating the strategic rivalry. Undoubtedly, the two shocks of 1963 and 1975 have had a consequential impact on the evolution and "the commitment to long-term animosity" (Valeriano 2013, 31). The rivalry has been an enduring one; although there have been periods of cooperation, Algerian-Moroccan relations have largely been more competitive than cooperative. The two states fought two limited wars and have since avoided direct military confrontation, limiting themselves to the projection of the rivalry beyond their immediate vicinity. Thus, the rivalry extended to their activities in the OAU/AU, their dealings with the European Union, their relations with major powers, and their policies on the African continent. However, while the rivalry had long been limited to a rivalry between governments, it has progressively spilled over into the Algerian and Moroccan society. The construction of the enemy is no longer confined to the decision-makers but now affects the two peoples' image of each other. The hostility between Algeria and Morocco in the media would be insignificant but for the fact that the citizens in each country hold negative views of the other, at least on the question of Western Sahara. It is unlikely the rivalry will result in an eventual war; however, an accidental event, another shock, or an uncontrolled escalation in Western Sahara might result in war with unforeseen consequences. Certainly, a definitive resolution of the Western Sahara conflict will not necessarily mean an end to the mistrust that exists between countries, as the negative perceptions that have built up will surely persist. At the same time, however, the resolution of that conflict would greatly facilitate both cooperation between the two countries and regional integration.

NOTES

1. An expert on defense issues in the Middle East and North Africa (MENA) provides a more insightful explanation about the defense-heavy spending of the two countries. See Kharief (2017).

2. Algerians often trace the mistrust back to 1845, when colonial France and Morocco signed the Treaty of Lalla Maghnia, which denied protection to Algeria's first resister to France, the Emir Abdelkader, who sought refuge in Morocco. The treaty is available in De Clercq et al. (1907).

3. At the end of the 1960s and early 1970s, despite the mistrust, the two states established a mechanism for conflict resolution in the Maghrebi system as a pattern of trade-offs between economic and political interests. Today, though not optimal, there is cooperation between the two states on antiterrorism.

4. Interviews the author conducted with many Algerian national security leaders reveal that they are concerned that France has not accepted its loss of the rich Sahara and that it could someday find pretext, such as terrorism in the Sahel, which borders the Sahara, to weaken Algeria. They fear that in case of a weakening of the state, as happened in Libya or Syria, France would attempt to reconquer the Sahara to exploit its resources, an idea that had emerged from 1957 onward, when the French intended to make the Sahara an autonomous region.

5. Houari Boumedienne coined this expression in the 1960s, but Algerians repeat it in unison to this day.

6. The author witnessed firsthand the reactions of the population at that time. As a boy scout, the task was to collect foodstuffs to send to the troops fighting Moroccan forces in southwest Algeria. The author vividly recalls people saying, "How could our own brothers [Moroccans] betray us in this manner?" and "How could they do this to us while our blood from the war against France is still fresh?" Ben Bella had given a televised speech in which he declared that the Moroccans *hagrouna* (they bullied us). Some volunteers showed up at barracks to go fight Moroccan troops.

7. Referring to Morocco's military intervention, an Algerian journalist stated, "In Algiers, the trauma was terrible. The later creation of a powerful 'popular' army was a direct consequence" (Alilat 2007).

8. For Algerians, the memorandum of understanding of 1961 "was a political compromise of circumstances and not a legal one per se, it had been dictated by the imperatives of the War of Independence and therefore could not commit the future of a sovereign Algeria" (Yousfi 1989, 121, cited in Lounnas and Messari 2018, 6).

9. The United Nations did not recognize the Madrid Accords and still considers Morocco as the occupier in Western Sahara and Spain as the administering power.

10. During an interview, the then–head of the directorate of intelligence told me that he personally said to King Hassan, "Do not think that because Algeria is on its knees that we cannot hurt Morocco. We, too, have means to do damage to the kingdom" (interview by the author, March 5, 1993).

11. The founder of the Armed Islamic Group, Abdelhak Layada, asserted in 2005 that he was not detained in Morocco in 1993; he claims that Moroccan officials sought to use him against Algeria. See Amrani (2005).

12. Polisario officials told the author that they repeatedly informed the Algerian military about cross-border arms shipments. This was confirmed to me in 2000 by a Moroccan scholar (anonymous) close to the Moroccan regime. See also *Jeune Afrique* 1757 (September 18–24, 1994): 8–11.

13. King Mohamed VI stated this in his speeches in November 2009 and again in 2014. See *Maroc Agence Presse* (2014).

11

Conclusion

Assessing Shocks and Rivalry Processes in the Middle East and North Africa

Imad Mansour and William R. Thompson

This book presented an explicit and empirically driven analysis of the impact of shocks on rivalries in the Middle East and North Africa (MENA). Not surprisingly perhaps, we believe this volume validates our initial position that rivalries are worth examining as rivalries. By identifying specific conflict relationships as rivalries, we do not mean to suggest that no one was aware of these conflicts before their identification. On the contrary, much has been written about pairs of states that share intense conflicts with each other. But most of what has been written describes interpretations of the history of their foreign policy activities. These descriptions can be invaluable. Yet they fall short of capturing the full nature of the rivalries and what rivalries entail. Rivalries are more than merely two feuding states. They have distinctive structures, processes, and life cycles. Moreover, they can be compared and theorized about. We think we gain some value added in doing so. This last statement does not imply that invoking the term "rivalry" suffices for understanding what is going on. It is only a starting point but one that we think is more advantageous than starting without invoking the term "rivalry."

From the findings of the chapters in this volume, we draw two central lessons on theorizing shocks within the study of rivalry and on why the "rivalry field" analytical prism advances our understandings of rivalries as well as regional dynamics. We conclude with a demonstration of how the rivalry field shifted with time from Arab-Israel confrontations toward rivalries including Iran and others.

LESSON ONE: SHOCKS IN RIVALRIES

A shock is an event or process whose effects are reflected in change on material or ideational relational levels. A shock could be endogenous to a group or state (such as at the level of leadership or ideas), or it could be exogenous (such as an invasion, economic collapse). Shocks are important given that they act on the level of decision-makers' perceptions, collective societal narratives, domestic political-economic coalitions, or international alliances. Pertaining to the importance of shocks in rivalry analysis, the chapters in this volume provide empirical demonstrations of how shocks work.

A central lesson to come out of the chapters is how shocks are useful analytical constructs for explaining rivalry onset or origins à la Goertz and Diehl (1995a), rivalry initiation and termination à la Diehl and Goertz (2000), and rivalry termination à la Rasler, Thompson, and Ganguly (2013). The chapters' findings are consistent with arguments in the rivalry literature that shocks can occur in the onset phase and thus spur on a rivalry (such as in the Morocco-Algeria or the Iran–Saudi Arabia rivalries) and that shocks can also terminate a rivalry (such as the impact of the 2003 American invasion of Iraq on the Iran-Iraq rivalry). However, our chapters also provide strong evidence on the importance of shocks in accounting for rivalry fluctuations along the rivalry continuum in between commencement and endings, serving, thus, as spurs to the inflammation or dampening of rivalry (see table 11.1).

Moreover, chapters have revealed how shocks can occur in clusters. This is the idea that there are, at least occasionally, circumstances in which a series of shocks in rapid succession significantly affect rivalry intensity or dynamics. We see such clusters in the period between 1988 and 1991 affecting the Iran–Saudi Arabia rivalry: the Iran-Iraq War ends, leadership changes occur in both countries, the Cold War ends, Iraq invades Kuwait, and another Gulf War takes place. The convergence of these events into a cluster led to a temporary détente between Iran and Saudi Arabia.

LESSON TWO: RIVALRY FIELDS

The chapters in this book have demonstrated how analyzing regional dynamics through an application of the prism of a rivalry field, as a conceptual structure, has powerful explanatory value. As explained in the introduction of this volume, a rivalry field is composed of multiple and interacting rivalries whose dynamics intersect; the dynamics in one rivalry in a field carries consequences for the others. For example, change in the Iran-Iraq rivalry in 1991 contributed to détente in the Saudi Arabia–Iran rivalry, while change in the Iran-Iraq rivalry in 2003 contributed to increased hostilities in the Iran–Saudi Arabia one.

Our volume underlines the utility of interpreting the international relations of MENA in terms of rivalries as conceptual structures and processes rather than simply referring to groups of hostile states by proper place names and various decades. This is carried over in how we theorize shocks; in essence, our volume's novel emphasis on the impact of shocks on rivalries expands the analysis of rivalries and seems particularly relevant to MENA political-economic history. A rivalry frame helps channel explanations from descriptions. Issue areas underpinning rivalry onset are explicated. Factors that sustain rivalries and have been responsible for varied trajectories are highlighted by tracing progressions in different dyads, a triad, and rivalry fields. Termination dynamics can be pinpointed better as well.

Shocks, Rivalry Fields, and Shifting Dynamics in the MENA

As became readily apparent in the chapter sequence, shocks can originate in the domestic, regional, or extra-regional environments. Most significant, and supported by evidence in several of the case studies, has been the centrality of domestic-level shocks. Between the 1950s and 1979 the important shocks that stimulated the beginning of many of the rivalries we see today were domestic. Occurring in the forms of national independence or domestic demands for political change, these shocks included, for example, revolutions leading to changes in government and ideas or narratives: this was the case in Egypt (1952), Iraq (1958), and Iran (1979). Interstate contestation related to independence was also the case with the persistent North African rivalry between Morocco and Algeria. Other forms of domestic shocks have been the collection of domestic revolts commonly now known as the Arab Spring. These are revolts leading to changes in government, but they have had much less impact on narratives or the overhauling of state institutional structures. A third type of domestic shock is related to changes in individual leadership, which can bring about changes in perceptions and preferences at the decision-making levels, hence foreign policy in general and rivalry relations in particular.

At the regional level the chapters provide a collection of shocks that affected the rivalry field. These have included the termination of colonial rule, which meant the ushering in of statist independence; we observed the impact of such shocks in North Africa as we did with the Levant, especially with the creation of Israel. At the regional level have also been various wars that shocked the rivalry field, and these have included several confrontations between Israel and Arab states as well as non-state actors (most prominently Hezbollah in Lebanon). Also important regionally was the Iran-Iraq War, which acted as a proxy theater (among other locations) for the Iran–Saudi Arabia rivalry to play out.

Finally, an important shock at the regional level was the Camp David Accords between Egypt and Israel, which came as a conclusion to the almost decade-long process of trying to dampen the militancy of the various Arab-Israel rivalries without abandoning the centrality of the Palestinian question. This shock was actually a multilevel one. Emanating technically from a site selected by the leading global power, it could easily be categorized as a global shock. The main regional component, however, was Egypt's decision to abandon a leading militant position in exchange for American aid.

We also observe how the MENA, like many global regions, has been, and remains, susceptible to extra-regional penetration or intrusion by major powers. These intrusions include, for example, Britain before 1971, the United States since the 1970s, and France in the Maghreb. What emerges, however, is that the Levant and the Gulf are most susceptible to direct intervention by a major power to alter the regional order. In particular, the United States has been the dominant extra-regional power in the MENA. The importance of the end of the Cold War as a shock to regional rivalries, especially in the sense of options for rivals, such as Saudi Arabia and Iran, or a "sole" voice guiding peacemaking processes in the set of Levantine rivalries emerged fairly clearly in the chapters.

Since the early 1990s American dominance has surely affected various patterns of local-global alliances, conflict, and accord as well as the space for other powers to act locally (such as Russia or China, especially in the last decade). It surely was the case that the 2003 American invasion of Iraq (a specific type of violent shock) carried significant influence on the Iraqi state and thus also on the various relevant relations, including with Iran, Turkey, Saudi Arabia, and others. It seems to us, however, that the definitive impact on regional rivalries has largely been a result of "local" (regional and domestic) shocks. This meant that systemic-level shocks are filtered through local dynamics at the level of domestic politics of states as well as individual decision-makers.

The claim we make about the importance of decidedly local dynamics seems to be supported by analyzing the effects of various shocks. In the case of North Africa, shocks acted to alter Moroccan and Algerian decision-makers' perceptions toward the other. Moreover, in the case of Iran, shocks acted to alter decision-makers' preferences toward domestic and foreign policy issue areas. Shocks also acted at the domestic level of rival states. In the case of Iran, for example, socioeconomic grievances fed a revolutionary momentum that itself resulted in a changed societal narrative, thus setting the ideational groundwork for rivalry with Israel. Also in the case of Iran, shocks left an impact on policy inasmuch as they interacted with, and were filtered through, domestic institutional roles and functions, altering, therefore, coalition formation and intra-political system balances.

The previously mentioned localization confirms the explanatory usefulness of the rivalry field construct in general. It also highlights an interesting way of thinking of the lingering puzzle or question: Why is there so much conflict in the MENA? If we look at regional dynamics through the prism of rivalry field, we observe two dynamics happening: the Levant and the Gulf seem to be the scenes of significant shocks that occur at least every decade, if not almost every year. This empirical observation allows us to modify the question on conflict persistence in the MENA and ask specifically about the Levant and the Gulf.[1] Analysis of multilevel shocks in the case chapters shows that there seems to be a neighborhood effect driving conflict propensity. That is precisely why understanding the configuration of rivalry fields is so important.

To elaborate more, one of the main "findings" of this book is that conflict begets conflict in the MENA. This is not exactly an unknown idea, but we have exposed a concrete causal mechanism. External wars and internal turmoil cause, selectively, realignments in rivalry relationships that in turn alter the probabilities of further conflict between and among rivals. Given a sufficiently complex rivalry field, movement toward a rivalry-free region is made especially difficult when closure in one rivalry may lead to the emergence of a new rivalry somewhere else in the field.

More recent evidence is suggesting, moreover, that neighborhood effects may be greater than dyadic effects in terms of peace and conflict. Rivalry fields, a manifestation of neighborhood effects, have not diminished all that much in MENA; they may shrink a bit from time to time but manage to maintain themselves by reflecting the reinvention of reasons for intense conflict over time. Thus, one of the main reasons MENA, or the Gulf and the Levant to be specific, is so highly conflictual is that it is highly conflictual. It is difficult to disengage from complex causalities. An important lesson from these empirically driven observations comes in the form of an invitation for rivalry scholarship to rethink the dominance of dyadic analysis. Kabalan's chapter 6, in particular, highlights the advantages of giving more attention to the neighborhood than the dyad.

In mapping out the shocks studied in this volume (table 11.1), and while recognizing that shock occurrence has been continuous since the beginning of the twentieth century, we can discern five temporal concentrations:

- 1950–60s: statist independence (and reactions)
- 1978–79: Camp David Accords, Iranian Revolution
- 1988–91: termination of Iran-Iraq War, end of Cold War, several Iraq-related wars
- 2003: American invasion of Iraq
- Since 2011: Arab Spring revolts

The sequence of these shocks had the effect of weakening the Arab-Israel rivalry field. This happened most significantly with the conclusion of the Camp David Accords, which effectively withdrew Egypt from the regional competition, leaving Syria with reduced military options to confront Israel. While Syria maintained rhetorical support for Palestinian resistance, Egypt's new foreign policy in the region eliminated the option of Damascus relying on the then-strongest Arab confrontation state. With these changes in the Arab-Israel system, the 1979 Iranian Revolution moved the active field toward the Gulf—this is another powerful, if indirect, finding of this book.

Empirically, the rivalry field in the MENA since the first half of the twentieth century has undergone a rare sea change, shifting from the Arab-Israel confrontations to Iran versus a wide range of regional state actors, including Arab states, Turkey, and Israel. With time the shifting of the rivalry field toward an "Iran-centric" one was coupled with a diminishing of interstate militarized confrontations (traditionally fought wars) across the MENA, with much of these rivalries taking on indirect proxy means, such as through alliances with state and non-state actors. While non-state actors, such as the Palestine Liberation Organization or the Frente Popular para la Liberación de Saguia el Hamra y Rio de Oro (Polisario), have historically had critical roles in the formation and direction of MENA rivalries, we can discern with the shifting of the rivalry field southward a marked increase in the numbers and activity of non-state actors with credible material, ideational, and strategic assets to allow us to note that they are in rivalry relations with states (and with other non-state actors). To be sure, the proliferation of actor types in rivalry relations is a significant development.[2]

With states and non-state groups engaged in rivalry, interstate conflict seems to have ceased being the only means of rivalry or the only dominant form of international relations in the MENA. Examples include Saudi Arabia (allied with the Yemeni government it recognizes) versus Houthi groups. Israel has been in rivalry with Hezbollah for decades; while Hezbollah receives support from Iran and Syria, it has exhibited effective tactical and operational independence as well as material and ideational capacities to sustain the rivalry with Israel. Turkey has been in rivalry with Kurdish groups for decades and, to be

Table 11.1. Shocks studied in this volume

	Shocks (single and clustered) in temporal progression						
	1950	1975	1980	1990	2000	2010	2018
Zoubir	Sands War (1963)	Western Sahara (1975–76)					
Altunışık	Emergence of modern states	Rise of the Cold War	Iranian Revolution	Cluster: end of the Cold War and the Gulf War	Cluster: US invasion of Iraq and domestic transformations	Arab Spring	Building of post-ISIL Syria
Volgy, Gordell, Bezerra	1952 Egyptian Revolution		Iranian Revolution	End of Cold War	2003 US invasion of Iraq		
Calabrese			Iranian Revolution	Cluster in 1990s: • Iran exhausted its military capabilities, swallowed the bitter pill, transition to a new political elite in Tehran • new leadership in Riyadh • end of the Cold War and demise of the Soviet Union	2003 US invasion of Iraq	Arab Spring	
Rasler	1952 Egyptian Revolution		1979 Iranian Revolution			Arab Spring	

Kabalan	Iraqi Revolution (1958) + derivative shocks or sub-shocks • collapse of Iraq's Qasim government to pro-Nasir officers (1963) • Iraqi Ba'ath Party assumed power (1968) • British withdrawal from the Gulf (1971) • signing of Iraqi-Soviet Treaty of Friendship (April 1972)	1979 Iranian Revolution	2003 US invasion of Iraq	2011 Syria Uprising / Civil War
Mansour		1979 Iranian Revolution	2002 reports surface of Iranian nuclear activities	2015 JCPOA
Wilson	• American intervention at various moments and in the form of military and political aid to allies (Saudi Arabia) as well as pressures on opponents (Iran) • Saudi Arabia policies as triggers (e.g., regarding the Hajj) • Leadership change (inducing changes in preferences and perceptions) and domestic institutional interests in Iran			
Thompson	1948-49 war; Egyptian Revolution; 1956 war; 1967 war; 1973 war; Camp David Accords; Iranian Revolution; Iran-Iraq War; First Gulf War; Second Gulf War; Arab Spring; Trump administration			

precise, with the Kurdistan Workers Party since 1984. Egypt has been in rivalry with the Muslim Brotherhood all over the MENA, which has had direct implications on regional relations as well as on Egyptian foreign policy globally. At times, state versus non-state group relationships have taken precedence over state versus state conflict. The expansion in the activity of multiple actors has had the dual effect of exacerbating local conflicts (but where local combatants or opponents have invited or welcomed external intervention) and fed back into and further fueled the multiple regional rivalries. Thus, we believe that rivalry scholarship should be interested in expanding its ontological scope to account for the activities of non-state groups.

NOTES

1. Implicit to this observation is the comparison with the Maghreb, in which shocks seem relatively scarce.

2. But then non-state groups were not unimportant even in the old Arab-Israel-centric rivalry field. Perhaps it is not so much the increased status of non-state groups that we need to acknowledge as much as it is their proliferation and increased status.

References

ABC News. 2003. "U.S. Shut Down Oil Pipeline to Syria." April 16, 2003. http://www.abc.net.au/news/2003-04-16/us-shut-down-oil-pipeline-to-syria/1837422.

Abdoh, Hannah Louise. 2017. "How Saudis Pushed Gulf Unity but Got the Qatar Crisis." *Bloomberg*, August 15, 2017. https://www.bloomberg.com/news/articles/2017-08-15/how-saudis-pushed-gulf-unity-got-qatar-crisis-quicktake-q-a.

Abdulghani, Jasem M. 2011. *Iraq and Iran: The Years of Crisis.* New York: Routledge.

Abed-Jabri, Mohamed. 1985. "Evolution of the Maghrib Concept: Facts and Perspectives." In *Contemporary North Africa*, edited by Halim Barakat. Washington, DC: Center for Contemporary Arab Studies.

Abisaab, Rula Jurdi. 2004. *Converting Persia: Religion and Power in the Safavid Empire.* London: I. B. Tauris.

Abrahamian, Ervand. 2004. "Empire Strikes Back: Iran in U.S. Sights." In *Inventing the Axis of Evil: The Truth about North Korea, Iran and Syria.* Edited by Bruce Cumings, Ervand Abrahamian, and Moseh Ma'oz. New York: New Press.

Abu-Nasr, Donna. 2009. "Saudi Government Cracks Down on Shiite Dissident." Fox News, April 1, 2009. https://www.foxnews.com/printer_friendly_wires/2009/Apr01/0,4675, MLSSaudiShiites.00html.

Acemoglu, Daron, Ufuk Akcigit, and William Kerr. 2015. "Networks and the Macroeconomy: An Empirical Exploration." Working Paper No. 21344, National Bureau of Economic Research, Cambridge, MA. https://www.nber.org/papers/w21344.

Acharya, Amitav. 1989. *U.S. Military Strategy in the Gulf: Origins and Evolution under the Carter and Reagan Administrations.* London: Routledge.

Acheson, Dean. 1969. *Present at the Creation: My Years in the State Department.* New York: Norton.

Achouri, Houari. 2017. "Révélation: le FIS a sollicité l'aide de Hassan II pour prendre le pouvoir." *Afrique-Asie*, October 3. http://www.afrique-asie.fr/revelation-le-fis-a-sollicite-laide-de-hassan-ii-pour-prendre-le-pouvoir/.

Afkhami, Gholam Reza. 2009. *The Life and Times of the Shah.* Berkeley: University of California Press.

Agence France Presse. 2001. "AFP Middle East News Summary." March 7, 2001. Nexis Uni.

———. 2007. "Iran's Ahmadinejad to Perform Hajj: Official." December 19, 2007. Nexis Uni.

Ahmadian, Hassan. 2016. "Four Reasons Sisi Won't Turn against Iran." *Al-Monitor*, May 3, 2016. www.al-monitor.com/pulse/originals/2016/05/iran-saudi-egypt-sisiprapprochement-salman-visit.html.

Ahren, Raphael. 2015. "Would a Nuclear Iran Truly Pose an Existential Threat to Israel?" *Times of Israel*, February 21, 2015. https://www.timesofisrael.com/would-a-nuclear-iran-truly-pose-an-existential-threat-to-israel/.

Akbarzadeh, Shahram, and James Barry. 2016. "Iran and Turkey: Not Quite Enemies but Less than Friends." *Third World Quarterly* 38 (4): 980–95.

Al-Alkim, Hassan Hamdan. 2000. "The Gulf Subregion in the Twenty-First Century: US Involvement and Sources." *American Studies International* 38 (1): 72–94.

Alam, Asadollah. 2008. *The Shah and I: The Confidential Diary of Iran's Royal Court, 1968–77.* New York: I. B. Tauris.

Alaoui, Mohamed Chakir. 2012. "Hamid Chabat demande à Alger la rétrocession des régions marocaines du Sahara oriental." *Le360*. http://fr.le360.ma/politique/hamid-chabat-demande -a-alger-la-retrocession-des-regions-marocaines-du-sahara-oriental-63376.

Al-Arabiya. 2016a. "Arab League Brands Hezbollah 'Terror' Group." March 11, 2016. http:// english.alarabiya.net/en/2016/03/11/Arab-League-declares-Lebanon-s-Hezbollah-terror -group.html.

———. 2016b. "Turkey-GCC Call for an End to Iran Interventions." October 14, 2016. http:// english.alarabiya.net/en/News/middle-east/2016/10/14/Turkey-GCC-call-for-end-to-Iran -interventions.html

Al Bawaba News. 2016. "Germany Tries to Mediate Iran, Saudi Tensions in Upcoming Meetings." February 1, 2016. http://www.albawaba.com/news/germany-tries-mediate-iran-saudi-tensions -upcoming-meetings-800446.

Alhasan, Hasan T. 2011. "The Role of Iran in the Failed Coup of 1981: The IFLB in Bahrain." *Middle East Journal* 65 (4): 603–17.

Al-Hatlani, Ibrahim. 2015. "Saudis Investigate Mina Stampede." Translated by Sami-Joe Abboud. *Al-Monitor*, October 5, 2015. http://www.al-monitor.com/pulse/originals/2015/10/iran -accuse-saudi-arabia-mina-stampede-Hajj.html.

Al Hayat. 2005.

Alilat, Farid. 2007. "Début de la guerre des Sables." *Jeune Afrique*, October 9, 2007. http://www .jeuneafrique.com/124805/archives-thematique/d-but-de-la-guerre-des-sables/.

Aljabiri, Satar Jabar. 2007. "Alalaqat aliraqiya alsouriya: dirasa fi dour alfae'l alsouri kfae'l muather fi alsha'n aldakhili aliraqi." *Majlat Dirasat Douliya* 33: 17–32.

Al-Jubeir, Adel. 2016. "Can Iran Change?" *New York Times*, January 19, 2016. http://www.ny times.com/2016/01/19/opinion/saudi-arabia-can-iran-change.html.

Al-Khoei, Hayder. 2013. "Syria: The View from Iraq." European Council on Foreign Relations. https://www.ecfr.eu/article/commentary_iraq.

Allison, Graham. 2016. "Is Iran Still Israel's Top Threat?" *Atlantic*, March 8, 2016. https://www .theatlantic.com/international/archive/2016/03/iran-nuclear-deal-israel/472767/.

Allouche, Adel. 1980. *The Origins and Development of the Ottoman-Safavid Conflict (906/962– 1500/1555)*. Berlin: K. Schwarz Verlag. https://archive.org/stream/Ottoman/the%20origins %20and%20development%20of%20the%20ottoman-safavid%20conflict#page/n47 /mode/2up.

Al-Mani, Saleh A. 1996. "Of Security and Threat: Saudi Arabia's Perception." *Journal of South Asian and Middle Eastern Studies* 20 (1): 74–87.

Al-Mazrouei, Noura S. 2015. "Disputed Islands between UAE and Iran: Abu Musa, Greater Tunb, and Lesser Tunb in the Strait of Hormuz." Cambridge: Gulf Research Centre. http://gulf researchmeeting.net/publication_pdf/Noura%20paper.pdf.

Al Omran, Ahmed, and Asa Fitch. 2016. "Iran Accuses Saudi Arabia of Bombing Its Embassy in Yemen." *Wall Street Journal*, January 7, 2016. http://www.wsj.com/articles/iran-accuses -saudi-led-coalition-of-bombing-its-yemen-embassy-1452171232.

Al-Saud, Faisal bin Salman. 2003. *Iran, Saudi Arabia and the Gulf: Power Politics in Transition, 1968–1971*. London: I. B. Tauris.

Alsultan, Fahad M., and Pedram Saied. 2017. *The Development of Saudi-Iranian Relations since the 1990s: Between Conflict and Accommodation*. London: Routledge.

Altoraifi, Adel. 2012. "Understanding the Role of State Identity in Foreign Policy Decision-Making." PhD diss., London School of Economics and Political Science.

Altunışık, Meliha. 2014. "Turkey's 'Return' to the Middle East." In *Regional Powers in the Middle East: New Constellations after the Arab Revolts*, edited by H. Fürtig, 123–42. New York: Palgrave.

Amirahmadi, Hooshang. 1994. "Iran and the Persian Gulf: Strategic Issues and Outlook." In *Islam, Iran, and World Stability*, edited by Hamid Zanganeh, 97–134. New York: St. Martin's Press.

Amiri, Reza Ekhtiari, Ku Hasnita Binti Ku Samsu, and Hassan Gholipour Fereidouni. 2011. "The Hajj and Iran's Foreign Policy towards Saudi Arabia." *Journal of Asian and African Studies* 46 (6): 678–90.

Amrani, K. 2005. "Le Fondateur du GIA écrit à Bouteflika: Le Maroc a soutenu les groupes armés." *Le Soir d'Algérie*, February 13, 2005. http://www.lesoirdalgerie.com/articles /2005/02/13/article.php?sid=19240&cid=2.

Amuzegar, Jahangir. 1997. "Adjusting to Sanctions." *Foreign Affairs* 76 (3): 31–41.

Anderson, Collin, and Karim Sadjadpour. 2018. *Iran's Cyber Threat: Espionage, Sabotage, and Revenge*. Washington, DC: Carnegie Endowment for International Peace.

Anderson, Harry, Richard Sandza, Robert Cullen, and Christopher Dickey. 1987. "A Sting in the Gulf." *Newsweek*, August 3, 1987.

Aourid, Hassan. 2013. "Au nom des nationalismes." *Zamane*, April 24, 2013. http://zamane.ma /fr/au-nom-des-nationalismes/.

Arjomand, Said Amir. 1988. *The Turban for the Crown*. New York: Oxford University Press.

———. 2009. *After Khomeini: Iran under His Successors*. New York: Oxford University Press.

Armstrong, David. 1993. *Revolution and World Order: The Revolutionary State in International Society*. Oxford: Clarendon Press.

Arraf, Jane. 2009. "Baghdad Bombing Leaves Hole in Diplomatic Corps." *Christian Science Monitor*, August 24, 2009. https://www.csmonitor.com/World/Middle-East/2009/0824/p06s01 -wome.html.

Asharq Al-Awsat. 2016. "Prince Turki Al Faisal, at the Paris Rally to Free Iran: The Muslim World Supports You Both in Heart and Soul." July 9, 2016. http://english.aawsat.com/2016/07 /article55354150/prince-turki-alfaisal-paris-rally-free-iran-muslim-world-supports-heart -soul.

Ashford, Douglas. 1962. "The Irredentist Appeal in Morocco and Mauritania." *World Politics* 15 (4): 641–51.

As-Safir. 2003.

Associated Press. 1990. "Pilgrims Wind Up Rituals, Iran Accuses Saudis of Incompetence." July 10, 1990. Nexis Uni.

———. 2016. "Iran Accuses Saudis of 'Murdering' Pilgrims in Hajj Stampede." *Guardian*, September 6, 2016. https://www.theguardian.com/world/2016/sep/06/iran-accuses-saudi-arabia -of-murdering-pilgrims-during-Hajj-stampede.

Avishai, Bernard. 2017. "Why Israeli Nuclear Experts Disagree with Netanyahu about the Iran Deal." *New Yorker*, October 24, 2017. https://www.newyorker.com/news/daily-comment/why -israeli-nuclear-experts-disagree-with-netanyahu-about-the-iran-deal.

Badeeb, Saeed M. 1993. *Saudi-Iranian Relations, 1932–1982*. London: Centre for Arab and Iranian Studies and Echoes.

Bahgat, Gawdat. 2000. "Iranian-Saudi Rapprochement. Prospects and Implications." *World Affairs* 162 (3): 108–15.

———. 2006. "Nuclear Proliferation: The Islamic Republic of Iran." *Iranian Studies* 39 (3): 307–27.

Bakhash, Shaul. 2004. "Iran and Iraq: 1930–80." In *Iran, Iraq, and the Legacies of War*, edited by Lawrence G. Potter, 11–27. New York: Palgrave Macmillan.

Baktiari, Bahman. 1996. *Parliamentary Politics in Revolutionary Iran*. Gainesville: University Press of Florida.

Balyuzi, Hasan M. 1976. *Muhammad and the Course of Islam*. Oxford: George Ronald.

Balzacq, Thierry. 2010. "Constructivism and Securitization Studies." In *The Routledge Handbook of Security Studies*. Edited by Cavely Myriam Dunn and Victor Mauer. Abingdon, UK: Routledge.

Bank, Andre, and Morten Valbjorn. 2012. "The New Arab Cold War: Rediscovering the Arab Dimension of Middle East Regional Politics." *Review of International Studies* 38 (1): 3–24.

Barbieri, Katherine and Omar Keshk. 2012. Correlates of War Project Trade Data Set. Codebook, Version 3.0. http://correlatesofwar.org.

Barbieri, Katherine, Omar Keshk, and Brian Pollins. 2009. "Trading Data: Evaluating Our Assumptions and Coding Rules." *Conflict Management and Peace Science* 26, 5: 471-491.

Barnett, Michael N. 1992. *Confronting the Costs of War: Military Power, State and Society in Egypt and Israel.* Princeton, NJ: Princeton University Press.

———. 1998. *Dialogues in Arab Politics: Negotiations in Regional Order.* New York: Columbia University Press.

———. 1999. "Culture, Strategy and Foreign Policy Change: Israel's Road to Oslo." *European Journal of International Relations* 5 (1): 5–36.

BBC. 1980. "Iranian Warning to Arab Regimes against Supporting Iraq." In *BBC Summary of World Broadcasts. Part 4: The Middle East and Africa.* September 22, 1980. Nexis Uni.

———. 1983. "Iranian Denial of Pledge about Pilgrims' Behavior." In *BBC Summary of World Broadcasts. Part 4: The Middle East.* September 19, 1983. Nexis Uni.

———. 1987a. "Iran: Rafsanjani on 'Avenging the Blood of Martyrs.'" In *BBC Summary of World Broadcasts. Part 4: The Middle East.* August 4, 1987. Nexis Uni.

———. 1987b. "Iranian Protest to Saudi Arabia over Hajj Expulsions." In *BBC Summary of World Broadcasts Part 4: The Middle East.* August 19, 1987. Nexis Uni.

———. 1989. "Iran Blames Saudi Arabia for Mecca Bombs." In *BBC Summary of World Broadcasts. Part 4: The Middle East.* July 12, 1989. Nexis Uni.

———. 1995. "Friday Prayers: Emami-Kashani Gives Reasons for US Pressure on Iran." In *BBC Summary of World Broadcasts. Part 4: The Middle East.* May 20, 1995. Nexis Uni.

———. 1998. "Rafsanjani Meets Saudi King, Favours Expanding Cooperation." In *BBC Summary of World Broadcasts. Part 4: The Middle East.* March 3, 1998. Nexis Uni.

———. 1999. "World: Middle East Saudi King Urges Rapprochement with Iran." July 6, 1999.

———. 2012. "Israel 'Prepared for 30-Day War with Iran." August 15, 2012. https://www.bbc.com/news/world-middle-east-19274866.

Ben-Gurion, David. 1958. *Mishnato shel David Ben-Gurion* [David Ben-Gurion's journal]. Tel Aviv: Yavne.

Bennett, Scott D. 1996. "Security, Bargaining and the End of the Interstate Rivalry." *International Studies Quarterly* 40 (2): 157–83.

———. 1997a. "Democracy, Regime Change, and Rivalry Termination." *International Interactions* 22 (4): 369–97.

———. 1997b. "Measuring Rivalry Termination, 1816–1992." *Journal of Conflict Resolution* 41: 227–54.

———. 1998. "Integrating and Testing Models of Rivalry." *American Journal of Political Science* 42 (4): 1200–1232.

Bergen, Peter. 2013. "Strange Bedfellows—Iran and al Qaeda." CNN.com, March 10, 2013. http://www.cnn.com/2013/03/10/opinion/bergen-iran-al-qaeda/.

Berramdane, Abdelkhaleq. 1987. *Le Maroc et l'Occident—1800–1974.* Paris: Karthala.

———. 1992. *Le Sahara Occidental—Enjeu maghrébin.* Paris: Karthala.

Bially Mattern, Janice, and Ayse Zarakol. 2016. "Hierarchies in World Politics." *International Organization* 70 (3): 623–54.

Bin Huwaidin, Mohamed. 2015. "The Security Dilemma in Saudi-Iranian Relations." *Review of History and Political Science* 3 (2): 69–79.

Black, Ian. 2014. "Assad and Maliki Unite against Common Enemy Isis." *Guardian,* June 26, 2014. https://www.theguardian.com/world/2014/jun/26/iraq-syria-air-strikes-isis.

———. 2016. "Saudi Talk of 'Regime Change' Takes Hostility to Iran to New Level." *Guardian,* July 12, 2016. https://www.theguardian.com/world/on-the-middle-east/2016/jul/12/saudi-talk-of-regime-change-takes-hostility-to-iran-to-new-level.

Black, Ian, and Simon Tisdall. 2010. "Saudi Arabia Urges US Attack on Iran to Stop Nuclear Programme." *Guardian,* November 28, 2010. https://www.theguardian.com/world/2010/nov/28/us-embassy-cables-saudis-iran.

Borzorgmehr, Najmeh. 2018. "Thousands of Iranians Take Part in State-Organised Rallies." *Financial Times*, January 3, 2018. https://www.ft.com/content/0064cb72-efac-11e7-ac08 -07c3086a2625.

Braithwaite, Alex. 2006. "The Geographic Spread of Militarized Disputes." *Journal of Peace Research* 43 (5): 507–22.

Brecher, Michael. 1972. *The Foreign Policy System of Israel: Setting, Images, Process*. London: Oxford University Press.

Brecher, Michael, and Jonathan Wilkenfeld. 1997. *A Study of Crisis*. Ann Arbor: University of Michigan Press.

Brown, Carl L. 1984. *International Politics and the Middle East: Old Rules, Dangerous Game*. Princeton, NJ: Princeton University Press.

Brumfield, Ben. 2015. "Leaked Audio: Israeli Leaders Drew Up Plans to Attack Iranian Military." CNN, August 22, 2015. https://edition.cnn.com/2015/08/22/middleeast/israel-plan-iran -military-target-strike/index.html.

Brzezinski, Zbigniew, Brent Scowcroft, and Richard Murphy. 1997. "Differentiated Containment." *Foreign Affairs* 76 (3): 20–30.

Buchta, Wilfried. 2000. *Who Rules Iran? The Structure of Power in the Islamic Republic*. Washington, DC: Washington Institute for Near East Policy.

Butt, Ahsan I. 2013. "Anarchy and Hierarchy in International Relations: Examining South America's War-Prone Decade, 1932–41." *International Organization* 67 (3): 575–607.

Calabrese, John. 1994. *Revolutionary Horizons: Regional Foreign Policy in Post-Khomeini Iran*. London: Macmillan.

———. 1998. "Turkey and Iran: Limits of a Stable Relationship." *British Journal of Middle Eastern Studies* 25 (1): 75–94.

Cammack, Perry, Michele Dunne, Amr Hamzawy, Marc Lynch, Marwan Muasher, and Yezid Sayigh. 2017. *Arab Fractures: Citizens, States and Social Contracts*. Washington, DC: Carnegie Endowment for International Peace.

Campbell, David. 1998. *Writing Security: United States Foreign Policy and the Politics of Identity*. Minneapolis: Minnesota University Press.

Çetinsaya, Gokhan. 2003. "Essential Friends and Natural Enemies: The Historic Roots of Turkish-Iranian Relations." *Middle East Review of International Affairs* 7 (3): 116–32.

Charbel, Ghassan. 1998. "Jalal Talibani yatathaker." *Al-Wasat*, no. 355 (November 16, 1998).

Choucri, Nazli, and Robert C. North. 1989. "Lateral Pressure in International Relations: Concept and Theory." In *Handbook of War Studies*, edited by Manus I. Midlarsky, 289–326. Ann Arbor: University of Michigan Press.

Chubin, Shahram. 1992. "Iran and Regional Security in the Persian Gulf." *Survival* 34 (3): 62–80.

———. 1996–97. "U.S. Policy towards Iran Should Change: But It Probably Won't." *Survival* 38 (4): 16–18.

Chubin, Shahram, and Charles Tripp. 1996. *Iran-Saudi Arabia Relations and Regional Order*. London: Oxford University Press.

Chulov, Martin. 2017. "Saudis in Talks over Alliance to Rebuild Iraq and 'Return It to the Arab Fold.'" *Guardian*, August 18, 2017. https://www.theguardian.com/world/2017/aug/18/saudi -arabia-talks-alliance-rebuild-iraq-return-arab-fold.

Clarke, Richard. 2004. *Against All Enemies: Inside America's War on Terror*. New York: Free Press.

Cline, Kirssa, Patrick Rhamey, Alexis Henshaw, Alesia Sedziaka, Aakriti Tandon, and Thomas J. Volgy. 2011. "Identifying Regional Powers and Their Status." In Volgy et al., 2011.

Cohen, Avner. 1998. *Israel and the Bomb*. New York: Columbia University Press.

Colaresi, Michael P. 2001. "Shocks to the System: Great Power Rivalry and the Leadership Long Cycle." *Journal of Conflict Resolution* 45 (5): 569–93.

———. 2005. *Scare Tactics: The Politics of International Rivalry*. Syracuse, NY: Syracuse University Press.

Colaresi, Michael P., and William R. Thompson. 2002. "Strategic Rivalries, Protracted Conflict, and Crisis Escalation." *Journal of Peace Research* 39 (3): 263–87.

Colaresi, Michael P., Karen Rasler, and William R. Thompson. 2007. *Strategic Rivalries in World Politics: Position, Space and Conflict Escalation.* Cambridge: Cambridge University Press.

Colgan, Jeff D. 2013. *Petro-Aggression, When Oil Causes War.* New York: Cambridge University Press.

Commins, David. 2006. *The Wahhabi Mission and Saudi Arabia.* New York: I. B. Tauris.

Conesa, Pierre. 2011. *La fabrication de l'ennemi ou comment tuer avec sa conscience pour soi.* Paris: Robert Laffont.

Coppedge, Michael, John Gerring, Staffan I. Lindberg, Svend-Erik Skaaning, Jan Teorell, David Altman, Frida Andersson, et al. 2016. *V-Dem Codebook v6.* Gothenburg, Sweden: Varieties of Democracy (V-Dem) Project.

Cordesman, Anthony. 2015. *Military Spending and Arms Sales in the Gulf.* Washington, DC: Center for Strategic and International Studies. https://csis-prod.s3.amazonaws.com/s3fs-public /legacy_files/files/publication/150428_military_spending.pdf.

Council on Foreign Relations. 2005. "The Fight against Extremism and the Search for Peace," September 20, 2005. http://www.cfr.org/radicalization-and-extremism/fight-against-extrem ism-search-peace-rush-transcript-federal-news-service-inc/p8908.

Cox, Eric W. 2010. *Why Enduring Rivalries Do—or Don't—End.* Boulder, CO: Lynne Rienner.

Crist, David. 2012. *The Twilight War: Secret History of America's Thirty-Year Conflict with Iran.* New York: Penguin.

Cullinane, Susan. 2015. "Iran's Khamenei Threatens 'Harsh' Retaliation over Hajj Stampede at Mina." CNN.com, September 30, 2015. http://edition.cnn.com/2015/09/30/middleeast/Hajj -deaths-saudi-iran-yemen/.

Daily Star. 2010. "Saudi-Iran Friction Get Personal at Medina Graves Revered by Shiites." January 5, 2010. Nexis Uni.

Damis, John. 1985. "The Western Sahara Dispute as a Source of Regional Conflict in North Africa." In *Contemporary North Africa*, edited by Halim Barakat. Washington, DC: Center for Contemporary Arab Studies.

Danielson, Robert E. 2007. "Nasser and Pan-Arabism: Explaining Egypt's Rise to Power." Master's thesis, Naval Post-Graduate School, Monterey, California.

Dawisha, Adeed. 1976. *Egypt in the Arab World: The Elements of Foreign Policy.* New York: John Wiley.

———. 2016. *Arab Nationalism in the Twentieth Century: From Triumph to Despair.* Princeton, NJ: Princeton University Press.

De Borchgrave, Arnaud. 2016. "Analysis: Arabian Medicis." UPI, December 27, 2015. http:// www.upi.com/Top_News/Opinion/de-Borchgrave/2006/12/27/Analysis-Arabian-Medicis /UPI-28221167225848/.

De Clercq, M., et al. 1907. *Recueil des Traités de la France.* Vol. 5, *1843–1849.* Paris: Amyot.

Dehghanpisheh, Babak. 2015. "Iran Recruits Pakistani Shi'ites for Combat in Syria." Reuters, December 10, 2015. http://www.reuters.com/article/us-mideast-crisis-syria-pakistan-iran -idUSKBN0TT22S20151210.

———. 2016. "To Iranian Eyes, Kurdish Unrest Spells Saudi Incitement." Reuters, September 4, 2016. http://www.reuters.com/article/us-iran-politics-kurds-idUSKCN11A0BD.

Dekkar, Taieb. 2016. *Maroc-Algérie—La méfiance réciproque.* Paris: L'Harmattan.

Diehl, Paul F., and Gary Goertz. 1992. "The Empirical Importance of Enduring Rivalries." *International Interactions* 18 (2): 151–63.

———. 2000. *War and Peace in International Rivalry.* Ann Arbor: University of Michigan Press.

Dittmer, Lowell. 1981. "The Strategic Triangle: An Elementary Game-Theoretical Analysis." *World Politics* 33 (4): 485–515.

Dreyer, David R. 2012. "Issue Intractability and the Persistence of International Rivalry." *Conflict Management and Peace Science* 29 (5): 471–89.

Economic and Political Weekly. 1982. "OPEC: Saudi Arabia-Iran Tussle." December 25, 1982.

Economist. 2017. "A New Confrontation: Donald Trump Intends to Take on Iran. Right, but Risky." February 25, 2017. http://www.economist.com/news/middle-east-and-africa/21717 384-how-far-new-administration-prepared-go-donald-trump-intends-take.

Edmonton Journal. 2009. "Saudi Organizers Vow to Keep Hajj Peaceful Despite H1N1, Political Unrest." Nexis Uni.

Esfandiary, Dina, and Ariane Tabatabai. 2016. "Saudi Arabia Cares More about Iran than Iran Does about Saudi Arabia." *National Interest*, October 18, 2016. http://nationalinterest.org /feature/Saudi-arabia-cares-more-about-iran-iran-does-about-saudi-18091.

Ehteshami, Anoushiravan. 1995. *After Khomeini: The Iranian Second Republic.* New York: Routledge.

———. 2002. "The Foreign Policy of Iran." *The Middle East in the International System.* London: Lynne Reiner Publishers.

———. 2013. *Dynamics of Change in the Persian Gulf: Political Economy, War and Revolution.* London: Routledge.

Eilts, Hermann. 2006. "Saudi Arabia's Foreign Policy." In *Diplomacy in the Middle East: The International Relations of Regional and Outside Powers.* Edited by L. Carl Brown. London: I. B. Tauris.

Elik, Suleyman. 2012. *Iran-Turkey Relations, 1979–2011: Conceptualising the Dynamics of Politics, Religion, and Security in Middle Power States.* Abingdon, UK: Routledge.

El-Maslouhi, Aberrahim. 2011. "Le syndrome statocratique. Les relations civilo-militaires à l'épreuve de la transition politique en Algérie." In *Maroc-Algérie, Analyses croisées d'un environnement hostile.* Paris: Kathala, 2011.

Ensor, Josie. 2016. "Muslim Leaders Call for Sunni and Shia to Unite against Islamist Terror after Prophet's Mosque Bombing in Saudi Arabia." *Telegraph*, July 5, 2016. http://www.telegraph .co.uk/news/2016/07/05/leaders-call-for-muslims-to-unite-against-islamist-terror-after/.

Erdbrink, Thomas. 2016. "Kurdish Rebels Clash with Iran's Revolutionary Guards." *New York Times*, June 27, 2016. http://www.nytimes.com/2016/06/28/world/middleeast/kurdish-rebels -clash-with-irans-revolutionary-guards.html.

Fadlallah, Muhammad Hussein. 1997. *Min Wahi A'shoura'* [Inspirations from Ashoura]. Beirut: Dar al-Malak lil-Tiba'a Wal-Nashr Wal-Tawzee'.

Fahim, Karim, and Nick Cumming-Bruce. 2016. "Expedited Weapons Deliveries to Saudi Arabia Signal Deepening U.S. Involvement." *New York Times*, April 5, 2016. http://www.nytimes .com/2015/04/08/world/middleeast/yemen-houthis.html?_r=0.

Faramarzi, M., H. Yang, J. Mousavi, R. Schulin, C. R. Binder, and K. C. Abbaspour. 2010. "Analysis of Intra-Country Virtual Water Trade Strategy to Alleviate Water Scarcity in Iran." *Hydrology and Earth System Sciences* 14 (8): 1417–33.

Farsoun, Karen, and Jim Paul. 1976. "War in the Sahara: 1963." *MERIP Reports* 45: 13–16.

Fatemi, Faramarz S. 1980. *The U.S.S.R. in Iran: The Background History of Russian and Anglo-American Conflict in Iran, Its Effect on Iranian Nationalism and the Fall of the Shah.* South Brunswick, NJ: A. S. Barnes.

Ferris, Jesse. 2013. *Nasser's Game, How Intervention in Yemen Caused the Six Day War and the Decline of Egyptian Power.* Princeton, NJ: Princeton University Press.

Filkins, Dexter. 2013. "The Shadow Commander." *New Yorker*, September 30, 2013. http://www .newyorker.com/magazine/2013/09/30/the-shadow-commander.

Friedman, Brandon. 2017. "Russia, Turkey, and Iran: Cooperation and Competition in Syria." *Tel Aviv Notes* 11 (2): 1–8. https://dayan.org/content/russia-turkey-and-iran-cooperation-and -competition-syria.

Fromkin, David. 1989. *A Peace to End All Peace: The Fall of the Ottoman Empire and the Creation of the Modern Middle East.* New York: Holt.

Fürtig, Henner. 2002. *Iran's Rivalry with Saudi Arabia between the Gulf Wars.* Reading, UK: Garnet Publishing.

———. 2007. "Conflict and Cooperation in the Persian Gulf: The Interregional Order and US Policy." *Middle East Journal* 61 (4): 627–40.

Ganguly, Sumit, and William R. Thompson, eds. 2011a. *Asian Rivalries: Conflict, Escalation and Limitations on Two-Level Games*. Stanford, CA: Stanford University Press.

———. 2011b. "Two-Level Games in Asian Rivalries." In Ganguly and Thompson 2011, 195–210.

Gao, Shuqin. 2017. "China and Global Energy Governance: Integration or Confrontation?" *Global Governance* 23 (3): 307–25.

Gartzke, Eric. 2007. "The Capitalist Peace." *American Journal of Political Science* 51 (1): 166–91.

Gause, F. Gregory, III. 2009. *The International Relations of the Persian Gulf*. Cambridge: Cambridge University Press.

———. 2014. *Beyond Sectarianism: The New Middle East Cold War*. Brookings Doha Center Analysis Paper No. 11. Washington, DC: Brookings Institution.

Gerges, Fawaz A. 1996–97. "Washington's Misguided Iran Policy." *Survival* 38 (4): 5–15.

Gibler, Douglas M. 2009. *International Military Alliances, 1648-2008*, 2 vols. Washington, D.C.: Congressional Quarterly Press.

———. 2012. *The Territorial Peace: Borders, State Development and International Conflict*. Cambridge: Cambridge University Press.

Gibler, Douglas M. and Steven V. Miller (2014) "External Threat, State Capacity, and Civil War." *Journal of Peace Research* 51,5: 634-646.

Gibson, Bryan Robert. 2013. *U.S. Foreign Policy, Iraq and the Cold War, 1958–1975*. PhD diss., London School of Economics.

Gillespie, Kate, and Clement Henry, eds. 1995. *Oil in the New World Order*. Gainesville: University Press of Florida, 1995.

Gladstone, Rick. 2015. "Death Toll from Hajj Stampede Reaches 2411 in New Estimate." *New York Times*, December 10, 2015. http://www.nytimes.com/2015/12/11/world/middleeast /death-toll-from-Hajj-stampede.html.

Globalist. 2016. "Can Iran and Saudi Arabia Coexist?" April 30, 2016. http://www.theglobalist .com/can-iran-and-saudi-arabia-co-exist/.

Gochman, C. S., and Zeev Maoz. 1984. "Militarized Interstate Disputes, 1816–1976: Procedures, Patterns and Insights." *Journal of Conflict Resolution* 28 (4): 585–616.

Goertz, Gary, and Paul F. Diehl. 1995a. "The Initiation and Termination of Enduring Rivalries: The Impact of Political Shocks." *American Journal of Political Science* 39 (1): 30–52.

———. 1995b. "Taking 'Enduring' out of Enduring Rivalry: The Rivalry Approach to War and Peace." *International Interactions* 21 (3): 291–308.

———. 1997. "Linking Risky Dyads: An Evaluation of Relations between Enduring Rivalries." In *Enforcing Cooperation: "Risky" States and Intergovernmental Management of Conflict*, edited by G. Schneider and P. Weitsman, 132–60. New York: Macmillan.

Goertz, Gary, Paul F. Diehl, and Alexandru Balas. 2016. *The Puzzle of Peace: The Evolution of Peace in the International System*. New York: Oxford University Press.

Goertz, Gary, Bradford Jones, and Paul F. Diehl. 2005. "Maintenance Processes in International Rivalries." *Journal of Conflict Resolution* 49 (5): 742–69.

Goldstone, Jack A. 1997. "Revolution, War, and Security." *Security Studies* 6 (2): 127–51.

Goodarzi, Jubin M. 2008. *Syria and Iran: Diplomatic Alliance and Power Politics in the Middle East*. London: I. B. Tauris.

———. 2013. "Syria and Iran: Alliance Cooperation in a Changing Regional Environment." *Ortadogu Etutleri* 4 (2): 31–54.

Gordell, Kelly M. 2017. "What Does the Literature Teach Us about Political Shocks?" Unpublished manuscript.

Graham, David A. 2015. "Israel and Saudi Arabia: Togetherish at Last?" *Atlantic*, June 5, 2015. http://www.theatlantic.com/international/archive/2015/06/israeli-saudi-relations/395015/.

Gresh, Geoffrey. 2006. "Instigating Instability: Iran's Support of Non-State Armed Groups in Iraq." *Al Nakhlah* (Summer): 1–12.

Grunet, Tali Rachel. 2015. *New Middle East Cold War: Saudi Arabia and Iran's Rivalry.* Electronic Theses and Dissertations. digitalcommons.du.edu/cgi/viewcontent.cgi/articles/2027 &context=etd.

Guardian. 1987. "Iran Threatens US with Crushing Blow." June 22, 1987. Nexis Uni.

———. 2003. "Charges against Damascus." *Guardian*, April 15, 2003. https://www.theguardian.com/world/2003/apr/15/iraq.syria.

———. 2008. "US Embassy Cables: Saudi King Urges US Strike on Iran." April 20, 2008. https://www.theguardian.com/world/us-embassy-cables-documents/150519.

———. 2009. "US Embassy Cables: Saudi King's Advice for Barack Obama." March 22, 2009. https://www.theguardian.com/world/us-embassy-cables-documents/198178.

Gündogan, Ünal. 2003. "Islamist Iran and Turkey, 1979–1989: State Pragmatism and Ideological Influences." *Middle East Review of International Affairs* 7 (1): 1–12. http://www.rubincenter.org/meria/2003/03/gundogan.pdf.

Gurr, Ted R. 1988. "War, Revolution, and the Growth of the Coercive State." *Comparative Political Studies* 21 (1): 45–65.

Haaretz. 2013. "Israel, Saudi Arabia Cooperating to Plan Possible Iran Attack." November 17, 2013. https://www.haaretz.com/israel-saudis-now-allies-on-iran-1.5291205.

Haeri, Safa. 1990. "Crisis in the Gulf: Assad Leaves, but the Differences with Iran Remain." *Independent*, September 26, 1990.

Halliday, Fred. 1996. "Arabs and Persians beyond the Geopolitics of the Gulf." *Cahiers d'Etudes sur la Méditerranée Orientale et le monde Turco-Iranien* 22: 251–76.

———. 2000. *Nation and Religion in the Middle East.* London: Saqi Books.

———. 2002. "A New Global Configuration." In *Worlds in Collision—Terror and the Future of Global Order.* Edited by Ken Booth and Timothy Dunne. New York: Palgrave Macmillan.

———. 2012. *The Middle East in International Relations: Power, Politics and Ideology.* Cambridge: Cambridge University Press.

Halperin, Morton H., Priscilla Clapp, and Arnold Kantor. 1974. *Bureaucratic Politics and Foreign Policy.* Washington, DC: Brookings Institute.

Hanna, Michael Wahid, and Dalia Dassa Kaye. 2015. "The Limits of Iranian Power." *Survival* 57 (5): 173–98.

Harbi, Mohammed. 2010. *Les Archives de la Révolution algérienne.* Algiers: Dahlab Editions.

Harbi, Mohammed, and Gilbert Meynier. 2004. *Le FLN. Documents et histoire, 1954–1962.* Algiers: Casbah Editions.

Harkabi, Yehoshafat. 1970. "Liberation or Genocide?" *Society* 7 (9–10): 62–67.

Harris, Kevan. 2015. "The Breakaway Boss: Semiperipheral Innovations and the Rise of Mahmoud Ahmadinezad." *Journal of World Systems Research* 21 (2): 417–47.

———. 2016. "All the Sepah's Men: Iran's Revolutionary Guards in Theory and Practice." In *Businessmen in Arms: How the Military and Other Armed Groups Profit in the MENA Region.* Edited by Elke Grawert and Zeinab Abul-Magd. Lanham, MD: Rowman & Littlefield.

Haseeb, Khairuddin. 1998. *Arab–Iranian Relations.* Beirut: Centre for Arab Unity Studies.

Hashem, Ali. 2015. "Khamenei Criticizes Saudi Airstrikes, Nuclear Agreement." *Al-Monitor*, April 9, 2015. https://www.al-monitor.com/pulse/originals/2015/04/iran-khamenei-saudi-airstrikes-yemen.html.

———. 2017. "Gulf of Mistrust Mars Kuwaiti Initiative for Iran-GCC Dialogue." *Al-Monitor*, January 30, 2017. http://al-monitor.com/pulse/originals/2017/01/iran-gcc-saudi-tension-kuwait-dialogue-initiative-visit.html.

Hauslohner, Abigail. 2013. "Iraqi Shiites Fight for Syrian Government." *Washington Post*, May 26, 2013. https://www.washingtonpost.com/world/middle_east/iraqi-shiites-fight-for-syrian-government/2013/05/26/6c3c39b4-c245-11e2-914f-a7aba60512a7_story.html.

Hazbun, Waleed. 2012. "The Middle East through the Lens of Critical Geopolitics: Globalization, Terrorism, and the Iraq War." In *Is There a Middle East? The Evolution of a Geopolitical Concept.* Edited by Michael E. Bonine, Abbas Amanat, and Michael Ezekiel Gasper. Stanford, CA: Stanford University Press.

Hegghammer, Thomas. 2010. *Jihad in Saudi Arabia: Violence and Pan-Islamism since 1979.* Cambridge: Cambridge University Press.

Heistein, Ari, and James West. 2015. "Syria's Other Foreign Fighters: Iran's Afghan and Pakistani Mercenaries." *National Interest*, November 20, 2015. http://nationalinterest.org/feature /syrias-other-foreign-fighters-irans-afghan-pakistani-14400.

Hensel, Paul R. 1994. "One Thing Leads to Another: Recurrent Militarized Disputes in Latin America, 1816–1986." *Journal of Peace Research* 31 (3): 281–98.

———. 1999. "An Evolutionary Approach to the Study of Interstate Rivalry." *Conflict Management and Peace Science* 17 (2): 175–206.

Hentov, Elliot. 2011. *Turkey's Global Strategy: Turkey and Iran.* Edited by Nicholas Kitchen. IDEAS Report SR007. London: London School of Economics and Political Science.

Hermassi, Mohamed El-Baki. 1972. *Leadership and National Development in North Africa.* Berkeley: University of California Press.

Hernando de Larramendi, Miguel. 2018. "Doomed Regionalism in a Redrawn Maghreb? The Changing Shape of the Rivalry between Algeria and Morocco in the Post-2011 Era." *Journal of North African Studies.* DOI:10.1080/13629387.2018.1454657.

Hernando de Larramendi, Miguel, and Beatriz Tomé. 2017. "The Return of Morocco to the African Union." In *Iemed Mediterranean Yearbook*, 229–32. http://www.iemed.org/observatori /arees-danalisi/arxius-adjunts/anuari/med.2017/IEMed_MedYearbook2017_morocco _african_union_Larramendi_alonso.pdf/.

Hinnebusch, Raymond A. 2003. *The International Politics of the Middle East.* Manchester: Manchester University Press, 2003.

———. 2005. "The Politics of Identity in Middle East International Relations." In *International Relations of the Middle East*, edited by Louise L'Estrange Fawcett, 151–71. Oxford: Oxford University Press.

———. 2014. *Syria-Iraq Relations: State Construction and Deconstruction and the MENA States System.* LSE Middle East Centre Paper Series No. 4, London.

Hodgson, Marshall. 1974a. *The Venture of Islam: The Classical Age of Islam.* Chicago: University of Chicago Press.

———. 1974b. *The Venture of Islam: The Expansion of Islam in the Middle Periods.* Chicago: University of Chicago Press.

———. 1974c. *The Venture of Islam: The Gunpowder Empires and Modern Times.* Chicago: University of Chicago Press.

Hokayem, Emile. 2014. "Iran, the Gulf States and the Syrian Civil War." *Survival* 56 (6): 59–86.

Holden, David, and Richard Johns. 1981. *The House of Saud.* London: Sidgwick & Jackson.

Hormozgan Steel Company. 2012. "Iran's Self-Sufficiency in Steel Industry Imminent." October 28, 2012. http://www.hosco.ir/en/News/item/68/Iran.

Hubbard, Ben. 2016a. "Iranian Protesters Ransack Saudi Embassy after Execution of Shiite Cleric." *New York Times*, January 2, 2016. http://www.nytimes.com/2016/01/03/world /middleeast/saudi-arabia-executes-47-sheikh-nimr-shiite-cleric.html.

———. 2016b. "Saudi Arabia Cuts Ties with Iran amid Fallout from Cleric's Execution." *New York Times*, January 3, 2016. http://www.nytimes.com/2016/01/04/world/middleeast/iran -saudi-arabia-execution-sheikh-nimr.html.

———. 2017. "Iranian Pilgrims Can Participate in Hajj This Year, Saudi Arabia Says." *New York Times*, March 17, 2017. https://www.nytimes.com/2017/03/17/world/middleeast/hajj-mecca -saudi-arabia-iran.html.

Hubbard, Ben, and Nick Cumming-Bruce. 2017. "Rebels in Yemen Fire Second Ballistic Missile at Saudi Capital." *New York Times*, December 19, 2017. https://www.nytimes.com/2017/12/19 /world/.../yemen-rebels-missile-riyadh.html.

Hudson, Valerie. 2014. *Foreign Policy Analysis: Classic and Contemporary Theory*. 2nd ed. Lanham, MD: Rowman & Littlefield.

Hunter, Shireen. 2010. *Iran's Foreign Policy in the Post-Soviet Era: Resisting the New International Order*. Santa Barbara, CA: Praeger.

Huntington, Samuel P. 1968. *Political Order in Changing Societies*. New Haven, CT: Yale University Press.

Hurrell, Andrew. 1995. "Regionalism in Theoretical Perspective." In *Regionalism in World Politics: Regional Organization and International Order*. Edited by Louise Fawcett and Andrew Hurrell. Oxford: Oxford University Press.

Hurwitz, J. C. 1972. "The Persian Gulf: British Withdrawal and Western Security." *Annals of the American Academy of Political and Social Science* 40 (1): 106–15.

Hussain, Mushahid. 1987. "A Clash of Credos Now Writ in Blood." *Sydney Morning Herald*, August 29, 1987. Nexis Uni.

Ibrahim, Fouad. 2013. "Reform, Security in Saudi Arabia." *Al-Monitor*, October 16, 2013. http:// assafir.com/Article/50/333304/AuthorArticle.

İdiz, Semih. 2017. "Turkish-Iranian Rivalry Hits Peak as Syria Talks Kick Off." *Al-Monitor*, February 22, 2017. https://www.al-monitor.com/pulse/originals/2017/02/turkey-iran-rivalry -spills-over-with-angry-exchanges.html.

IHS Markit. 2015. "Saudi Arabia Replaces India as Largest Defence Market for US, IHS Study Says." March 7, 2015. http://press.ihs.com/press-release/aerospace-defense-terrorism/saudi -arabia-replaces-india-largest-defence-market-us-ihs-.

Independent. 1991. "Iran Wants to Shout Cries of Hatred." May 8, 1991. Nexis Uni.

Inskeep, Steve. 2015. "Ex-Mossad Chief Supports Iran Nuclear Deal." National Public Radio, July 31, 2015. http://www.npr.org/2015/07/31/427990359/ex-mossad-chief-supports-iran -nuclear-deal.

International Crisis Group (ICG). 2004. "Syria under Bashar: Foreign Policy Challenges." Middle East Report No. 23, International Crisis Group, Brussels.

———. 2009. "Reshuffling the Cards? Syria's Evolving Strategy." Middle East Report No. 92, International Crisis Group, Brussels.

———. 2016. "Turkey and Iran: Bitter Friends, Bosom Rivals." Briefing No. 51, December 13, 2016. https://www.crisisgroup.org/middle-east-north-africa/gulf-and-arabian-peninsula/iran /b051-turkey-and-iran-bitter-friends-bosom-rivals.

International Institute for Strategic Studies. 2006. "Iran and Turkey." *Strategic Comments* 12 (4): 1–2. DOI:10.1080/1356788061244.

Iran Daily. 2016a. "Captured Militant: Turkey Training Daesh on Its Soil." December 4, 2016.

———. 2016b. "ISIL Oil Trucks Cross into Turkey Everyday: Captured Terrorist Admits." January 2, 2016.

Jaabouk, Mohammed. 2018. "En l'absence d'Alger, Bourita affirme que le 'Sahel n'est le champ exclusif de personne.'" *Yabiladi* (Morocco), February 23, 2018. https://www.yabiladi.com /articles/details/62141/l-absence-d-alger-bourita-affirme-sahel.html.

Jafari, Saeid. 2016. "Why Was Iran So Quick to Rally behind Erdogan?" *Al-Monitor*, July 29, 2016. http://www.al-monitor.com/pulse/originals/2016/07/iran-turkey-coup-attempt-erdogan -rouhani.html#ixzz54AElfuaZ.

James, Laura M. 2006. *Nasser at War, Arab Images of the Enemy*. New York: Palgrave Macmillan.

Jenkins, Gareth H. 2012. *Occasional Allies, Enduring Rivals: Turkey's Relations with Iran*. Silk Road Paper, Central Asia–Caucasus Institute and Silk Road Studies Program, Washington, DC. http://isdp.eu/content/uploads/images/stories/isdp-main-pdf/2012_jenkins_occasional -allies.pdf.

Jervis, Robert. 1968. "Hypotheses on Misperception." *World Politics* 20 (3): 454–79.

———. 1976. *Perception and Misperception in International Politics*. Princeton, NJ: Princeton University Press.

Jones, Seth G. 2012. "Al Qaeda in Iran: Why Tehran Is Accommodating the Terrorist Group." *Foreign Affairs*, January 29, 2012. https://www.foreignaffairs.com/articles/iran/2012-01 -29/al-qaeda-iran.

Jones, Toby. 2009. "Embattled in Arabia: Shi'is and the Politics of Confrontation in Saudi Arabia." Combating Terrorism Center at West Point, June 3, 2009. http://arabia2day.com/wp -content/uploads/2010/12/Embattled-in-Arabia-Shiis-and-the-Politics-of-Confrontation-in -Saudi-Arabia.pdf.

Jones, Toby Craig. 2006. "Rebellion on the Saudi Periphery: Modernity, Marginalization and the Shia Uprising of 1979." *International Journal of Middle East Studies* 38 (2): 213–33.

Juneau, Thomas. 2016. "Iran's Policy towards the Houthis in Yemen: A Limited Return on a Modest Investment." *International Affairs* 92 (3): 647–63.

Kabalan, Marwan. 2007. "Iran's Response to Annapolis." *Gulf News*, December 7, 2007. https:// gulfnews.com/opinion/thinkers/iran-s-response-to-annapolis-1.217257.

———. 2009. "Syrian Foreign Policy: Between Domestic Needs and the External Environment." In *Syrian Foreign Policy and the United States, from Bush to Obama*, by Raymond Hinnebusch, Marwan J. Kabalan, Bassma Kodmani, and David Lesch. Boulder, CO: Lynne Rienner.

———. 2012. "Al Maliki's Ploy to Gain Legitimacy." *Gulf News*, March 30, 2012. http://gulf news.com/opinion/thinkers/al-maliki-s-ploy-to-gain-legitimacy-1.1001580.

———. 2013. "Syrian-Turkish Relations: Geopolitical Explanations for the Move from Conflict to Co-operation." In *Syrian-Turkish Relations between Enmity and Amity*, edited by Raymond Hinnebusch and Ozlem Tur. Burlington, VT: Ashgate.

Kamrava, Mehran. 2009. "Iran's Regional Foreign and Security Policies in the Persian Gulf." International Relations of the Gulf, Working Group Summary Report No. 1, Center for International and Regional Studies, Georgetown University School of Foreign Service in Qatar, Doha.

———. 2010. "The 2009 Elections and Iran's Changing Political Landscape." *Orbis* 54 (3): 400–412.

———. 2011. "Iranian and Foreign Security Policies in the Persian Gulf." In *International Politics of the Persian Gulf*. Edited by Mehran Kamrava. Syracuse, NY: Syracuse University Press.

Kamrava, Mehran, and Houchang Hassan-Yari. 2004. "Suspended Equilibrium in Iran's Political System." *Muslim World* 94 (October): 495–524.

Karagiannis, Emmanuel. 2016. "The Rise of Iran as a Regional Power: Shia Empowerment and Its Limits." *NATO Review*. http://www.nato.int/docu/Review/2016/Also-in-2016/iran-regional -power-tehran-islamic/EN/index.htm.

Karami, Arash. 2016. "IRGC Head Calls House of Saud 'Clear Enemy' of Iran." *Al-Monitor*, July 21, 2016. http://www.al-monitor.com/pulse/originals/2016/07/irgc-head-saudi-arabia-clear -enemy-iran.html.

Karsh, Efraim. 2002. *The Iran-Iraq War, 1980–1988*. London: Osprey.

Katz, Yaakov. 2010. "Stutnex Virus Set Back Iran's Nuclear Programs by 2 Years." *Jerusalem Post*, December 15, 2010. https://www.jpost.com/Iranian-Threat/News/Stuxnet-virus-set-back -Irans-nuclear-program-by-2-years.

Katzman, Kenneth. 2005. "US-Syria Relations after the Fall of Saddam." Emirates Center for Strategic Studies and Research, February 6, 2005. http://ecssr.com/ECSSR/print/ft.jsp?lang =en&ftId=/FeatureTopic/Kenneth_Katzman/FeatureTopic_0073.xml.

Kayaoglu, Barın. 2014. "The Limits of Turkish–Iranian Cooperation, 1974–80." *Iranian Studies* 47 (3): 463–78.

Kaye, Dalia Dassa, Alireza Nader, and Parisa Roshan. 2011. *Israel and Iran: A Dangerous Rivalry*. Santa Monica, CA: RAND.

Kéchichian, Joseph A. 1999. "Trends in Saudi National Security." *Middle East Journal* 53 (2): 232–53.

———. 2001. *Succession in Saudi Arabia*. New York: Palgrave Macmillan.

Keddie, Nikki R., and Rudolph P. Matthee. 2002. *Iran and the Surrounding World: Interactions in Culture and Cultural Politics*. Seattle: University of Washington Press.

Kerr, Malcolm. 1967. *The Arab Cold War, 1958–1967*. 2nd ed. London: Oxford University Press.

———. 1971. *The Arab Cold War: Gamal 'Abd al-Nasir and His Rivals, 1958–1970*. Oxford: Oxford University Press.

Keshavarzian, Arang. 2005. "Contestation without Democracy: Elite Fragmentation in Iran." In *Authoritarianism in the Middle East: Regimes and Resistance*, edited by Marsha Pripstein Posusney and Michele Penner Angrist. Boulder, CO: Lynne Rienner.

Keynoush, Banafsheh. 2016. *Saudi Arabia and Iran: Friends or Foes?* London: Palgrave Macmillan.

Khalilzad, Zalmay. 1995. "The United States and the Persian Gulf: Preventing Regional Hegemony." *Survival* 37 (2): 95–120.

Kharief, Akram. 2017. "Armement : trente ans de compétition entre l'Algérie et le Maroc." *Middle East Eye*, March 7, 2017. https://www.middleeasteye.net/fr/reportages/armement-trente-ans -de-comp-tition-entre-lalg-rie-et-le-maroc-1425398824.

Kheel, Rebecca. 2018. "State Official Indicates US Military Role in Syria Post-ISIS Centered on Iran." *The Hill*, January 11, 2018. http://thehill.com/policy/defense/368525-state-official -indicates-us-military-role-in-syria-post-isis-centered-on-iran.

Khomeini, Ruhollah. 1980. "We Shall Confront the World with Our Ideology." *MERIP Reports* 88: 22–25.

———. 1981. *Islam and Revolution: Writings and Declarations of Imam Khomeini (1941–1980)*. Translated by Hamid Algar. Berkeley, CA: Mizan.

Kiastevan, Hossein, ed. 1978. *Siasat-e Movazeneh-ye Manfi dar Majlis-e Chahardahom* [The policy of negative equilibrium in the 14th parliament]. Tehran: Islami.

Kienle, Eberhard. 1991. *Ba'th versus Ba'th: The Conflict between Syria and Iraq, 1968–1989*. London: I. B. Tauris.

Kifner, John. 1987. "400 Die as Iranian Marchers Battle Saudi Police in Mecca: Embassies Smashed in Teheran." *New York Times*, August 2, 1987. http://www.nytimes.com/1987/08/02/world /400-die-iranian-marchers-battle-saudi-police-mecca-embassies-smashed-teheran.html ?pagewanted=all.

Kinsella, David. 1994. "Conflict in Context: Arms Transfers and Third World Rivalries during the Cold War." *American Journal of Political Science* 38 (3): 557–81.

Kirişçi, Kemal. 1997. "Post-Cold War Turkish Security and the Middle East." *Middle East Review of International Affairs* 1 (2). http://www.rubincenter.org/1997/07/kirisci-1997-07-06/.

Klein, J. P., Gary Goertz, and Paul Diehl. 2006. "The New Rivalry Dataset: Procedures and Patterns." *Journal of Peace Research* 43 (3): 331–48.

———. 2008. "The Peace Scale: Conceptualizing and Operationalizing Non-Rivalry and Peace." *Conflict Management and Peace Science* 25 (1): 67–80.

Knights, Michael. 2010. "The Evolution of Iran's Special Groups in Iraq." *Sentinel* 3 (11–12): 12–16.

Koch, Christian. 2007. "Kingdom Come—Saudi Arabia Asserts Its Position as Regional Actor." *Jane's Intelligence Review*, July 19, 2007.

Koelbl, Susanne, Samiha Shafy, and Bernard Zand. 2016. "Saudi Arabia and Iran: The Cold War of Islam." *Der Spiegel Online*, May 9, 2016. http://www.spiegel.de/international/world /saudia-arabia-iran-and-the-new-middle-eastern-cold-war-a-1090725-3.html/.

Korany, Bahgat, and Moataz Fattah. 2008. "Irreconcilable Role-Partners? Saudi Foreign Policy between the Ulama and the US." In *The Foreign Policies of Arab States: The Challenge of Globalization*, edited by Bahgat Korany and Ali E. Hillal Dessouki, 343–96. Cairo: American University in Cairo Press.

Kurzman, Charles. 2004. *The Unthinkable Revolution in Iran*. Cambridge, MA: Harvard University Press.

Laitin, David. 1998. *Identity in Formations: The Russian-Speaking Populations in the Near Abroad*. Ithaca, NY: Cornell University Press.

Lake, Anthony. 1994. "Confronting Backlash States." *Foreign Affairs* 73 (2): 45–55.

Lake, David A. 2011. *Hierarchy in International Relations*. Ithaca, NY: Cornell University Press.

Lake, David A., and Robert Powell, eds. 1999. *Strategic Choice and International Relations*. Princeton, NJ: Princeton University Press.

Lawson, Fred. 2016. "International Relations Theory and the Middle East." In *International Relations of the Middle East*. Edited by Louise Fawcett. Oxford: Oxford University Press.

Lebovic, James, and William R. Thompson. 2006. "An Illusionary or Elusive Relationship? The Arab-Israeli Conflict and Repression in the Middle East." *Journal of Politics* 68 (3): 502–18.

Lenczowski, George. 1994. "Iran: The Big Debate." *Middle East Policy* 3 (2): 52–62.

Leng, Russell. 1983. "When Will They Ever Learn? Coercive Bargaining in Recurrent Crises." *Journal of Conflict Resolution* 27 (3): 379–419.

———. 2000. *Bargaining and Learning in Recurring Crises: The Soviet-American, Egyptian-Israeli, and Indo-Pakistani Rivalries*. Ann Arbor: University of Michigan Press.

Levy, Jack S., and William R. Thompson. 2010. *Causes of War*. West Sussex, UK: Wiley-Blackwell.

Lieberman, E. 1995. "What Makes Deterrence Work? Lessons for the Egyptian-Israeli Enduring Rivalry." *Security Studies* 4: 851–910.

Long, David E. 1985. *The United States and Saudi Arabia: Ambivalent Allies*. Boulder, CO: Westview Press.

Lounnas, Djallil, and Nizar Messari. 2018. "Algeria–Morocco Relations and Their Impact on the Maghrebi Regional System." MENARA Working Papers No. 20. http://www.iai.it/sites/default/files/menara_wp_20.pdf.

Lynch, Marc. 2009. "The Syrian-Iraqi Spat." *Foreign Policy*, September 2, 2009. http://foreignpolicy.com/2009/09/02/the-syrian-iraqi-spat/.

———. 2013. *The Arab Uprising: The Unfinished Revolutions of the New Middle East*. New York: Public Affairs.

Mabon, Simon. 2013. *Saudi Arabia and Iran: Power and Rivalry in the Middle East*. London: I. B. Tauris.

Macfarquhar, Neil. 2003. "Syria, Long Ruthlessly Secular, Sees Fervent Islamic Resurgence." *New York Times*, October 24, 2003. https://www.nytimes.com/2003/10/24/world/syria-long-ruthlessly-secular-sees-fervent-islamic-resurgence.html.

Macintyre, Donald. 2012. "Israel 'Does Azerbaijan Airbase Deal' in Plan to Attack Iran." *Independent*, March 30, 2012. https://www.independent.co.uk/news/world/middle-east/israel-does-azerbaijan-airbase-deal-in-plan-to-attack-iran-7601132.html.

Maddy-Weitzman, Bruce. 2012. "The Arab Regional System and the Arab Spring." In *The Arab Regional System and the Arab Spring*. Edited by Stephen Callega and Monica Wohlfield. Malta: Mediterranean Academy of Diplomatic Studies. https://www.um.edu.mt/_data/assets/pdf_file/0009/150399/chapter 5_-_Maddy\.

Mahdavi, M. 2011. "Post-Islamist Trends in Post-Revolutionary Iran." *Comparative Studies of South Asia, Africa and the Middle East* 31 (1): 94–109.

Mahmoud, Aly. 1981. "2 Million Moslems Climax Annual Pilgrimage to Mecca." Associated Press. October 7, 1981. Nexis Uni.

———. 1982. "Iran Protests Crackdown on Pilgrims." Associated Press. September 9, 1982. Nexis Uni.

———. 1989. "Bomb Kills One, Hurts 16, during Holy Pilgrimage." Associated Press, July 11, 1989. Nexis Uni.

Malmvig, Helle. 2015. "Coming in from the Cold: How We May Take Sectarian Identity Politics Seriously in the Middle East without Playing to the Tunes of Regional Power Elite." Project on Middle East Political Science, Elliot School of International Affairs, Washington, DC. https://pomeps.org/2015/08/19/coming-in-from-the-cold-how-we-may-take-sectarian-identity-politics-seriously-in-the-middle-east-without-playing-to-the-tunes-of-regional-power-elites/.

Maloney, Suzanne. 2015. *Iran's Political Economy since the Revolution.* New York: Cambridge University Press.

Mamouri, Ali. 2017. "Will Iraq Succeed in Bringing Iran, Saudi Arabia Closer?" *Al-Monitor,* January 25, 2017. http://www.al-monitor.com/pulse/originals/2017/01/saudi-iran-iraq-pilgrim-hajj-nimr.html.

Mansour, Imad. 2008. "Iran and Instability in the Middle East: How Preferences Influence the Regional Order." *International Journal* 63 (4): 941–64.

———. 2016. *Statecraft in the Middle East: Foreign Policy, Domestic Politics and Security.* London: I. B. Tauris.

———. 2018. "The State of Hezbollah? Sovereignty as a Potentiality in Global South Contexts." In *The Oxford Encyclopedia of Empirical International Relations Theory,* edited by William R. Thompson, 3:433–54. New York: Oxford University Press.

Maoz, Zeev. 1995. "Domestic Norms, Structural Constraints, and Enduring Rivalries in the Middle East, 1948–1980." In *Democracy, War and Peace in the Middle East,* edited by David Farnham and Mark Tessler. Bloomington: Indiana University Press.

———. 1996. *Domestic Sources of Global Change.* Ann Arbor: University of Michigan Press.

———. 2012. "Preferential Attachment, Homophily, and the Structure of International Networks, 1816–2003." *Conflict Management and Peace Science* 29 (3): 341–69.

Maoz, Zeev, and Kyle A. Joyce. 2016. "The Effects of Shocks on International Networks: Changes in the Attributes of States and the Structure of International Alliance Networks." *Journal of Peace Research* 53 (3): 292–309.

Maoz, Zeev, and Ben D. Mor. 2002. *Bound by Struggle: The Strategic Evolution of Enduring Rivalries.* Ann Arbor: University of Michigan Press.

Maroc Agence Presse. 2014. "SM le Roi adresse un discours à la nation à l'occasion du 39è anniversaire de la Marche Verte (Texte intégral)." November 6, 2014. http://www.mapnews.ma/fr/activites-royales/sm-le-roi-adresse-un-discours-la-nation-l%E2%80%99occasion-du-39e-anniversaire-de-la-march.

Marr, Phebe. 2012. *The Modern History of Iraq.* Boulder, CO: Westview Press.

Marschall, C. 2003. *Iran's Persian Gulf Policy: From Khomeini to Khatami.* London: Routledge.

Marshall, Monty G., Ted Robert Gurr, and Keith Jaggers. 2016. Polity IV Project: Political Regime Characteristics and Transitions, 1800-2015. Dataset User's Manual. data.nber.org/ems/Feldstein/ENSA_Sources/CSP/Polity%20Score/p4manualv2015.pdf.

Matthiesen, Toby. 2010. "Hezbollah al-Hijaz: A History of the Most Radical Saudi Shi'a Opposition Group." *Middle East Journal* 64 (2): 179–97.

———. 2012. "A 'Saudi Spring?' The Shi'a Protest Movement in the Eastern Province, 2011–2012." *Middle East Journal* 66 (4): 628–59.

McClelland, Charles. 1999. *World Event/Interaction Survey (WEIS) Project, 1966–1978.* ICPSR05211-v3. Ann Arbor, MI: Inter-University Consortium for Political and Social Research.

McDowall, Angus. 2016a. "Exclusive: Saudi Warns against 'Nefarious Activities' by Iran." Reuters, January 21, 2016. http://www.reuters.com/article/us-saudi-nuclear-idUSKCN0UX2HK.

———. 2016b. "Saudi Arabia Expands Its Anti-Iran Strategy beyond the Middle East." Reuters, June 5, 2016. http://www.reuters.com/article/us-saudi-security-diplomacy-iran-idUSKCN0YR08N.

McGinnis, Michael D. 1990. "A Rational Model of Regional Rivalry." *International Studies Quarterly* 34 (1): 111–35.

McLaughlin Mitchell, Sara, and Brandon C. Prins. 2004. "Rivalry and Diversionary Uses of Force." *Journal of Conflict Resolution* 48 (6): 937–61.

Mekki, Abdelhamid. 2016. *La construction de l'image de l'ennemi dans les discours politiques et médiatiques marocains : exemple de l'Algérie.* Master's thesis, University Jean Moulin 3, Paris.

Messari, Nizar. 2001. "National Security, the Political Space, and Citizenship: The Case of Morocco and Western Sahara." *Journal of North African Studies* 6 (4): 47–63.

Middle East Media Research Institute. 2017. "Saudis Optimistic on Trump Administration's Middle East Policy, Express Hope It Will Act against Iran." Special Dispatch No. 6807, March 1, 2017. https://www.memri.org/reports/saudis-optimistic-trump-administrations -middle-east-policy-express-hope-it-will-act-against.

Middle East Monitor. 2018. "Yemen: Three Days of Airstrikes on Houthi-Controlled Hudayeh." February 26, 2018. https://www.middleeastmonitor.com/20180226-yemen-three-days-of-air -strikes-on-houthi-controlled-hudaydah/.

Middle East Research and Information Project. 1972. "Nixon's Strategy in the Middle East." *MERIP Reports,* no. 13: 3–8.

Milani, Abbas. 2010. "The Shah's Atomic Dreams." *Foreign Policy,* December 29.

Milani, Mohsen M. 1992. "Iran's Active Neutrality during the Kuwaiti Crisis: Reasons and Ramifications." *New Political Science* 11 (1–2): 41–60.

———. 1994. "Iran's Post-Cold War Policy in the Persian Gulf." *International Journal* 49 (2): 328–54.

———. 2006. "Iran's Relations with Iraq, 1921–1979." *Encyclopedia Iranica* 13 (2): 564–72.

———. 2013. "Why Tehran Won't Abandon Assad(ism)." *Washington Quarterly* 36 (4): 79–93.

Milner, Helen. 1991. "The Assumption of Anarchy in International Politics Theory: A Critique." *Review of International Studies* 17,1: 67-85.

Mojtahed-Zadeh, Pirouz. 2007. *Boundary Politics and International Boundaries of Iran.* Boca Raton, FL: Universal Publishers.

Mor, Ben, D. 2004. "Strategic Beliefs and the Formation of Enduring International Rivalries: Israel's National Security Conception, 1948–1956." *International Relations* 18 (3): 309–29.

Morrow, J. D. 1999. "The Strategic Setting of Choices: Signaling, Commitment and Negotiation in International Politics." In *Strategic Choice and International Relations.* Edited by D. A. Lake and R. Powell. Princeton, NJ: Princeton University Press.

Mortimer, Robert A. 1993. "The Greater Maghreb and Western Sahara." In *International Dimensions of the Western Sahara Conflict.* Edited by Yahia H. Zoubir and Daniel Volman. Westport, CT: Praeger.

Moslem, Mehdi. 2002. *Factional Politics in Post-Khomeini Iran.* Syracuse, NY: Syracuse University Press.

Mousavian, Seyed Hossein. 2016. "Saudi Arabia Is Iran's New National Security Threat." *Huffington Post,* June 3, 2016. http://www.huffingtonpost.com/seyed-hossein-mousavian/saudi -arabia-iran-threat_b_10282296.html.

Mozaffari, Mehdi. 1999. "Revolutionary, Thermidorian and Enigmatic Foreign Policy: President Khatami and the 'Fear of the Wave.'" *International Relations* 14 (5): 9–28.

Nader, Alireza. 2013. *Nuclear Iran in the Persian Gulf.* Santa Monica, CA: RAND.

Nareim, Vivian. 2017. "Saudi Arabia Says It Will Work with Trump to Contain Iran." *Bloomberg,* January 24, 2017. https://www.bloomberg.com/politics/articles/2017-01-24/saudi-arabia -will-work-with-trump-on-containing-iran.

Nasr, Vali. 2006. *The Shia Revival: How Conflicts within Islam Will Shape the Future.* New York: Norton.

Nasrawi, Salah. 2006. "Death Toll Rises to 345 in Hajj Stampede." Associated Press, January 12, 2006. Nexis Uni.

Nasseri, Ladane, and Glen Carey. 2016. "Saudi Arabia Has a Plan B to Stop Iran's Economic Rise." *Bloomberg*, May 25. http://www.bloomberg.com/news/articles/2016-05-25/a-rear guard-action-by-saudi-arabia-to-stop-iran-s-economic-rise.

Nezzar, Khaled. 1999. *Mémoires du Général Khaled Nezzar.* Algiers: Chihab Editions.

Noble, Paul. 2008. "From Arab System to Middle Eastern System? Regional Pressures and Constraints." In *The Foreign Policies of Arab States: The Challenge of Globalization,* edited by Bahgat Korany and Ali E. Hillal Dessouki, 67–166. Cairo: American University Cairo Press.

Ojo, Olatunde, D. K. Orwa, and C. M. B. Utete. 1985. *African International Relations.* London: Longman Group.

Okruhlik, Gwen. 2003. "Saudi Arabian-Iranian Relations: External Rapprochement and Internal Consolidation," *Middle East Policy* 10 (2): 113–25.

Olson, Robert. 2001. *Turkey's Relations with Iran, Syria, Israel, and Russia.* Costa Mesa, CA: Mazda.

Oneal, John R., and Bruce Russett. 1999. "The Kantian Peace: The Pacific Benefits of Democracy, Interdependence, and International Organizations." *World Politics* 52 (1): 1–37.

Ottaway, David, and Marina Ottaway. 1970. *Algeria: The Politics of a Socialist Revolution.* Berkeley: University of California Press.

Ottaway, Marina. 2013. "The MENA Region: Regional Equilibria Stable Despite Turmoil." Analysis No. 204, Italian Institute for International Political Studies, Milan.

Ozcan, Gencer. 2001. "The Military and the Making of Foreign Policy in Turkey." In *Turkey in World Politics: An Emerging Multiregional Power.* Edited by B. Rubin and K. Kirisci. Boulder, CO: Lynne Reiner.

Palmer, Glenn, Vito D'Orazio, Michael Kenwick, and Matthew Lane. 2015. "The MID4 Dataset, 2002–2010: Procedures, Coding Rules and Description." *Conflict Management and Peace Science* 32 (2): 222–42.

Pamuk, Hümeyra. 2015. "Turkey's Erdogan Says He Can't Tolerate Iran Bid to Dominate." Reuters, March 26, 2015. http://www.reuters.com/article/us-yemen-security-turkey-idUSKBN 0MM2N820150326.

Parsi, Trita. 2006. "Israel and the Origins of Iran's Arab Option: Dissection of a Strategy Misunderstood." *Middle East Journal* 60 (3): 493–512.

Paul, T. V., ed. 2005. *The India-Pakistan Conflict: An Enduring Rivalry.* Cambridge: Cambridge University Press.

———. 2006. "Why Has the India-Pakistan Rivalry Been So Enduring? Power Asymmetry and an Intractable Conflict." *Security Studies* 15 (4): 600–630.

———, ed. 2018. *The China-India Rivalry in the Globalization Era.* Washington, DC: Georgetown University Press.

Perlo-Freeman, Sam, Aude Fleurant, Pieter Wezeman, and Siemon Wezeman. 2016. "SIPRI Trends in World Military Expenditure 2015." Fact Sheet, Stockholm Peace Research Institute, Solna. http://books.sipri.org/files/FS/SIPRIFS1604.pdf.

Perry, Tom, and Laila Bassam. 2017. "Saudi Reopens Lebanon Front in Struggle with Iran." Reuters, November 7, 2017. https://www.reuters.com/article/us-lebanon-politics-hariri-analysis /saudi-reopens-lebanon-front-in-struggle-with-iran-idUSKBN1D72BA.

Petterson, Therese and Peter Wallensteen. 2015. "Armed Conflicts, 1946-2014." *Journal of Peace Research* 52, 4: 536-550.

Phillips, Christopher. 2016. *The Battle for Syria: International Rivalry in the New Middle East.* New Haven, CT: Yale University Press.

Plommer, Leslie. 1987. "Iran Mined Gulf, War Official Says." *Globe and Mail*, August 21, 1987. Nexis Uni.

Pollack, Kenneth M. 2004. *The Persian Puzzle: The Conflict between Iran and America.* New York: Random House.

Porter, Gareth. 2014. *Manufactured Crisis: The Untold Story of the Iran Nuclear Scare.* Charlottesville, VA: Just World Books.

Prados, Alfred B. 2006. "Syria: U.S. Relations and Bilateral Issues." CRS Issue Brief for Congress, Congressional Research Service, Washington, DC. https://fas.org/sgp/crs/mideast/IB92075.pdf.

Press TV. 2015a. "Captured Militant: Turkey Training Daesh on Its Soil." *Iran Daily*, December 29, 2015. http://www.iran-daily.com/News/133883.html.

———. 2015b. "Turkey Deploying Troops to Iraq Endangers Regional Security." *Iran Daily*, December 6, 2015. http://www.iran-daily.com/News/132271.html.

———. 2016. "Iran Foreign Ministry Categorically Rejects GCC, Turkey Allegations." October 15, 2016. http://www.presstv.ir/DetailFa/2016/10/15/489190/Iran-GCC-Turkey-Foreign-Ministry-Riyadh-JCPOA-islands-Syria.

———. 2018. "American Military Bases in Middle East. Why Does US Have Them?" January 30, 2018. http://www.presstv.com/Detail/2018/01/30/550726/How-many-military-bases-US-has-in-Middle-East.

Putnam, Robert D. 1988. "Diplomacy and Domestic Politics: The Logic of Two-Level Games." *International Organizations* 42 (3): 427–60.

Qaidaari, Abbas. 2016. "Who Sent Iranian Green Berets to Syria?" *Al-Monitor*, April 28, 2016. https://www.al-monitor.com/pulse/fr/originals/2016/04/iran-army-brigade-65-green-berets-syria-deployment.html.

Quandt, William. 1981. *Saudi Arabia in the 1980s.* Washington, DC: Brookings Institution.

Radio Free Europe. 2017. "Iran Says New Refinery Will Make Country Self-Sufficient in Gasoline Output." May 1, 2017.

Radio Free Europe / Radio Liberty. 2016. "Thousands in Iran Protest against Saudis as Hajj Begins." September 10, 2016. http://www.rferl.org/content/thousands-protest-iran-against-saudi-arabia-Hajj-begins/27978664.html.

Rageh, Rawya. 2004. "244 Killed as Muslim Pilgrims Stampede in Saudi Arabia." *Gazette*, February 2, 2004. Nexis Uni.

Rakel, Eva. 2008. *Power, Islam and Political Elite in Iran: A Study on the Iranian Political Elite from Khomeini to Ahmadinejad.* Leiden, Netherlands: Brill.

Ramazani, R. K. 1972. *The Persian Gulf: Iran's Role.* Charlottesville: University Press of Virginia.

———. 1986. *Revolutionary Iran: Challenge and Response in the Middle East.* Baltimore, MD: Johns Hopkins University Press.

———. 1992. "Iran's Foreign Policy: Both North and South." *Middle East Journal* 46 (3): 393–412.

———. 2013. *Independence without Freedom: Iran's Foreign Policy.* Charlottesville: University of Virginia Press.

Randall, Jonathan C. 1984. "Saudi Supertanker Is Attacked in Gulf." *Washington Post*, May 17, 1984. https://www.washingtonpost.com/archive/politics/1984/05/17/saudi-supertanker-is-attacked-in-gulf/aa9a546f-24d0-491f-a802-af2246550dbb/.

Rasler, Karen. 2000. "Shocks, Expectancy Revision and the De-escalation of Protracted Conflicts: The Israeli-Palestinian Case." *Journal of Peace Research* 37 (6): 699–720.

———. 2001. "Political Shocks and the De-escalation of Protracted Conflict: The Israeli-Palestine Case." In *Evolutionary Interpretations of World Politics.* Edited by William R. Thompson. New York: Routledge.

Rasler, Karen A., and William R. Thompson. 2005. *Puzzles of the Democratic Peace: Theory, Geopolitics and the Transformation of World Politics.* New York: Palgrave Macmillan.

———. 2014. "Strategic Rivalries and Complex Causality in 1914." In *The War of 1914: Analytic Perspectives on Historical Debates.* Edited by Jack S. Levy and John A. Vasquez. Cambridge: Cambridge University Press.

Rasler, Karen, William R. Thompson, and Sumit Ganguly. 2013. *How Rivalries End.* Philadelphia: University of Pennsylvania Press.

Reuters. 2009. "Iraq PM Challenges Syria to Explain Militant Aid." September 3, 2009. https://www.reuters.com/article/idUSANS349705.

———. 2010a. "Iraq Recount Fails to Overturn Allawi Election Win." May 16, 2010. https://www.reuters.com/article/us-iraq-election/iraq-recount-fails-to-overturn-allawi-election-win-idUSTRE64F11A20100516.

———. 2010b. "Iraq's Maliki in Syria to Mend Strained Ties." October 13, 2010. https://www.reuters.com/article/us-syria-iraq-maliki/iraqs-maliki-in-syria-to-mend-strained-ties-idUSTRE69C3TW20101013.

———. 2011. "Iraq's Maliki Warns over Syrian Sectarian Turmoil." September 30, 2011. https://www.reuters.com/article/us-iraq-syria/iraqs-maliki-warns-over-syrian-sectarian-turmoil-idUSTRE78T2WJ20110930.

———. 2012. "Iraqi Shi'ite Militants Fight for Syria's Assad." October 16, 2012. https://www.reuters.com/article/us-syria-crisis-iraq-militias/iraqi-shiite-militants-fight-for-syrias-assad-idUSBRE89F0PX20121016.

———. 2016. "Saudi Arabia Halts $3 Billion Package to Lebanese Army, Security Aid." February 19, 2016. http://www.reuters.com/article/us-saudi-lebanon-idUSKCN0VS1KK.

Reyner, Anthony S. 1963. "Morocco's International Boundaries: A Factual Background." *Journal of Modern African Studies* 1 (3): 313–26.

Rich, Ben. 2012. "Gulf War 4.0: Iran, Saudi Arabia and the Complexification of the Persian Gulf Equation." *Islam and Christian-Muslim Relations* 23 (4): 471–86.

Riedel, Bruce. 2015. "Why Did It Take Saudi Arabia 20 Years to Catch Khobar Towers Bomber?" *Al-Monitor*, August 27. http://www.usnews.com/news/articles/2015/08/27/why-did-it-take-saudi-arabia-20-years-to-catch-khobar-towers-bomber.

———. 2016. "Saudi Arabia Turns Up the Heat on Hezbollah." *Brookings Brief* (blog), March 29, 2016. http://www.brookings.edu/blogs/markaz/posts/2016/03/29-saudi-arabia-hezbollah-riedel.

Risen, James, and Duraid Adnan. 2012. "U.S. Says Iraqis Are Helping Iran to Skirt Sanctions." *New York Times*, August 18, 2012. http://www.nytimes.com/2012/08/19/world/middleeast/us-says-iraqis-are-helping-iran-skirt-sanctions.html.

Rustow, Dankwart A. 1956. "Defense of the Near East." *Foreign Affairs* 34 (2): 271–86.

Ryan, Curtis. 2012. "The New Arab Cold War and the Struggle for Syria." *Middle East Report* 262: 28–31.

Saab, Bilal Y. 2016. "Why an Iran–Saudi Arabia Conflict Is More Likely Today than Ever Before." *Newsweek*, October 18, 2016. www.newsweek.com/why-iran-saud-arabia-conflict-more-likely-today-ever-511317.

Sabet, Farzan. 2017. "The April 1977 Persepolis Conference on the Transfer of Nuclear Technology: A Third World Revolt against US Non-proliferation Policy?" *International History Review* 40 (5): 1134–51. DOI:10.1080/07075332.2017.1404483.

Sadjadpour, Karim. 2009. *Reading Khamenei: The World View of Iran's Most Powerful Leader*. Washington, DC: Carnegie Endowment for International Peace.

Saeidi, Ali A. 2004. "The Accountability of Para-governmental Organizations (Bonyads): The Case of Iranian Foundations." *Iranian Studies* 37 (3): 479–98.

Safran, Nadav. 1985. *Saudi Arabia: The Ceaseless Quest for Security*. Ithaca, NY: Cornell University Press.

Safshekan, Roozbeh, and Farzan Sabet. 2010. "The Ayatollah's Praetorians: The Islamic Revolutionary Guard Corps and the 2009 Election Crisis." *Middle East Journal* 64 (4): 543–58.

Sahimi, M. 2011. "The Canny General: Quds Force Commander Ghasem Soleimani." *PBS Frontline*, December 31, 2011. http://www.pbs.org/wgbh/pages/frontline/tehranbureau/2011/12/profile-the-cannygeneral-quds-force-commander-ghasem-soleimani.html.

Saïd Zahlan, Rosemarie. 1989. *The Making of the Modern Gulf States: Kuwait, Bahrain, Qatar, the United Arab Emirates, and Oman*. London: Unwin Hyman.

Saïdy, Brahim. 2009–10. "La politique de défense Marocaine: articulation de l'interne et de l'externe." *Maghreb-Machrek* 202:117–32.

Sakthivel, Vish. 2014. "Morocco's Move in Mali: What Rabat Gained in the Battle against Islamic Extremism." *Foreign Affairs*, January 14, 2014. https://www.foreignaffairs.com/articles /africa/2014-01-14/moroccos-move-mali.

Salami, Habibollah, and Mohammad Saeid Noori Naeini. 2014. "Prospects for Food Self-Sufficiency in Iran in 2025." In *Food Security in the Middle East*, edited by Zahra Babar and Suzi Mirgani, 115–35. Oxford: Oxford Scholarship.

Salehi-Isfahani, Djavad. 1995. "The Oil Sector after the Revolution." In *Iran after the Revolution: Crisis of an Islamic State*, edited by Saeed Rahnema and Sohrab Behdad, 150–73. London: I. B. Tauris.

Salehyan, Idean, and Kristian Skrede Gleditsch. 2006. "Refugees and the Spread of Civil War." *International Organization* 60 (2): 335–66.

Salih, Mohammed A. 2016. "Why Iranian Kurdish Party Is Stepping Up Fight against Tehran." *Al-Monitor*, July 1, 2016. http://www.al-monitor.com/pulse/originals/2016/07/iran-kurd ish-party-attack-irgc.html.

Salloukh, Bassel F. 2013. "The Arab Uprisings and the Geopolitics of the Middle East." *International Spectator* 48 (2): 32–46.

Sariolghalam, Mahmood. 2002. "Siasat-e Khareji-ye Jomhuri-ye Islami: Naghd-e Nazari va Tarh-e Etelaf" [The Islamic Republic's foreign policy: Theoretical critiques and reconciliation]. *Majlis va Pajuhesh* 35: 65–82.

Sarkees, Meredith Reid, and Frank Wayman. 2010. *Resort to War, 1816–2007*. Washington, DC: Congressional Quarterly Press.

Saunders, Bonnie F. 1996. *The United States and Arab Nationalism: The Syrian Case, 1953–1960*. London: Praeger.

Savage, Charlie. 2016. "James Cartwright, Ex-General, Pleads Guilty in Leak Case." *New York Times*, October 17, 2016. https://www.nytimes.com/2016/10/18/us/marine-general-james -cartwright-leak-fbi.html.

Sayigh, Yezid. 2016. "Who Made the Arab Spring into an Arab Crisis?" *Al Jazeera*, November 20, 2016. http://carnegie.mec.org/2016/11/20/who-made-arab-spring-into-arab-crisis-pub-6.

Schedler, Andreas. 2013. *The Politics of Uncertainty: Sustaining and Subverting Electoral Authoritarianism*. New York: Oxford University Press.

Scheff, Thomas J. 2005. "The Structure of Context: Deciphering Frame Analysis." *Sociological Theory* 23 (4): 368–85.

Schelling, Thomas. 1966. *Arms and Influence*. New Haven, CT: Yale University Press.

Schemm, Paul. 2016. "Iran Suspends Participation in the Hajj as Relations with Saudi Arabia Plummet." *Washington Post*, May 12. https://www.washingtonpost.com/world/iran-sus pends-participation-in-annual-Hajj-pilgrimage-as-relations-with-saudi-plummet/2016 /05/12/a0e1c970-1848-11e6-924d-838753295f9a_story.html.

Schmidt, Michael S., and Yasir Ghazm. 2011. "Iraqi Leader Backs Syria, with a Nudge from Iran." *New York Times*, August 12, 2011. http://www.nytimes.com/2011/08/13/world/middleeast /13iraq.html.

Seale, Patrick. 1965. *The Struggle for Syria: A Study of Post-War Arab Politics, 1945–1958*. London: Oxford University Press.

———. 1989. *Assad of Syria: The Struggle for the Middle East*. Berkeley: University of California Press.

Sela, Avraham. 2004. "'Abd al-Nasser's Regional Politics, A Reassessment." In *Rethinking Nasserism, Revolution and Historical Memory in Modern Egypt*, edited by Elie Podeh and Onn Winckler, 179–204. Gainesville: University Press of Florida.

Shafy, Zamiha, and Bernhard Zand. 2016. "Interview with Saudi Foreign Minister Adel Al-Jubeir." *Der Spiegel Online*, February 19, 2016. http://www.spiegel.de/international/world/interview -with-saudi-foreign-minister-adel-al-jubeir-on-syrian-war-a-1078337.html.

Shapiro, Michael J. 1988. *The Politics of Representation: Writing Practices in Biography, Photography and Political Analysis*. Madison: University of Wisconsin Press.

Sharnoff, Michael. 2011. "Looking Back, Nasser's Inter-Arab Rivalries, 1958–1967." *Middle East Observer* 2 (4).

Sherwell, Philip. 2009. "Israel Launches Covert War against Iran." *Telegraph*, February 16, 2009. https://www.telegraph.co.uk/news/worldnews/middleeast/israel/4640052/Israel-launches -covert-war-against-Iran.html.

Shih, Chih-yu. 1992. "Seeking Common Causal Maps: A Cognitive Approach to International Organization." In *Contending Dramas: A Cognitive Approach to International Organizations*. Edited by Martha L. Cottam and Chih-yu Shih. New York: Praeger.

Simon, Herbert A. 1985. "Human Nature in Politics: The Dialogue of Psychology with Political Science." *American Political Science Review* 79 (2): 292–304.

———. 1991. "Bounded Rationality and Organizational Learning." *Organizational Science* 2 (1): 125–34.

Sinkaya, Bayram. 2005. "Turkey-Iran Relations in the 1990s and the Role of Ideology." *Perceptions: Journal of International Affairs* 10 (1): 1–15.

———. 2017. "The Kurdish Question in Iran and Its Effects on Iran-Turkey Relations." *British Journal of Middle Eastern Studies* 45 (5): 840–59. DOI:10.1080/13530194.2017.1361315.

Skocpol, Theda. 1979. *States and Social Revolutions: A Comparative Analysis of France, Russia and China*. New York: Cambridge University Press.

Smith, Ben. 2007. "The Quds Force of the Iranian Revolutionary Guard." SN/IA/4494, UK House of Commons, International Affairs and Defence Section, London. http://researchbriefings .files.parliament.uk/documents/SN04494/SN04494.pdf.

Smolansky, Oles M., and Bettie Moretz Smolansky. 1991. *The USSR and Iraq: The Soviet Quest for Influence*. Durham, NC: Duke University Press.

Snyder, Jack. 1991. *Myths of Empire: Domestic Politics and International Ambition*. Ithaca, NY: Cornell University Press.

Sofer, Sasson. 1998. *Zionism and the Foundations of Israeli Diplomacy*. Translated by Dorothea Shefet-Vanson. Cambridge: Cambridge University Press.

Solingen, Etel. 2012. "Of Dominoes and Firewalls: The Domestic, Regional and Global Politics of International Diffusion." *International Studies Quarterly* 56, 4: 631-644.

Solomon, Erika. 2017. "Riyadh's Lebanon Intervention Driven by Wish to Curb Hizbollah." *Financial Times*, November 13, 2017. https://www.ft.com/content/de2f3002-c886-11e7 -ab18-7a9fb7d6163e.

Solomon, Jay. 2016. *The Iran Wars: Spy Games, Bank Battles, and the Secret Deals That Reshaped the Middle East*. New York: Random House.

Sorli, Mirjam E., Nils Petter Gleditsch, and Havard Strand. 2005. "Why Is There So Much Conflict in the Middle East?" *Journal of Conflict Resolution* 49 (1): 141–65.

Spencer, Richard. 2012. "Iraqi Sunni Tribal Sheikh Admits Sending Men to Fight against Bashar al-Assad in Syria." *Guardian*, March 11, 2012. https://www.telegraph.co.uk/news/world news/middleeast/syria/9137115/Iraqi-Sunni-tribal-sheikh-admits-sending-men-to-fight -against-Bashar-al-Assad-in-Syria.html.

Spencer, William. 2000. *Iraq: Old Land, New Nation in Conflict*. Brookfield, CT: Twenty First Century Books.

Spindle, B., and M. Coker. 2011. "Saudi Arabia and Iran Wage a New Cold War in the Middle East." *Wall Street Journal*, April 16, 2011.

Stein, Aaron, and Philipp C. Bleek. 2012. "Turkish-Iranian Relations: From 'Friends with Benefits' to 'Its Complicated.'" *Insight Turkey* 14 (4): 137–50.

Stein, Janice Gross. 2013. "Threat Perception in International Relations." In *The Oxford Handbook of Political Psychology*. 2nd ed. Edited by Leonie Huddy, David O. Sears, and Jack S. Levy. New York: Oxford University Press.

Steinberg, Guido. 2014. *Leading the Counter-Revolution, Saudi Arabia and the Arab Spring*. SWP Research Paper, Stiftung Wissenschaft und Politik, German Institute for International and Security Affairs, Berlin.

Stratfor. 2009. "Yemen: The Persian–Arab Proxy Battle." September 1, 2009. http://www.stratfor .com/analysis/20090831_yemen_persian_arab_proxy.

———. 2010. "The US–Saudi Arms Deal and Riyadh's Military Challenge." October 21, 2010. http://www.stratfor.com/sample/analysis/us-saudi-arms-deal-and-riyadhs-military -challenge.

Streich, Philip, and Jack S. Levy. 2016. "Information, Commitment and the Russo-Japanese War of 1904–1905." *Foreign Policy Analysis* 12 (4): 489–511.

Strout, Richard L. 1981. "Reagan Prestige, US Influence Ride on AWACS." *Christian Science Monitor*, October 27, 1981.

Svolik, Milan W. 2012. *The Politics of Authoritarian Rule*. New York: Cambridge University Press.

Takeyh, Ray. 2009. *Guardians of the Revolution, Iran and the World in the Age of the Ayatollahs*. Oxford: Oxford University Press.

Takeyh, Ray, and Suzanne Maloney. 2011. "The Self-Limiting Success of Iran Sanctions." *International Affairs* 87 (6): 1297–1312.

Tal, Israel. 2000. *National Security: The Israeli Experience*. Westport, CT: Praeger.

Tastekin, Fehim. 2015. "Are Turkey, Saudi Arabia Working Together against Iran?" *Al-Monitor*, March 5, 2015. http://www.al-monitor.com/pulse/originals/2015/03/turkey-saudi-plan-anti -iran-sunni-bloc.html.

Tavernise, Sabrina. 2006. "Syria and Iraq Restore Ties Severed in the Hussein Era." *New York Times*, November 21, 2006. https://www.nytimes.com/2006/11/21/world/middleeast/21iraq .html.

Tazmini, Ghoncheh. 2013. *Khatami's Iran: The Islamic Republic and the Turbulent Path to Reform*. New York: I. B. Tauris.

Thompson, William R. 1970. "The Arab Sub-system and the Feudal Pattern of Interaction: 1965." *Journal of Peace Research* 7,2: 151-167.

———. 1973. "The Regional Subsystem: A Conceptual Explication and a Propositional Inventory." *International Studies Quarterly* 17 (1): 89–117.

———. 1995. "Principal Rivalries." *Journal of Conflict Resolution* 39 (2): 195–223.

———. 1999. *Great Power Rivalries*. Columbia: University of South Carolina Press.

———. 2001. "Identifying Rivals and Rivalries in World Politics." *International Studies Quarterly* 45 (4): 557–86.

———. 2003. "A Streetcar Named Sarajevo: Catalysts, Multiple Causation Chains, and Rivalry Structures." *International Studies Quarterly* 47:453–74.

———. 2018. "Constructing a General Model Accounting for Interstate Rivalry Termination." In *The Oxford Encyclopedia of Empirical International Relations Theory*, edited by William R. Thompson, 1:362–81. New York: Oxford University Press.

Thompson, William R., and David Dreyer. 2011. *Handbook of International Rivalries, 1494– 2010*. Washington, DC: Congressional Quarterly Press.

Torbati, Yegani. 2017. "Trump Administration Tightens Iran Sanctions, Tehran Hits Back." Reuters, February 3, 2017. http://www.reuters.com/article/us-iran-usa-idUSKBN15H253.

Torres-Garcia, Ana. 2013. "US Diplomacy and the North African 'War of the Sands' (1963)." *Journal of North African Studies* 18 (2): 324–48.

Touval, Saadia. 1967. "The Organization of African Unity and African Borders." *International Organization* 21 (1): 102–27.

Trevino, Javier A. 2003. "Introduction: Erving Goffman and the Interaction Order." In *Goffman's Legacy*. Edited by A. Javier Trevino. Lanham, MD: Rowman & Littlefield.

Trofimov, Yaroslav. 2016. "Feuding Friends Frustrate Saudi Efforts to Counter Iran: Egypt and Turkey Disagree on Greater Threat: Shiite Iran or Political Islam." *Wall Street Journal*, June 30, 2016. http://www.wsj.com/articles/feuding-friends-frustrate-saudi-efforts-to-counter-iran 14677279000.

Ünver, H. Akin. 2012. "How Turkey's Islamists Fell out of Love for Iran?" *Middle East Policy* 19 (4): 103–9.

Unver Nois, Aylin. 2013. "A Clash of Islamic Models." *Current Trends in Islamist Ideology* 15: 92–114.

Valbjorn, Morten, and Andre Bank. 2012. "The New Arab Cold War, Rediscovering the Arab Dimension of Middle East Regional Politics." *Review of International Studies* 38 (1): 3–24.

Valeriano, Brandon. 2013. *Becoming Rivals: The Process of Interstate Rivalry Development*. New York: Routledge.

Valeriano, Brandon, and Matthew Powers. 2016. "Complex Interstate Rivalries." *Foreign Policy Analysis* 12 (4): 552–70.

Vasilogambros, Matt. 2016. "Iran's Own Internet." *Atlantic*, August 2016.

Vasquez, John A. 1993. *The War Puzzle*. Cambridge: Cambridge University Press.

———. 1996. "Distinguishing Rivals That Go to War from Those That Do Not." *International Studies Quarterly* 40 (4): 531–58.

Vassiliev, Alexei. 1998. *The History of Saudi Arabia*. London: Saqi.

Voice of America News. 2009. "Yemen, Iran Trade Accusations about Houthi Rebels." Nexis Uni.

Volgy, Thomas J., Paul Bezerra, Jacob Cramer, and J. Patrick Rhamey Jr. 2017. "The Case for Comparative Regional Analysis in International Politics." *International Studies Review* 19 (3): 452–80.

Volgy, Thomas J., Renato Corbetta, Keith A. Grant, and Ryan G. Baird. 2011. *Major Powers and the Quest for Status in International Politics*. New York: Palgrave Macmillan.

Volgy, Thomas J., Kelly Gordell, J. Patrick Rhamey, and Paul Bezerra. 2018. "Conflicts, Regions, and Regional Hierarchies." In *The Oxford Encyclopedia of Empirical International Relations Theory*, edited by William R. Thompson, 1:335–62. New York: Oxford University Press.

von Maltzahn, Nadia. 2013. *The Syria-Iran Axis: Cultural Diplomacy and International Relations in the Middle East*. London: I. B. Tauris.

Wallish, David. 2013. "Syrian Alliance Strategy in the Post-Cold War Era: The Impact of Unipolarity." *Fletcher Forum of World Affairs* 37 (2): 107–23.

Walt, Stephen M. 1987. *The Origins of Alliances*. Ithaca, NY: Cornell University Press.

———. 1996. *Revolution and War*. Ithaca, NY: Cornell University Press.

Waltz, Kenneth N. 1979. *Theory of International Politics*. Long Grove, IL: Waveland Press.

Ward, Steven R. 2009. *Immortal: A Military History of Iran and Its Armed Forces*. Washington, DC: Georgetown University Press.

Warrick, Joby. 2011. "Iraq, Siding with Iran, Sends 'Lifeline to Assad.'" *Washington Post*, October 8, 2011. https://www.washingtonpost.com/world/national-security/iraq-siding-with-iran -sends-lifeline-to-assad/2011/10/06/gIQAFEAIWL_story.html?utm_term=.08cedd74615b.

Wayman, Frank. 2000. "Rivalries: Recurrent Disputes and Explaining War." In *What Do We Know about War?*, edited by John Vasquez, 219–34. Lanham, MD: Rowman & Littlefield.

Wehrey, Frederic C. 2014. *Sectarian Politics in the Gulf: From the Iraq War to the Arab Uprisings*. New York: Columbia University Press.

Wehrey, Frederic C., Theodore W. Karasik, Alireza Nader, Jeremy Ghez, Lydia Hansell, and Robert A. Guffey. 2009. *Saudi-Iranian Relations since the Fall of Saddam: Rivalry, Cooperation, and Implications for U.S. Policy*. Santa Monica, CA: RAND.

Weller, Marc. 1999–2000. "The US, Iraq and the Use of Force in a Unipolar World." *Survival* 41 (4): 81–100.

Wells, M. C. 1999. "Thermidor in the Islamic Republic of Iran: The Rise of Muhammad Khatami." *British Journal of Middle Eastern Studies* 26 (1): 27–39.

White House. 2017. "Remarks by President Trump on Iran Strategy." October 13, 2017. https:// www.whitehouse.gov/briefings-statements/remarks-president-trump-iran-strategy/.

Wild, Patricia B. 1966. "The OAU and the Algerian-Moroccan Border Conflict: A Study of New Machinery for Peacekeeping and for the Peaceful Settlement of Disputes among African States." *International Organization* 20 (1): 18–36.

Willis, Michael, and Nizar Messari. 2003. "Analyzing Moroccan Foreign Policy and Relations with Europe." *Review of International Affairs* 3 (2): 152–72.

Wilson, George C. 1988. "Navy Missile Downs Iranian Jetliner over Gulf." *Washington Post*, July 4, 1988. Nexis Uni.

Wilson, Peter W., and Douglas F. Graham. 1994. *Saudi Arabia: The Coming Storm*. New York: M. E. Sharpe.

World Bank. n.d. *World Development Indicators*. https://databank.worldbank.org/source/world-development-indicators.

Yesilbursa, Behçet K. 2001. "The American Concept of the 'Northern Tier' Defence Project and the Signing of the Turco-Pakistani Agreement, 1953–54." *Journal of Middle Eastern Studies* 37 (3): 59–110.

Yousfi, M'hamed (1989), Le pouvoir 1962-1978 , Alger, ANEP (this citation is used by the current author from another work by Djallil Lounnas and Nizar Messari which he cites).

Zaanoun, Adel. 2009. "Iran's Mottaki to Reassure Saudi on Hajj: Iranian Official." Agence France Presse, November 11, 2009. Nexis Uni.

Zarif, Mohammad Javad. 2014. "What Iran Really Wants: Iranian Foreign Policy in the Rouhani Era." *Foreign Affairs* 93 (3): 49–59.

———. 2016. "Mohammad Javad Zarif: Saudi Arabia's Reckless Extremism." *New York Times*, January 10, 2016. http://www.nytimes.com/2016/01/11/opinion/mohammad-javad-zarif-saudi-arabias-reckless-extremism.html?_r=0.

Zatarain, Lee Allen. 2010. *America's First Clash with Iran: The Tanker War, 1987–1988*. Haverton, PA: Casemate.

Zoubir, Yahia H. 1987. "Soviet Policy in the Maghreb," *Arab Studies Quarterly* 9 (4): 399–421.

———. 2001. "Algerian-Moroccan Relations and Their Impact on Maghribi Integration." *Journal of North African Studies* 5 (3): 43–47.

———. 2004. "The Dialectics of Algeria's Foreign Relations from 1990 to the Present." In *Algeria in Transition-Reforms and Development Prospects*. Edited by Ahmed Aghrout. London: Routledge.

———. 2010. "Conflict in Western Sahara," In *Interpreting the Modern Middle East: Essential Themes*. Edited by David Sorenson. Boulder, CO: Westview Press.

———. 2012. "Tilting the Balance toward Intra-Maghreb Unity in Light of the Arab Spring." *International Spectator* 47 (3): 64–80.

———. 2015. "Algeria's Roles in the OAU/African Union: From National Liberation Promoter to Leader in the Global War on Terrorism." *Mediterranean Politics* 21 (1): 55–75.

———. 2018. "Algeria and the Sahelian Quandary: The Limits of Containment Security Policy." In *The Sahel: Europe's African Borders*. Edited by Dalia Yazbeck-Ghanem. Barcelona: European Institute of the Mediterranean.

———. Forthcoming. "The Giant Afraid of Its Shadow: Algeria, the Reluctant Middle Power." In *Middle Power Politics in the Middle East: Aspirations and Limitations*. Edited by Adham Saouli. Oxford: Oxford University Press.

Zunes, Stephen, and Jacob Mundy. 2011. *Western Sahara: War, Nationalism, and Conflict Irresolution*. Syracuse, NY: Syracuse University Press.

Contributors

Meliha Benli Altunışık is a professor in the Department of International Relations at Middle East Technical University (METU) in Ankara. She has written mainly on international relations of the Middle East and Turkey's foreign policy. She is the author (with O. Tur) of *Turkey: Challenges of Continuity and Change* (Routledge 2005) and coeditor (with O. Tanrısever) of *The South Caucasus: Security, Energy and Europeanization* (Routledge 2018). Some of her recent publications focus on cusp states, rentier state theory, regional powers, humanitarian diplomacy, soft power, and social movements and international relations.

Paul Bezerra is an assistant professor of military and strategic studies at the US Air Force Academy. He previously worked as the National Security Affairs Postdoctoral Fellow at the US Naval War College (2018) and earned a PhD from the University of Arizona (2017). His research takes advantage of emerging data and technologies, such as geographic information systems (GIS), to understand the local geography and context of political action as well as the way state actors transform humanitarian/development assistance into foreign policy cooperation. To date, his research has appeared in *International Interactions*, *Foreign Policy Analysis*, *Public Choice*, and *International Studies Review*, and he is a coauthor on the Militarized Interstate Dispute Location (MIDLOC) data set. Before pursuing his PhD, Paul worked in nonprofits and city government in Dallas and New York, served as an AmeriCorps national service volunteer in Fresno County, California, and helped develop and deliver a management training program for nongovernmental organizations in Duhok, Iraq. More information can be found at www.paulbezerra.com.

John Calabrese, PhD, teaches US foreign policy at American University in Washington, DC. He also serves as a scholar in residence at the Middle East Institute (MEI), where he directs MEI's project on the Middle East and Asia (MAP). He is the book review editor of *The Middle East Journal* and previously served as general series editor of *MEI Viewpoints*. He is the author of *China's Changing Relations with the Middle East* and *Revolutionary Horizons: Iran's Regional Foreign Policy*. He has edited several books and has written numerous articles on the international relations of the Middle East, especially on the cross-regional ties between the Middle East and Asia. He codirected the MEI-FRS project for the European Commission on Transatlantic Cooperation on Protracted Displacement.

Kelly Marie Gordell is a doctoral candidate in the School of Government and Public Policy, University of Arizona. Her work focuses on the involvement by both international and regional communities on the improvement of postconflict conditions, specifically exploring their impact on different dimensions of human security. Additional information can be found at www.kellygordell.com.

Marwan J. Kabalan is the head of policy analysis at the Arab Center for Research and Policy Studies (ACRPS) in Doha, Qatar. He is also chair of the Gulf Studies Forum (GSF) and head of Contemporary Syria Studies at the ACRPS. He is an adjunct professor in public policy at the Doha Institute for Graduate Studies. Kabalan served as dean of the Faculty of International Relations and Diplomacy at the Kalamoon University in Damascus, Syria. He taught international political theory at the University of Manchester and at the Faculty of Political Sciences, Damascus University. He was a member of the board of directors at the Damascus University Center for Strategic Studies and Research. Kabalan's research interests include theory of international politics and foreign and security policy in the Middle East. Select publications include *Syrian Foreign Policy and the United States, from Bush to Obama* (2009) and *Turkey-Syria Relations: Between Enmity and Amity* (2013). Marwan's most recent research publication is *Qatar Foreign Policy: Elite v. Geography* (in Arabic).

Imad Mansour is adjunct professor in the Department of Political Science at McGill University and is a nonresident scholar at the Middle East Institute (Washington, DC). He was previously at Qatar University and at Sciences Po Paris (Campus Moyen-Orient Méditerranée à Menton). His research interests are in interdisciplinary approaches to studying the influence of narratives in government and state building as well as the social roots of international politics, especially conflicts, rivalries, and regional orders. He is author of *Statecraft in the Middle East: Foreign Policy, Domestic Politics and Security* (I. B. Tauris 2016).

Karen Rasler is professor emerita of political science at Indiana University. She is the author of articles on repression, political violence, long cycles of world leadership, and war and state-building. She has coauthored five books: *War and Statemaking: The Shaping of Civil Wars* (1989); *The Great Powers and Global Struggle, 1490–1990* (1994); *Puzzles of the Democratic Peace* (2005), with William R. Thompson; *Strategic Rivalry: Space, Position, and Conflict Escalation in World Politics* (2008), with Michael Colaresi and William R. Thompson; and *How Rivalries End* (2013), with Sumit Ganguly and William R. Thompson.

William R. Thompson is Distinguished Professor and Donald A. Rogers Professor of Political Science (emeritus) at Indiana University. He is editor in chief of the *Oxford Research Encyclopedia of Politics* and a past president of the International Studies Association, as well as a previous editor of International Studies Quarterly. Recent publications include the *Oxford Encyclopedia of Empirical International Relations Theory* (4 volumes) and *Racing to the Top: How Energy Fuels Systemic Leadership in World Politics* (with Leila Zakhirova).

Thomas J. Volgy (PhD, University of Minnesota) is professor of political science in the School of Government and Public Policy, University of Arizona, and the previous executive director of the International Studies Association. He has published extensively, including numerous books and over seventy research articles. His present research agenda focuses on status competition in international politics; the identification and impact of major and regional powers; the effects of hierarchy on interstate conflict; the comparative analysis of regions in international politics; and assessments of governmental effectiveness on rivalries and other conflict processes. A longer version of his background is available at www.volgy.org.

Thomas Keith Wilson is a PhD candidate in political science at Indiana University, with emphasis in international relations, comparative politics, and Central Eurasian studies. He holds an MA in international relations from Creighton University and a BA in political science from the University of Michigan. Wilson is also an active duty military officer of seventeen years, a period that includes operational and strategic work with Middle Eastern politics. His research interests include rivalry studies, contestation across regime types, electoral authoritarian regimes, religion and religious political networks, media, cognitive theory, and the influence of bureaucracy on decision-making.

Yahia H. Zoubir is professor of international studies and international management and director of research in geopolitics at KEDGE Business School, France (since 2005). He has been visiting faculty in various universities in China, Europe, the United States, India, South Korea, and the Middle East and North Africa. His publications include *The Politics of Algeria: Domestic Issues and International Relations* (Routledge 2020); *North African Politics: Change and Continuity* (Routledge 2016); *Building a New Silk Road: China and the Middle East in the 21st Century* (World Affairs Press 2014); *Global Security Watch—The Maghreb: Algeria, Libya, Morocco, and Tunisia* (ABC/CLIO 2013); and *North Africa: Politics, Region, and the Limits of Transformation* (Routledge 2008). He has published in *Third World Quarterly, Mediterranean Politics, International Affairs, Journal of North African Studies, Middle East Journal, Middle East Policy, Arab Studies Quarterly*, and the *Encyclopedia of Nationalism*. In 2019 he published a major study, "Civil Strife, Politics, and Religion in Algeria," in the *Oxford Research Encyclopedia of Politics*. Other recent publications include "China's Participation in Conflict Resolution in the Middle East and North Africa: A Case of Quasi-Mediation Diplomacy?" *Journal of Contemporary China* (March 2018) and "Algeria and the Sahelian Quandary: The Limits of Containment Security Policy," *IMed/EuroMeSCo* (2018).

Index

Figures and tables are indicated by f and t following the page number.

www.ingramcontent.com/pod-product-compliance
Lightning Source LLC
Chambersburg PA
CBHW081737270326
41932CB00020B/3307